Selves, Symbols, and Sexualities

Selves, Symbols, and Sexualities
An Interactionist Anthology

Thomas S. Weinberg
SUNY Buffalo State

Staci Newmahr
SUNY Buffalo State

Editors

Los Angeles | London | New Delhi
Singapore | Washington DC

Los Angeles | London | New Delhi
Singapore | Washington DC

FOR INFORMATION:

SAGE Publications, Inc.
2455 Teller Road
Thousand Oaks, California 91320
E-mail: order@sagepub.com

SAGE Publications Ltd.
1 Oliver's Yard
55 City Road
London, EC1Y 1SP
United Kingdom

SAGE Publications India Pvt. Ltd.
B 1/I 1 Mohan Cooperative Industrial Area
Mathura Road, New Delhi 110 044
India

SAGE Publications Asia-Pacific Pte. Ltd.
3 Church Street
#10–04 Samsung Hub
Singapore 049483

Acquisitions Editor: Jeff Lasser
Associate Editor: Nathan Davidson
Editorial Assistant: Nick Pachelli
Production Editor: Libby Larson
Copy Editor: Patrice Sutton
Typesetter: C&M Digitals (P) Ltd.
Proofreader: Sally Jaskold
Indexer: Jean Casalegno
Cover Designer: Janet Kiesel
Marketing Manager: Erica DeLuca

Printed in the United States of America

Library of Congress Cataloging-in-Publication Data

Selves, symbols, and sexualities : contemporary readings / [edited by] Thomas S. Weinberg, SUNY Buffalo State, Staci Newmahr, SUNY Buffalo State.

pages cm
Includes bibliographical references and index.

ISBN 978-1-4522-7665-6 (pbk. : alk. paper) —
ISBN 978-1-4833-1267-5 (web pdf : alk. paper)
1. Sex. 2. Sexual orientation. 3. Identity (Psychology)
I. Weinberg, Thomas S. II. Newmahr, Staci.

HQ21.S4436 2015
306.7—dc23   2014000279

This book is printed on acid-free paper.

14 15 16 17 18 10 9 8 7 6 5 4 3 2 1

CONTENTS

PREFACE

This coedited volume was conceived as a supplemental reader for courses in the sociology and social psychology of human sexuality. Its consistent symbolic interactionist approach makes it unique among the few readers in the topic area. Our goal was to produce a highly readable book without sacrificing intellectual rigor. We therefore decided that instead of using previously published selections, written for a professional audience, we would only include new, fresh contributions that were designed for undergraduate students.

Since human sexuality is a complex phenomenon, the treatment in this book is expansive, in order to cover the diversity of relevant topics. The readings vary in terms of their conceptual or practical approaches. For example, there is a mixture of conceptual and research contributions as well as first-person accounts, which makes this volume unique.

Both editors bring a strong background in the sociology of sexuality to the project, spanning two generations of constructionist thought. Both of us have engaged in ethnographic research in sexuality and have published our work in leading refereed journals in the field. Both of us are also contributors to *The Routledge Handbook of Deviant Behavior,* edited by the late Clifton Bryant and published in 2012.

Dr. Thomas S. Weinberg is the author or editor of four books (two monographs and two edited volumes) on sexuality. His work in gay studies and the sociology of sadomasochism appears in sociological and interdisciplinary journals, such as the *Journal of Sex Research,* the *Journal of Homosexuality, American Journal of Sexuality Education, Annual Review of Sex Research, Journal of Psychology & Human Sexuality,* and *Social Analysis.* He is an associate editor of *Ethnographic Studies* and *Sexuality & Culture* and a referee for the *Journal of Sexual Medicine.*

Dr. Staci Newmahr is an ethnographer and the author of *Playing on the Edge: Sadomasochism, Risk and Intimacy* (Indiana University Press, 2011), an ethnography of an SM community that theorizes risk-taking and emotion from an interactionist perspective. She has published several papers in sociology and interdisciplinary journals, including *Symbolic Interaction, Journal of Contemporary Ethnography,* and *Qualitative Sociology.* Dr. Newmahr is associate editor of *Symbolic Interaction* (Wiley-Blackwell). She is currently working toward a book on nonsexual erotic proliferations.

ACKNOWLEDGMENTS

We are both indebted to the brilliance, enthusiasm, and tremendous work ethic of all of our contributors for this exciting collection of original and cutting-edge research. We are grateful to our departmental colleagues at SUNY Buffalo State, particularly Gerhard Falk and Allen Shelton, for their support and for their friendship. We thank the editors and staff at SAGE, including Dave Repetto, who helped us get this book off the ground, and the editorial team of Diane McDaniel, Jeff Lasser, and Lauren Johnson, who supported and managed this project throughout the process.

Tom Weinberg: I would like to thank my wife, Bonnie, for her support in this project and her patience when working on the volume took time away from her and our domestic projects. Carolyn Englehardt went well beyond her duties at our library's help desk to figure out some of the formatting problems we had with the manuscript.

Staci Newmahr: I owe a warm and hearty thank-you to Tom Weinberg for approaching me with this idea, for his attention to detail, and for being nothing less than a wonderful collaboration partner. This collection was shaped in part by dozens of sessions and conversations with sexuality scholars and symbolic interactionists over the past few years. I am always inspired by those people, by their work, and by our conversations: Chuck Edgley, Clare Forstie, Kate Frank, Thaddeus Muller, Susie Scott, Allen Shelton, Nicolas Simon, Brandy Simula, J. Sumerau, Beverly Thompson, Dennis Waskul, and D J Williams. More broadly, and perhaps a tad sentimentally as I emerge from the process of editing a determinedly interactionist book, I am deeply appreciative of the Society for the Study of Symbolic Interaction (SSSI) and all of its members for being an intellectual home to many of us. Finally, as always, I am grateful to my family for weathering the storm of frazzled intensity that I bring home through every edit, revision, and new deadline.

INTRODUCTION

Thomas S. Weinberg

The readings for this book reflect a common theme: Sexualities are sociological realities. In fact, biological responses are initiated, structured, and understood through the meanings that people bring to sexual situations. As humans, we continually interpret our own situations, identities, motivations, and behaviors as well as that of others through those meanings that we learn in social interaction. These meanings are continually reinforced and validated by others. This is true of all social phenomena, including sexualities. For example, we learn who and what is sexy, and this, not hormones, triggers our responses. Americans have a consistent image of the sexy man and woman, as reflected in the occasional lead stories in popular supermarket publications on "The 100 Sexiest Men," "The Sexiest Women," and so on. *Sexy* in American culture means young, slim, and physically fit. But in other places, this is not the case. Among the Hima tribe in Uganda and the Annang and Efik of Nigeria (Malcolm 1925), young women enter a fattening hut to increase their marriage desirability. In Mauritania, girls are force-fed to make them gain weight. In these cultures, obesity is a sign of wealth and, ultimately, beauty and sexual attractiveness.

In our own society, standards of female attractiveness and hence, beauty, have changed over the years. One hundred years ago, full figured women were desirable. By the 1920s, the era of the "flapper," women were binding their breasts, as being flat chested was sexy. The actress Clara Bow, known as the "It Girl," was seen as the epitome of sexiness during that time. In the 1940s, the curvy woman was back in vogue, as illustrated by the actress Betty Grable, the "pinup" of American servicemen. In the 1950s, screen sirens, such as Jane Russell, Marilyn Monroe, and Jayne Mansfield, all well-endowed women, were the fantasy objects of young men.[1] During that time period, Dagmar, a model, actress, and popular guest on television, was so well endowed that the bullet nosed bumper guards on Cadillacs, Packards, and Buicks of the day were called "Dagmars." In the 1960s, thin was the new sexy, and an aptly named popular recording star, "Twiggy," epitomized sexuality.

Even within our own contemporary society, there are subcultural variations in what is considered to be attractive and sexy. For example, Thio (2010) points out that the meaning of weight as it relates to sexiness varies according to race. The African American community is much more accepting of fat[2] women and more likely to see them as sexy than is the white community. In fact, during the spring 2012 semester, one of the African American student organizations on our college campus sponsored a "PHAT" beauty contest. According to their poster advertising this event, PHAT stands for "Pretty, Hot and Thick." Contrast this with McLorg and Taub's (1987) finding that anorexia and bulimia are predominantly found among young middle-class white women.[3]

Men, as well as women, are seen as sex symbols. In the 1910s and 1920s, the actor Douglas Fairbanks, who played in what were called "swashbuckling" roles (i.e., in what we now call action films), was seen as the ideal man. In the 1920s, his status as a sex symbol was challenged by Rudolph Valentino, who was seen by women as the romantic ideal. Men, however, compared him negatively to Fairbanks, and there were those in the media who considered him effeminate because of his impeccable dress and slicked down hair (Ellenberger and Ballerini 2005).

In the 1930s, movie stars who were seen as sex symbols, such as Errol Flynn, who was another swashbuckler, Gary Cooper, and Clark Gable, were the epitome of masculinity. The 1940s found men with a more sophisticated persona like Cary Grant still masculine but more refined. The 1950s was the era of the "bad boy" image, personified by James Dean, who played a troubled teen in 1955's *Rebel Without a Cause,* and Marlon Brando, who played a motorcycle gang leader in the 1953 film *The Wild Ones.*

Unlike the status of female sex symbols, historically, the sexiness of males has depended more on perceived personality and romantic presentation than on body type. In patriarchal systems built around gender binaries (that is, structures in which people are viewed as occupying one of two mutually exclusive gender categories), cultural capital is accorded to men based on their capacities for action, or what they can do. Men gain social status (and therefore desirability, or what we come to think of as sexiness) based on the skills they possess (e.g., intelligence, physical competence, or leadership skills) or the indicators of those skills (e.g., high-status jobs, expensive possessions). Women, in turn, become valued for the status they confer onto men. In other words, in a social system in which only men had access to economic and political resources, women came to symbolize men's success; the more attractive a woman, the more impressive a man appears for attracting her. Despite the profound changes in the world since women were denied access to political and economic power, women's desirability, or sexiness, continues to reside less in symbols of what they can *do* in the world than in their aesthetic value.

One interesting development does seem to have occurred by the 1960s, however. It has to do with chest hair, rather than physique. The early swashbucklers, when they appeared shirtless, were always shaved. By the 1960s, actors like Paul Newman, Robert Redford, and Sean Connery exposed themselves in hairy glory. This hirsute trend reached a new level when Burt Reynolds, the 1970s sex symbol, posed nude and hairy with only an arm discreetly covering his male parts. From the 1980s to the present, as gender roles have changed drastically, there seems to have developed a greater emphasis on the male body and fitness. Sharply defined abdominal muscles ("abs") are now seen as sexy. Pictures of celebrity abs are regularly found in supermarket fan magazines, and there are numerous television infomercials promising to enable one to define one's abdominals, if only a particular piece of exercise equipment, diet, or program is purchased. In 1989, the actor Patrick Swayze showed off his toned physique in the film *Roadhouse,* and in the 1990s, Brad Pitt also displayed his abs, as did Fabio, a male model, actor, romance novel author, and spokesman for a number of businesses and products, whose career as a sex symbol spanned two decades.

Most of the examples cited above come from the media: magazines, movies, and television. There is no denying the power of the media in modern American society as an arbiter of cultural tastes and trends. Idealized images of sexual attractiveness, however, both contemporary and historical, are also found elsewhere in, for example, literature (Singh, Renn, and Singh 2007) and art (Haughton 2004). Haughton notes that Renaissance painters depicted an idealized woman with symmetrical features, "alabaster skin," a small waist, and large breasts and broad hips. He describes Venus in Botticelli's painting, *Venus and Mars,* painted between 1480 and 1490, as follows: "Note the high forehead, the sharply defined chin, pale skin, strawberry blond hair, high delicate eyebrows, strong nose, narrow mouth and full lips . . . a full figure with an ample bosom, rounded abdomen and wide hips" (Haughton 2004:231). A contemporary artist, Anna Utopia Giordano, has Photoshopped paintings of Renaissance masters, such as Bouguereau, Cabanel, Botticelli, Bronzino, Hayez, Ingres, and Velazquez, bringing them, tongue in cheek, up to modern standards of beauty.[4] Like the Renaissance paintings, modern romance novels present idealized images of both men and women. The description of the heroine in the following excerpt is startlingly like that described by Haughton above:

. . . no man worth his salt would have missed the surprisingly lush curves of breasts and hips, guaranteed to stop traffic and haunt dreams. . . . Her hair was that rare, striking color between red and gold, and it hung thick and shining to the middle of her back . . . and that silky, burnished hair framed a face that was almost too delicately perfect to be real. She was like a painting: every feature was finely drawn with artistic excellence, from her straight nose to the sweet curve of her lips. And in that strikingly perfect face, her eyes were simply incredible: a clear, pale green; huge and shadowed by long, thick lashes. (Hooper 2012:12–13)

Here is how the author describes the central male character:

[H]e was over six feet tall and powerfully built. He was dressed casually . . . but the informal attire did nothing to conceal the physical strength of broad shoulders and powerful limbs, or the honed grace of his movements. . . . He was dark, black-haired, and black-eyed, his lean face handsome. (Hooper 2012:18)

Few people, whether living in the 15th or 21st centuries, can measure up to these idealized images. We learn from our culture or subculture not only who is sexy, but also what is sexy. For example, American males' preoccupation with female breasts as erotic objects is not shared by men in many other cultures in which women usually are bare breasted. In these cultures, breasts are viewed simply as sources of milk for babies. Our culture also teaches us who are appropriate sexual partners and the situations in which sexual behaviors are appropriate. Even more fundamentally, the very concept of "sexual" is culturally constructed. We learn what "counts" as sex and what does not. We learn the connections between our ideas about sex and our ideas about relationships, feelings, monogamy, and gender. We learn, and teach each other, what should turn us on and what should not. We learn to understand and define ourselves in relation to our sexual behavior and sexual desires, and these understandings underpin the way we present ourselves to the world. All of these sexual meanings are created through our social interactions, and what comes to be defined as erotic, and decidedly unerotic, can be traced back to the level of everyday life.

Standards of sexuality are not fixed, but they are constantly changing through a process of interaction. We humans are not in any sense captives of our culture; rather, cultures are continually in flux as new norms and values are created in response to societal changes. The discussion of the first section of the book, "Theorizing Sex," succinctly makes this point.

Our definitions of sexiness extend beyond our judgments of others to our self-appraisals. Through a process of interpreting other people's responses to us, which early social psychologist Charles Horton Cooley (1902:183–184) termed the looking glass self, we form opinions of our own attractiveness. We are able to do this because we humans, unlike animals, have the ability to use symbols and thus are able to treat ourselves as objects, to stand outside ourselves and see ourselves as we might see others.

CONTROLLING SEXUALITIES

People's sexualities and their expression are controlled in two ways. The first of these is through socialization. Children learn the norms, attitudes, values, and perspectives of their group through their parents and other significant figures in their lives. This process illustrates what George Herbert Mead (1934), an important founder of the perspective, which later became known as "symbolic interaction" theory, termed the "generalized other." Through this process, children come to internalize certain views of the world, including those of sexuality. Not so very long ago, in the days of your grandparents' or great grandparents' youth, romance and sexuality between members of different nationalities (e.g., Italian Americans and Irish Americans) and religious groups (e.g., Catholics and Protestants) were strongly opposed by each group. The focusing of romance and eroticism only on members of one's own group was facilitated in many communities by de facto segregation by nationality. For example, in the authors' city of Buffalo, New York, South Buffalo has traditionally been Irish, the upper West side was predominantly Italian, the lower West side was mainly Hispanic, the near East side was populated by African Americans, and the far East side was the Polish section. Jews were found mostly in North Buffalo, but there were small communities on the East side along with small Italian populations. Old timers have told us that men who attempted to date a young woman from another group were sometimes met with violence by men in her neighborhood. While there have been population shifts over the last 40 years or so, large segments of the original populations remain in the old areas.

A more restrictive way in which groups focus their members' sexualities is through arranged marriages, often made at very young ages. For example, in colonial India in the early 20th century, girls as young as 8 years old were often betrothed to an older man (Southgate 1938). My great grandparents had their marriage arranged for them when they were 16 and 19. They, in turn, were so angry that their 17-year-old daughter (my maternal grandmother) had married a man from outside their religious group that they sent her, along with her younger brother, to America. Even today, the practice of arranged marriages continues. In fact, during the fall 2012 semester, I was approached by a male student, whose immigrant family had arranged a marriage for him with a young woman whom he had never seen, who lived on another continent thousands of miles away. He was also being pressured by the woman's father, who kept sending him e-mails, asking when he was coming to see his daughter.

The second way in which sexualities are structured is through formal laws, which may prescribe not only with whom one may have sex but also what kind of sex one may have. In the southern United States, before civil rights, for example, some jurisdictions passed miscegenation laws, which prohibited the "mixing" of the races. All states have age of consent laws, which make it illegal to have sex with someone under a certain age. This age varies from state to state. Many states had sodomy laws, prohibiting specific sex acts (or contact between certain body parts), which were periodically enforced. While theoretically applying to both heterosexuals and homosexuals, in the past, they were usually only enforced against gay men.[5]

Although prostitution is illegal in the United States in all jurisdictions other than a few counties in Nevada, a number of European countries have decriminalized it and restrict sex workers to "red light" districts. In Amsterdam, the chamber of commerce provides maps of these areas and instructions about how to deal with prostitutes.

In addition to laws specifically aimed at controlling sexuality, such as sodomy, age of consent, and miscegenation laws, there are other laws, not originally developed for that purpose, which, nevertheless, are used to regulate sexual behavior. For example, state or municipal ordinances pertaining to nudity, disorderly conduct, suspicion, trespassing, loitering, parking, and liquor laws have been selectively used to limit sexualities. Police in some cities are known to ticket cars parked near gay bars. State liquor authorities can control the spread of gay bars by revoking liquor licenses. One gay man I interviewed (Weinberg 1994a) claimed that he had been arrested for "drunken parking," while sitting in his car and talking with another man outside a gay bar. He was asked, the man said, whether he wanted to be put in the regular drunk tank or the gay drunk tank. Loitering and trespassing laws are often invoked in an attempt to prevent gay men from "cruising" (i.e., looking for sexual partners) in parks and other settings. Public health laws have similarly been used to close gay bathhouses and heterosexual "swingers" clubs. Men acting "suspiciously" in areas where children play may be picked up for loitering or suspicion pending an investigation.

In summary, sexualities are not merely reflections of biological imperatives. They are controlled through socialization and formal mechanisms. Most important to remember is that the meanings that are conveyed through these processes play the major role in how people perceive, define, and act out sexuality.

THE SYMBOLIC INTERACTION PERSPECTIVE

While there are other ways of understanding human sexualities (see Weinberg 1994b, for examples), we have chosen symbolic interaction as the sociological framework to use in this book because we see the production of meaning as central to all human activity, including sexuality. Symbolic interactionism focuses on individuals and how they understand themselves and others. It is an example of a *microsociological* theory in sociology.

For the symbolic interactionist, roles, relationships, and meanings are socially constructed. That is, they are negotiated during a process of social interaction rather than being fixed and predetermined (Hewitt and Shulman 2011; Sandstrom, Martin, and Fine 2010). From this point of view, the individual has considerable control over his or her identity and behavior. He or she is seen as possessing a self, which is developed through a continuing process of interaction and interpretation. That is, who and what we think we are is at least partly a reflection of how we believe we are viewed by others, as Cooley (1902), cited above, tells us. Thus, at the core of symbolic interaction theory is the idea that people are sense-making creatures. Humans have the capacity to interpret situations, which we do in terms of significant symbols. We continually construct, apply, and act in terms of the *meanings* we place on ourselves, others, and situations. This is succinctly summed up by William I. Thomas's statement in the early 20th century: "If men define situations as real, they are real in their consequences" (Thomas and Thomas 1928:571–572). People, and the world around us, are seen as dynamic processes, rather than as the static structures assumed by *macrosociological* level theories, such as structural functionalism. We humans are in a continual state of becoming. Identities, for example, can be created, tried on, and discarded by the individual. We are not simply passive recipients of labels; we do interpretive work to figure out who and what we are. Nor are meanings immutable. At any given time, we can reinterpret a situation or behavior and choose from among a number of alternative meanings. For example, an adolescent male who has sex with another boy may see this behavior as "meaning" that he is gay, or that he is bisexual, or that he is going through "an adolescent stage," just "experimenting," or having no meaning at all, "just what guys do" when they get together. He may define and redefine his behavior several times, taking into account new knowledge and new circumstances (Weinberg 1983).

Erving Goffman (1959, 1963, 1967) notes that we attempt to control the way we appear to others by taking into account their probable responses to us. To do this, we have to be able to identify with them, to put ourselves in their position, and attempt to see things from their perspective. This ability to take the role of the other is a uniquely human trait. Engaging in reciprocity thinking by putting ourselves in other people's situations is dependent upon our capacity to create and use symbols. This type of thinking is developmental. It, too, is learned through a process of interacting with others. While young children have only the rudiments of this ability, it becomes much more critical during adolescence. Adolescents develop this capacity through identifying with groups of their peers. These people of their own age serve as what we call "reference groups." Reference groups are used by the individual as a guide for his or her feelings and behavior. They become "significant others" with whom we compare ourselves. How these others think and feel, especially about us, become critical for our feelings about ourselves.

Symbolic interaction is not a single unified perspective, but one that contains a number of variations and developments. There are, however, some unifying concepts upon which all symbolic interactionists agree. According to Herbert Blumer, who was the first to use the term "symbolic interaction" (Blumer 1937),

> Symbolic interactionism rests in the last analysis on three simple premises. The first premise is that human beings act toward things on the basis of the meanings that the things have for them. . . . The second premise is that the meaning of such things is derived from, or arises out of, the social interaction one has with one's fellows. The third premise is that these meanings are handled in, and modified through, an interpretative process used by the person in dealing with the things he encounters (Blumer 1969:2).

Blumer's fundamental concepts are reflected in the variety of chapters in this volume. Although they take different approaches to study a wide range of sexualities, these premises form a unifying theme in all of them.

NOTES

1. For a contemporary account of Ms. Monroe's ample hips and derrière, as described by show business manager Milton Ebbins, who was struggling to help her get into a dress she was wearing for president John F. Kennedy's 45th birthday celebration in Madison Square Garden (in which she sang the now famous, "Happy Birthday, Mr. President"), see Bill O'Reilly and Martin Dugard, *Killing Kennedy, the End of Camelot*. 2012. New York: Henry Holt and Company, page 82.

2. I am not using the word *fat* pejoratively, but rather following its usage in both the fat-activist and contemporary scholarly literature (Gullage 2010; Murray 2004, 2005a, 2005b; Scott-Dixon 2008). As I point out in this chapter, "fatness" is socially constructed.

3. This is becoming an increasing problem for boys and young men, as well. "[T]he latest data, from 2011, showed that Los Angeles boys were nearly as likely as girls to purge through vomiting or laxatives. They were also as likely as girls to use diet pills, powders, or liquids without the advice of a doctor" (Alpert, 2013:F3).

4. For examples of her work, especially her Venus Project, go to http://annautopia giordano.it/.

5. This was generally true until June 26, 2003, when the U.S. Supreme Court, in Lawrence v. Texas, 539 U.S. 558 (2003), decided 6–3 that the state's sodomy laws were invalid, thus nullifying a previous decision and making sexual acts between consenting adults no longer illegal throughout the country.

PART I

THEORIZING SEX

The first section of the book, Theorizing Sex, describes, discusses, and illustrates various interactionist approaches to understanding sexuality. We intend these chapters to provide a foundation for thinking about sex from sociological, anthropological, and broader cultural perspectives. All of the chapters share a constructionist approach; that is, they view sex and sexuality as a product of our culture.

The idea of *social construction* moves away from the perspective that things are the way they are because "society makes it that way." Social constructionism shifts the focus to the fact that the abstraction *society* is *us;* there is no society outside what its people say, do, create, and destroy. We are the agents of social construction. When we say things like, "society says it should be this way," or "the media forces that viewpoint," we reify concepts instead of examining how it is that we, in our everyday lives, reproduce, reinforce, or challenge these ideas. Social constructionism pushes us to be aware of, and accountable for, the actions we take that, in turn, contribute to particular constructions of cultural meanings. Chris Brickell's opening chapter introduces the fundamentals of social constructionism and a symbolic interactionist approach to sexuality. It illuminates sex—by which we mean not only sexual behaviors but also thinking, feeling, talking, and legislating about sex—as a social process. It explores how some things come to be considered "sexual" (while others do not), and it provides examples of the ways in which sexuality is, like all social processes, fundamentally about meaning. This chapter illustrates how social construction of sexuality works through social interaction—"on the ground," as interactionists sometimes like to say.

Therefore, the second thing the chapters share is that they are concerned with thinking about sexuality at the level of interaction. They are concerned not only with sexuality as it relates to "society" but also with understanding sexual practices, interactions, and meanings—at the level of the individuals and their lives. A symbolic interactionist studies the meanings created in and evidenced by social interaction as the ideal site for understanding society and culture. Where the first chapter explores the intersections of interactionism, constructionism, and the study of sexuality, the second chapter in this section provides a developed example of how one can think about the significance of sexual meaning-making processes. Don Kulick's exploration of fantasy among the Gapun of New Guinea provides a compelling example of both social constructionism of sexuality and the importance of understanding social phenomena at the level of the individual. By focusing on another culture, we can recognize that sexuality is not the same for all human beings, because meanings are not the same for all human beings. Kulick's chapter (2) is a powerful demonstration that even something thought to be as basic as sexual fantasy—what is "hot" and what is not—differs according to what meanings we accord to behaviors, words, body parts, symbols, and spaces. It delivers an important challenge to the general assumption that our erotic fantasy lives are private, disconnected from our cultural values and our public lives. It encourages us to think about the relationship of fantasy and imagination to broader cultural meanings.

Another way of thinking about how sexuality is socially constructed at the level of interaction is to examine social control mechanisms, such as laws, police, courts, and formal social organizations, and their relationships to individuals' sexualities and sexual lives. In Chapter 3, Misty Luminais explores these complex relationships in a community of bondage/discipline/domination /submission/sadism/masochism (BDSM) participants. Luminais uses the concept of cultural hegemony to explain how the dominant values around sexuality are supported and reproduced. This chapter demonstrates exactly how dominant ideas about sexuality are deployed, through interaction, to oppress individual sexual expressions, ultimately strengthening those values.

Still another approach to a symbolic interactionist study of sexuality is to focus on the way people *talk* about sex, rather than on sexual behaviors themselves. In Chapter 4, Jackson and Ying Ho provide a glimpse into the discourse about premarital sex among young women in Britain and Hong Kong. Their account utilizes scripting theory as applied to sexual discourse, and in so doing, they illustrate cross-cultural differences in sexual values around virginity and risk.

Finally, Charles Edgley's chapter (5) provides a thorough and detailed introduction to dramaturgy, a core microsociological approach within symbolic interactionism. Edgley demonstrates a dramaturgical approach to sexual social behavior, or what Erving Goffman might call a "sexual situation." As an approach, dramaturgy torques the symbolic-interactionist concern with meaning slightly, by shifting from a focus on how individuals make meaning in interaction to how they communicate and collaborate on those meanings. Edgley thus illustrates how a dramaturgical approach to sex might begin to explore how sex actually "works" as a social interaction.

Taken together, these five chapters constitute an overview of symbolic-interactionist and social constructionist perspectives on sexuality, emphasizing interaction between individuals. We intend these chapters to provide theoretical tools for reading, thinking, discussing, and writing about the material in the rest of the book, and sexuality far beyond it.

Staci Newmahr

CHAPTER 1

SEX, SYMBOLIC INTERACTIONISM, AND SOCIAL CONSTRUCTIONISM

Chris Brickell

Sexuality is a profoundly social phenomenon. When we talk about sex, we use the language provided by our culture. We may be "horny," "celibate," or "lesbian"—all three at once, perhaps—"puritanical," "bisexual," or "vanilla." When we have sex, we work with numerous social expectations: Who should we get together with, where should we do it, and what should it feel like? Our media tells us all about sexuality on a daily basis. Newspapers, magazines, and websites reveal celebrity relationships and affairs, show us the sexiest bodies, and instruct us on the secrets of better sex. The social construction of sexuality is even more profound than this. What activities count as sexual in the first place? Flirting? Erotic massage? Oral sex?

Sexuality takes its meaning from its social, cultural, and historical contexts. It comes into being as human bodies, sensations, and experiences are interpreted and organized among prevailing interpretations and power relations (Seidman 2010; Vance [1989] 1998). Across time and space, sexuality is constructed in a range of contexts: families, educational institutions, religious settings, and the visual and textual representations that saturate our culture (Plummer 2003:515). From television advertisements to the gritty realities of everyday life, from the classroom to the bedroom, sexuality takes form in social settings.

A social constructionist perspective on sexuality can be distinguished from *essentialism*, the presumption that sexuality is a "natural" characteristic that flows from an individual's mind or body and forces its way outward. Instead, our sexual lives reflect broader social contexts. Social constructionist scholars challenge the view that we are slaves to our sexual desires, human robots who endlessly reiterate some kind of biological destiny. Instead, the very notion of an inherent sexuality is open to challenge, as we consider how our bodies and their capacities take shape within particular social, cultural, and historical moments. The very idea of a sexual essence, a kernel of sexual truth common to everyone and all contexts, is a social artifact in itself (Delphy 1993:5).

Language is an important element of the process of social construction. Words—*celibate*, *vanilla*, and the rest—form frameworks for knowledge. Language is an important resource with which humans construct meaning and subjectivity. It binds us into wider communities of meaning, and we share our understandings of the social and sexual world with others. In our domestic, workplace, and leisure settings, we immerse ourselves in exchanges of words, symbols, and ideas. These help to define ourselves, "our communities, our age-groups, our genders, and our era in history" (Lemke 1995:1).

This is not a predetermined process though. Even though our social worlds furnish us with possibilities and limits, words and relationships, we do not take on others' dictates wholesale. Humans rarely run mouse-like through a maze of social expectations. Instead, we negotiate our places in the sexual world when we interact with each other and with wider communities of meaning (Plummer 2002). We exist in dynamic relationships with words, symbols, and other people.

Let us have a look at an example. It is frequently assumed that people pair off in life, forging a relationship with one intimate other at a time. Legal and cultural codes buttress this assumption. A range of marriage and property laws privilege coupledom, as do most representations in the popular media (Ménard and Cabrera 2011). Weddings are the basis of a multibillion dollar industry (Ingraham 2008). Even so, rather a lot of people take part in more complicated relationships than that. More than a few have occasional casual sex or an "affair," some take up "swinging," and a few embrace nonmonogamy. The newer term *polyamory* suggests multiple love relationships that may or may not involve a sexual component (Klesse 2006). People do not necessarily live out dominant views of what a relationship "is"; there are spaces in which we might imagine sex and intimacy differently. The social construction of sexuality, then, is a negotiated process, in which prevailing assumptions give way to debate, change, and recalibration across time and location.

Some key symbolic interactionist principles help us to further explore these processes of negotiation. Harold Blumer suggests people act toward "things"— objects, other people, institutions, ideals, and activities—"on the basis of the meanings that the things have for them" (Blumer 1969:2). Like all areas of social life, aspects of sexuality have meaning only insofar as they become meaningful to their participants. As we will see, these meanings can—and do—vary profoundly between contexts.

Social and sexual worlds develop as their participants interact with each other and with the meanings that circulate around them (Craib 1984:73–79). In any given situation, a "common world" comes into being (Berger and Luckmann 1969). Within this common world, people's actions coalesce around shared "definitions of the situation," a term developed by Thomas ([1923] 1931:41). In sexual terms, the definition of the situation would involve shared assumptions about what sex means and how it ought to be experienced (with whom, in what context, in which order, and in which way, for instance).

These definitions operate within particular "interaction orders," domains of face-to-face interaction between people. Any interaction order is governed by specific rules and conditions, and participants are judged by their adherence to those rules (Goffman 1983). As a result, participants involve themselves in processes of "impression management." They put up a performance of self that others will (hopefully) regard as culturally competent and appropriate to the situation. People manage impressions of themselves in the presence of others and conduct themselves in ways that demonstrate their competence within an interaction order. We see this in recent literature on Internet life. On dating sites, for instance, participants manipulate text and photographs in ways that allow them to "come across as credible" and attractive to others (Waskul 2004b:85). The truth can be stretched a bit in these interaction orders—by displaying photos which hide or accentuate particular physical features, for instance—but participants strive to maintain a good overall impression (Zhao, Grasmuck, and Martin 2008:1819).

These contexts are rarely fixed. Meanings change within and between situations, as do definitions of situations and the rules that govern interactions (Blumer 1969). At a dinner party of traditionally minded, long-married couples, one would probably not argue that polyamory is more fulfilling than monogamy, for instance. We would probably save that discussion for those likely to be more receptive to our point of view. Only if we felt like setting the cat among the pigeons and cared little for impression management, would we disrupt the understanding that sexual intimacy is a matter for couples in enduring relationships.

These kinds of situations gesture toward the importance of space, a container in which sexuality takes on specific meanings for its participants. "Cruising" and "dogging" are two evocative examples. In his work on cruising, Brown explores the use of public spaces—toilets and parks, in particular—for sex between men (Brown 2008). Neither type of space is "constructed with cruising in mind" (916), he notes, but they allow erotic interaction orders to take shape nevertheless. Cruising encounters are "established and progressed" through a particular "sequence of gestures and movements" (917). A "flash of [the] eyes, a smile and a raised eyebrow or two" signals interest, at which point men usually head off together to a rather more private spot (920). Glances between strangers in a park or a toilet can take on meanings, not experienced by most other users of those spaces.

"Dogging"—a term coined in the United Kingdom—refers to heterosexual practices of public or semipublic sex, sometimes in combination with voyeurism and exhibitionism (Bell 2006). "Urban fringe green spaces," parks, picnic spots, and car parking areas are key locations. Dogging's technological paraphernalia—websites, mobile phones, and cars—function in symbolic ways: a text message or a flash of the headlights signals availability. When other people are invited into a sexual situation, through an open car door, for instance, they enter a spatially and temporally specific interaction order. Like cruising, dogging also redefines, albeit momentarily, public space as sexual space (Ashford 2012:43).

In these examples, sexuality emerges as a situation-specific phenomenon, one that involves variable definitions, codes, and interpretations. A car door or headlight, for instance, takes on a new symbolism in this new sexual world. In such moments, sexual selves are constituted—at least in part—through "'grounded' connections to spaces, places and people" (Gorman-Murray 2007:6).

In the world of sexuality, nothing stays the same. Simon and Gagnon point out that sexual behavior, like other aspects of social life, is always molded by the context of "pervasive social change" (Simon and Gagnon 2003:496). This comes to the surface when we consider symbolic interactionism's own sexual history. During the early part of the 20th century, University of Chicago sociologists researched the sexual spaces of their own city. Many of their subjects were hobos or bohemians, sex workers, homosexual men and women, and heterosexuals living out a philosophy of free love. In his 1907 book titled *Sex and Society,* Thomas described how "changing social conditions inevitably produced shifts in the construction of sexual norms and practices" (Heap 2003:462).

These were "grounded connections," to borrow Gorman-Murray's phrase. Researchers poked their noses into the homosexual life of the Near North Side, the hobo worlds of the cheap flophouses and otherwise-deserted alleyways. Places and situations constituted the very experience of sexuality. They gave rise to specific definitions of the situation, embedded in locally particular interaction orders. Among hobos, for instance, all-male social groups and a mobile population produced particular sexual forms: commercialized, casual heterosexual contacts, and relationships between older men and younger male "wives" (Heap 2003:466).

Sex work featured in another piece of research, this one from the early 1970s. George Lee Stewart, a graduate student, conducted ethnographic research in a brothel. He sought to investigate, as he put it, "boredom; waiting; fantasies; sex and Sex; the body; the creations, transformations, destructions, and constructions of realities, worlds, and selves" among the women who worked there (Stewart 1972:256). Stewart was a novice in the world of sex work. His inexperience produced a lively account of the construction of sexuality within this new setting. His article was titled "On First Being a John," and Stewart wrote: "I did not know what I was supposed to do. I was unskilled because I did not know what behavior was permissible, possible or required by the situation." For this researcher, at least, the brothel "was not the everyday world" (266).

Stewart wrote of his experiences in this "new meaning world" (257). On his first visit to the brothel, he delivered a letter to be passed on to the manager. The second time around, he paid for the services of one of the workers. He then discovered the "rules of interaction" that governed sex-for-pay in this particular location. The brothel's sex workers imposed a particular definition of the situation: a choreographed ritual of bodily pose, eye contact, tone of voice, and a sequence of events. One woman escorted the nervous researcher to a room, took control of the situation, and inspected and washed his genitals. As sexual activity took place, she uttered such stock phrases as "Oh wow, you sure have got me hot" and "Are you getting hot, honey?" (269–270). The sex worker showed her "situational competence," Stewart reported, a clear contrast with his own inexperience.

The unfamiliar rules and definitions of the encounter produced a sense of unreality in one unused to such a setting. "[W]hat would she do? What would I do?" Stewart wrote. "How was the situation to be managed?" (267). "I felt that I had stepped into a reality enclave as alien as the Land of Oz, a universe constituted of some different kind of reality which had its own, unknown to me, rules of operation" (268). Stewart's sexual encounter took place in a specific location—a brothel—with its own rules and definitions.

Symbolic interactionist principles can be applied to even earlier examples. Some of my own work explores a 19th-century case from a New Zealand mental hospital. This, I suggest, reveals the relationships between history, symbols, and social interactions. In 1891, 21-year-old Percy Ottywell was committed to the Seacliff Asylum. He had threatened to commit suicide when adults disapproved of his intense attraction for another young man. Under questioning within the institution, Ottywell accounted for his sexual interests this way:

> I was perfectly right until about two years ago when I happened to read a notice of a case of sodomy in a newspaper [. . .] I looked up the subject in a book and gradually I came to read things like that until after a while they seized quite a fascination over me. I don't know why I read them either because they were quite repugnant to my feelings but somehow I could not help it; one thing led to another. I actually took a pleasure in reading the beastly things about sodomy and masturbation (cited in Brickell 2006:424).

This young man drew upon a range of symbolic prompts: a story in a newspaper and other material in books. "One thing led to another," and, over time, Ottywell forged a sense of sexual difference. When the asylum's superintendent continued his questioning, other symbolic influences came to the surface: sex advice tracts and a range of "health books and pamphlets." A few of these were available in the local book store, while Ottywell borrowed some from "other young fellows." In this instance, human interactions mediated this young man's reading of written texts.

As a space for the reformulation of subjectivity, the asylum provided a setting for further interaction and reflections. Here is an excerpt from one of Ottywell's letters, sent to a contact outside the institution's walls:

> You will naturally wonder how I came to be here. I do not intend to trouble you with details of the circumstances connected with my removal here, nor of the ridiculous conduct on my part which rendered such a thing apparently necessary, suffice it to say that I conceived a very violent and unnatural affection [. . . and] announced my intention of committing suicide, because my absurd infatuation was not approved of. [. . .] At first I was in a state of great indignation but now that I have been here 10 weeks I do not look upon it quite in the same light as I did then (cited in Brickell 2006:426).

The hospital proved to be as much an interlocking set of interaction orders as a collection of buildings. Over time, Ottywell redefined his definition of the situation. Initially, with "great indignation," as he later put it, he had defended his feelings for his male companion. "You will admit that a man may love a woman—then why not one of the other sex?" he asked the asylum superintendent. "The bible says 'love one another' does it not?" (cited in Brickell 2006:425). Ten weeks later, when he wrote the letter shown here, he had redefined those feelings as "unnatural" and "absurd." Still, we cannot know whether Ottywell truly shifted his views: It is possible he wanted to manage impressions of himself—and his sexual subjectivity—to those inside and outside of Seacliff.

So far, we have seen how sexuality is constructed in a range of settings: across a dinner table, in a brothel, in a car park late at night, and in an asylum. These settings provide frameworks and interaction orders within which people understand and negotiate their sexual involvements. Symbolic interactionists evoke another location too: the theatre. The stage, they argue, is a powerful metaphor for daily life. We prepare our performances privately, "back stage," and present them "front stage" (Goffman 1959; Longmore 1998). Just as an actor's words and actions are scripted, Gagnon and Simon argued in *Sexual Conduct,* so too are our daily interactions with others. Sexuality, like other elements of social life, is played out dramaturgically. Unlike stage scripts though, sexual scripts are not hard and fast; there is no director to pull us into line if we stumble. They suggest broad plots or schemas that we might reiterate and/or deviate from. In any given time and place, people adopt and adapt scripts to varying degrees (Laumann et al. 1994:6). Gagnon and Simon's scripts are best understood as guidelines that we "actors" work with.

Whether or not given activities are even considered sexual, Gagnon and Simon suggested, depends on their social locations. "Without the proper elements of a script that defines the situation, names the actors, and plots the behavior," they contended, "nothing sexual is likely to happen" (1973:19). *Sexual Conduct* offers the medical examination as an example. Its elements, Gagnon and Simon suggested, are homologous to sexual situations in certain respects: "[T]he palpation of the breast for cancer, the gynecological examination" involve touching parts of the body that are often touched in sexual contexts (Gagnon and Simon 1973:23). In a medical setting, however, "the social situation and the actors are not defined as sexual or potentially sexual, and the introduction of a sexual element is seen as a violation of the expected social arrangements" (23). As others have argued, medical personnel project and maintain "the definition of nonsexuality" (Henslin and Briggs, cited in Longmore 1998:49).

As patterned constellations of language and action, convention and expectation, sexual scripts link specific social contexts to individuals' sexual experiences on the other. Scripts "specify with whom people have sex, when and where they should have sex, what they should do sexually, and why they should do sexual things" (Laumann et al. 1994:6). There are three elements to sexual scripts: cultural scenarios, interpersonal scripts, and intrapsychic scripts (Simon 1996; Simon and Gagnon 1987). Cultural scenarios prescribe the what and how of sexual conduct. With whom might we engage sexually, why, and when?

What is expected of us in a sexual situation? How ought we to act, and what might we expect to feel? Cultural scenarios can be highly gendered. Men are often presumed to take the role of initiators and pleasure seekers while women are expected to act as gatekeepers and satisfiers:

> The sexual script for men has been identified as including elements such as: actively seeking out sexual partners; endorsement of sexual exploits by peers; uncontrollable sexuality once aroused; and seeking sex as a source of pleasure for its own sake. For women, the sexual script is said to include elements such as: passively waiting to be chosen rather than actively seeking a partner; desire for affection or love rather than sex; and the desire to please men. (Frith and Kitzinger 2001:214)

Within social science writing, sexual scripting approaches are applied to a range of topics, from romance novels to dating behavior and scripted sex in prisons. For instance, magazines and popular novels are important sources of cultural scenarios. They offer us "cultural signposts" to guide our sexual understanding and activity: the who, what, where, when, how of sex. Ménard and Kleinplatz (2008) analyzed a range of magazines whose writers told their readers about the secrets of "great sex." Men were portrayed as sexually insatiable, while women were instructed to appear attractive to men—but not too eager. At the same time, women were instructed in techniques to enhance men's sexual pleasure rather than their own. Although men wanted sexual variety, the magazine writers suggested, romance was women's priority. Heterosexuality and monogamy were taken for granted within the scenarios offered in these magazines, whose writers proposed that "all readers want a monogamous, long-term relationship with the partner with whom they have great sex" (14).

Similar themes emerged in best-selling romance novels (Ménard and Cabrera 2011). The vast majority of novels conformed to dominant sexual scripts. Story lines revolved around young, heterosexual, attractive pairs in which men usually initiated sex and the encounter took place in the "correct order": Characters "would engage in kissing, touching and penile-vaginal intercourse in a bedroom, at night" (243). Public sex and sexual encounters between multiple partners had no place in these scenarios.

While magazines and novels offer a window into the cultural scenarios circulating in society at large, interpersonal scripts bring together individual experience and the wider world of sexual meanings. Social actors shape these broader scenarios when they go about the business of intimate relations. Some U.S.-based studies of dating scripts suggest that people often do adhere to the cultural scenarios laid out for them (Bartoli and Clark 2006; Laner and Ventrone 2000). Laner and Ventrone's research on first dates, for instance, suggest that many young people followed highly gendered scripts. Their male and female participants agreed that a man asks a woman out, decides on plans, buys flowers, picks up his date, and makes the affectionate moves later on, while a woman waits to be asked out and is taken to the venue. She attends most closely to her appearance before and during the date (493). Participants in this study often wove these scenarios into their own interpersonal scripts. Social interaction is the defining dynamic of interpersonal scripts. "Talking with friends about dates," Laner and Ventrone added, "may also reinforce culturally expected notions about expected behaviors and dating activities" (489).

Still, dominant cultural scenarios are collective reference points, not absolutes. Although there is often a strong similarity between these scenarios and interpersonal scripts, actors may also draw from "alternative cultural scenarios" (Stokes 2007). One study suggests that young Chinese and Japanese people follow both dominant and alternative scenarios (Farrer, Suo, and Tsuchiya 2012). While many research participants valorized sex within long term monogamous relationships, they also recognized—and sometimes participated in—a range of casual sexual arrangements: "one night love" (*yiyeqing*), "sex friend" (*sefure*) and "fuck buddy" (*yaritomo*), among others (277).

Intrapsychic scripts operate at the level of the sexual self, where actors internalize wider sexual meanings (Whittier and Simon 2001). A person's relationship to scripts generally stabilizes once he or she attains a sufficient degree of "sociosexual competence" and sexual satisfaction. Interpersonal and intrapsychic scripts might be renegotiated, however, if the individual moves to a new cultural context (Simon 1996:51). In a new set of interaction orders, then, sexual situations may be defined differently. Stewart's 1972 article on the brothel hints at this—with its sense of adapting to an apparently "strange" sexual world—even though Stewart did not write about scripts in particular. Keys's (2002) work on prison sexuality offers another example. Keys explains that in men's prisons, inmates construct scripts around sex between men that differ from those prevalent elsewhere. A prison's interaction orders are typically characterized by rigid hierarchy, and many inmates leave behind the scripted identities that pertained on the "outside." In this new setting, they suspend their usual understandings of one's own and others' sexual identity.

In Keys's research, the categories of "homosexual" and "heterosexual" are abandoned in favor of a distinction between dominant men (defined as "men," "jockers," "studs," or "wolves") and those positioned as subordinate ("women," "punks," "bitches," or "queens"). The second category included physically weaker men, or those with less persuasive ability. A slightness of build, an absence of facial hair, or a high-pitched voice were "signs and symbols through which the requirements and practice of specific roles are given" (Simon and Gagnon, cited in Keys 2002:265). These situations were incorporated into intrapsychic scripts. As one inmate put it, "A guy has to at least accept that going away changes your mind" (266). In prison, interpersonal and intrapsychic scripts are carefully reworked into a role that fits the context.

A scripting approach is relentlessly social. Although the "private world" of desire is often experienced as "originating in the deepest recesses of the self" (Simon 1996:43), this "world" in fact emerges at the intersection of social meanings and ongoing processes of self-creation. Sexuality depends upon the constructed character of the scripts that people use in order to make sense of individual and collective experiences.

Symbolic interactionism offers an account of agency within constraint. This applies as much to sexuality as it does to other aspects of human life. People "actively shape and re-produce scripts in multiple ways" (Mutchler 2000:33). They use, adapt, revise, and edit the symbols and meanings offered by their culture. Through these processes, social actors play out and reconstruct their "sexual fantasies and thoughts" (Lauman et al. 1994:5). The very meaning of sex is up for grabs.

We often assume sexuality to be a natural matter, an unchangeable set of drives and desires. A symbolic interactionist approach suggests another way to think about sex. Rather than expressing a sexual essence, we construct the idea of essence through our relationships with symbols and other people. Within overarching sexual contexts, we arrange information and meaning in order to construct the very notion of an inherent, essential sexuality (Plummer 2002:28). We live out what we believe to be natural and inevitable, until a new interaction order—with its own meanings—prompts us to rethink what we thought we knew for certain.

This is not to say, of course, that the sexual body is nonexistent or unimportant. Symbolic interactionism leaves room for those fleshy pleasures and pains, the "lustful desires" we come to know so well (Plummer 2003:522). However, social situations render these meaningful and provide the channels through which they take shape. Stewart describes his approach to the brothel this way: "I arrived [. . .] in a state of high anxiety. I was extremely nervous and tense; my stomach was fluttering; my joints were twinging—knees, elbows, and wrists; my chest seemed constricted; my mind went out of focus" (Stewart 1972:264). Once inside, these visceral feelings took new forms. Stewart entered the interaction order of the brothel, with its highly specific spaces, scripts, and expectations. In this unfamiliar definitional environment, even Stewart's bodily sensations seemed unreal somehow:

> Colette told me it would be necessary for her to inspect me for venereal disease. She did so, manipulating me in a manner reminiscent of someone milking a cow. Under familiar circumstances, I might have found this procedure degrading, or odd, or sexually stimulating, depending on the manipulator and the situation. However, here and now I felt nothing, as if I were not an active participant (Stewart 1972:266).

As Stewart's experience vividly suggests, contexts—both familiar and otherwise—mold bodily experience.

Although our bodies offer one important means through which we experience sexuality, we become sexual subjects not by expressing an already-meaningful, sexualized inner impulse. Instead, we assemble sexual meanings during our interactions with other members of society. Precisely how we do this depends on the meanings given to feelings and situations by ourselves and others, the resources through which these might form into scripts, and our wider social relationships. We are always involved in negotiating and modifying sexual scenarios as we put together interpersonal and intrapsychic scripts. Meanings and interactions are not only the building blocks of symbolic interactionist theory: They are the stuff of human life.

CHAPTER 2

MUSCLE AND BLOOD

Erotic Fantasy in Theory and Practice

Don Kulick

*E*DITORS' NOTES: *Fundamentally, symbolic interactionism is concerned with meaning-making processes. That is, interactionists are interested in how we understand our social realities, how we come to understand them as such, and how these understandings are grounded in social interaction. In this chapter, Don Kulick draws on conceptual tools from psychoanalytic thought, in order to explore aspects of sexual life in Gapun, Papua New Guinea. Although psychoanalysis and symbolic interactionism differ in important ways from one another, they often share an inclination to interpret and explain social behavior through interaction with others. The empirical and theoretical contributions of this chapter address the broader symbolic interactionist question of meaning-making. (Kulick's concern with psychoanalysis is itself a meaning-making endeavor, turning to cultural articulations of nonerotic fantasy in order to understand constructions of desire.)*

This chapter illustrates the extent to which what we find erotic is culturally constructed and socially situated. In other words, what we find sexually arousing is powerfully related to culture. It demonstrates that many of the things that we consider to be sexual universals—such as masturbation and orgasm—are not consistent across societies, but bounded by broader cultural values. By illuminating the extent to which these things operate differently within different meanings across cultures, Kulick challenges essentialist views of sexuality. Finally, his experiences in the field and conversations with his informants demonstrate the crucial role that social interaction plays in the construction of the erotic and of the sexual. The eroticism of the fantasies Kulick relays is a product of a different relationship to the social interactions of abstinence and denial.

If you have a strong reaction to the stories Kulick tells, explore those reactions as cultural products. What cultural conditions and values might lead you to react this way? What, for example, does the penis symbolize in Western culture, and how does this affect our reactions? How do social interactions in our societies shape the way we think and feel about blood? What can we learn about our

broader social values from an inquiry into the fantasy lives of the men in Gapun?
What does masturbation mean for us? What meanings around abstinence are
operating in these fantasies? How do our social interactions inform, shape, and
reproduce different relationships to sexual abstinence and sexual denial?

⊗⊗⊘

One dimension of sexuality that presents special problems of understanding
is the realm of fantasy. We know from our own experience that people have
fantasies and that fantasies do things—they inspire, they repel, they motivate,
they fulfill, they disgust, they enliven. But how we might consider fantasy in the
analysis of ethnographic data about sexuality is a question that vexes.

One reason it vexes is because many social scientists have a weak
understanding of what fantasy is. Many think of fantasy in the commonplace
way as illusion, or, as a flight or an escape from reality. That, however, is too
simplistic. Fantasies are not opposed to reality. Instead, they help to constitute
reality. A psychoanalytic truism is that fantasy is always in dynamic interplay
with social life. Fantasy arises from unresolved relations to other people and
out of our particular positions as subjects in society. It influences one's
perceptions of the world and one's actions in it. If I believe that my neighbor
or my boss or my mother or my cat loves me, or can love me, or doesn't love
me, then that will influence what happens in the real world, in my social
relations and my interactions with others.

In psychoanalytic theory, fantasies are understood as the stagings or the
settings of desire. They are not exactly the same thing as desire. A helpful way
of thinking about fantasies is to consider them like a movie or a play where the
script is written by desire, and all the characters represent different dimensions
or aspects of desire. Fairy tales have been analyzed in this way. The child
psychologist Bruno Bettelheim argued in his book *The Uses of Enchantment*
that a fairy tale is the expression of fantasy—one that both formulates
unconscious dilemmas and attempts to resolve them: the fear of abandonment
in a fairy tale like "Hansel and Gretel," of sibling rivalry in "Cinderella," of
feelings of inferiority and inadequacy in the "Ugly Duckling" (Bettelheim
1976). An analysis like Bettelheim's is helpful in drawing attention to the
accessibility of fantasy—to the way that fantasy can be articulated in language,
in culturally legible fashions. Bettelheim's analysis also makes it easier to see
that fantasy is not the same as desire. An abandonment fantasy like the one
staged in "Hansel and Gretel" does not represent the desire to be abandoned.
A more adult example would be a rape fantasy, which does not represent the
literal desire to be raped; or a killing fantasy, which does not represent the
straightforward desire to murder.

An important psychoanalytic point about fantasy is that it choreographs particular desires and identifications and it scrambles and codes them in ways that need to be interpreted. One identifies with different features of a fantasy in different ways and with different intensities—and those identifications may not be approving avowals. In thinking about this, it is important to maintain a conceptual distinction between "identifications" and "identities." The feminist scholar Diana Fuss, in her book on the concept of identification, has defined it as "a process that keeps identity at a distance, that prevents identity from ever approximating the status of an ontological given." Identifications are "mobile, elastic and volatile," Fuss writes, and approaches to identity need to come to terms with the way that identity "is continually compromised, imperiled, one might even say *embarrassed* by identification" (1995:2, 8, 10, emphasis in original). Cultural critic Laura Kipnis agrees, arguing that "identification doesn't mean you like it or want to do it. It may be ambivalent, or based on relics and repressions from the past. All it means is that something hooks you about the scene, and you don't necessarily know what" (1998:197). Identifications are staged, evoked, and materialized in fantasy.

Freudian psychoanalysts have debated what they call the topographical location of fantasies—do they arise in the unconscious, the preconscious (that is, in that level of the psyche that can be brought to consciousness with a bit of thought), or the conscious? There are clearly different kinds and degrees of fantasy—daydreaming about being on a warm beach or eating chocolate mousse is not exactly the same as dreaming about being attacked by two-meter tall spiders that look like your mother. But it ought to be possible for social scientists to work with the concept of fantasy without worrying too much about where it is located in the psyche or how it arises. Freud himself expressed different views, at different points during his long life, about the genesis and location of fantasy. His main concern, though, was not so much to typologize as it was to explore the ways in which fantasies act as dense transfer points between processes that are unconscious and those that are conscious.

SNEAKING OFF INTO THE RAIN FOREST IN PAPUA NEW GUINEA

With those considerations about fantasy as a theoretical concept in mind, I now turn to the empirical example I will discuss, which is one of erotic talk, taken from my fieldwork in the country of Papua New Guinea. I have conducted a total of over three years of fieldwork there, in a small, isolated village called Gapun. I went to Gapun for the first time in the mid-1980s. I spent 15 months in the village then, gathering material for a study of language shift. Papua New Guinea is compelling in terms of language because it is the most linguistically diverse country on Earth (almost 1,000 different languages, most of them undescribed, spoken by a population of about six million people). Many of those languages are disappearing. The little ("literally small") language with which I worked in Gapun is called Tayap by its speakers. There is nothing to indicate that Tayap was ever spoken by more than about 200 people. But by the 1980s, children no longer spoke it as their first language, and only about 87 people spoke it actively. I documented the sociocultural reasons why the villagers were allowing their ancestral language to die.

I left Gapun in 1987 and returned in 1992, planning to gather more linguistic material that would allow me to write a grammar and dictionary of the dying Tayap. By that time, however, Papua New Guinea had become a very dangerous place, and I left the village after only a few months (Kulick 1992, 1993). The country is still a staple on lists of "Top 10 Most Dangerous Places in the World"—usually coming soon after Chechnya, Somalia, and South Sudan—but I did return 17 years later, in 2009, and I spent 8 months living in the village again. I also went back for a month in 2010.

The point of going back to Gapun in 2009 was to gather the linguistic material I had hoped to collect in 1992. I also wanted to see whether the predictions about language shift that I had made in the 1980s had come to pass. To assess that, I spent a lot of time with young women and men between the ages of about 14 to 26, to try to observe their linguistic practices and gauge their linguistic competence.

With the young men, I engaged in activities like going into the rain forest to look for birds to shoot with arrows or slingshots. I sat with them, drinking homemade alcohol that they only recently had learned to brew. I also accompanied them when they went off together in groups to perform a variety of secret practices. These practices are what I will analyze here. There are ethical problems in writing about them, because women are not supposed to know about them. Women do know about them, unsurprisingly—in a village of only 200 people in the middle of a rain forest, not much about people's intimate lives remains a mystery. The young men publicly pretend that women don't know anything about what they do, even if, in private, individual men concede that women do know about it. Women, too, readily described to me what the men go off into the rain forest to do, sometimes taking the opportunity to scoff at the men's pretension that they are too unobservant to know. The young men gave me permission to write about their activities. They reason that it doesn't matter to them one way or another if people outside Papua New Guinea know about them.[1]

Here is what happens when young village men go off together into the forest: When someone has been able to obtain a steel razor blade, young men between the ages of 14 and 26 go, in groups that range between two and five young men or more. The young men go to places usually at least a 40 minute walk from the village, to places where there is some source of water, ideally a stream or a creek, and where they are both sheltered from the view of anyone who might happen to walk by or they will hear anyone approaching. Once they all get to this place, they use a machete to divide the razor blade into sharp shards. Everybody gets a shard. Then, they undress, and they stand tugging at their penises. Some men walk away from the others and stand on their own, others stand only slightly apart from others, and others stand close to others and whisper erotic stories to one another. These erotic stories are all about fantasy, and I'll return to them in a minute.

In order to help their penis "get muscle" (*kisim masel*), as they say in their colorful way, some young men chew coconut meat and spit onto their penises thus providing lubrication. But interestingly, they never touch, caress, or stroke any other parts of their bodies, such as their stomach, chest, balls, nipples, or backside. All they do is shake and pull at their penises. When the penis becomes hard from the combination of manual stimulation and mental stimulation aided by the erotic stories, a young man is ready to do what he came to do. He takes the sharp shard of the razor blade, raises it up, and jabs it straight into the head of the penis. As one might imagine, the engorged organ releases a geyser of blood that spurts from the puncture. This action is what gives the practice the name the young men call it in Tok Pisin—the creole language that is replacing Tayap. They call the practice *sut,* which means "shoot," or "pierce."

This first blood that gushes into the forest is bad blood. It is blood that has remained in your body from when your mother gave birth to you. It is black, the men say. You want to get rid of it. This blood is either expelled directly into flowing water, which will wash it away, or onto a leaf that will be thrown into the rain forest. The rest of the blood—and there is usually quite a lot—is better blood. It is still something you want to expel, but it is freshly produced blood and redder than the blood that comes directly from the body of your mother. This better, redder blood is milked into half a coconut shell that the young man has prepared and has handy by his side. When he has milked all the blood he can from the puncture that he has made in the one side of his penis, he ideally starts all over again, tugging at the penis until it is hard again, and then he jabs it on the other side of the head, repeating the process once again. If a young man is afraid to pierce his own penis, one of the other young men will stand beside him and jab it for him.

Once you've pierced your penis twice and have milked the blood into a coconut shell, you chew more coconut and spit some of the chewed up mixture into your hand. You then take your coconut shell full of what by this time is rather coagulated blood and you pour some of the blood from the coconut shell into the same palm that contains the coconut. You smear this white and red mixture all over your body. When you have covered much of your body, you go to a stream and wash it all off. Then, in the short version of the act, you come back and dry yourself by a fire, get dressed, and go back to the village. In the longer version of this act, which young men do if they have the time and the inclination, they take the blood that remains in the shell, and they climb a kind of tree with light bark, known as the Kandum tree. They smear the remaining blood on it, in order to make their own skin appear as light and bright as the bark of the tree, and, so that the black ants that are found on the trees will fight over the blood, just like women will fight over the young man. Then, the young man climbs down, rubs a bit more blood on his body to enliven it, dries off by a fire, gets dressed, and goes.

Why do they do it? The simple reason is in order to pep themselves up—to restore vigor and look more beautiful. Penis piercing is similar to the old European custom of bloodletting. The young men think that by letting blood they will become healthier and stronger. Generally speaking, blood—especially the blood that one retains in one's body from the time before birth—is a bad, hot fluid. One never wants too much blood. Too much blood can cause headaches and feelings of tiredness and despondency. In children, too much blood is thought to cause temper tantrums, and kids who cry too much are held down and cut on the face and stomach with a razor blade, to help their bodies expel the bad blood that is causing them to cry. Both women and men regard menstruation as something good—menstrual blood is potentially deadly to men, but the act of menstruation is great, because it flushes out old, bad, debilitating blood from the body. Men can't menstruate, but they can bloodlet, and this is what they do when they pierce their penis. Men recognize the parallel and even insist on it. Some young men told me that they time their sessions in the rain forest with the moon, to correspond to female menstruation.

So the point of bloodletting is to feel better, to "strengthen the skin" (*strongim skin*), and look more beautiful. Men go off and pierce their penises when they are feeling lethargic, when they haven't been having much success hunting, or when they want to attract women for sex or perhaps a relationship. The men say that the blood they rub on their skin heats it up, and they emerge from the forest looking luminous. Men who see them, perceiving their sudden and intense glow, will immediately know the reason. Women, the young men say, won't know what hit them when they see the newly bloodlet men. They will simply be bowled over and find them irresistible.

Penile cutting like this exists in various forms throughout Papua New Guinea and has been described by many anthropologists. One classic book about the area is even titled *The Island of Menstruating Men* (Hogbin [1970] 1996). In Gapun, penile bloodletting has existed forever[2], but it used to take a different form—a vine with stiff, hooked bristles used to be inserted into the urethra and yanked out. This ceased after WWII, when the elaborate initiation cycles that used to exist in the area were definitively abandoned and when young men of the time refused to perform such painful acts that left them incapacitated for weeks afterward.

Until recently, penile bloodletting used to be a private act. Adolescent men would be instructed in what to do by a maternal uncle, and they would go off into the rain forest and do it privately by themselves. This changed because of soccer. The villagers used to play games of soccer every Sunday with teams from other villages on the grounds of a school located about 2 hours from Gapun. In the early 1990s, the captain of the village soccer team initiated a ritual whereby he took the team into the forest on the afternoon before a game and had everyone pierce their penis and cut their legs so that blood would flow and they would all be strong and swift and invincible on the playing field the following day. This initiated the practice of going off together in groups, which continues today.

GOOD EROTIC STORIES

Going off into the bush in groups also initiated the practice of telling erotic stories. Before I examine those in detail, I want to make explicit what I have only been hinting at until now. And that is this: The purpose and the effect of the stories are not orgasm—at least not orgasm in the way most people probably imagine it. It took me a long time and much observation of these activities to work up the courage to talk about masturbation, but in the conversations I had with various men, both individually and in groups, I came to the unexpected realization that masturbation is not a universal sexual act. Men in Gapun never actually masturbate to ejaculation. They find the whole idea strange and rather disgusting. They have wet dreams, but the pleasure they derive from those dreams does not get translated into the idea that one might do it oneself. What happens instead when they masturbate is that as soon as their penis gets erect, they jab it with a razor blade and spurt blood. So while the men can be said to excite themselves sexually through masturbation, the sexual release they achieve as a result of this masturbation is not the ejaculation of semen, it is the ejaculation of blood.[3]

To get to this desired endpoint, young men tell each other erotic stories as they stand next to one another pulling on their penises. Anyone might tell such a story, but some young men are acknowledged experts in the genre and are sought after by men who want to hear a thrilling tale.

The stories that the young men tell to excite one another have two basic narrative trajectories. The stories are short formulaic tales of a man meeting a woman and having sex with her—or, and this is what I'll spend some time discussing below—of *not* having sex with her. Here is a typical example of the first kind of erotic story—it was told by a 19-year-old villager in the context I've described. Here is a translation of the story, which was told in Tok Pisin:

> So Sakoko took Mbopai and went inside [into the rain forest; laughs]. He like took her and went inside, took her and went inside, he fucked her. Fucked her, fucked, fucked her for a long time (*kuapim em i go go go*). I was standing watching the house. I was watching the house and she came by. She came by and she broke a branch and I heard her and I thought to myself "Oi, she's coming." I stood there and watched her as she came. "What were you doing in there?" She told me, "I went and Sakoko sent word for me, but I didn't feel like it." When I put out my hand and felt her cunt it was wet. So I got up and I didn't waste any time, I lifted her and laid her down, just lifted her and laid her down, and I didn't waste any time, I put my big man [i.e., penis] inside her. I put the big man and when I was putting it inside she suddenly closed her legs. "Fuck that [*kaikai kan*, lit. "eat cunt"]. You're a big girl, open your legs." Like that. She opened her legs, opened her legs, and me too I didn't waste any time, I fucked her. I fucked her for awhile and my cock suddenly fell out and she held my cock—I'm telling you, it felt nice. I went to it, I didn't waste any time, I fucked her. I finished fucking her, I told her "I'm gonna stay here, you like go first, you take off first. I'll come [back into the village] later." She took off first, I came later.

Here is the second kind of erotic story. In this kind of narrative, the erotic charge lies not in having sex; the erotic charge lies in *not* having sex.

> Listen to the story about Kokom [this is the village's Mrs. Robinson—a married, now divorced, woman in her 40s with six children]. Listen Kokom, Kokom. We came and she was making a sago pancake. She was making a sago pancake and she got up, me and Devid came and she went inside her house. And she was wearing trousers. She was wearing trousers. She went inside and took off the trousers and put on just a skirt. Just a

skirt and she came outside. She came outside and she lifted her leg to make a sago pancake and her cunt was really open. I saw it and my cock got really tight [i.e., erect]. I saw it and I said to Devid, "Enough, let's run away." We got up and went to the men's house.

This story, where young men are invited to have sex but they decline the invitation, is a variation on what young men in Gapun agreed was the *ki stori*, the key erotic story, the master erotic narrative, in the village. This is the story that will give any man erection, I was told. It is the New Guinean erotic equivalent of a coronary defibrillator—this story will shock even the most recalcitrant penis into an erection, which can then be pierced.

This story was told to me privately, late one night in my house, by a young man in his 20s. He told me the story in a tone that suggested that an important secret was being revealed. Here is the translation of the transcript of the story:

This boy [a young village man whom everybody knows and who was a young man of about 15 at the time of the event], he went to work sago. He finished and he was really feeling sleepy and he went up into a bush house and lay down. He was lying down and this woman, the same one we were just talking about [also Kokom, the woman who appeared in the previous story], she also came. She arrived and she went up into the bush house, sat on the floor and put her skirt—but she wasn't wearing any trousers or underpants . . . OK, she went up into the bush house and sat down. She sat down and raised her two legs [i.e., she sat on her bottom with her legs bent at the knees in front of her, as opposed to the usual cross-legged style in which women sit].

Don: Did she know he was there?

She was feeling. She was feeling. It's like feelings came and she felt like, she felt like "having sex" [in English] right then.[4] So she sat there and raised her legs, and she showed everything. She turned and faced the boy and she opened her legs. The boy was lying down. He was lying down and she faced him and opened her legs. Showed him again. And the boy turned and looked. Oh no, the boy felt shame. He tried to turn his eyes away; he looked back and saw the same thing. She pulled her skirt all the way up and she opened her legs again at the boy. She opened them really wide, showed everything.

Don: And what was the boy doing? Just lying there?

The boy was lying there. His big man was "alert" [in English]. It was like that and the boy felt that this wasn't right. OK, a little girl came. I don't know who. She came and . . . the big woman told her "Come and look for lice in my hair." The girl came and looked for lice and she turned again and opened her legs again at the boy again. The man looked for a long time and he was sick of it. The woman was really feeling and she wanted to fuck right then.

So she said to the boy, "I've hidden some bananas up over there. If you'd like to eat bananas, OK, the two of us can go get them." She tried to butter him up now.

The boy said to her, "No, I don't want to go. The sun is hot and I don't want to go."

"Sss, get up and let's go," the woman said to him. "Get up and let's go. Or if you don't want to go [together], I'll tell you where they are, where the bananas are, and you can go."

The boy said, "No, I don't want to."

"Don't be like that, come, let's go," the woman was really pushing him, really strongly. She really wanted the boy to go with her. But she pushed in vain. The boy knew that if he went with her, the two of them would fuck, and he was afraid. He was afraid of fucking this big mama. Like the woman was feeling like she wanted to fuck right then. He was afraid of the mama. Her thing is a really big thing [laughs]. So the boy said no. OK, so the boy just stayed there. The woman went by herself and got the bananas and came back. She gave one to him but he didn't want to eat it. The boy had seen the thing [i.e., the woman's vagina] and he didn't want to eat. He said he didn't want to.

That's it. This is the story, as I mentioned above, which is the most erotically charged story that the young village men know. It is guaranteed to give you "muscle."

Obviously, this is very rich material that might be analyzed in a variety of ways. But here, I want to focus on how the fantasies enunciated here stage desire. At the most transparent level, it is obvious that in these stories, sex is highly desirable, and the male protagonists are always prepared. No foreplay is necessary to arouse a man; his "big man" is ready for action. These men don't "waste any time"; their members are "tight" and "alert." Women in these stories are presented as though they are naturally enchanted by this zestful male aura. In the first story, the woman has sex with the narrator after having just had sex with another man. She has a moment of hesitation, but that resistance is easily overcome.

Notice the contrast with the other two stories, where *male* hesitation is not overcome. The erotic allure of the woman in the second and third stories—an older, experienced, childbearing woman, a "big mama" who has a "really big thing" that refuses to be cloaked and who, in the third story, offers "the boy" a banana, of all things, to eat—this is a scenario practically screaming out for a Freudian reading. But while the *mis-en-scène* of erotic tension here is important and revealing, perhaps most telling is the way the anxieties raised in the stories are resolved. Rather than succumbing to the big mama's big thing, protagonists refuse the demand the thing makes on them. In the second story, the two young men resolve the narrative's tension by "running away." In the "key story," the young protagonist does what feminist self-empowering advice tells women to do in the face of sexual solicitation they do not want: he just says "no." This is not a resolution, needless to say, that features prominently in erotic stories produced by Western men. Note that one thing the refusal does, though, is keep desire in play. Desire is not fulfilled here; it is postponed. Even after the flight or the refusal, the demand remains present. In neither story does the source of the demand—the big thing—disappear or go away. In the second story, the two young men run away from it—it remains where it was. And in the key story, the boy says no, but the thing goes nowhere, and it will, it seems implied, keep on repeating its coercive solicitation and elicit desire, deferring it, keeping it possible and alive, in the diegesis of the narrative, forever.

Why is the fantasy of running away from sex, or refusing it, erotic for these young men? In order to understand that, we need cultural contextualization. We need to be able to interpret why the narrator of the key story twice says that the young man was "afraid" of the mama and her really big thing, and we need to be able to comprehend why this fear is pleasurable. The fear expressed here is an acknowledgment that sex in New Guinea is fraught with danger for men. Heterosexual sex strengthens women, because they become infused with male semen. But it weakens men, who absorb female blood and vaginal fluids. This menace, of course, in many cases adds to the allure of sex. It certainly does in this fantasy—note how the anxiety that surrounds the sex act is both acknowledged and resolved by the man's refusal. And note how that refusal is productive—it affects the erotic charge that makes a young man's penis tight and ready for jabbing with a razor blade. From a psychoanalytic perspective, the narratives are quintessentially phallic, not because they are about the penis—in many senses, they are not—but because the scenario they construct is an articulation of structure; of both having and not-having: The men don't have sex because they refuse to, but they also *have sex* because as they hear the story, their penis gets hard, and they obtain sexual release by stabbing it with a razor blade. So the narratives conjure up a kind of utopian phantasmal nirvana of plenitude, where men can experience themselves as alluring, where they can enjoy erotic pleasure, and where they can obtain sexual release—all while being in absolute control and without exposing themselves to the danger of decay that necessarily results when they actually have intercourse with a woman. This is all fantasy, but it is a productive fantasy, with affective appeal, interactional substance, and demonstrable social force.

Note that this kind of analysis in no way suggests that the young men who tell a story like the key story and listen to it are necessarily identifying with the young male protagonist. For all we know, individual men may be identifying with the big mama's seduction of the young man or with the little girl who strokes the big mama's scalp as the mama flashes her thing—or even with the lice the girl unfastens from their embrace of the skin and the hair of the mama. Tellers and listeners may be switching identifications or multiply identifying throughout the narrative. We don't know, and they may not know either, in the sense of being consciously aware of their identifications and how those produce the erotic charge that they experience. The point is that the narrative articulates a range of relations and positions and makes them available to be identified with, or against. And the identifications animated by the narrative provide various measures of pleasure, or displeasure; varying measures of investment, or disavowal.

This is what fantasy does, and this is why examples like the ones presented here can help us think about sexuality in ways that extend our engagement with social theory—including psychoanalytic theory, which I, and many others along with me, regard as a species of social theory. Just as fantasy in psychic life is a transfer point between unconscious and conscious processes and relations, so ought we be able to use explicit engagement with fantasy as a transfer point between different theories of subjectification—between those that highlight knowing and intentionality, and those (like psychoanalysis, or poststructuralism) that argue that language always expresses more, always expresses differently, than speaker intention. An exploration of fantasy could facilitate a more expansive and supple understanding of speaking subjects, and of how people use language to materialize different kinds of desires. To think seriously about "fantasy" opens up analyses to other, related concepts, like "identification" and "desire." It frees up analysis to explore, with a greater array of perceptions and poetics, how language moves people, touches them, and affects them. It would complicate notions of investment and interaction.

But most of all, thinking seriously about fantasy in narratives and interactions moves our thought about sexuality beyond the view that people's psychic lives must remain unknowable and unanalyzable by social scientists. If we can identify the persistence, the structure, and the meaning of *that* fantasy, then we might be able to resolve some of our own analytic anxieties, and push our analysis of sexuality onto exciting, fresh, more open ground.

1. Obviously, this matter is more complex than that, given the fact that a book like the one in which this chapter appears may well end up not only in Papua New Guinea, but also it may, one day in the probably distant future, be read by individual villagers or people who know them. This kind of ethical quandary haunts the study of intimate sexual practices, and different people will advocate different resolutions to it. I am, myself, not entirely decided on the best way to handle material like this, and one reason for publishing it here is to encourage discussion and debate. I am not convinced, however, by the sometimes-voiced argument that the best way of handling these kinds of data is to simply *not* write about it. I think that exploring sexual diversity is important, both as a scholarly project and a political one. And while I acknowledge that material like this is sensitive, I have concluded that discussing it in a publication like this will most likely not result in harm or embarrassment for any individual, partly because all the names in this chapter are pseudonyms and some details have been changed and partly because, as I mention in the text, the kinds of practices described here are widespread throughout Papua New Guinea. The "secret" nature of the acts I discuss is rhetorical rather than real, which means that even if a villager were to read this account, it would not tell him (or, I stress, her) anything more than he or she already pretty much knows about the practices that take place when groups of young men suddenly go off together into the rain forest.

2. The Tayap term is the euphemism *mirinan awinni tuwku*—"to bathe in rain forest water."

3. Another dimension of the practice that surprised me is that, as far as I was able to tell (and I concentrated very hard on being able to tell), there was no homoerotic exchange or tension during these sessions in the rain forest. This is surprising partly because in other parts of the country, bloodletting acts like the ones described here used to be part of a complex of relations between men that included sex (Herdt 1981, 1993). As far as I have been able to determine, though, sex between men does not occur in Gapun. The young men I observed clearly enjoyed being together, and they liked the thrill of the erotic stories and of doing something secretive together with others. But I never witnessed anyone's eyes linger over the bodies of his masturbating friends and relatives; there were no comments or jokes—defensive or affirmative—about homosexuality; no one ever had a spontaneous, ready erection before the storytelling began; and no one ever ejaculated semen or looked like they were about to or wanted to. The atmosphere during the sessions was jocular, but businesslike. The men were there to produce blood, and as soon as the penis became hard enough to jab, they jabbed it.

4. English is the main language of instruction in Papua New Guinean schools. Most village children learn almost nothing because of poor instruction and frequent strikes by teachers. Talk about sex is an area where some villagers do pick up some English, however, through contact with young villagers outside Gapun, and, also through songs by Papua New Guinean bands that are played on the radio or circulated on cassette tapes.

CHAPTER 3

STATING DESIRE

Sexuality, the State, and Social Control

Misty Luminais

The state, through laws and enforcement, acts as the guardian of morality, constructing appropriate sexualities. While we might like to believe that desire is a personal choice or a natural urge, the state has a distinct role in shaping who is a suitable object and what methods can be used to express that desire. As a group, one kinky community in Texas sees itself as resisting vanilla hegemony by flaunting some aspects of the law. However, to paint all actions in this kinky community as resistance misses the internal tensions within the group. Elites in the community mimic the power of the state for their own purposes to maintain the status quo. In this "outlaw" community, particular laws are mocked, and yet members hold fast to a belief in the rule of law. Although many people question the law as it pertains to their behavior particularly, this does not lead to questions about the fundamental nature of the law, where the authority to enforce it derives from, nor whom the law benefits or oppresses. When a final account is tallied, most members of the kinky community reap the benefits of living in this law-abiding society. The state, in both its concrete and spectral forms, informs the construction of sexuality.

I worked as an anthropologist in a kinky community of a large city in Texas I call Cactus for twenty months between 2009 and 2011, conducting ethnographic research that focused on participant-observation and semistructured interviewing. The term *kinky* refers to a set of physical and relational practices based on a consensual, unequal distribution of power in a sexual setting. This community consists of roughly 100 core members involved in several umbrella groups that unite the community and a number of smaller specialty groups. People participate in the community through bondage/discipline/dominant/submissive/sado/masochism (BDSM) parties, social events in vanilla (non-kinky) settings, study groups, conferences, and online social networking. Many of the larger groups are pansexual, meaning that anyone of any sexuality or gender presentation is welcome. In practice, however, these groups are predominantly heterosexual. This kinky community serves as an illustration of the way larger forces shape what are considered intimate experiences, in part due to the public display of sexuality and the community's explicit self-reflection on what it means to be kinky in relation to the self and to others.

In order to understand how the state shapes and controls desire, one must understand the possible direct interventions of the state, meaning "a formal government that has the capacity and authority to make laws, and use force to defend the social order" (Haviland et al. 2008:656), in kinky affairs. The justice system has access to municipal, state, and federal laws to monitor and censure participants in the kinky community, including laws on prostitution, kidnapping, rape, assault, unlawful restraint, indecent exposure, and human trafficking. Some of the basic activities which lead to legal scrutiny include flogging, branding, cutting, electrocution, and rope bondage. More complex situations also enter a legally gray area, including the commercial aspect of kinky parties and the concept of "consensual nonconsent." Consensual nonconsent is a contested term in various communities, but in Cactus it usually referred to a type of play where a person acts (and sometimes feels) as if the attention (sexual or otherwise) is unwanted, such as in a rape fantasy or a punishment scene, while retaining the power to stop the scene by using a safe word. These acts could lead to serious charges being levied. Members of the kinky community take great pains to demonstrate that they are not violating these laws by focusing on the consent of participants, but whether or not intention is taken into account in possible charges depends on the individual officer who responds to any given situation. Part of what leads to such intense self-monitoring in the community is the capriciousness with which the law may be applied. Community members try to preempt possible sanctions by creating explicit interpretations of the acts the law legislates and structuring their own activities and others' in such a way as to avoid violating the intention of the law.

The police play a particular role in the kinky community, which is a distillation of the wider American society's uneasy relationship with law enforcement. On the one hand, the police are admired and even lionized. On the other, they are feared as agents of oppression. In the kinky community, masculinity is often performed as an imitation of military bearing and discipline. The kinky community traces its roots to the gay male leather community, which was founded, according to lore, by gay service men returning from World War II. Historically, some men (and now some women) with military backgrounds found themselves drawn to the kinky community. It functions as a feedback loop—ex-military people intensify the militant feel of a community, which in turn attracts more veterans and other people who admire the military. It makes sense that this militant atmosphere engenders a sense of fraternity with the police. Both groups serve the country in potentially violent situations, to enforce order and distribute justice, at least ideally. Even people who have not served in the military emulate the example of law enforcement in dress, mannerisms, and attention to protocol to project a sense of masculinity.

Simultaneously, the police are seen as agents of vanilla oppression. In their role as enforcers of morality, their power is anxiety provoking. One reason for the community's uneasy relationship with law enforcement is that the police's power reveals the constructed nature of the power exchange relationships between community members. Haviland defines power as "the ability of individuals or groups to impose their will upon others and make them do things even against their own wants or wishes" (Haviland et al. 2008:655). Consent is the bedrock on which the kinky community is based, making it a society of peers. Not everyone has the same influence or prestige, but there is no raw, awesome power. The presence of the police, with their ability to strip away freedom backed up by the authority of the state, exposes the performative nature of kinky relationships. Police can serve as a rupture in what is otherwise a mutually agreed upon pretense. It is for this very power that the police inspire awe. Additionally, people suspect the capricious nature of law enforcement. Although they believe that a rational examination of the facts will reveal that no transgression has taken place, community members also acknowledge that how the law is applied depends on the context. The more a person resembles a model citizen, the more liberties it is assumed one has. A white, heterosexual, middle-class man is perceived to be able to stretch the law with fewer repercussions than a poor, queer, woman of color.

Another aspect of state control involves the civil courts. Most of the people I interviewed either did not have children or their children were grown. Logistically, it is difficult to juggle small children with involvement in a community where children are banned. Children make participating in the kinky community more risky by their very existence. For parents with traditional-looking relationships (for example, married with no acrimony), there is always the outside possibility that their fitness as parents could be called into question by someone in authority. Things escalate when parents are in the midst of a divorce and child custody is at stake. It is in this role that the courts are seen as most dangerous. Many ex-spouses use whatever ammunition they can to paint their former partner as a poor parent. All too often, involvement with the kinky community is used as part of the basis for denying a parent custody, even if it is clear that there is no child abuse (Klein and Moser 2006).

The state as both the shaper of and distillation of hegemony influences the construction of sexuality beyond the scope of specific laws. Cultural hegemony is a concept used by social scientists and philosophers to explain the existence and reproduction of oppression. Following Borón, by "hegemony" I refer to "the Gramscian concept of an ideology-based dominance that is exercised by the state and enjoys consensus, thus legitimating the interests of the upper-classes" (Martínez and Breña 2007:47). The concept of hegemony has been used fruitfully to examine how ideologies can reinforce, and in some cases replace, traditional state power by manipulating and shaping consciousness to allow the elite to exploit people with lower status, economically, intellectually, sexually, and culturally (Alison 1999; Ling 1996; Myers 1998; Quinlan 1998; Salter and Salter 2007).

A complicated example of hegemony in the United States is the beauty standard for women. In a simplified analysis, women and girls are taught by society through media and peer pressure that only certain body types are desirable. Many women are unhappy with their bodies and strive to achieve the "perfect" body type, despite the fact that it causes physical pain (extreme exercise, restrictive clothing) and costs money (diet aids, gym memberships, etc.). There is no police force dictating beauty standards, coercing women into behaving contrary to their own interests. However, certain segments of the society benefit from women's discontent with their bodies such as the media and the fashion industry. Less directly, the people with political and economic power gain because the time and effort women might otherwise use to question the status quo is instead spent on attempting to achieve an unachievable ideal. Using the framework of hegemony allows us to analyze how the overt meanings of social practice obscure power structures which benefit the few at the expense of the many.

I focus less on the economic forces of hegemony than the ideological and social implications of cultural domination. Intellectual and cultural hegemony is often teased out as the relationship between the colonizer and the colonized. The kinky community is certainly not colonized territory, but the concept of hegemony is useful in understanding how the dominant ideology of the United States, especially as codified and enforced as law, is both contested and embraced by members of the kinky community. For example, the belief that sex should necessarily be procreative, rather than simply pleasurable, has been enshrined in both popular understanding and in the law. For years, there were laws against adultery (extramarital affairs) and sodomy (including oral and anal sex between people of any gender). Recently, there has been a shift in both arenas, notably the growing acceptance of gay marriage. However, the belief that sex should still be private and shared only between two people remains. The kinky community, with its embrace of public displays of eroticism (and sometimes sex) and expectation of multiple partners, questions the sanctity of these beliefs about sex. In its embodied practices, the kinky community resists the hegemonic ideal of monogamous sex as the only valid form of sexual expression.

While under threat of state interference from legislators, the police, the judicial system, and the medical community, members of the kinky community also deploy these same threats toward their own ends through mimicry of the state, using laws and mainstream cultural conventions to functionally exclude certain groups of people from parties or to monitor behavior and membership. The reproduction of hegemony in the kinky community illustrates how fully integrated this group is in a state-level society.

I had my own experience with how hegemony functioned in the form of state interference and the resulting discourse at a Libidinousness United in Sadomasochism, Texas (LUST)[1] party. What follows is an excerpt based on my field notes:

I had been hesitant to play in public, for a number of reasons. However, my interviews were wrapping up, and I felt my research would benefit from the subjective experience of public play. I admired Stephanie for her commanding presence, her skill with many different toys, and her ease in navigating a predominantly heterosexual scene as queer woman. I finally screwed up the courage to ask her to play with me. She specialized in using fire in her scenes and never lacked for play partners. That night, she was surprisingly free. After much stumbling and awkwardness on my part, she said yes and began to orchestrate the scene. We found an area in the fire room that was open. She notified the DM (dungeon master, who is responsible for monitoring the safety of scenes) that we were going to do a fire scene and made sure that the fire extinguisher was close by. She sent me to find a towel and soak it in water, just in case. Her friend acted as her second, a person appointed to help put out any potential problems, a necessity in a fire scene. I lay face down on a massage table and Stephanie swabbed my skin with rubbing alcohol. I felt the whoosh as it was ignited. I had seen her play before with fire wands, metal rods tipped with cotton soaked in alcohol, so I knew what she was doing, but I was lost in the experience. The amazing thing about this kind of play was that by the time I had processed that there was fire on my skin, Stephanie had extinguished the flames. She had me flip over and laid out spirals of flash cotton over my chest and belly then ignited them with a wand. It did not exactly hurt but I understood the word "intense" in a new light. My body began to physically react to the fire, shivering uncontrollably as endorphins washed over me. I felt present and connected to Stephanie. I stopped worrying about the anthropological implications of ritual or counting how many people were in the room. My eyes began fluttering and I recognized a trance state setting in.

Then I heard, "The cops are here." Later, Stephanie and I joked that this was my safe word. Although I had admired Stephanie prior to playing with her, what she did next made me trust her. I was startled, not a good thing when there is open flame on skin. She pressed her hand against my chest and kept me from bolting upright into her lit fire wand. She then said, "You are not a minor. We are not doing anything wrong. It will be fine." I believed her. All the while, she continued to play the fire across my skin. People became more insistent, saying, "No, the cops are here. Get her dressed." Stephanie's calm demeanor reassured me, in my dazed state, that it would in fact be ok. After a few more passes with the wand, she announced, "Now, I am done." She helped me sit up and got me dressed in short order. Partly due to the endorphin high, I was in a happy place and she seemed to be taking care of everything, if moving expeditiously. I dimly recalled my advisor's [sic] admonition to avoid arrest because the university would take it poorly. By the time she had wiped down the table and I had my shoes on, the all clear rang up the stairs. The police had gone. Stephanie acted as if the cops had no impact on her at all. Downstairs, she got me some water and then we collapsed on the couch.

Later, I pieced together what had been going on in other parts of The House (as the house converted into a permanent dungeon was known) while I was engaged. A neighbor called the town police, complaining of noise. As the police pulled into the long driveway, people in costume or undressed made their way into The House. One of the men, a former board member with a military background, appointed himself as spokesperson. He explained that there was an adult-oriented party taking place with no minors or alcohol. The police warned the group to keep it down and left. On the whole, it was not a threatening encounter. By the time Stephanie and I made it downstairs, the police had been gone for 5 minutes, and everyone chattered in manic relief. At the time, I was too spaced out on endorphins to truly appreciate the threat presented by the police. The consequences of a raid and arrest could have been far-reaching for anyone at the party. Everyone felt chastened, and most people decided against playing the rest of the night. However, people remained at the party, retelling where they had been when the police came and what role, if any, they had in the encounter. Stephanie was much lauded for maintaining her composure and not ending our scene abruptly as soon as the first cries of "the cops are here" were heard. Much later, she confessed to me that she was "freaked out," but the situation elicited her contrary streak and she "would be damned if someone was going to *make* [her] finish [her] scene." I mistakenly believed the encounter ended once the police left, but the story took on a life of its own. After that party, I concentrated on my transcripts, keeping in touch with members of the community through e-mail while sitting out a month of parties. At the next event I went to, I heard the story of the LUST party retold, only this time as something bigger, more grandiose. To hear it again, it was a veritable showdown between the kinky community and the forces of vanilla oppressors, not quite a Cactus Stonewall[2], but certainly a skirmish. In the retelling, the threat presented by the police in that particular situation was emphasized. The harmful consequences of disturbing hegemonic ideals created a sense of shared adversity which served to turn a collection of individuals into a community.

This encounter with the police illustrated the fact that self-policing may smooth over interactions with the authorities. In the shared narrative, people emphasized how the spokesperson's intercession with the police prevented a more threatening encounter. Even though this spokesperson was not part of the current board of LUST, he had been previously and felt comfortable speaking for the club. No one questioned whether he was the best choice, in part because he was effective. Characteristics that he shared with the police were highlighted, such as being male and having a military background. Unspoken but implied were his whiteness and heterosexuality. By demonstrating promptly the group's knowledge of and adherence to the law (no minors) and social standards (no alcohol), he deflected negative attention. In this manner, kinky organizations, called clubs, take on the role of enforcers of the law. There is motivation to maintain the appearance of law-abiding citizens in order to minimize contact with the police.

Building on the threat of state intervention, laws are selectively applied by different groups, usually to the advantage of the elites rewarded by the status quo. The most universally espoused edict is "no children." The definition of child is occasionally debated, but whatever it is, it should never occur in the kinky community. In Texas, an adult can be prosecuted for having sex with someone under the age of 17. In the kinky community, the lower limit is usually set at 18, although in some cases the age limit is 21 to reflect the drinking age. I can understand this paranoia: In my own experience with the Institutional Review Board, the committee was very concerned that I not even discuss possibly illicit sex with someone under the age of 18 and emphasized it was my duty to report child abuse. I did not have to confront that situation, in large part due to the kinky community's very public stance against involving children. It is difficult to imagine a person more abhorred in the United States than the child molester, and people go to extraordinary lengths to avoid accusations of pedophilia. In most cases, people do not even discuss kink with younger people for fear of sounding as if they are promoting it. Jenna found this problematic and questioned the wisdom in it:

Jenna: Age is not a hard limit [a personal line that cannot be crossed] for me. It gets me in a lot of trouble. Even when I started at eighteen, it was so double standard. Kinky people are crazy like that. They all say, "Oh yeah, I was doing kinky stuff when I was in high school and I had fantasies early on" and then you say, "Why don't we talk to these now sixteen-year-olds and let them know they don't have to go through that dark period that you did?" And, no, no, no, can't do that. That's horrible. I'm not like that. I will not start some "educate teenagers about kink now" but if someone came to me I would be totally out to them.

Misty: Would you play with them?

Jenna: Yes. If I felt they could give informed consent, absolutely. I wish I had been given that option. (Interview transcripts)

Among my respondents, commonly people's narratives revealed they had kinky predilections early in life but felt that it was somehow wrong or they were the only ones who felt that way. In some ways, the Internet alleviates some of this pressure, but most people refrain from even discussing kink with people under 18. Jenna is a maverick in the community, outspoken in her beliefs, even when they do not match the social mores of the larger community. She feels it her duty to question everything, making a case that while some hegemonic ideals are furthered in the community, people do not buy into them wholesale. However, Jenna had an uneasy relationship with the community, constantly threatened with expulsion due to her unconventional beliefs. Her focus on a person's ability to give informed consent does not rely on the dictates of the state about a clear line in the sand but rather privileges the relationship between individuals. By promoting these beliefs, Jenna not only risks her personal safety with regards to the authorities but also jeopardizes the wider kinky community's image as upstanding citizens.

Applying age standards leads to some behaviors which have implications beyond preventing an underage person slipping in. Some groups check identification, such as driver's licenses, to make sure that everyone is at least 18 (or 21). This is an embrace of the state and lends an air of officialization to the process. People who do not have proper identification are barred from attending certain parties.[3] In this way, clubs vet attendees, taking on a paternal role. People trade their anonymity and some of their autonomy for the protections offered by the club. At one club in particular, people have to show their identification while signing a waiver, and the information is taken down. Sophia explained,

> [The other club], when you go there, they have waivers but you can just sign them with an X, which doesn't protect your members. [Our club] has the waivers, if somebody came here and said, "Hey, let's go have some coffee and talk" and you went off with them and they took you off and raped you or something, then you could come to me and I could find out who it was because they have to show me their driver's license. We send those to our lawyer's office and he keeps those. If the police gave a warrant, they could only get the one waiver, not the whole bunch. We've done it that way on purpose. If you just go and sign an X and somebody took you off and no one had ever seen them before and no one would know who they were, so we're really careful about that. We want to keep our members safe and coming back. And the people who are no longer members of [the other club] had a really big issue with those waivers so they rammed everybody's face in them for years and years and told us how terrible we are and that we just want to out people and that's so not true. (Interview transcripts)

There were people who would not attend that club's parties because of the need to show identification. Despite Sophia's protestations that the only reason to check identification so closely is for the safety of the members, it is a display of power to have physical proof that a person attended a kinky party. Police may not have ready access to the waivers, but if they focus on a particular individual, it would not be difficult to obtain a warrant. Sophia used the threat of rape to emphasize the unreliability of new people and reinforced the protective role the club played. It is hard for me to judge how valid this threat was, but I am reminded of how women are often warned about rape for doing things unbecoming to their sex, like wearing short skirts or walking after dark. The club takes on a paternal role, functioning much like the state in surveillance of members.

Another example of the paternal nature of the clubs was the prohibition on alcohol at LUST parties. The ostensible reason for the ban on alcohol is due to the fact that people under the legal drinking age are allowed at the party. Underage drinking can bring the wrong sort of attention to an organization. Rather than bar people between the ages of 18 and 21, LUST outlaws alcohol. This decision, however, is not simply a rational response to legal pressure. For reasons too complex to be addressed in this paper, the heterosexual kinky community in Cactus has chosen to differentiate itself from previous incarnations of BDSM (or s/m or leather) by its stance on using substances. The shared, public understanding at LUST is that engaging in play while impaired in any way is inherently unsafe. For this reason, alcohol and drugs are not allowed at parties. Many of the same community members who advocate teetotaling for public parties admit that they occasionally imbibe during private play. In comparison, many other kinky organizations in other parts of the country are bar based, and alcohol is considered part of the experience. LUST, however, acts as the arbiter of morality by passing judgment on whether people can be trusted to act safely if drinking alcohol. The leaders of the club note that the loss of drinking privileges is outweighed by the protection against raids and the increase in safety. This is the same reasoning that has Americans removing their shoes at the airport for security reasons.

In clubs that require more than ostensible membership, participants are subjected to more paternal oversight in areas of their lives outside of parties. Members are held accountable for their behavior. Generally, rules of conduct are explicit in membership clubs, more so than the unspoken customs of the wider kinky community. Abigail, a leader of a leather club, explained,

> I go on [online social network site] if somebody calls me up and says so-and-so did such-and-such and I'll go on [the social network site] to read it, but I don't go there for gossip purposes. I do it because I am a leader in the community. It will be like, especially in the [my] group, because they have a code of conduct, and if you don't abide by the code of conduct you can get kicked out. So they will say "so-and-so did this, said that, I don't think it's appropriate." It's usually not even them tattling on one another, it's the other leader in the group calling me, saying, you have to read this. Then they usually get told, "if you want to be part of the [. . .] group, you can't represent yourself like that," and usually, "stop doing that." (Interview transcripts)

By becoming a member, a person acknowledges the club has a stake in its members projecting a certain image for the good of the group. Leaders of the club are expected to moderate disagreements and legislate violations of code in much the same way people turn to the authority of the state in legal matters.

One of the major reasons people accept the paternal attitudes of different clubs is due to the perceived protection from the authorities offered by the clubs. Many clubs made allowances for prostitution laws. Legally, "a person commits an offense [prostitution] if he knowingly: (1) offers to engage, agrees to engage, or engages in sexual conduct for a fee; or (2) solicits another in a public place to engage with him in sexual conduct for hire" (Texas Penal Code

2012:section 43.02). Introducing money into an otherwise legal activity creates illicit sex, regardless whether it is kinky or vanilla. To avoid this, clubs draw a line between what is paid for and sex; often what is bought is access to a party or membership in the club. By examining the ways in which people separate or conflate sexuality, the law, and the economy, I demonstrate how the legal definition of sex and people's subsequent interpretation of that definition are clear illustrations of how the state constructs sexuality.

There are four strategies to avoid looking as though people are paying for sex, each with its own repercussions: only sell tickets ahead of time, only take donations, require a membership fee, or do not allow sex at the party. The first strategy, practiced by LUST and other groups, requires an investment in the community. Most groups in Cactus value relationships more than activities and focus on making a community rather than a party circuit. By only selling tickets in nonparty venues, members (both new and old) are forced to engage with other people socially, making it more likely for people to be involved in the community outside of parties. The economy of the transaction supports the infrastructure of the parties, such as rental fees or dungeon maintenance. One of the arguments made against equating buying tickets to buying sex is that it is possible that no one at a party will have sex. Having a ticket is not a guarantee one will witness sex, much less participate in it. At pro-sex parties, the definition of sex is nebulous and left to individual interpretation. Removing money from the physical location allows sex to remain subjective.[4]

Membership dues are a more stringent form of enforced community than selling tickets beforehand. Clubs that require more than nominal membership usually mandate some sort of service in addition to participation in social events. Membership allows a person access to parties which are not publically available. Again, because money is one step removed from the transaction, the definition of sex is left open. These venues tend to be smaller and more intimate due to the limited number of people, creating an atmosphere where sex is more likely to occur regularly than at public parties.

In the community, taking donations is felt to be the riskiest strategy, since it places money and sex in the same physical location. I am not sure how successful this strategy is; I did not spend a lot of time with this particular group. It seems to have the function of leveling income disparity, with people paying what they can afford. These parties would not have been possible without the patrons offering their spacious house as a play space for free. I can also see how this setup could easily lead to a "tragedy of the commons" situation, with many people taking advantage of what is offered without contributing equally. Despite this group's promotion of a "sex-positive" credo, people felt wary about engaging in behaviors that included male orgasm. As discussed in the next section, female orgasm was not considered sex and therefore not legislated. Many people in the community cited fears of prostitution charges when explaining why they did not participate in these parties.

The final strategy to avoid prostitution charges, and perhaps the most explicit response to state pressure, is to ban "sex" at parties. The Collective of unNamed Desires (CaNDy), another large umbrella group, adopted this approach. According to CaNDy bylaws, sex is considered penetration, with penis, fingers, or dildos. This is a rather arbitrary line, since exchanging money for any "sexual conduct" (including "any touching of the anus, breast, or any part of the genitals of another person with intent to arouse or gratify the sexual desire of any person"; Texas Penal Code 2012:section 43.02) is prohibited. In practice, this rule works to exclude gay men from these predominantly heterosexual parties because penetrative sex is considered an integral part of play for many men in the gay male leather scene. I do not think most people actively try to exclude classes of people from parties, but the legal justification for some of the rules reinforce hegemonic ideals of appropriate behavior. This focus on penetration ignores female orgasm as a sufficient condition of sex, resulting in parties where there is supposedly "no sex" yet women are expected to enact orgasms as a sign of a good scene. Even among queer female respondents, many people differentiated sex as penetration from female orgasm from other stimulation. People privilege a heteronormative definition of sex, despite the Texan law's attempt to be gender neutral and unspecific, in order to protect themselves from prosecution for prostitution.

Although members of small-scale societies are under great pressure to conform to community standards due to the limited size of the group, the pressures to conform in a state-level society manifest differently. Large urban areas attract people who are otherwise out of place in small communities, such as immigrants or people in sexual minorities, granting them a measure of freedom in the anonymity of the vast city and the ability to find others with similar experiences. Clubs in the kinky community monitored and controlled behaviors through methods which were drawn from living in a state-level society. In the larger community, iteration of community standards via party and club rules and the proliferation of waivers cast the club in the role of the state, with a vested interest in maintaining order, thereby avoiding adverse interactions with the police.

Unlike the state, the kinky community can only enforce adherence to community standards through ostracism, which is still an effective form of social control, as any social scientist knows from the example of the !Kung (Shostak 1981). People in the kinky community are very indulgent with many forms of behavior. One of the credos is "Your kink is ok by me." However, if a person transgresses accepted behavior (for example, a kinky relationship with a child or violating consent), the group makes them unwelcome. It is worth noting that both of those examples are against the law, yet most people did not discuss the possibility of involving the authorities if people transgress in such a manner. Because any kinky behavior could be suspect if investigated by the police, people hesitate to invoke the wrath of the state lest it focus on them as well. Community members feel they do an adequate job of protecting their own from both predators and the authorities. Word of mouth travels relatively rapidly, resulting in the offender being barred from events. Stan explained,

> In the BDSM community, your reputation is your coin so you're safe to walk through an event because if someone misbehaves, their reputation suffers and they become ostracized by the outsiders [the kinky community]. Reputation is so important and peer pressure is hugely influential in our community. At our parties, there are certain kinds of activities that are frowned on. Scat play, animals. You'll find very few groups where they will say, "bring your dog, we don't mind." We all have our limits of what we're willing to watch, what we're willing to participate in. Most of the parties that you'll find with the local groups, they are very much the same—floggers, canes, violet wands, different kinds of play but it's always the same. Very seldom will you see someone step outside that box and do something truly edgy. If it's too edgy, we all go "Eww, we don't like you." Your reputation in our eyes is lessened because you do this kind of stuff. While the BDSM group is pretty accepting, we have our limits too. Once you get ostracized by the outsiders, where do you have left to go? (Interview transcripts)

Some small-scale society tactics are effective in the Cactus kinky community due to its small size and exclusivity, yet this subculture remains firmly entrenched in a wider American experience of living in a state-level society. In certain ways, the state directly informs people's definition of sexuality through its legislation of prostitution law. People interpret these laws through a heteronormative lens, deciding what acts count as sex and what is "other." In my experience, community members' ambiguous feelings about the police were manifested in the response to a minor confrontation. The need to appear as upright citizens to avoid scrutiny and possible sanctions conflicted with the countercultural ideology of resistance promoted by the kinky community's self-identification as outlaws. Behind this uneasy relationship lies the fact that the police have the very real power to strip people of liberty and cause social ruin. Community members know that their sexuality makes them a target for law enforcement should they step too far out of bounds. This in turn leads to high levels of self-policing and surveillance. Clubs mimic the state in an effort to mitigate the risks of pursuing this type of sexuality. Elites in the clubs are able to maintain the status quo by selective application of certain laws, invoking the threat of the power of the state yet acting paternally to protect members from that power. The interpretation of laws, such as the age of consent, is used not only to prevent overt threats but also to perpetuate the social control exerted by community leaders in the form of hegemonic ideals.

The authority of the state to construct sexuality is, in some ways, contested by people who create a space for nontraditional sexualities within the context of a finite community. However, the process is marked by the ways the state can directly or indirectly intervene in what most would consider a private matter. More than simply a collection of individual predilections, sexuality is always situated in a web of social interactions, influenced by the state, the economy, religion, ethnicity, class, gender, and the list could go on. It does not spring like Athena from Zeus's head, fully formed and without history. Specific social interactions inform the construction of complex cultural experiences such as sexuality. It is in these details social scientists may hope to discover universal truths.

NOTES

1. All names of groups and individuals have been changed to protect confidentiality.

2. In 1969, the Stonewall Riots occurred in New York City as members of the gay community violently protested a police raid on the Stonewall Inn, an important gathering place for this marginalized group.

3. In a state with a booming immigrant population, it was amazing to me that I only met one Mexican national. There are a number of deterrents, both cultural and economic, to immigrant involvement in this particular kinky community, the requirement for state identification being only one.

4. Although beyond the scope of this paper, it is interesting to note that when defining sex ideally, most people said it was up to individuals to decide what counts as sex. In practice, however, when people in the heterosexual community spoke about having sex, it centered on whether a male partner penetrated a person of any gender or if male orgasm occurred.

CHAPTER 4

SCRIPTING SEXUAL PRACTICE IN DIFFERING SOCIAL CONTEXTS

Young Women Negotiating Mothers' Expectations in Hong Kong and Britain

Stevi Jackson

Petula Sik Ying Ho

In this chapter, we present and discuss some data from a study of young adult women and their mothers in Hong Kong and Britain. Both Hong Kong and Britain are wealthy, developed societies (despite being hit by recent economic crises). Hong Kong is a little richer than the United Kingdom, but with far greater poverty and economic inequality owing to its low tax, low welfare-spending regime. Hong Kong, moreover, has developed very rapidly and at the time when the mothers in our sample were growing up was characterized by third world levels of poverty. Hong Kong families, partly because of these conditions and partly because of the Chinese emphasis on family continuity and solidarity, are more close-knit than British families with much more contact among extended kin. Whereas most of the young British women we talked to lived apart from their parents, all of those in Hong Kong still lived in the parental home, reflecting both cultural practices and the exorbitantly high cost of housing in Hong Kong (see Jackson, Ho, and Na 2013).

Sexual morality in Britain is generally more relaxed than in Hong Kong, and the young women in our British sample had far more sexual experience than those in Hong Kong. Heterosexual histories were in keeping with what has been found in large-scale surveys. In the UK National Survey of Sexual Attitudes and Lifestyles (Wellings et al. 2001), the median age of first sexual intercourse (male and female) was 16 and those aged 16 to 24 had an average of three heterosexual partners in their lifetime. Data from Hong Kong Youth Sexuality Studies (Family Planning Association of Hong Kong, 2009) show an increase of premarital sexual activity since the late 20th century, but slightly less than half of women aged 19 to 27 had experienced sexual intercourse (only 4% before age 15) and most of this was with a future spouse. While there is evidence of a decline in the emphasis on premarital virginity in Hong Kong, it is still a value held by many (Chan 2008). Indeed, the issue of virginity loomed large in our discussions with the Hong Kong young women.

We conducted individual, in-depth life-history interviews with young, university educated women aged 20 to 26 (below the average age at marriage in both locations), and their mothers. We interviewed 13 young British women and 12 of their mothers and 14 young Hong Kong women and 12 of their mothers. All the British participants were white British and all Hong Kong participants were Chinese. The mothers were all heterosexual, as were most of the daughters; one young British woman was bisexual, and there were two lesbian daughters in the Hong Kong sample. We also held focus groups with young women, and during these, we discussed with each group some of our data and findings from the other location, enabling Hong Kong women to comment on British women's accounts and vice versa. We draw on this "exchanged" data in what follows.

SEXUAL SCRIPTS

In interpreting these data, we have applied the concept of "sexual scripts" developed by Gagnon and Simon (1974, 2004; Simon and Gagnon 1984b). Gagnon and Simon challenge the idea that sexual conduct is biologically driven, arguing that sexuality is fully social and that it is socially scripted. According to Gagnon and Simon, we are not born with innate sexual drives that are repressed and molded by the effects of culture but *become* sexual through the interactive processes whereby we learn sexual scripts and begin to locate ourselves within them, actively interpreting the sexual world and making sense of our place in it. Like all interactionists, Gagnon and Simon emphasize the meanings underpinning human conduct: We act on the basis of our interpretations of situations rather than simply playing predefined roles, but our interpretations are shaped by commonsense knowledge and expectations derived from interactions with others. Sexual scripts act as sources of meaning and general guides for action: They enable us to make sense of our own bodily feelings, to identify a situation as potentially sexual, to interpret what is then expected of us, and to act accordingly. Because they are subject to interpretation and negotiation in interaction, scripts are not fixed and therefore can change over time and vary with context.

Gagnon and Simon identify three levels of scripting: cultural scenarios, interpersonal scripting, and intrapsychic scripting (Gagnon 2004; Gagnon and Simon 2004; Simon and Gagnon 1984b). *Cultural scenarios* are the "cultural narratives" constructed around sexuality that circulate within a society, what others might call discourses. They define shared meanings of sexuality within a given culture or cultural group, for example, what is seen as sexual and how sex should be done, and they derive from numerous sources such as films and novels, public controversies around sexual morality, scientific constructions of sexuality, and commonsense assumptions about sex. These scenarios do not *determine* sexual conduct, but they represent resources on which we draw in making sense of the sexual. In contemporary societies, moreover, there are competing sexual scenarios available—so not everyone will draw on the same cultural scripts.

Interpersonal scripting is what goes on within everyday interaction. In negotiating a sexual relationship with someone and engaging in sex with them, we draw on wider cultural scenarios but interactively shape them "into scripts for behavior in specific contexts" (Simon 1996:41). This might involve considerable negotiation if sexual partners are mobilizing different variants of cultural scenarios; in heterosexual relationships, for example, women and men may bring gendered versions of cultural scripts into play. *Intrapsychic scripting* occurs at the level of our individual thoughts and desires, through reflexive "conversations with ourselves," which enable us to construct fantasies or think about sexual encounters. Thus, we reflexively process material from cultural scenarios and interpersonal experience and make sense of our own and others' sexuality. Our personal intrapsychic scripts inform, in turn, our engagement in interpersonal scripting and our interpretations of cultural scenarios.

The interplay between these three levels of scripting allows for the complexity and fluidity of human sexuality while always locating it in social context. Furthermore, Gagnon and Simon repeatedly emphasize the interrelationship between sexual and nonsexual aspects of social life, which is helpful to us in locating sexuality within broader patterns of intimate life and practices. In seeing sexuality as part of wider sociality, its gendered dimension is brought to the fore, making this perspective useful for feminist analysis (see Jackson and Scott 2010a, 2010b). Because this conceptual framework does not specify the content of scripts but sees them as contingent on social context, it is applicable to comparative research. This approach does have one drawback, however: its lack of attention to material structural inequalities. We would argue that scripting always occurs within particular material socioeconomic parameters that affect the kinds of cultural scenarios that can emerge, the contexts of our interpersonal interaction, and the resources on which we can draw in reflexive self-construction. Nonetheless, since interactionism is a "modest" theory (Plummer 2003), with no claim to explaining all of human social life, there are no barriers to supplementing it with wider observations on material social conditions, as we have done in analyzing our data.

Engaging in qualitative research on sexuality involves scripting processes. Researchers and the researched draw on wider cultural scenarios in framing questions and answers; the interchanges between them, and among participants in focus groups, involve elements of interpersonal scripting. Whereas Gagnon and Simon use the term *interpersonal scripting* primarily in relation to interaction within sexual encounters, we see it as having wider applicability. After all, much of our everyday understanding of sexuality derives from interaction with others—from exchanging information, discussing sexual issues, or gossiping about friends' or celebrities' sexual relationships. We therefore use this concept in making sense of interaction within the focus groups.

DISCUSSING SEX: INTERACTION IN THE FOCUS GROUPS

One of the passages from the British transcripts that we shared with the Hong Kong focus group came from an interview with Zoë, a young British woman, complaining that her parents had not allowed her to sleep with her boyfriend in the parental home until she turned 18—despite the fact that her mother had earlier facilitated her "going on the pill"; therefore, Zoë acknowledged that she was heterosexually active. We explained to the Hong Kong group that it was common in Britain for young women to have their boyfriends sleeping over while they were still living with their parents. In the following responses of the young Hong Kong women, a process of interpersonal scripting occurred in which a shared account of local cultural scenarios was co-constructed, potentially challenged, and then reinforced:

Jacqueline: My mum would allow um, my boyfriend to sleep over, but not together, he would be sleeping on the sofa and I'll be in my room.

Researcher: What about other people?

Lola: No, not for me.

Researcher: No?

Lola: I'm still living with my family . . . my mother don't, she express actually that she can't take them stay overnight and it didn't happen, yep.

Researcher (turning to other participants): Do you think your mother would accept this?

Carrie: No, no way!

Vicky: No sleeping over.

Donna: Anywhere!

Celia: Now my boyfriend is currently staying at my house, he's living there because we're saving up money to get our own apartment so my parents allow him to stay in our house.

Jane: So if you have a marriage plan that's different. (Focus group, January 2011)

Jacqueline and Lola begin by explaining the impossibility of the British situation being replicated in their own homes. When the researcher throws the issue open to others in the group, Carrie, Vicky, and Donna provide reinforcing comments in quick succession, each confirming the previous speaker's experience and ending with Donna's emphatic "anywhere!" At this point, a dissident opinion is voiced when Celia announces that her boyfriend *does* stay over. Jane then intervenes to explain that imminent marriage makes a difference—effectively saying that the exception proves the rule. Consensus is thus restored, and we are left with a shared account of local family practices in relation to young women's sexuality.

What this interchange tells us about the restrictions placed on young women's sexual activity should be placed in its wider sociocultural context. First, most of these young women live with their parents in very small apartments, where there is little privacy for sexual exploration. Indeed, a subsequent exchange involved one of the participants, Jacqueline, questioning the British researchers on Zoë's family background, assuming that she must have very wealthy parents for them to own a home large enough to afford space for her to sleep with her boyfriend in privacy. The revelation that Zoë's parents were quite "ordinary"—both were teachers—served to underline the contrast between the living conditions of the women in the British and Hong Kong samples. In addition to material constraints, Hong Kong women live within a culture in which premarital virginity is still prized, at least by the older generation.

Earlier in the Hong Kong focus group discussion, there had been a lively conversation among the young women about the value placed on virginity by their mothers—and our interviews with their mothers did reveal a widespread concern with preserving their daughters' virginity; some were assiduous in policing it. The young women themselves expressed a range of views on the issue, some determined to remain chaste until marriage and others not, with some indicating that they were no longer virgins. What was clear, however, was that even if they shared their mothers' views they had not simply "internalized" them as a result of "socialization." They had been exposed to competing cultural scenarios, to traditional Chinese cultural mores as well as a range of alternative perspectives from the media and from interpersonal interaction with peers. They had actively, reflexively negotiated their own positions and were keen to represent themselves to us as possessing agency and arriving at their own opinions. They did not directly challenge their mothers, but in sharing their accounts with us and each other, they used humor to put some distance between their mothers' vigilance and themselves. Donna told the following story with considerable dramatic verve and to laughter from the group:

> My mum . . . keeps checking and she scares me, like erm, she does still say it's very important to be a virgin until you get married . . . and you know before er, HPV protection injection, our doctor says it's better to get the injection when you're still a virgin because it works better and my mum say, "oh do you want to do that?" "No," because I don't like injections, I don't want like pain and she says "wow, why don't you want the injection? Is it because you're not a virgin anymore?" [I say] "Okay I'll do it." [Mum says] "Don't waste money if you're not a virgin anymore, don't do it." I say, "I'll take the injection." [Mum says] "Are you wasting money?" and then she will also ask me, "oh ask your friends, does any of your friend want to take the injection?" She just wants gossip, you know, which friend is not a virgin anymore. (Focus group, January 2011)

In recounting this conversation with her mother, Donna does not present herself as rebelling but as ultimately agreeing to have the injection while sidestepping the question of her virginity status. Yet in representing her mother's surveillance humorously, she maintains her self-presentation as an autonomous "modern" woman who "knows" her mother's views and attitudes are likely to be seen as absurd and excessive. This "knowingness" itself derives from wider social and immediate interactional contexts. The way the story is told relies on a shared (interpersonally scripted) understanding of mothers' concerns that probably preceded the focus group event, but which had already been established within the group as a framework within which such stories were told.

The section of the Hong Kong focus group interview in which virginity was discussed was played back to the British focus group in the expectation that their experience would be very different. It had become clear from the interviews we had conducted that being sexually active was simply taken for granted among the young British women and therefore not in need of explanation or elaboration: The only British participant who justified her stance on premarital heterosexual activity, Julie, was married and claimed to have been a virgin prior to her wedding. Giving a group of young British women access to the Hong Kong data encouraged them to make explicit assumptions that usually remained implicit:

Carla: Yeah I don't think my mum would ever expect me to wait for marriage, I don't think it was ever on the cards, so yeah, it's never really been an issue.

Emily: Erh yeah, I never thought my mum was nosey as this but er no, I don't really [think] my mum really expected me to stay a virgin till I was married either, I don't know if she would have preferred me to or not, but I don't think she expected it.

Bryony: Oh there was never any assumption I'd stay a virgin till marriage, not least because they hoped I wouldn't be getting married really young anyway so um, if I had they would have been a bit worried.

Researcher: Worried about?

Bryony: Worried about me being some kind of thirty-five year old virgin or something. (Focus group, February 2011)

Superficially, these responses attest to a greater freedom from maternal surveillance enjoyed by young British women than their Hong Kong counterparts, but there is more going on in this interchange. As in the Hong Kong group's account of not being allowed to have boyfriends sleeping over, these women co-constructed a consensus based on a shared sexual script. Here, premarital heterosexual conduct appears to have been thoroughly normalized. This normalization, however, cannot be read simply as "sexual freedom" in an absolute sense. What is evident from Bryony's response to being asked for clarification is the importance of *being* sexual, where becoming "a thirty-five year old virgin" would be cause for concern. In the approach taken by Gagnon and Simon, sexuality is never outside the social, can never be "free" from its social shaping. Translated into Foucauldian terms, power is productive, working through incitement as much as prohibition (Foucault 1981). The expectation that one should be sexually active is as much a form of social control as injunctions against sexual activity.

The sexual world inhabited by our British sample is not one in which mothers have no anxieties about their daughters' sexual lives. There was not a total lack of surveillance when the women were younger—although now that most live apart from their parents, mothers no longer interfere in their lives. At the time when they became, or were expected to become, heterosexually active, their mothers were concerned to keep them safe from unwanted pregnancy and sexually transmitted infections. The amount of information received from mothers, and the degree of openness of communication about sexual matters, was highly variable among our British sample. Almost all daughters, however, had received some advice on safe sex and contraception, and many of their mothers had ensured they had access to contraception. Some mothers also expressed concerns about daughters avoiding abusive sexual relationships or being coerced into sexual activities against their will and had discussed these issues with them. Allowing boyfriends to sleep over could also be seen as a kind of benign supervision, ensuring that sex was practiced in a safe space.

The limits to mother-daughter interaction on sexual matters are hinted at by Emily in the extract above where she says she does not know if her mother would have preferred her to remain a virgin. The limits to sexual disclosure reappear in her interview. While it seems that her mother expected her to be heterosexually active from her teens in that she left condoms for Emily and her boyfriend to use, they preferred to buy their own. She said, "We never used the condoms that were in the bathroom cupboard because it would have been too embarrassing like, oh there's one missing . . . could have been used but they never were." For this reason, she was not sure whether her mother was aware when she first started having sex.

CONCLUDING COMMENTS

Interaction with mothers on sexual issues (or the lack of it) matters. Parental evasions on the one hand, or information, advice, and admonitions on the other, derive from already circulating sexual scripts and form an element in the resources young women draw upon in making sense of sexuality and reflexively constructing their sexual selves. In the data we have presented, there is clear evidence of active interpretation of their mothers' views, whether in young Hong Kong women's negotiation of their mothers' concern with virginity or the British women imputing motives to their mothers (as in Bryony's assertion that her parents would have been "worried" by long-term maintenance of her virginity). Our data also demonstrate the importance of taking account of wider sociocultural conditions. Living arrangements and housing differentially enable and constrain young women's sexual opportunities; not only does living with parents increase possible surveillance, but it might also heighten parents' sense of responsibility for their daughters' conduct. The past history of Hong Kong and Britain plays a part too. The British mothers came to adulthood at a time when sexual mores were already shifting markedly in Britain, and many of them had experience of premarital and nonmarital sexual relationships, which may account for their more relaxed attitudes toward their daughters' sexuality. Hong Kong mothers, on the other hand, often grew up with considerable hardship and with little opportunity for sexual freedom and still hold to many of the values with which they grew up. We have discussed these issues only in relation to heterosexuality and have not had space, in this short article, to discuss the experience of the lesbian and bisexual minority—where parental attitudes are even more polarized, impacting particularly on young Hong Kong lesbians (cf. Tang 2011). We have only been able to offer a few snippets from our data here but hope that, in so doing, we have established the utility of an interactionist approach to cross-cultural analysis of sexuality.

CHAPTER 5

SEX AS THEATER
Action, Character, and the Erotic*
Charles Edgley

We are in this together, my dear. All damned to the theater. Condemned to live through our art. For we do not know how to live through our lives—we are islands.

From the film *Trust the Man* (2005)

ACT I

Preliminaries

Appearance and the Sexual Self

Sex as theater? Absurd, you say. Theater is public. Sex is private—at least most of the time—and we are no more inclined to see sex as a staged activity than we are of seeing ourselves as actors on a stage. But before we dismiss the idea too quickly, let us run through a daring thought experiment. Here, we'll try to think of as many matters of appearance as we can that could complicate or ruin sex.[1] We'll start with a hypothetical example. A sexually aroused couple climbs into bed. Having only recently met, they've never seen each other naked, much less had sex. Both are primed with the kind of anticipation that comes only from the "first time." The lead-up has been perfect in every way. But how many things can ruin this idyllic scene if not turn it into an encounter memorable only for its failure? For starters, the narratives of sex can go badly. What if she spends the time during foreplay talking about her former boyfriend and comparing her new partner's penis to his? Somewhere in mid act, she asks if he's had any sexually transmitted diseases (STDs), and he mentions herpes

---

*I am indebted to Beth McLin and Dennis Waskul for a helpful critical reading of an early draft of this chapter.

but says that it seems to be "dormant" at the moment. He hears a toilet flush through the paper-thin walls of her apartment, and his erection flags, but only briefly. She blurts out a joke about STDs—but was it really a joke? My God, does she have something?! The garlic from dinner is making it difficult to concentrate. He notices that her breasts, which looked so beautifully natural in her clothes, are actually the result of the artifice of a plastic surgeon. He stifles a laugh, but a split-second too late, and she notices the look on his face. He notices that she notices, but it's too late, and it can't be taken back. Later, it is she who laughs at the wrong time, and since he thinks she's laughing at him, his penis temporarily suffers what sociologist Erving Goffman might call a "prop failure" (Goffman 1959), a critical matter which has to be attended to before things can proceed. As a preliminary, the two had agreed that he should use a condom since she isn't on the pill, but it fails just as they're really getting into it. "Oh, God don't stop now," she murmurs. Torn between passion and responsibility, he thinks, "What the hell," and pulls the damaged condom off his penis rather than trying to repair it. The excitement of the "first time" is moving him toward orgasm, but way too soon. Embarrassingly, he climaxes long before she's ready, and they finish with her trying to stuff his rapidly shrinking penis back into her vagina.

We could go on and on with this litany of dramaturgical horrors, but this thought experiment is already starting to look like an X-rated *Saturday Night Live* routine. Besides, it's overkill. As anyone experienced in sex knows, any one of these expressive faux pas might be sufficient to ruin a sexual encounter. But that said, the list is also incomplete. Literally, *thousand*s of things could go wrong as participants in erotic acts make tacit comparisons between how they are performing and what an ideal performance is supposed to look like.

In spite of these deficiencies, though, this thought experiment is useful. For when we have sex in any number of its countless forms, sexual selves are being continually created by virtue of a dramaturgical imperative—we *must* necessarily appear to the other. Sex is social precisely because it is dramatic, and our very self is on the line with all of its potential doubts and vulnerabilities. "The actor taught us this," says Camus ([1942] 1991): "There is no difference between appearing and being." To appear is to be and sex is no different. Sex *requires* that we appear in a communicative guise and that guise is the province of drama.[2] Even online sex where we are connected to the other not by bodily proximity but only by the invisible ether of the Internet requires us to appear (Waskul 2004a). But as precise and straightforward as it sounds, this is not how we ordinarily understand sex, at least not initially. Everybody "knows" that sex is a biological drive and a physical act. It has reproductive functions and solves the problem of death through the regeneration of the species. But theater?

What does theater have to do with sex? Sex may be the subject of countless theatrical *performances* ("No Sex, Please. We're British!"). It may occur *in* a theater. But in most people's minds, sex emanates from powerful physical and biological sources, not fundamentally social ones (Gecas and Libby 1976). Yet with all due respect to the voluminous science of sex, all the biological information in the world tells us precious little about what will happen when persons having sex actually encounter each other. The physical mechanisms of desire are quite different from the objects of desire, as well as their social meaning and purpose. Biology knows nothing about relationships. So while some of the equipment of sex is biologically provided, none of its meanings are, and this fact alone makes sex in human beings far more than the howls and grunts of rutting creatures. For people, sex is not simply a physiological need but an intensely social and interactional experience where we ultimately craft, negotiate, and otherwise creatively deploy whatever "nature" has given us, a point made nicely by Plummer:

> Sexuality, for humans, is not simply a free-floating "desire," but is always grounded in wider material . . . forces. There is no essential "sexuality" with a strictly biological base that is cut off from the social. From the social acts of rape to the social processes surrounding reproduction, sexuality has no reality *sui generis*. Any concern with "it" must harbor wider social issues, for human sexuality has to be socially produced (no human can ever just "do it"), socially organized, socially maintained, and socially transformed. Overlapping with and omnipresent in all of social life, human sexualities are always conducted at an angle: they are never "just sex." (Plummer 2007:16)

So whatever else sex may be, it is also a socially constructed act that includes friction, fantasy, and talk—both verbal and nonverbal. It also includes every other communicative dimension of the setting in which it occurs. This includes such things as clothing, hair, makeup, odors, body art, ambient sounds, and literally anything else that intrudes and/or appears.

Indeed, when it comes to the relationship between the meaningful world of eroticism and the mundane matter of bodies, libido doesn't create fantasy as much as fantasy creates libido.[3] So how do we conceptualize, study, and analyze something as complex as sex? First, we must recognize that human beings are symbolic creatures who approach life armed with their primary capacity: the ability to use and be used by symbols (Mead 1934). Humans respond sexually the way they respond to everything else in their worlds of experience: with definitions, images, and symbols—all in the service of meaning. What would a definition of human sex look like? To use a historical example, while his enemies thought he was just being evasive—as he almost surely was—when former president Bill Clinton was asked under oath whether he had ever had sexual relations with a White House intern, it became clear that by "sex," he meant "sexual intercourse" and not the oral, anal, and masturbatory behavior to which both had earlier confessed. He was not alone. If a person were asked to compile an honest list of how many people with whom they had had sex, would that list include those with whom they'd "only" had oral sex? Would most respondents include themselves as sex partners (masturbation)? Does "sex" include failed attempts? How about "everything but"—a fiction that countless participants have used to remain "technical virgins" while still engaging in a vast array of sexual activities, many of which would have made previous generations blush (Medley-Rath 2007)? What about fantasies? Are they "sex"? Moreover, given the heteronormative nature of our discourses about sex (Page and Peacock 2013), straight people regard the subject differently from gays as illustrated by the following observation:

> My gay friends schooled me on this point. While one professed to be saving his ass for marriage (literally), he didn't consider himself to not be having sex when going down on men; my lesbian pals wondered aloud what the hell kind of terrible oral sex I was having by comparison that I didn't consider it "sex."[4]

Obviously a definition of sex is not a simple matter. Such an approach which concentrates on symbols and meaning is the traditional contribution of symbolic interaction to the study of sex. However, in this chapter, we move the focus slightly from a narrow concern with symbols to communication in the widest sense as we did with the thought experiment, and suggest that one of the best frameworks for elucidating human sexuality is to use a variant of symbolic interactionism, the metaphor of theater, or, simply put, to approach the subject dramaturgically. So our purpose in this chapter is to show the usefulness of dramaturgical analysis to the study of sex without any consideration of other frameworks often used to study this most intimate of human acts.[5] We also move the focus from individuals to the entire scene of sexual actions, showing how self emerges in sexual acts as it does anytime we are in the awareness context of others. As a result, the chapter may look quite different from other accounts of sexuality—even those within this volume—for the material out of which we construct these descriptions comes from diverse sources: literature, social science studies, pornography, popular culture, and direct accounts of sexual experience.

What Is Dramaturgy?

Action is character.

F. Scott Fitzgerald

At its heart, dramaturgy is the study of how human beings accomplish meaning in their lives. Its fundamental principle is that "the meaning of people's doing is to be found in the manner in which they express themselves in interaction with similarly expressive others" (Brissett and Edgley 2006:3).[6] Moreover, this concern with meaning is construed behaviorally, not cognitively or psychologically. Meaning is what happens to an act. Among the many things people do, sex is omnipresent. People do sexual things. They may even do sexual things of which they are unaware since sometimes we are key players in someone else's sexual scene. A shoe salesman with a foot fetish comes to mind as well as the celebrated case of ESPN sports reporter Erin Andrews who was stalked by an insurance salesman who took nude photographs of her through hotel peepholes over the course of several months. For this crime, he got two-and-a-half years in prison even though he never touched her, and she didn't know until later what had happened. She testified that 30 months in prison wasn't nearly enough, and much of the public agreed. So meanings may be assigned to what we do sexually during all phases of the act: preparatory, the act itself, and its aftermath, and these meanings are not altogether ours. New dalliances may hold all the excitement of the first time, and old affairs may come back to haunt us, especially if they are brought up at inconvenient moments. So just what does sex dramaturgically considered look like?

Kenneth Burke (1969), the godfather of dramaturgy, contended that social life involved a demonstration of the ratios between five critical elements in social life which he labeled the "pentad," a conceptual scheme that applies closely to the study of sex. These are the five elements:

1. Act—what happened, what is going on? How is the situation defined?

2. Scene—all action occurs somewhere, and this element involves questions of where and when. Time and timing become important in scenes. Situation and place are central. Pauses and rhythms affect what happens.

3. Agent—who are the performers? Burke thinks of *agent* not in a psychological or subjective sense, but dramaturgically, in the sense of a defined role or part. One's being resides in one's doing.

4. Agency—this element addresses the question of "how" and defines the dramaturgical insight as much as any other. The meaning of an act is agency sensitive in the sense that how something is done conditions the meaning of an act as much or more than any other element. It is the key dramaturgical preoccupation.

5. Purpose—a consideration of purpose answers the question of "why," not in the mechanical sense of cause, but in the human sense of purpose. Unlike the conditioned responses of other animals, human beings are concerned with rationales that give meaning to what they are doing. Dramaturgists think of this element in terms of "accounts"—excuses and justifications which arise when conduct is questioned. (Hewitt 2013)

When we apply these five elements to sex, we get a clear picture of how meaning arises in sexual situations. Sexual acts are a continuous source of speculation about what they mean, just as sexual scenes and their arrangement are common topics of conversation. Because of the relationship between character and action, we also care very much about who we are and what we have become when we have sex. In our thought experiment, how many different characters emerged from a single act? Who were the participants when they began? Who were they when they finished? Sex is transformative and for better or for worse, we never see a person the same way again once we have had sex with them—an observation confirmed at countless high school and college reunions. The hows of sex (agency) are also an unending source of fascination and speculation for human beings. Volumes have been written about what makes a person good in bed, how to please one's partner, and so on. The popular press and self-help manuals regularly promote this kind of narrative. Changing the ratios between the elements of the pentad changes the entire meaning of an act. As Gloria Leonard famously put it: "The difference between pornography and erotica is lighting."

Dramaturgical thinking about sex, then, takes us to a world of appearances, surfaces, images, and talk. It takes seriously Cooley's dictum that "the imaginations people have of each other are the solid facts of society" (Cooley 1908:87). Dramaturgy is not—at least superficially—about depth, essences, or any of the other frameworks which regard communicative action as merely epiphenomenal to something more essential. It is about very small things because those small things constitute human worlds of experience even more than the larger ones that are allegedly more important. A story attributed to evangelist Billy Graham—probably apocryphal—has an interviewer asking him what the last thing he does before taking the stage to preach to the multitudes.

"I make sure my fly is zipped," he is supposed to have said. This is the dramaturgy of small things. One would be hard-pressed to find a framework more suitable to the study of sexual conduct than dramaturgy where people in society make so much of "small things" (Bourdieu 1983). A man puts his penis into a vagina, a mouth, or an anus or between breasts, armpits, or thighs. He moves it around until some white stuff comes out the end. Everyone has a cigarette. Nothing could be smaller or less significant. And nothing could be larger or of more importance. This is the paradox of the "small things" with which dramaturgy is occupied, so let us turn our attention to a close-up look at how these "small things" are staged.

ACT II

Setting the Stage

Staging the Sexual Self

> I may not be a great actress but I've become the greatest at screen orgasms. Ten seconds of heavy breathing, roll your head from side to side, simulate a slight asthma attack and die a little.
>
> Candice Bergen

The sexual stage, like any other, is set by and develops in the course of interaction. Staging may occur deliberately with careful attention to minute detail, or, spontaneously with little or no planning at all. Much has been written by sociologists and others about sexual scripts (Long and Schwartz 1989; Simon and Gagnon 1984a)—the latter envision three types of scripts: cultural scripts, interpersonal scripts, and intrapsychic scripts, which they claim guide sexual encounters. But without doubting the existence of such blueprints, a dramaturgical understanding of sex does not consider such scripting to be either central or necessarily desirable. Participants often report that unscripted improvisations produce the best sex of all. As with all other encounters, the measure of a sexual scene is not whether it followed a script properly but whether it was meaningful.

Whether deliberate or spontaneous, a sexual stage is composed of props and settings, all of which interact to produce a scene. Most sexual scenes have common features, but some have their own unique requirements. Much of this discussion presumes a kind of generic treatment of the subject of sexual dramaturgy with an emphasis on heterosexuality. But these processes also are staged in gay, lesbian, and transsexual scenes, as well as in the entire sadism and masochism (S&M) arena where other categories of dramatic action each have their own content. The process of "queering" conventional approaches to sexuality usefully shows how arbitrary and conventional our assumptions are about sex (Ahmed 2006).[7] In the world of S&M where people create consensual scenes of pain, power, and domination and submission, for example, the participants do not regard themselves as "performing," and indeed, the entire point is to perform in such a way that the participants get the sense that through these sexual scenes they are moving toward the experience of a more authentic self[8] (Newmahr 2012).

Returning to the more conventional world of heterosexual scenes, the popular press, as well as the Internet, is full of advice for setting sexual stages, moods, and characters. However, Goffman's observation that the best performance is one that comes off, not as a performance at all, but as the "real thing" seems to have been lost on most advice mongers who devote their instruction to the question of how to create a stage that sets the proper mood for sex. Popular scripts cover such details as room temperature, coupling angles, lighting, birth control, and lubricants. But such scripts get lost in the details. What does one do if they find they've missed a step or gotten things in the wrong order? A dramaturgical view of sex stresses spontaneity and ambiguity as key features of performances since the point is the creation of meaning. When there is not enough information, nonsense leads to the death of the encounter just as when things are too predictable, as strict fidelity to a script would almost guarantee, boredom ensues. Both constitute the death of meaning (Becker 2010). As with all our nonsexual encounters, sometimes we want sex to go on and on, and at other times, we want it over with as quickly as possible, the latter underscoring the observation that men don't pay hookers for sex, they pay them to leave when it's over. The scene sets the stage for all such possibilities but dictates none of them.

TIME AND TIMING

While sex can occur anytime and anywhere, it is usually reserved for bedrooms where privacy can be ensured, and for what Davis calls "that vague temporal ghetto called nighttime" (Davis 1983:33). Nighttime has many advantages when it comes to sexual stages. It is at the end of the day. The domineering and insistent world of everyday reality may have put aside its hegemony long enough for people to think about other things. Because day's end also corresponds to nightfall, darkness offers unique qualities for the production of erotic selves. Soft lights mask physical imperfections; darkness offers the illusion of privacy, candles set an erotic mood, and as the night wears on, there is less possibility of interruption.[9] In addition, nighttime is accompanied by either a change of clothing or their complete removal, acts easily given to sexual meanings. Paradoxically, partial nudity as clothes fall away is more erotic than total nudity, a point well-known to strippers who make their living creating sexual fantasies by the strategic manipulation of clothing in an effort to extract money from customers (Pasko 2002).

While such features of sexual stages offer conventional ways of constructing eroticism, it is also important to note that since true eroticism turns on a perception of limitations (Bataille 1984), the violation of any of these elements of staging may also enhance the thrill of an erotic encounter. Sex in broad daylight, sex in public places, sex between taboo partners, S&M, and other forms of kinky play, all hold the potential for boasting the erotic payoff. This helps us to understand the thrill of adultery, why public figures from Pee-Wee Herman to Fred Willard risked their professional careers by masturbating in movie theaters, to all the voyeuristic entertainment provided the public by the Clinton-Lewinsky scandal as the most powerful man in the free world risked it all for a blow job. Endorsed and legitimated, desire may wane; shackled and repressed, few forces are as powerful. This also accounts for why long-term passion may be difficult to keep up. Whatever else it may be, marriage is a legitimating ritual designed to give societal blessing and approval to sexual acts. Consequently, couples who couldn't keep their hands off each other before marriage may find it difficult to maintain the same level of desire for long periods of time once what was previously taboo is now not only legitimate but also expected. This is such a pronounced experience for married couples that Murray Davis suggests that "marriage seems almost intentionally designed to make sex boring" (Davis 1983:119). Moreover, the fact that sex always deals with two or more people— even masturbation typically involves imagined others—women and men may develop quite different conceptions of what a stimulating sexual scene looks like. At their best, sexual scenes move like a symphony, as Anatole Broyard in his memoir of life in Greenwich Village in the 1930s discovers with an artist named Sheri Martinelli, a protégée of Anaïs Nin: "She made love the way she talked—by breaking down the grammar and the rhythms of sex. Young men tend to make love monotonously, but Sheri took my monotony and developed variations on it, as if she were composing a fugue" (Broyard 1997:17).

THE BACK- AND "FRONTSTAGES" OF SEX

In Goffman's version of dramaturgy, he makes an oft-quoted distinction between front- and backstages and their relationship to performance. Backstages are places sequestered from the eyes of audiences. They are any place that is "bounded by barriers to perception" (Goffman 1959). Among other reasons, secure backstages are critical to performances because the impression left by a properly staged show is compromised if the audience "frontstage" is privy to the backstage where the performance is prepared. Backstages are typically guarded by signs—"Employees Only," "No Admittance," and the like—and these places count on the fact that those who are not privy to the backstage typically honor the rules of access to it. Because of the centrality of place to sex, backstage and frontstage define the meaning of a sexual act. Consider that the difference between "normal" and "deviant" sex, lies not so much in *what* is done but *where* it is done. The normal bodily routines of anyone would have a far different meaning if done in a public square as opposed to a bathroom. Dramaturgically, the meaning of an act is in the response of the other, so how the audience interprets the act presumes access to it. In private residences, locks on interior doors may be absent all over the house, but they are almost always present on doors guarding bathrooms and bedrooms. In bathrooms, we regularly do to bodies what chefs do to food. We plump it, clean it, coif it, perfume it, and generally make it presentable to an audience who will later review the performance. Since all it takes to turn something into a performance is an audience, we use locks to ensure that what we are doing to our bodies doesn't become a show. This is necessary because if something shows, it is part of the show—whether we want it to be or not—and the only way to keep this from happening is to secure our preparations from a potential audience. This sequestration may even be one partner from the other before sex as bathrooms become final staging areas for the performance that will occur in the bedroom. By the same token, the way we keep sex lives "private" is to secure the places where they occur with a lock. These examples presume, of course, that we are dealing with a couple in a conventional sexual relationship. But increasingly, the idea of "conventional" is problematic. The frontstage of a middle-class home may look conventional, but the backstage may contain an orgy which must be shielded from outsiders by carefully controlling access to the scene. Swingers engage in either "open" or "closed" swinging—designations based on who watches and where the acts take place. Cybersex (Waskul, Douglas, and Edgley 2000) is typically shielded from family members and friends who "wouldn't understand," or even see it as "virtual adultery." Identity and role are critical as well, for as Goffman observes "the obscene invitations of a stranger to a woman are the spicy endearments of a man to his wife" (Goffman 1971:412). Again, we see that in the drama of social life, context and identity reign supreme.

A Myriad of Motives for Sex

Women need a reason to have sex. Men just need a place.

Billy Crystal, "*City Slickers*" 1991

Sex is made even more complicated dramaturgically because of the countless possible motives for sex and the necessity of offering up an appropriate vocabulary when questions of reason and purpose arise. Sometimes, partners don't care why they're having sex, but often, and perhaps especially for women as Billy Crystal famously asserts, they do. Motives typically arise in the context of a challenge (Mills 1940), and while we often assume and impute motives to a partner and avoid challenges, sometimes the act is interrupted by the question of why? It is at that point that motives are articulated, and whether or not the act continues may well depend on the answer. Possible vocabularies of motive include such things as love ("Because I love you and I want to make you feel good"); reproduction ("I want your baby")—often assumed but seldom articulated; reasons that are virtually never articulated such as obligation or duty; boredom; recreation (known in the argot of sex talk as "sport fucking"— recreational sex with no commitments); "mercy sex" (having sex with someone because you feel sorry for him or her); "farewell fucking," which occurs in the context of "one last time" for partners who are breaking up or have broken up; and the "birthday bang," the more-or-less unwritten rule that if you're in a sexual relationship and it's your birthday, your partner is obligated to give you what you want.

Indeed, research—to say nothing of experience—has identified hundreds of different reasons why people have sex, the number of accounts far eclipsing the actual number of sexual behaviors. Psychologists Meston and Buss (2007), claim to have uncovered 237 separate and distinct motives for sex. These reasons range from the mundane, "It just happened," to the bizarre, "I wanted to feel closer to God," to the therapeutic, "I wanted to have sex to get rid of menstrual cramps."

As might be expected, the reasons men claim to have sex differ in priority from the reasons articulated by women. Men maintained that they have sex primarily because of lust, physical attraction, fun, adventure, excitement, and love. The primary reasons women said they had sex were love, physical attraction, pleasing one's partner, a romantic setting, and it made them feel sexy. In short, even when the motives were the same, their priorities were different. Meston's and Buss's study was based on a sample of 20-year-old college students and might be very different if we were to talk with older people, exclusively married couples of any gender, gays, or any other subset. But it does suggest that the motives for one partner might be quite different than the motives for another, and we are confronted with yet another methodological problem in the study of sex, namely, that the motives people articulate to researchers in a nonerotic context are often quite different than the vocabularies they use with each other when trying to negotiate sex.

THE VULNERABILITY OF SEXUAL SELVES

Because sex is tied up with our most intimate feelings, doubts, and values, the presentation of a sexual self is a potential exercise in vulnerability. During sex, we take off our clothes; we allow our partner to see us in poses and moments that are intensely private. Organs that are ordinarily closed now open, and bodily fluids that are usually hidden or otherwise kept at bay are revealed. In the earliest stages of romantic involvement, we may see the other in ways we have never seen them before. As parties to sexual encounters engage in what Murray Davis calls "the lascivious shift from everyday reality to erotic reality," new selves replace old ones (Davis 1983:12). As in other situations, proffered selves may be rejected thus making a sexual encounter full of potential obstacles if not downright disaster. Our recognition of this precariousness of the sexual self may account for the observation that we often hold a special place in our hearts for first loves. Our bumbling efforts to show ourselves as sexual beings may border on the ludicrous and can lead to ridicule as easily as arousal. But our first love is indulgent—perhaps because they are as inept as we are—and we often remember them fondly and with the kind of appreciation reserved for those who see through our acts but take us seriously anyway. Appearances—especially poorly constructed ones—are easily undermined, and we are therefore grateful to sympathetic audiences who protect our face. So when an 18-year-old emerges from a movie theater with his date after seeing a James Bond film, he may be emboldened to act out parts of the script which involve such dimensions as self-assurance, technical competence, savoir faire, and other elements of a sophisticated production of the self that few 18-year-olds can master. Over his head and therefore teetering between glory and ruin ("Am I pulling this off or not?"), his audience may not know whether to laugh or cry.

This move out of everyday reality and into erotic reality is astonishing in its complexity, for as phenomenologists tell us, it involves a complete disruption of the assumptions of everyday life. In everyday reality, we are caught up in a routine world that is decidedly nonerotic and actively discourages all efforts to make it erotic. Eroticism is seen to be incompatible with work, most forms of play, and the rest of the quotidian routines with which most people spend much of their day. When the barrier that separates everyday from erotic reality is breached, such as when sex talk occurs at work,[10] trouble usually ensues. Further complicating the matter is that the walls that separate these two worlds are primarily enforced by talk and are therefore quite porous. How do we talk about body parts? They belong to both worlds, and we have to act toward them in ways that are consistent with the reality in which they are supposed to belong at that moment. Gagnon and Simon put the matter this way:

> Most of the physical acts [involved in sex] occur in many other situations—the palpation of the breast for cancer, the gynecological examination, the insertion of tampons, mouth-to-mouth resuscitation—all involve homologous physical events. But the social situation and the actors are not defined as sexual or potentially sexual, and the introduction of a sexual element is seen as a violation of expected social arrangements. (Gagnon and Simon 2005:16)

When violations of this proprietary separation occur in medical settings, patients are often gently re-educated to the use of proper terminology: "vagina" instead of "pussy," "penis" in place of "cock," and so on in an effort to maintain the definition of a medical situation. A wonderfully comprehensive treatment of this subject, which shows just how precarious medical definitions of a situation are, may be found in Emerson (1970:80–85).

Erotic reality, in contrast to the uptight requirements of everyday life, is built out of acts which flagrantly violate those requirements. Bodily parts normally concealed are lasciviously exposed. Fluids that are ordinarily unspeakable become the measure of how well the encounter is going. Emotions usually held in check are breached. Panting, sweating, screaming, and moaning occur, sometimes in wild abandon. If there is verbal talk, it may take on a quality usually reserved for pornography. Eyes that are normally open during everyday reality close to further heighten erotic sensations, a simple change that has enormous implications as participants fall further into erotic reality. The famous Paris seductress and literary figure Anaïs Nin describes the sensations in her famous erotic novel *Delta of Venus*:

> When she closed her eyes she felt he had many hands, which touched her everywhere, and many mouths, which passed so swiftly over her, and with a wolf-like sharpness, his teeth sank into her fleshiest parts. Naked now, he laid his full length over her. She enjoyed his weight on her, enjoyed

being crushed under his body. She wanted him soldered to her, from mouth to feet. Shivers passed through her body. (Nin 2004:44)

Erotic literature revels in this kind of description of the shift from the everyday to the erotic and at each stage of the change; the sexual selves being produced are subject to the precariousness of their own unstable production.

WHEN THINGS GO AWRY

The dramaturgical dimensions of the self do not ordinarily reveal themselves when things are going well. This was the reason for beginning this chapter with our thought experiment. We usually take for granted that we are who we claim to be—even when we know that our performances owe more to pretense than to authenticity. The audience that reviews us most of the time willingly suspends disbelief and goes along with the proffered appearances. But when performances go awry, those dimensions reveal themselves to be the fictions that they are, and the meltdown is often quick and cruel. Goffman's version of dramaturgy is replete with close-up descriptions of what happens when appearances fail and how hapless performers try to extricate themselves from the meltdown of embarrassment. These descriptions are so poignant and reveal so much about ourselves as human beings in this dilemma together that London writer Alan Bennett says reading Goffman leaves him in a "cold sweat"[11] (Bennett 1981). The opening example to his review of Goffman's work pushes all the buttons of the terror of the absurdity of everyday life (Scott and Lyman 1989) that readers of Goffman are accustomed to:

> I am waiting in an office for an appointment. A secretary sits at the desk. I shift in my seat and the leather upholstery makes a sound that could be mistaken for a fart. I therefore shift in my seat again, two or three times, making the same sound deliberately in order to demonstrate that I have not inadvertently farted. The secretary looks up inquiringly. She may just be thinking I am uncomfortable. She may, on the other hand, be thinking I have farted, and not once but three times.[12] (Bennett 1981:12)

Life is full of these kinds of situations. "What have I done?" "How might it be interpreted?" "What do things look like?" "Have I been found out?" Applied to sex, an even more poignant and telling instance is the crucial scene in director Neil Jordan's 1992 political thriller *The Crying Game* set in the turmoil and conflict of Northern Ireland in which the protagonist, an Irish Republican Army (IRA) operative named Fergus, falls in love with a fellow operative, Nil, a beautiful and sexually alluring woman. As they move toward their first encounter in the bedroom, he removes her clothing, and as his eyes wander downward, he reacts in horror as he sees for the first time that she is a man. The impact is so devastating that he lurches to the bathroom and vomits as she helplessly mumbles, "I thought you knew." Suddenly, we see clearly that gender is a social accomplishment based on appearances that most of us take utterly for granted (Lorber 1995). When it turns out that a person does not have the biological credentials for what they claim in appearances, the performance is ruined and the damage to the proffered selves incalculable.

PROPS AND PROP FAILURES

The Crying Game is an extreme example of what happens when a critical performance prop (in this case genitals which establish gender identity) fails. As actors, human beings are dependent on properly working props to maintain the appearances that produce the self. The most common kind of meltdown revolves around the failure of clothing and props.

A sexual scene works in part because the props do. A prop is a physical accompaniment to an act that serves to define a situation. Props may be anything that participants incorporate into a sexual scene, and they are usually more mundane than the example of Fergus and Nil. For heterosexual and male homosexual performances, an erect penis fits the definition of a prop too—and a critical one at that, a point we made early in this chapter in our thought experiment. But because it is composed of aberrant flesh, it sometimes fails. A flaccid penis at the wrong time kills the definition of the situation as quickly as an erect one does in church.[13] Self-help manuals often encourage women to manage this situation gracefully by attributing the failure to such outside factors as fatigue, medications, or the weaknesses to which flesh is heir. "It happens to everyone." This is one area of sexual life in which the medicalization of human problems has proceeded with abandon. Conceived of as a disease called "erectile dysfunction" concurrently with the development of Viagra in the late 1990s, Viagra and its imitators Cialis and Levitra promise through their extensive marketing campaigns a solution to the prop failure of a soft penis in any situation demanding a hard one. They now constitute a $3 billion a year business. Owing perhaps to the success of feminism in raising awareness about women's needs, the entire idea of a growing epidemic of erectile dysfunction, as well as the way these drugs are marketed, also suggests a sea change in the way men are expected to relate to women. For most of the world's history, women have been expected to be ready to have sex anytime men wanted it. But these drugs are marketed to men with the tagline "Now you can be ready when she is," thus offering entirely different dramaturgical possibilities.

ACT III

Closing Curtain

Through its single-minded determination to see the erotic as expressive behavior, dramaturgy provides a window to the most intimate aspect of life that few other frameworks can. Sex offers up an entire panoply of human meaning: "bodies, souls, proofs, purities, delicacies, results, promulgations, commands, pride . . . benefactions, bestowals, passions, loves, beauties, and delights of the earth" as the poet Walt Whitman put it (Whitman 1986:136).

The dramaturgical insight reminds us that life is a process, not a thing. "Theater occurs," says Beckman. "Theater does not exist except when it is occurring . . . the script may exist as well as the scenery . . . a poem is a thing made. Theater is not. It is something happening" (Beckerman 1976:4). So following Goffman and the rest of the dramaturgists, an account of the erotic centers on how people do sex, what people do *about* sex, what they *make* of sex, how they *account* for sex, and how they *talk* about sex. Sex is a party in which people play society:

> That is[,] they engage in many forms of social interaction, but without their usual sting of seriousness. Sociability changes serious communication to noncommittal conversation, *eros* to coquetry, ethics to manners, aesthetics to taste . . . the world of sociability is a precarious and artificial creation that can be shattered at any moment by someone who refuses to play the game. (Berger 1984:139)

A fully developed dramaturgical account of sex and its relationship to the self has yet to be written. I hope that this chapter, with all its inspirations and imperfections, will help hasten that day.

NOTES

1. If we reverse the thought experiment, of course, we come up with a list of appearances which makes things go well. The anomic is related to the nomic (See Berger 1967 for a classic statement about the relationship between the anomic—things gone wrong—and the nomic—things gone right).

2. It is not within the scope of this chapter to explicate the differences between theater and drama, a point that many critics of dramaturgy seem unable to get straight. Suffice it to say here that theater is an artificial construction in which we pull action out of the drama of daily life in order to emphasize it in certain ways: to instruct, to entertain, or to politicize.

3. The fact that erectile dysfunction medications do not produce erections in the absence of some kind of sexual imagery and stimuli underscores this point.

4. From the web blog *Jezebel*, http://jezebel.com/5305545/few-people-agree-on -the-definition-of-sex.

5. I engage this exercise fully aware of the deficiencies of this framework. Dramaturgy does not model the actor's consciousness, does not explain why action occurs in the first place, pays no attention to the multiplicity of independent variables alleged to "cause" action, and often seems to focus more on when things go badly than when they go well. For more sociological traditionalists these are fatal flaws. But the dramaturgical preoccupation with *how* action occurs and *how* meaning is established is useful in its own terms, if for no other reason than the fact that participants in sexual acts generally care little about anything *except* the meaning of the experience (Davis 1983).

6. For a full explication of dramaturgical thinking, see Brissett and Edgley 2006 and Edgley 2013.

7. To "queer" a subject, Ahmed says, is simply to take that which is ordinarily interpreted from a heterosexual set of assumptions and frame it homosexually. The results are often striking and surprising.

8. This example demonstrates nicely that dramaturgy is a behavioral, not a phenomenological, account of human activity. It is an attempt to describe the process of behaving, not an effort to model the consciousness of the actor. We often perform in ways which communicate that we are not performing at all. But at other times—especially when things go badly—we incorporate into our actions the idea that our performance was "just" a performance and therefore not to be taken seriously.

9. Such observations about time and mood also help us understand why the incidence of sex tends to go down after the birth of children. Given the strict wall of segregation this society requires between children and adults when it comes to sexuality and given the physical ecology of most homes, nothing kills an erotic mood quicker than the sudden appearance of children on a sexual scene. "Mommy, I'm thirsty," is a demand that evaporates eroticism as couples grab for clothing and search for explanations.

10. Much of the sexual harassment dilemma can be seen in this sense as what happens when talk appropriate to the world of erotic reality enters the workplace where it is seen as decidedly inappropriate. Here, as elsewhere, the dramaturgy of situation and place are critical to the definition of occurrences as constituting harassment.

11. This quality of Goffman's writing leaves the reader with the impression that his work is a kind of pornography in the sense that it reveals that which is supposed to be kept private. Sexual pornography is not judged to be "obscene" or "dirty" merely because of its content, but mostly because it takes the form of making intensely public things regarded as private. Goffman does this for everyday life and its most sacred construction—the self.

12. Bennett goes on to say that these "common predicaments and awkward moments appeal" to any reader of Goffman.

    There was a time when I imagined those readers were few. As with all the best books, I took Goffman's work to be somehow a secret between me and the author, and incidents such as I have detailed above are our private joke. Individuals knew they behaved in this way, but Goffman knew everybody behaved like this and so did I. Only we were both keeping it quiet. (Bennett 1981:12)

13. Male ministers often wear robes when performing their roles, a dramaturgical necessity when it comes to making certain their genitals are secure from inadvertent public view. The capacity of erections to ruin a show was one of the aspects of sex that troubled the early Christian fathers and influenced the development of Puritan ideologies with which even modern day sex is shackled. By the same token, as Lorentzen (2007) has shown, males can get erections under all kinds of nonsexual circumstances, and these can lead to catastrophic embarrassment. Prop activations at the wrong time are as embarrassing as prop failures.

PART II
CONSTRUCTING SEXUAL MEANINGS

This section deals with exploring changing cultural meanings around sex and sexuality, along with how they come to change. We view these four chapters as being in conversation with one another, about these changes on the one hand and responses to them on the other.

In Chapter 6, Elliott and McKelvy paint a picture that we suspect contemporary undergraduates will find familiar, but which veteran sex researchers may find shocking. From a "sex-positive" perspective, the implications are rather disturbing. Elliott and McKelvy reveal the extent to which contemporary sexual education appears to be committed to a discourse of sex as dangerous. Nationwide over the past two decades, sex education debates have resulted in a compromise of sorts: abstinence-focused or abstinence-only sex education. Elliott and McKelvy illustrate that the preferred way to convince adolescents to abstain, at least in the schools they studied, is to convince them that pre- and extramarital sex is dangerous.

Researchers (and everyone else) who came of sexual age before the AIDS crisis will remember a time during which sex was not considered dangerous. The desire to control adolescent sexuality existed during our lifetimes as well, but it was not couched in terms of danger, but as morality. This appears to us to be a post-AIDS shift, in which an increasingly medicalized culture has brought sexuality ever more strongly into the fold.

When one of us (Weinberg) was in high school, from the late 1950s to the early 1960s, there were no formal sex education courses. This was an era in which sexualities were never talked about in public. Television programs of that time rarely showed adults in a bedroom. When they did, these were married people, who both wore pajamas and robes and slept in twin beds. Adolescent sexuality was discreet. Mostly, it was confined to "heavy petting" and "dry humping." Girls who became pregnant rarely kept their babies; they were sent away to "visit an aunt," which meant that they went to a home for unwed mothers and came back without their baby. High school sex education for girls consisted of a movie shown once a year. Boys were not allowed in. Sex was not especially dangerous, but it was taboo. It was bound up in morality (or immorality) and mystique.

By the time Newmahr was in junior high school and high school in the 1980s, the sexual revolution of the 1960s and 70s had made talking about sex much less taboo. Sex education was in full swing—but only as a health issue. Sex ed became part of the curriculum of health classes, as opposed to, for example, part of physical education, a life skills curriculum, or its own subject. Sex education focused on preventing sexually transmitted diseases (STDs; then, called "venereal disease") and pregnancy, but it wasn't especially fear based. Students memorized the effectiveness rates of condoms as compared to the birth control pill and answered essay exam questions about how one could effectively combine multiple methods. The AIDS crisis led to an increased emphasis on conversations about "barrier methods," and even as we sifted through new research about whether HIV was transmitted through kissing, cunnilingus, or fellatio, the message was "use a condom just in case, at least until we know more."

Somewhere between the Clinton-Lewinsky affair and the end of the George W. Bush administration (which directed funds toward abstinence-only education), sex became scary. Children are increasingly vaccinated to protect against STDs, and sex before marriage is the boogeyman. This marks a radical shift from the adolescence of the last five decades, in which sex before marriage went from being morally wrong in the fifties and most of the sixties, to the key to sexual and spiritual liberation (in the late 60s and 70s), to the perhaps-unfortunate reality of adolescence (in the 80s and part of the 90s). At this particular moment, several social occurrences intersect that may help explain the construction of sex as scary in the contemporary United States: the sexual and religious morality of the 8-year Bush administration, the general trend toward risk aversion and "fear culture," the increasing medicalization of the body and the related influence of the pharmaceutical industry, and the identification of new sexually transmitted diseases. These cultural changes impact generations of people who think and feel differently about sex than previous generations.

At the same time, other aspects of our social world are also changing rapidly. Dennis Waskul's chapter (7) explores the role of technology in the sexual lives of people who have grown up in the digital age. Although it may seem just a matter of course for today's undergraduates, Waskul's analysis sensitizes us to the fact that, for the first time in history, sexual life simply cannot be adequately understood without thinking also about communication technologies. The Internet, cell phone cameras, texting, and Skype have all altered the landscape of the sexual. Writing an erotic note, once a form of flirtation, has given way to "sexting," a behavior increasingly understood as a sex act in its own right. The implications of technology-mediated sexuality include changes in the relationship of the body to sexuality; technologies can impact our erotic relationships to the skin and smells and textures, for example. One wonders if the sexual fantasies of digital generations will become increasingly text based through the role of words on a screen in their erotic lives—or whether, over time, the written word may lose its erotic potential for these generations, for the same reasons.

In addition to these potential changes to sexuality ushered in by new technologies, viewing Waskul's chapter as in conversation with Elliott and McKelvy's raises interesting questions about "safer" forms of sexuality. The flourishing of techno-sexualities at a time in which physical sexuality is increasingly constructed as threatening begs for a wider conversation about our ideas about sex, danger, the body, and privacy. In the early days of the Internet, public fears about sex hinged on chat rooms and the potential for sexual "predators" to access children. Later, concerns about sexuality and technology centered around privacy and the control of digital property; how did we know our pictures and stories would not "get out"? Among the contemporary techno-sexuals that Waskul describes, there seem to be relatively few concerns about information privacy . . . but several concerns about the dangers of physical sex.

Alison Better's chapter on sex shops further illustrates not only how sexual meanings are constructed but also the consistency with the discourse of sex as dangerous. Most explicitly, Chapter 8 illustrates the construction of sex and eroticism as gendered by exploring the marketing of sex shops to women. In its recognition of the construction of "romantic sex" as what women want, though, it also touches upon romance as the converse of "dangerous" sex. The marketing of "feminist" sex shops as romantic (that is, about love), clean, and safe upholds the notion that "other" sex—the kind that we think women do *not* want—is not about love and (therefore) dirty and dangerous.

In the particular shop that Better describes, the phallus is excluded, in order to maintain the safe feeling of the shop. The idea of the penis as dangerous, then, and the labeling of sex shops without phalluses as feminist designates feminist spaces as those without penises, while upholding the notion that what women want is "Barbie dream house sex"—pretty, clean, standardized, and rooted in monogamous, dyadic relationships. Better's exploration of this so-called feminist vision therefore helps to illuminate the cultural irony here: Through the marketing of sex shops as feminist, women's sexuality is constructed in a particular and monolithic way, with particular traits, and in direct contrast to men's sexuality, thereby upholding gendered constraints on sexual expressions.

The discourse that Elliott and McKelvy uncover in Chapter 6, then, runs through each of the chapters in this section, if we concern ourselves with the construction of meanings of, around, and through sexuality. Though this was not intentional on our part, the discourse that emerged from each of the chapters on constructing meanings illustrated for us a pervasive perspective of sex, and particular sexualities and behaviors, as dangerous and therefore undesirable.

Staci Newmahr

CHAPTER 6

TALKING SEX

Parents, Schools, and Sexuality

Sinikka Elliott

Josephine Ngo McKelvy

A few years ago, a broad swath of Texans—parents, community leaders, teachers, physicians, and others—came together for a series of public school board meetings to debate the adoption of new student health textbooks for the state. Of contention was whether the students' books would contain information about contraception. The people who attended the meetings were clearly divided on this issue—some were for the information appearing in the students' books while others were against it. With angry looks and high emotions, people lobbed accusations at one another and gave impassioned, sometimes tearful, speeches.

Yet regardless of which side of the sex ed debate people were on, what they said sounded remarkably similar. Those for teaching youth about contraception described ministering to young people who, in the hopes of avoiding pregnancy and sexually transmitted infections, use plastic bags as condoms and douche with Coke. Those opposed to offering students contraceptive information, other than failure rates, spoke of things like seeing herpes that resemble cigarette burns on young women's genitals. In short, despite the amount of dissension in the room, everyone agreed that teen sexual activity is a highly risky venture and deployed graphic and horrific descriptive language to emphasize the damage sexual activity can wreak on young people's—especially young women's—bodies. The two sides differed merely in their solution to the "problem" of teen sexuality.

The debates over sex education offer insight into prevailing ways of talking and thinking about teen sexuality. They also raise important questions: Why do we teach teens about sexuality? What do we hope to accomplish? What beliefs about teens, sex, and knowledge underlie these efforts? The idea of sex education has been around since the early 1900s, but sex education came to be systematically offered in public schools only starting in the 1970s. By the 1980s, sex education—and by association teen sexuality—had become a flash point in the culture wars (Fields 2008; Irvine 2002; Luker 2006). Over the past couple of decades, two approaches to sex education have dominated. The first approach emphasizes the importance of waiting to have sex until marriage—typically referred to as *abstinence-only sex education*. The second approach usually also emphasizes the value of abstaining from sex until adulthood but, in addition, provides contraceptive information to encourage safer sex—often referred to as *comprehensive sex education*.[1]

In this chapter, we discuss the tactics deployed by these two approaches to sex education and the constructions of teens and teen sexuality that underlie these approaches. We also explore parents' beliefs about teen sexuality as well as their efforts to teach their children about sex. Throughout the chapter, we use research the first author collected over a 3-year period (2004–2007), which involved attending community meetings where sex education was debated, observing school-based sex education classes—both abstinence-only and comprehensive—and interviewing in detail nearly 50 parents of teenagers about their views on sex education and their experiences talking with their teen children about sex.

READING BETWEEN THE LINES OF SEX EDUCATION

Abstinence-only and comprehensive sex education programs are often portrayed as diametrically opposed to one another, yet they share similar ideas about youth and sex. Both curricula construct teen sexuality as highly dangerous and focus on educating young people about the dangers of sex (Connell and Elliott 2009). Following Elliott (2012), we refer to this as "the danger discourse" of teen sexuality. In characterizing sexual activity as dangerous for teens, both approaches also routinely rely on and reproduce gendered, racialized, classed, and heteronormative meanings and inequalities (Connell and Elliott 2009; Fields 2008; Garcia 2009; Kirby 2002). Further, both tend to construct teens as irresponsible and immature yet, simultaneously, highly sexually motivated (Elliott 2012; Schalet 2009). In the next section, drawing from participant observation in sex education classes, we elaborate on these dimensions of abstinence-only and comprehensive sex education as they are illustrated by two sex educators. First, we detail the setting of the two schools from which observations were drawn during 2006.

EASTSIDE AND TAYLOR HIGH SCHOOLS

Eastside High School is located in a dense, predominantly black and Latino, urban area. A rusty wire fence surrounds the school; the front gate is open only during school hours. Warnings crisscross the entrance: No Trespassing, Guns Prohibited. Before the bell rings, students lounge on large boulders that act as barriers between the sidewalk and the front of the school building. Inside, the three-story school resembles a panopticon: Classrooms snake around a central courtyard with a see-through roof. This open, middle part of the school is not heated or cooled. Students are visible to staff whenever they are outside of class, making it more difficult to skip, and the intemperate temperatures make being out of class less inviting. The lack of privacy at Eastside extends into the girls' bathroom, where school officials have removed the stall doors. The school has a throbbing energy, and students' voices echo around the courtyard, building to a loud roar between classes.

In contrast to Eastside's urban setting, Taylor High School sits in the center of a large field, and it serves a rapidly growing immigrant-destination suburb. Befitting its wide-open location, the school is a sprawling, low building. Although the school is fairly new, it has already reached capacity and health classes are taught in one of several portable buildings located next to a wire fence enclosing the back of the school. The immediate area in front of the school is manicured, but the field surrounding the school is overgrown and does not look inviting. The lack of sidewalks funnels traffic in and out of the school through the front of the building where the office is located. Both the landscaping and lack of footpaths are purposeful elements, intended to discourage students from leaving campus without permission. The school itself is designed in a horseshoe, with a large, dusty outdoor courtyard. A security guard with a gun in his holster and a noisy walkie-talkie patrols this area on a golf cart, stopping occasionally to interact with students. "Things can get out of hand in the courtyard" (Field notes), says Taylor's health teacher Ms. Fox, explaining the continuous presence of security personnel. Inside the school, the tinted windows provide muted light, and the atmosphere is subdued except when students are between classes.

Schools both fear and promote teen heterosexuality (Pascoe 2007), and Taylor High and Eastside are no exception. Both schools have strict policies on public displays of affection (PDAs): Public displays of affection are not allowed on school property. Both adhere to a gendered and racialized dress code which prohibits girls from wearing "halter tops" and "shorts and/or skirts that distract" and admonishes boys against wearing "gang-associated clothing or colors" and "baggy pants or oversized clothing," among other specifications reminiscent of hip-hop apparel or thug culture. Yet at Eastside, handwritten posters hang from every available surface advertising Homecoming—one of many heternormative school rituals (Pascoe 2007)—and urging students to vote for Homecoming King and Queen—"Vote Lakeisha as Your Queen." And Taylor High's popular health teacher, Ms. Fox, routinely refers to former and current heterosexual student couples during her health lessons. Thus, the schools' informal curriculum and formal rituals (like Homecoming) assume and even stress heterosexuality, even as schools officially discourage hetero-sexual *behavior*. The next section takes us into the sex ed classrooms at these two schools where these contradictions are also evident.

THE DANGER DISCOURSE OF TEEN SEXUALITY

Mr. Marks, a white male in his mid thirties, is an abstinence-only sex educator. His thinning dirty blond hair is styled in a buzz cut, and he favors polo shirts, faded blue jeans, and loafers. He has been an abstinence presenter for 6 years, visiting 40 or more schools in the course of a year. During his 3-day presentation to a class of low-income, primarily black and Latino/a ninth graders at Eastside High School, Mr. Marks brings up the topic of boundaries. He asks the class,

> "Are boundaries good or bad?"
>
> A few students mutter, "Good."
>
> "Right," Mr. Marks says, adding cryptically, "boundaries can give you more freedom."

He then gives an analogy of elementary students on a playground without a fence:

> They're playing with a ball. It gets thrown into the street and a student runs out to get it. Now wouldn't that student have been safer if there'd been a fence around the playground?

Having established the necessity of boundaries, he makes a further analogy:

> Fire is good, but fire can be bad when it's not contained. The same applies to sex. So a fireplace is to fire what marriage is to sex—it contains it, makes it safe and good. (Field notes)

Across town, Ms. Fox is teaching a group of mostly low-income black and Latino/a students in one of her health classes at Taylor High School. Ms. Fox helped develop a comprehensive sex ed curriculum and travels around the state training other teachers in its use. She is in her early fifties, has blonde shoulder-length hair, and wears brightly colored Southwest-inspired clothing. A popular health teacher, she tells her students that sex outside of marriage is a risky enterprise akin to "running out into the middle of a busy interstate. It is fraught with danger." She frequently accuses her students, "You don't use contraception because you think you've got some sort of force field." (Field notes)

For both of these educators, the goal is to jolt young people into awareness of how dangerous sex is. Mr. Marks hopes that his lessons will convince youth to wait until they are safely married to have sex. Ms. Fox says her intent is to get at least some of her students who decide to have sex "to think ahead, to plan." The parents interviewed for this study generally agree that sex education "should just scare them to death," as one mother puts it (Elliott 2012). And students appear to be getting this message. After listening to Ms. Fox's presentation on sexually transmitted infections, a female student volunteers how the scare tactics have left a lasting mark, scarring her "for life": "I am scarred. I am *scarred* for life," she says.

Parents and sex educators also seem to agree that an effective way to scare youth away from sex is to scare them away from intimate relationships with their peers. For example, Mr. Marks's lesson on boundaries includes a class activity that subtly bolsters homophobia. He asks two of the boys to come to the front of the classroom. He tells one to pretend he is on an elevator and the other to step onto the elevator. The boy does so, turns, and faces outward, leaving plenty of space.

"What if he faced inward?" Mr. Marks asks, directing the boys to face one another.

Some of the students giggle, and one of the boys' raises his fists threateningly at the other.

"That's right," Mr. Marks concludes. "Boundaries also help you feel comfortable." (Field notes)

He thanks the boys and sends them back to their seats. By selecting two boys for this activity, Mr. Marks underscores that boys should not want intimacy with one another.

Mr. Marks dismisses homosexuality as a viable option, yet his depictions of heterosexual relationships are highly adversarial. After the elevator activity, Mr. Marks addresses the girls in the classroom:

> Girls, I don't mean to pick on you, but my wife says y'all are bad at this "come hither" stuff.

Mr. Marks giggles and makes his voice "girly." He says, "Stop that," in a completely unconvincing way and slaps at an invisible boy with a limp wrist. "What's that telling the guys?" he asks.

The boys in the class yell, "Go for it!"

Having established that boys actively lust after and push girls into sex, Mr. Marks then looks piercingly at the girls:

Girls, you have the most to lose. You have to stay in control more than anyone. Now guys, I know girls can be aggressive as well, especially in today's society, but . . .

Mr. Marks trails off. Momentarily, he introduces the possibility of female sexual desire, but this does not neatly fit Mr. Marks' abstinence-only formula because it acknowledges girls' active sexuality and contradicts gendered sexual stereotypes. Mr. Marks instead quickly dismisses the sexually desiring girl in favor of an emphasis on the importance of girls controlling boys' sexuality. He says to the girls,

You need to have an exit strategy. The number one thing 90 percent of girls say they want to know about sex is how to say no without hurting his feelings. Use humor: "I would, but my dad's a gun owner." Girls, you can say no. State your reason and say something nice, "I really like you, but. . ." (Field notes)

In this way and others, Mr. Marks paints heterosexual relationships as a zero-sum game. Boys want one thing. Girls need to keep them from getting it and protect their chastity—albeit remaining "nice" in the process. If girls are not able to say no on their own terms, they can appeal to a patriarchal authority figure—their gun-toting fathers—as an excuse to avoid sex. His lectures illustrate how the lessons of sex education construct teens as naturally heterosexual, even as they do not make heterosexual relationships seem very appealing (Fields 2008; Kirby 2002).

Parents also emphasize the dangers their children's peers pose. In their conversations with their teen children, parents focus on their children's vulnerability in the face of a highly sexualized peer culture comprising more sexually motivated peers. Often using coded racialized, gendered, and classed language, parents warn their teen children away from intimate relationships with their peers (Elliott 2012; Solebello and Elliott 2011). For example, parents caution their sons that girls will use sex to lure them into a relationship and may even try to trap them through a pregnancy. One working-class mother, Renae, desperately wants her teen sons to attend college and become middle-class professionals. Her older son was on his way to college when his girlfriend had a pregnancy scare. Rather than view her son as at least partially responsible for the potential pregnancy, Renae uses classed and gendered language to cast him as a victim. Describing the girlfriend as "streetwise"—a code word that has strong class overtones—Renae believes she faked the pregnancy in an effort to keep her son from going to college or to attach herself permanently to a young man with a promising future (Elliott 2012).

Parents of daughters also paint a grim picture of heterosexual relationships. Many tell their daughters that boys are only after one thing (sex) and will not respect the girl who gives it to them (Elliott 2012; Solebello and Elliott 2011). Corina, a black mother, asked a male friend to talk to her two teen daughters about the "male point of view." He told them "the truth," Corina says approvingly. Describing the friend in racialized terms as a "player," Corina says he told her daughters, "'I just want women for their body. I'm using them and if any other man tells you that's not what they're doing, then they're lying to you'" (as quoted in Elliott 2012, 119). Parents' lessons are heartfelt. They want to protect their teen children from heartache and victimization, but they also suggest "that adults have a monopoly on good relationships and may prevent parents from having frank discussions with their children about the complexities—the good, the bad, and the ambivalent—of romantic attachments" (Elliott 2012:97). These lessons also imply that their children are not responsible for their actions; their peers are to blame. Assigning responsibility is another primary lesson of sex education.

CONSTRUCTING (IR)RESPONSIBILITY

A major emphasis of abstinence-only and comprehensive sex education is teaching teens to be responsible. Ms. Fox, the health teacher, repeatedly asks her students,

> "If you have sex, what two things must you assume?"
>
> Her male and female students echo back, "She's pregnant and I've got an STD."
>
> "Who's to blame?" Ms. Fox asks.
>
> "I am," the students reply in unison. (Field notes)

In addition to emphasizing personal responsibility, as with other school-based sexuality lessons, Ms. Fox above constructs a generic male sexual agent ("*She's* pregnant and *I've* got an STD"); yet the "bad girl" looms in the implication that a willing female sexual participant is a transmitter of disease.

For the abstinence-only instructor, Mr. Marks, responsibility involves being future-focused. In demonstrating the importance of students focusing on goals to help them achieve their life pursuits, Mr. Marks spins a plate on a stick, vaudeville style. As long as he looks raptly at the plate, it remains balanced and spinning on the stick. When Mr. Marks looks up from the spinning plate, it wobbles and topples off the stick. The students enjoy this demonstration and several ask to try it themselves, with the same result. Mr. Marks then hammers home his point:

> You need to keep your eyes on your futures and not be distracted. Sex is distracting. It makes you think about sex in the here and now—you don't need to be doing that at this point. You need to be focusing on your goals in life. What do you want to achieve in life? (Field notes)

Yet in teaching responsibility, sex educators often stress teenagers' *irresponsibility*, implying that teens are incapable of making good choices, acting rationally, or taking responsibility for their actions. In the previous passage, Mr. Marks assumes that teenagers cannot handle the responsibilities of sex along with their other responsibilities. Ms. Fox confides to the first author that even though she teaches her students about contraception, she does not believe that her lessons make much of a difference:

> The harsh reality is, most teens don't use it, but maybe some will. If I can just get through to a couple [of them]. (Field notes)

Ms. Fox is not confident in her students' personal responsibility, and she is skeptical of their academic responsibility as well. For example, her students rarely take notes, unless she directs them to do so and tells them exactly what to write down. Even so, she requires her students to leave the notes they do take in the classroom, assuming they will lose them if left to their own devices. In other words, pedagogically, teenagers are often treated as remarkably irresponsible.

Sex educators also blame students' parents, whom they portray as irrational or uninformed. Mr. Marks tells the ninth graders that their "parents don't know all the sexually transmitted diseases that are out there" (Field notes) and thus cannot fully appreciate the dangers sex poses to them and properly guide their sexuality. Ms. Fox regularly portrays her students' parents as not only ignorant but also as impediments to their learning. She tells her students that their parents do not want her to teach them about condoms and birth control, but she is going to anyway because she cares about them.

Ms. Fox also informs her students that their parents too easily let them off the hook for responsibility. As an example, she says that if one of her own children got pregnant as a teenager, she would not let that child live under her roof as so many parents do:

> I would get them an apartment and they can live there and raise that child. They're not going to raise that kid under my roof—they're going to be responsible for that kid. (Field notes)

Given that Ms. Fox is a white, middle-class teacher addressing a class of mostly low-income black and Latino/a students, this suggestion is infused with racialized and classed meanings about responsibility. Ms. Fox implies that living independently means taking responsibility. Yet in securing an apartment for her child and presumably helping to cover associated expenses, she also points to the role family resources play in enabling independence, resources her low-income students' families likely lack. Thus, sex educators present themselves as caring, knowledgeable, and indispensable in large part by constructing their students as incapable, their students' parents as unaware, and both groups as irresponsible.

ADULT ACCOUNTABILITY AND THE (IM)POSSIBILITY OF PLEASURE

Reading between the lines of sex education's lessons reveals not only the fears adults have about teens behaving irresponsibly but also concerns about adult accountability for the safety of young people. Ms. Fox says she is tremendously invested in her students and feels responsible for their well-being. Early in his presentation, Mr. Marks confesses that he had sex as a teen and that not a day goes by when he wishes this was not so. "I want you to avoid the mistake I made." As a responsible adult, he adds, the only message he "can responsibly impart is one of abstinence—it is the one true way" (Field notes).

Like these sex educators, parents feel morally accountable for ushering their children safely to adulthood. Abstinence holds great allure in this context and many parents emphasize its value. But parents are also skeptical about the feasibility of abstinence (Elliott 2012). Some believe it is unrealistic to expect teens to abstain, given their raging hormones and hypersexualized peer culture, but say abstinence is the only unambiguous directive available to parents. Overall, parents feel a profound sense of responsibility for keeping their children safe from harm (Elliott 2012; Elliott and Aseltine 2012; Nelson 2010; Rutherford 2011). In their efforts to avoid the semblance of condoning sexual experimentation, parents avoid the subject of pleasure in their sex talks, saying it would be irresponsible to talk about pleasure with their teen children given the risks associated with teen sexual activity (Elliott 2012).

Hence, in a climate of sex panics—where fears about sex, from predatory adults to promiscuous teens, prevail—parents, schools, and sex educators also worry that their lessons about sexuality may expose *them* to accusations of impropriety and irresponsibility (Elliott 2012; Fields 2008; Irvine 2002). Ms. Fox can thus show her students a condom but cannot demonstrate how to put it on. She and other sex educators in her district can talk about contraception, but they must highlight their failure rates and constantly reinforce the message of abstinence. With its emphasis on neutral, "scientific" lessons, pleasure rarely enters the comprehensive sex ed classroom (Fields 2008). Much of Ms. Fox's lessons, for example, focus on the biology of sex. The students learn the anatomically correct terms for reproductive organs and recite after Ms. Fox in a monotonous chorus, "vas deferens, scrotum, penis, fallopian tubes, uterus, vaginal canal. . . ." Comprehensive sex educators adopt this "naturalist perspective" in an effort to protect themselves from charges of teaching students inappropriate or offensive material (Fields 2008:104; Pascoe 2007).

Abstinence-only sex ed, in contrast, creates discursive space to discuss pleasure, but it is pleasure within the confines of marriage, with an emphasis on the long-lasting emotional scars of sex outside of marriage. Thus, even though pleasure is present, the emphasis is still on the dangerous and negative consequences of sex outside of marriage, which is consistent with larger sex panics around teen sexuality. Mr. Marks regularly describes sex in very enthusiastic terms. "I think sex is amazing, fantastic, phenomenal, awesome, you name it," he gushes. However, the key to good sex for Mr. Marks is that it is contained within marriage. "Only marriage can create the relationship between two people that allows sex to be good," he tells the students. (Field notes)

If a person has sex before marriage, Mr. Marks cautions, it can destroy the possibility of ever establishing this bond because it can make the person guarded and less open. Mr. Marks uses an activity to illustrate this point, instructing two students, whom he refers to as "playas," to stick the same piece of masking tape onto several other students' arms and then stick the tape on a poster board. Using the term *playas* helps Mr. Marks present himself as hip and cool, but it is also a gendered and racialized term that codes sexual activity as the terrain of black and Latino males. By the end of the activity, the playas tape does not stick to the poster board as well as the tape of two students who simply held onto their tape, presumably saving themselves for marriage. This activity underscores Mr. Marks's point that sex before marriage can blunt the potency of sex in marriage and, given the significance of marital sex, place the marriage itself on tenuous ground.

In sum, sex education is ostensibly about "making healthy choices," as Ms. Fox routinely emphasizes. Yet because sex educators construct teens as irresponsible *and* simultaneously highly sexually motivated, a laundry list of bad choices is always accompanied by one good choice: abstinence. Sex educators tell teens they have the power to control their destinies and that any bad choices they make are theirs and theirs alone.

"These are your choices," Ms. Fox tells her students. "Your health is your choice. I can't do anything about it. It is up to you." (Field notes)

In this sense, then, despite sex educators' sense of moral accountability, sex education is also about absolving schools and the state of any responsibility for the "bad" decisions youth make. The mandate of individual accountability and personal choice precludes any responsibility of the state, any notion of the common good, and instead creates a perception of willfully bad, oversexualized young people—often coded male, black, Latino/a, and low income in the language that sex educators (and parents) use, as well as the dress code institutionalized by the schools. The "problem" of teen sexuality thus becomes a problem of individual, irresponsible, and hormonal teenagers (and their ill-informed, lax parents)—rather than a structural, endemic one.

CONCLUSION

As we have seen, how sex educators and parents talk to young people about sexuality is based on and reproduces dichotomies of pleasure versus danger and responsible versus irresponsible. Lessons in sexuality posit youth as both too young to have sex and too sexed to handle information about sex. They also construct all youth as heterosexual, even as they teach adversarial gender relations and promote stereotypes based on race, class, gender, and sexuality. These constructions thus offer insight into the reproduction of social inequality. They also offer a roadmap for new ways of thinking about teen sexual activity and teaching youth about sexuality. It is time to fundamentally rethink current constructions of teens and youth sexuality. The danger discourse of teen sexuality makes it more difficult for adults to accept that teens are sexual agents who, with support and resources, can carve out positive sexual lives *and* promising futures.

NOTE

1. At the time of the study, 33% of public schools offered abstinence-only sex education (Fine and McClelland 2006). According to a recent report by the Guttmacher Institute (2012), 17 states and the District of Columbia require that contraceptive information be provided when sex ed is offered. Overall, 37 states require that information on abstinence be provided to students while 19 states require information stressing the importance of sex within marriage.

CHAPTER 7

TECHNO-SEXUALITY

The Sexual Pragmatists of the Technological Age

Dennis D. Waskul

Melissa is a 20-year-old Caucasian freshman at an upper-Midwest university. Born August 1993 in a small rural community, Melissa enjoyed what most consider a typical American upbringing: Her mother and father are college-educated upper-middle class professionals; her older brother scored an athletic scholarship at a state university; she enjoyed close high school friendships with relatively little drama; she first kissed a boy when she was 14 but it would be another year until, in her own words, she had her first "real boyfriend, if you can call it that"; her family attended a Lutheran church (but not religiously), voted Democrat (but not doctrinally), and enjoyed annual family vacations (but never made it to Disneyland). It was a warm and loving upbringing, as stereotypically normative as it may be.

Undecided about her major, Melissa is currently content with a newfound enthusiasm for learning that university life has ignited. An academic world has just opened before her eyes on subjects she never learned about in primary and secondary education, in courses she did not anticipate, and with intellectual discoveries she could not have foreseen—including my own sexualities course, which she found especially provocative. Melissa graciously allowed me to share her story with you because, as you will soon see, things are not always what they seem.

Melissa told me that she always remembered being sexually curious, even as a young child. She vividly remembers, at the age of 13, when she first saw porn on the Internet: at her home computer, alone in the room, it was an innocent search that turned up not-so-innocent results. Melissa recalls being shocked by the images she saw—especially images of fellatio—"but" she says as she reflects on it now, "I think it's mostly because it was the first time I ever saw a hard cock." The shock did not last long.

Young Melissa had already discovered the pleasures of self-touching, typically before going to bed at night, although it would take a while before learning a proper word for what she was doing. Even after she labeled her semi-nightly ritual "masturbation," she never fully adopted the shame that often comes with that knowledge. Instead, as private opportunities would arise, Melissa would often return to the computer to gaze upon the images as her main source of information about sexual pleasure as well as her private experience of it. As her sexual desires were awakening, a plethora of Internet sites provided ready-made images of otherwise vague, even abstract passions. Some she liked, and others made her uncomfortable:

> I mostly liked penetration. Nothing anal, which kinda freaked me out. I liked all the positions, and imagined how they would feel. Like I said, I was really curious. It was more the softer stuff. Now I don't mind it a little rough, but back then I liked it more [pause]. What's the word? Romantic, I guess. Not so, I dunno, out there. You know? Like too hardcore.

Melissa remembers feeling guilty about her interest in sex, especially porn. Nonetheless, the pleasures trumped the guilt and, to this day, Melissa continues to enjoy watching Internet porn "about two times a week."

After the demise of her "first real boyfriend" relationship and a short string of dating that went nowhere, Melissa fell into a romance with Nick that lasted through her junior and most of her senior year of high school. She felt in love with him, and he would say the same words to her. While she kissed other boys, felt erections in their pants, and had her body explored by the hands of some of them, only with Nick would Melissa genuinely experience some sexual firsts.

After several months of kissing and heavy petting, sneaky fingers turned to oral sex—and that was sufficient for almost a year until, just prior to the age of 17, Melissa and Nick would go "all the way." Melissa found the first time disappointing, awkward, and even a bit painful, "but it got better." While on the surface there is nothing in this portion of Melissa's confession that is out of the ordinary, once more things are not always what they seem.

Melissa and Nick's relationship became increasingly physical in union with the ways they used technology to explore and express those experiences. Like most contemporary teens and young adults, cell phones were their preferred means of communication—and especially text messaging—"but sometimes when we would talk sexy on Facebook too." *Sexting*, as we now call it, was frequent between Melissa and Nick. At first, the two of them would use text to express desires "about every other day or so," Melissa recalls, but as the relationship grew more trusting, written words turned to images. "I wasn't real comfortable sending Nick sexy pictures, and it was usually just in my bra or panties. But he kept begging for them. I mostly did it for him at first." "God," Melissa reflects, "I think there was a time there where he saw my boobs more on his phone than he touched them on me!," accentuating the exclamation with a giggling smirk and adding:

"But it's not like that was anything new to me. I used to go to chatrooms when I was thirteen and fourteen. It was fun to talk dirty and pretend that I was older than I was. I mean, I didn't know what I was doing. It was all stuff I saw in porn. It made me feel more mature. I got a laptop when I was fifteen and it had a cam[era], and I'd sometimes send pictures—never my face, of course! I knew I shouldn't have been doing that but it made me feel so sexy! Like all these guys are so hot for me [laughs]."

Melissa feels fortunate that none of her erotic pictures ever reappeared in awkward or embarrassing ways and, as it turned out, Nick had enough respect to keep her images private. "He never kept them, or showed anyone. I told him if he did he wouldn't get any more from me!" While she was with Nick, Melissa would still sometimes view Internet porn and visit chat rooms to further explore sexual desires and fantasies—even using her webcam at times, and not always alone. Melissa used that same webcam to give Nick a very special gift on his 17th birthday: a video of Melissa giving him oral sex. "Honestly, I loved taking naughty pictures. I still do once in awhile."

Melissa and Nick broke up at the end of their senior year, although they remain friends (entirely on Facebook). Melissa has since had a few short-term relationships and a small number of sexual partners. She was gifted her first vibrator from a friend when she turned 18 and now owns two more—a technology that is central to her reply when I ask about her current love life:

I guess I'd like to have a boyfriend sometime. I always seem to have a cute guy that I want to be with. [giggles] I'm just focused on other things right now. I guess I'm kinda selfish cuz I really don't wanna be tied down or even do the whole relationship thing right now. I know I can get a guy if I want to get some. I'm not ashamed that I've had a couple relationships just for sex. But right now if I'm horny I've got my vibrator and if I'm feeling really naughty I can go to chatroulette. And, of course, I've always got my favorite porn sites to get me off!

Melissa's sexual coming of age is both normative and unique. Her vivid memory of her first encounter with porn is consistent with her peers; in a 2008 study of 594 young people, more than 50% of both boys and girls had seen pornography online by age 14 or 15—and boys are significantly more likely to purposely search for it (see Sabina, Wolak, and Finkelhor 2008). She discovered her ability to sexually please herself in normative ways (see Waskul, Vannini, and Wiesen 2007). Her tale reflects a progression of partnered physical intimacy that matches Western contemporary cultural scripts. Still, there is something in Melissa's story that stands out clearly, something decidedly unique—two things, in fact.

First, unlike any prior generation in history, Melissa's coming of age is situated in a highly technological era where sexual awakenings and discoveries are profoundly mediated by new media technologies, and especially communication technologies. Social interactions in general have never been so mediated by technology and, not surprisingly, so too are sexual interactions in the specific. Behind the electronic curtain of Melissa's otherwise tranquil exterior appearance, there is a seething technologically mediated erotic ether through (and in) which her sexual awakenings and desires have always been explored or expressed in one way or another. Second—and this is important— Melissa is not a real person.

"Melissa" is not a person, per se, but a persona I created from bits and pieces of biographical information that have been shared with me in recent years. Melissa is a fiction made of fact; every element of her story is true of one or more people who candidly revealed that information with me. Even the quotes that I attributed to Melissa are almost verbatim. Melissa is an assemblage of actual accounts and recollections that are simply woven into a single biography that isn't.

I created the Melissa persona for illustrative purposes—mainly to highlight how technology *can* extensively mediate contemporary sexualities. And, as I will soon illustrate, the Melissa persona also illustrates how technologies often *do* mediate contemporary sexualities. For the record, I will no longer exploit my privileges as an author to deceive you into fictions and half-truths. From here on, I will remain faithful to my duties as a broker of truth (although I will refer back to Melissa from time to time). Indeed, to that end I have gathered a nonrandom sample of 33 young adults[1] who replied to an open-ended qualitative survey on their sexual uses of technology. I'll base the remainder of this chapter in their words. No more shooting from the hip.

INSTITUTIONAL TECHNO-SEXUALITIES

We are in the midst of a technologically mediated reorganization of the social relations of sexuality.

–Steve Garlick. 2011. "A New Sexual Revolution?"
Canadian Review of Sociology 48(3):223

It is common to think of sexuality in the singular and as an innate essence of a person that is more-or-less reduced to biological conditions (e.g., hormones), psychological influences (e.g., drives), or fundamental units of a grand natural order (e.g., instincts). Regardless of merit, these reductionistic approaches obscure an equally important frame for understanding, and one that is especially vital for understanding contemporary sexualities: *sexualities are institutions*. Simply stated, an institution is a well-established and structured pattern of behaviors or relationships that are accepted as normative within a given culture. Hence, for one example, just as we may think of marriage as an institution so too are sexualities; just as marriage is made up of patterns of behaviors and relationships within a given culture, so too are sexualities.

It is crucial to understand sexualities as institutions for many reasons; however, for our purposes, doing so serves as a necessary corrective. Institutions are not universal in form and content. Institutions have a history. Institutions are social and cultural constructions. Institutions are codified for the purposes of order, and that process of ordering defines (in fact, creates) that which is considered "deviant." Institutions are ironically stable yet also quite sensitive to dynamics of social change. Institutions require processes of socialization whereby people learn the patterns of behavior (and corresponding values) that sustain them, while also presenting opportunities to reject or rebel against them. Seen as an institution, then, it is also clear why contemporary, first-world sexualities simply must be understood in the light of technology. Indeed, when Melissa "was born" in 1993, she entered a world that was about to undergo a sweeping transformation: Every major institution would soon be radically reshaped by an unprecedented implosion of new media and communication technologies—especially the Internet. Just as those technologies brought about dramatic change in all other institutions, so too has it been for sexualities.

As digital culture became increasingly pervasive and embedded in young people's everyday experiences (Weber and Dixon 2010), those technologies infiltrated how young people socialize among acquaintances *and* sexual partners. I use the term *techno-sexuality* to refer to these institutional dynamics of contemporary sexualities—an institution that comprises what I will call "techno-sexuals" (which is not specific to any gender or sexual identity). Like any other institution, techno-sexualities manifest themselves in a variety of related forms. Like any other institution, techno-sexuals are more or less acculturated. That is, to use an example, Melissa's techno-sexuality is more extensive than most—which is to say that Melissa makes extensive use of technology to mediate, explore, and express her sexual desires. Nonetheless, I strongly suspect that the vast majority of those who read her semifictional tale share one or more experiences in common with her use of technology for sexual purposes. *That* is precisely what I mean by techno-sexuality, and it may be fair to suggest that anyone under the age of 40 who is reading these words is to some extent a techno-sexual.[2] Indeed, of the 33 young adults (aged 19 to 27) who participated in this study, there was enormous variation in the extent to which they each used technology for sexual purposes, yet *every* one of them use at least *some* new media or communication technology for erotic purposes.

Thus, techno-sexuality simply refers to the increasingly ubiquitous use of technology to gather sexual information, express sexual desires, view or expose sexual bodies, experience sexual pleasure, and explore sexual fantasies. Expressions of techno-sexuality can be found in the sexual ways that people use the World Wide Web, e-mail, chat rooms, instant messaging, text messaging, digital cameras, webcams, and spoken voice in computer-mediated environments. These sexual uses of new media and communication technologies are sometimes solitary, sometimes with one or more copresent others, sometimes with one or more known partners on the other end of the technology, sometimes with anonymous virtual partners, or some combination thereof. Sometimes, the use of technology for sexual purposes involves isolated moments of curiosity or desire, other times technology is more persistently used in the processes of weaving emergent sexual selves over time. Other technologies also play an important role in techno-sexuality—especially the recently pervasive interest, acquisition, and use of vibrators among women. For now, I wish to remain focused on sexual uses of new media and communication technologies.

THE SEXUAL PRAGMATISTS OF THE TECHNOLOGICAL AGE

> That's one of the most beneficial aspects of technology for me. I love that I can find whatever gets me off on the Internet, it makes life easier.
>
> –Cindy, aged 20

A pragmatist is someone whose actions are guided by immediate practical consequences and intended outcomes. To be pragmatic is to creatively use available materials to directly accomplish tasks and goals. A pragmatist, in simple terms, is the opposite of the idealist who is guided by abstract ideas and intellectual principles (although these are not mutually exclusive characteristics). To some people, idealists are considered impractical because their deep commitment to abstractions hinders their ability to see immediate solutions to concrete problems. Those frustrated "some people" are the pragmatists among us—and they are particularly skilled innovators who, much to the chagrin of the idealists, have no problems whatsoever using things for undesignated purposes to achieve immediate, desired, and functional outcomes.

The one theme that consistently emerges in the data I have collected on the ways Midwestern young people use technology for sexual purposes is that it is most surely *pragmatic*. Available technologies can be used for many sexual purposes, and the meaning and value to those who use them hinge on immediate practical outcomes. As I will soon illustrate, the specters of idealism sometimes guiltily haunt; nonetheless, the sexual pragmatists of the technological age carry on with relative indifference. The main characteristics of techno-sexuality concern the pragmatics of sexual convenience, the pragmatic ways that technology is used for anticipatory sexual socialization, and the practical means of improvising with technology to supplement existing romantic relationships. Yet equally pragmatic are the outcomes of how young people use those technologies to render techno-sexuality both explicitly communicative and decidedly ludic. I will illustrate each of these characteristics in detail.

Considering that more than 90% of U.S. young people aged 12 through 18 use the Internet (Ybarra and Mitchell 2005), the capacity to use that technology for sexual purposes is undoubtedly *convenient* for those who are sexually curious, aroused, or would like to be. New media and communication technologies—especially the Internet—have made it far easier to gain immediate access to sexually explicit materials at virtually any moment and anywhere that the mood strikes. This kind of point-and-click for instant gratification (most often free of charge and complete with a wide variety of erotic choices) has obvious utility for immediate arousal and masturbatory inspiration:

> I did used to look at magazines when I was younger, but when the Internet boom hit it pretty much made that option obsolete. (Shaun, aged 24)

> I like using pornhub or other websites because they offer a large variety of videos and they are free so I don't need to go buy or rent a video. (Julie, aged 20)

These obvious, immediate uses of technology for sexual purposes are important for understanding contemporary techno-sexuality, but they are woefully superficial. Much more than a convenient means to a masturbatory end, the sexually pragmatic uses of contemporary technologies are far more deeply woven into the fabric of everyday, normative sexualities. For example, primarily because of the convenience of access, technology is highly instrumental in the processes of *anticipatory sexual socialization*.

Anticipatory socialization refers to voluntary preparations for anticipated future roles; it involves gathering knowledge, adopting necessary value sets, playing at or rehearsing required scripts, and otherwise grooming oneself—mostly in acts of mental preparedness—for the perceived expectations of future roles and identities. Because the majority of the privileged population born after 1990 has no recollection of any time in their lives when the Internet and other new media technologies were *not* available for immediate and convenient use, it is no surprise that those resources prove highly instrumental in the processes of *sexual* anticipatory socialization as young people imagine and prepare themselves to be future lovers. Tina (aged 20) provides one of the clearest examples:

> When I was around 12–13 I used to go on aol [America Online] chatrooms and pretend to be someone else. I would have one on one convos with strangers and have "cybersex." At the time I found it to be fun and guilty. I liked it because I was just starting to learn and explore my sexual self. I had maybe kissed a boy and that was as far as it had gone in my real life. Cybersex allowed me to express my sexuality without any real commitment or person I knew.

As Tina concisely explains, the veil of anonymity and physical distance allowed her to explore emerging sexual desires in online chat rooms—to quite literally rehearse or play them out and, as part of her anticipatory sexual socialization, provided a reasonably safe means for testing that sexuality or at least initially contending with her emerging desires. Tina admits, "As time went on I began to not like it as much. It became repetitive . . . I guess I kind of just grew out of it," yet she is quick to remind us, "it was kind of a nice start to learning about sexual experiences."

While Tina's early use of technology for sexual purposes occurred prior to significant embodied sexual experiences with another copresent person—as a means to communicatively explore her own desires on her own terms—the use of technology for anticipatory sexual socialization is most commonly reported in conjunction with embodied sexual experiences. That is, in short, when young people become sexually active in the flesh, they also concurrently use available technologies to further express or explore sexual desires. For example, Amy (aged 19) has "been sexting since I was 16 when I started having sex" whereas Laura (aged 27) began using technology for sexual purposes shortly after becoming sexually active—and mainly out of sheer curiosity:

> I have been using the Internet for sexual purposes since about the age of 17. I initially started in order to understand what was all out there. I was

16 when I first became sexually active, and I was curious to what other guys' bodies looked like. . . . white guys, black guys, Asian guys, etc.

In other processes of anticipatory sexual socialization, technology is an immediate precursor to in-the-flesh youthful sexual relationships, and, mainly for the practical purpose of gaining knowledge that compensates for inexperience:

I think that the only time I really used technology for sexual purposes and that was when I had my first boyfriend. I was 16 and I looked [on] Google and looked up "how to" do different things. I looked up how to give head and how to have sex, things like that. I think that it was actually very helpful and helped me feel more comfortable doing different things with my boyfriend. (Krista, aged 22)

Perhaps most importantly, the pragmatic use of technology for erotic purposes is overwhelmingly within the context of *existing* sexual relationships. As previous examples have hinted, techno-sexuality allows people to use technology to play at being someone they are not (as in the case of a young person who engages in cybersex pretending to be older and more experienced). However, those uses of technology for sexual purposes are much less common than the use of technology within the context of existing sexual relationships. In fact, the use of technology for explicitly sexual purposes (with another person) is nearly identical to how young people use Internet communications in general—like social networking sites—to reinforce existing relationships rather than to meet new people (see Valkenburg and Peter 2010). This is important, for it clearly illustrates how techno-sexuality is no substitute for embodied sexual relationships; it's an *additive*—or, as Susan (aged 19) phrased it "a flavor"—and one most often shared only with trusted partners. As Tina (aged 20) wrote,

I also only use it when I am in a trusting relationship. . . . I have used the webcam to film myself and my ex having sex and text naughty pictures or sext messages. Again I only do this when in a good trusting relationship.

Yet, here too, when technology is used as an additive to existing sexual relationships, it again appears in highly pragmatic forms. The most obvious is the innovative use of technology to sustain sexual relationships in circumstances where distance prevents physical contact:

It was difficult being away from my boyfriend for the whole summer after more than a year of having sex pretty often so having Skype was helpful for our sex life. We weren't actually able to have sex but it was the next best thing. (Julie, aged 20)

When I was stationed overseas, my ex girlfriend and I would frequently use this [webcam] as a means for pleasure. At that time, I would say we used in [it] a couple of times a week. (Shaun, aged 24)

In these ways, as Lynn (aged 21) reports, technology "keeps me happy knowing that I have so many ways to please the person I am with without physically being there." This sentiment is shared by Tina (aged 20) and many others for the pragmatic reason that "distance no longer has to mean lack of sexuality together."

Among young lovers who have immediate access to the body of one another, technology still occupies an instrumental role. Indeed, the participants in this study routinely report using available mediums to send sexy messages that stoke up desire and convey intentions—a kind of "technological foreplay"—that Brooke (aged 22) describes especially well:

I think that adding technology makes things really exciting, it amps it up. Texting someone something really dirty when they are at work or when you are at a party together. Telling them what you wish they were wearing or what they weren't wearing. Telling them exactly what wall you would like to shove them up against. What you want them to call you when you are fucking later.

The participants in this study generally express a casual, playful comfort with the use of technology for sexual purposes. In fact, boundaries and limits are far less determined by technology but, instead, with *whom* they are sharing with:

I feel like I'm comfortable with talking dirty or sexting if it's a guy I'm either seeing, hooking up with, or my boyfriend. I feel like if it's in any of those relationships I'm pretty comfortable. (Erika, aged 21)

I don't think I have a boundary or limits on using technology for sexual purposes. I guess my boundaries would be who I use technology with. I would use it with a partner or potential partner. I would want it to be something we shared together and to mean something for us. (Tina, aged 20)

Certainly, people who are not in a current sexual relationship will often use technology as a pragmatic alternative. As Emily (aged 20) wrote, "When registering for classes my first semester of college, I decided I wanted to be focused mainly on school and not social events or trying to have a boyfriend. I bought a vibrator to use instead of starting a relationship with someone." Still, it is significant to note that techno-sexuality isn't as hedonistic as one might think. In fact, the expressed morality of techno-sexuality is deeply utilitarian in that technology is explicitly used to maximize both utility and happiness and thus is easily woven into existing sexual relationships.

It [technology] helped me explore my sex life more. I have learned so much about myself from it. I realized I am a very sexual person and open to any kind of sex when I am in a relationship. Anything to make sure my partner and I are both satisfied. (Lynn, aged 21)

I didn't have a cellphone until I was 16 or 17, but I would say my "sexting" experiences started shortly after that. "Sexting" provides a way to keep in touch from a distance, and I found that it builds some great anticipation. I especially have used "sexting" with my significant other while in relationships. (Joel, aged 22)

TECHNO-SEXUAL RESERVATIONS AND PREFERENCES

I think we have to tread very carefully when using technology for sexual purposes because there are endless limits to what people can do with the things you give them.

–Alice, aged 19

Because social interactions in general have never been so mediated by technology, it is no surprise, at all, that contemporary sexual interactions are also profoundly mediated by technology. The utilitarian use of technology for sexual purposes—either as an alternative to embodied sex or as an additive to an existing sexual relationship—typically provides sufficient moral justification, but not always. In some cases, conflicting belief systems create a vexing war between desires and ideals that are at least as old as Augustinian theology:

Somewhere in my childhood I got the idea sex was bad, dirty, and wrong. It created polar opposite feelings that were hard to sort out as a teen and even as a young adult. On one hand, I loved and still love what a well-played sex scene will do. The feeling of arousal is so great! There isn't any other word for it. On the other hand, it was wrong and sinful that I was looking up these images and the feelings I was experiencing were sinful as well, according to the way I was raised. I felt sexual pleasure of any sort before marriage was wrong and one of the worst sins a Christian could commit. (Susan, aged 19)

Much more common, however, are reservations about the *medium*. As a passive consumer of, say, pornography the young adults in this study are generally comfortable with online porn. Twenty-one of the 33 participants in this study reported using the World Wide Web for sexual purposes, in all cases to access pornography, starting as young as the age of 12 and as old as 18. As previous data quotes have illustrated, many report using online chat and instant messaging in their early teenage years. Fifteen of the 33 participants in this study reported using chat rooms or instant messaging for sexual purposes— all for a very short period of time while young teenagers then quickly abandoning those mediums. Once in established sexual relationships, webcams were also frequently used—but in nearly all cases as a pragmatic "next best thing" when lovers were separated over an extended period of time (16 of the 33 participants reported using webcams for sexual purposes, and in all but one case between the ages of 18 and 19). Interestingly, e-mail is infrequently used for sexual purposes (only three of the 33 participants reported ever using e-mail for sexual purposes). As Jack (aged 22) reports, "E-mail was already a fairly 'dead' medium by the time I was becoming sexually active, so I never really used it to converse with anyone sexually or send anything." Others expressed similar sentiments:

The older I have gotten, the less I have used e-mail for sexual purposes because it's a little out-dated. If I really wanted to get sexual content or images to someone, I would use my phone. (Lora, aged 27)

I really don't do a lot of emailing. Honestly I like the immediacy of texting. If I am talking dirty I want someone to do it back right away, someone to engage me. (Brooke, aged 22)

As the above data quotes clearly illustrate, and consistent with other studies of romantic or sexual uses of technology (see Bergdall et al. 2012), cell phones are by far the preferred medium; only one participant in this study reported "never used" a cell phone for sexual purposes. In nearly all cases, the young people in this study report using cell phones for sexual purposes immediately following two occurrences: acquiring a cell phone in the first place and, more importantly, establishing a sexual relationship in the flesh. Virtually all of the participants in this study are comfortable with texting naughty messages which are playfully regarded as "fun, flirty and definitely creates sexual tension. It can be great if you're apart from a significant other, or you just wanna brighten someone's day" (Lora, aged 27).

Sex thrives in all communication environments, and that is hardly surprising. Sex—in all its forms—is fundamentally an act of communication, even when no words are spoken at all. Hence, eroticizing words results in a techno-sexuality that is *explicitly* communicative. Words allow for a concrete expression of otherwise private and sometimes abstract desires that, when shared in a text medium, can bring about a potentially immediate and enrapturing coauthored exchange:

> I was 18 when I started sexting. I did it because I enjoyed painting pictures with words about the things I wanted to [do with] my ex-girlfriend. There were times I would get lost in sexting that it would have my undivided attention. (Lynn, aged 21)

Whereas words represent, images present. The difference is subtle but important: between telling and showing, between saying and seeing, between poetry and photography. Words are most effective for expression; images are most effective for authentication. With words, communications are more thought-like, and we can playfully toy with *imagined* possibilities. Communications become more concrete and act-like when they include images. On first blush, the difference seems to merely boil down to language versus sight, but they are also two different symbolic forms that do not mean the same thing. Consider, for example, Lisa's (aged 20) recollection of a sexting session that ended badly, and precisely because of the differences between words and images:

> I have only had a full on sexting session once in my life. I remember it very well because I was 15 and dating an older guy who I really wanted to impress. At this time I was a virgin and had very little experience sexually. Needless to say I used sex scenes from movies and let my imagination run wild. The conversation ended with me receiving a "dick pic," and I was so shocked and weirded out I haven't talked to the guy since.[3]

The differences between words and images are also gendered, which is clearly seen in Lisa's account of receiving a "dick pic," yet it's also in the willingness of the young people in this study to experiment with various mediums for using technology for sexual pleasure. Consistent with the stereotypical norm, the young men in this study are much more likely to prefer visual mediums: All the young men in this study reported frequenting online pornography (only half the women reported ever visiting an online porn site), and all but two of the young men reported using webcams for sex (compared to less than half of the women). The young women reported far more use of text-mediums: 14 of the 26 women reported using chat rooms or instant messaging for sexual purposes (compared to only one of the men).

The young men in this study were remarkably nonchalant about sending nude images of themselves to others, in most cases reporting these erotic uses of technology as matter-of-factly as a weather report. For example, as Mike (aged 20) bluntly reports, "From age 16 to 19 I would send naked pictures to girls." And Jack (aged 22) straightforwardly recalls his fling:

> I remember sending some images of myself to a girl that had almost taken my virginity before we had gone our separate ways, I had also sent a video of myself having an orgasm with other pictures to a girl I had a fling with at age 19.

Even when those images were seen by unintended eyes, the potential embarrassment for young men was curiously casual:

> One time the picture I sent of my dick got seen by quite a few girls in my class. I was embarrassed but it didn't bother me too bad[.] I'm pretty proud of that area down there. (Brett, aged 21)

Like the "erotic looking glass" of people who enjoy webcam sex (see Waskul 2002), some women in this study relished the attention and positive feedback they received from sharing erotic self-images:

> Pictures are my favorite I think. When someone gets turned on by my pictures, it makes me feel good about the way I look, as stupid or insecure as that sounds. (Cindy, aged 20)

> I took erotic pictures for an anniversary present when I was 18. I had some where a friend took them of me in lingerie and then took some of myself in less clothing to no clothing. I love it! I felt so sexy. (Tina, aged 20)

In most cases, however, the women in this study were highly guarded and cautious with their naughty self-images, assuming they shared any at all. As several women reported in nearly identical words, "I'm not comfortable with sending pictures. My friend's girlfriend sends nude pictures to him and he has no problem showing them to his friends. I wouldn't want my boyfriend to do that to me, they are supposed to be private, but you never know who they are showing" (Holly, aged 21). And those images can awkwardly wind up in even more public spaces:

> Even though at one point I sent pictures of myself I'm sure I don't want to do that anymore. Once a topless picture of me found its way onto Facebook. Though it was brief and an "accident" I will never make that mistake again. (Emily, aged 20)

Because the women in this study were generally reserved about the use of visual mediums for techno-sexual expressions, and quite aware of the risks, they were especially cautious about how much of their sexual bodies they were willing to expose if they were to use visual mediums at all. Note, for example, how the women who report sharing erotic self-images would typically "only" reveal themselves in undergarments or "just" expose their breasts, using qualifying words like *only* and *just* to signify boundaries—namely, nothing below the belt:

> Sexting first came into my life when I was 16. My boyfriend at the time and I would send not fully nude photos, but just bra and underwear snap shots. (Molly, aged 21)

> Only when I was 19 years old and separated from my boyfriend is when I would webcam with him. I wouldn't go any further than just showing him my boobs. (Jill, aged 21)

> I only used my webcam to share myself one time to my ex boyfriend who went to a different school. It was nothing too bad just a little boob showing. (Eva, aged 20)

On one hand, it may seem odd that a young woman would trust someone enough to willingly share her physical body but not an image of it (or very little at least). On the other hand, that decision makes perfect pragmatic sense—and surely an indication that young people are not as ignorant, careless, or unthinking as they are often characterized. While it is true that all sexual activities leave trace records—even a single pubic hair can be convincing evidence for someone skilled in forensics (to say nothing of semen residue, or, what that residue might convict even a sitting president of doing!)—with techno-sexuality, those digital trace records do not have the half-life of biological ones, and they also have the infinite potential for replication. It is no surprise, therefore—especially considering the distinction between thought-like words and act-like images—that young people may be willing to integrate techno-sexuality into their normative sexual selves, but they are also often restrained unto what medium and with whom.

That restraint is especially salient for those who have the most to potentially lose, and not all techno-sexuality is equal. While much has changed in the technological era, some things remain the same—and especially the continued prevalence of the patriarchal sexual double standard by which sexual desire and expression in men is positively regarded (studs), while denigrated and stigmatized in women (sluts). That double-standard is an obvious reason why the young men in this study were not particularly concerned—and even proud—to have their erotic images seen by unintended eyes, while the young women were most often mortified by that same possibility. Yet there is another more insidious side. Young women's concern over sharing erotic self-images combined with young men's preferences for them often results in predictable power dynamics in which women sometimes give in to the persistent demands of their male lovers to technologically put out. Susan (aged 19) provides one of the best examples:

> As far as sexting images goes, I have only a few times sent images of myself in a swimsuit or a cleavage-revealing top. I probably sent the first image [of] me in a revealing shirt around 15 or 16 and immediately felt dirty, wrong, and bad about myself. I also feared the images would be leaked to other members of the school and my parents would find out. When I sent images of me in a bikini around age 18 I experienced the same feelings paired with anger as the images were sent to, again, get a boyfriend to stop asking for some. In fact, in both instances (there were only two times I sent images) they were begged for and sent to quill [*sic*] the irritating texts sent begging for them. . . . Only a couple instances [did I use a webcam] my freshman year of college when I was in a long distance relationship. It was only a quick glimpse of my breasts or I would join a Skype conversation while still in my lace bra. The quick glimpse of my breasts was only after continual begging by my boyfriend on the other line. I was annoyed most of the time and did it just to get him to shut up.

In this way, the use of contemporary technology for sexual pleasure potentially reveals much older micropolitics of gender within sexual relationships. Indeed, it is quite reasonable to conclude that, at least in some forms of techno-sexuality, "young women are more likely to be negatively impacted" and especially when "coerced or pressured to send images" (Walker, Sanci, and Temple-Smith 2011:14).

CONCLUDING REMARKS

Every technological innovation creates deviant as well as respectable possibilities . . . technology is morally quite neutral. . . . the machine itself simply does not dictate the moral choice; human beings do that. On the other hand, it would be foolish to believe that the availability of certain technologies did not make possible certain moral choices that were previously difficult or impossible to arrange.

Charles Edgley and Kenneth Kiser. 1982. "Polaroid Sex: Deviant Possibilities in a Technological Age." *Journal of American Culture* 59–64.

In the early 1980s, sociologists Charles Edgley and Kenneth Kiser (1982:59) published a witty and insightful analysis of the Polaroid camera as a *sexual* technology: "prior to the development and mass distribution of the Polaroid camera, homemade pornography was almost impossible to achieve, unless one of the participants had access to a developing laboratory and the skill with which to process his [or her] own prints." More than three decades later, a Polaroid camera can only be found in an antique shop, and in its place has emerged an implosion of other (and similar) technologies, and yet they all equally reflect the very same three themes that Edgley and Kiser explored: sexual relationships in a changing age, popular culture as an agent of social change, and the role of technology in mediating between the two. In contrast to the early 1980s, our contemporary world is utterly saturated with technologies that mediate social relationships—sexual and otherwise—yet that observation is not only obvious but also misses perhaps the most important point: New media technologies, in contrast to say the Polaroid camera, do not merely mediate social relationships and present new moral choices, they *re*mediate them and that's what makes them "new"—even to the extent of potentially obliterating awareness of the moral choices at all.

Bolter and Grusin (2000) convincingly argue that contemporary new media technologies do not merely mediate, but remediate in that they function to eradicate the experience of mediation primarily through two mutually dependent characteristics: immediacy and hypermediacy. That is, in short, new media technologies provide immediate moments of witness, within a saturation of layered media, so as to provide the sense that we can "know the objects directly" while simultaneously employing numerous forms of media in the process (Bolter and Grusin 2000:70). This would ultimately become the double logic of remediation: "to both multiply its media and to erase all traces of mediation" (Bolter and Grusin 2000:5; also see Curnutt 2012). In simple terms, one way to understand this state of remediation—at least in the context of sexualities—is that historically technology has long been in bed with sex (Lane 2001; Springer 1996) but never before so woven into normative, taken-for-granted everyday life within multiple mediums of expression.

No doubt the remediated state of contemporary techno-sexualities presents both opportunities and risks—with the latter much more represented in both academic literatures and the more generalized moral panic of popular culture as well. Most of the available literature on young people's use of technology for sexual purposes is obsessed with its potential as a "public health problem" and urges the need to educate young people on the dangers and risks (see, for one example, Walker et al. 2011). Very little scholarship has bothered to explore how young people understand and experience the sexual uses of technology. The unfortunate outcome is that we are blind to the nuances of techno-sexuality at precisely the time when we know there is no turning back while, simultaneously, contemporary new media and communication technologies are remediating at an increasingly rapid rate.

Now is precisely the time for bold new studies. Since the turn of the most recent century, I have published a steady stream of empirical studies on every major medium of Internet sex: text cybersex (Waskul, Douglass, and Edgley 2000), webcam cybersex (Waskul 2002), public posting of nude digital self-images (Waskul and Radeloff 2009), and avatar sex on Second Life (Waskul and Martin 2010). Elsewhere, I have written generalized accounts of the sexual uses of new media and communication technologies, and often highly critical accounts of the moral panic that pervades academic literatures on the erotic uses of contemporary technologies (Waskul 2006; Waskul and Vannini 2008). In this chapter, I have avoided referencing those works for they all fall short of the mark of what I have sought to convey in these pages. Erotic uses of new media and communication technologies continue to provide opportunities for people to play at sexual selves in the ether of an Other world that is apart and distinct from commonplace realities. However, as the participants in this exploratory study have clearly conveyed, new media and communication technologies have rapidly been remediated into the realities of *everyday* erotic life and *lived* experiences of sexual selves, and the emerging institution of techno-sexuality has yet to be understood in all of its transformative potential.

1. Twenty-six women and 7 men volunteered to answer eight open-ended questions about their history of using technology for sexual purposes. Ages ranged from 19 to 27; however, 29 of the respondents (88%) were between the narrow range of 19 and 21 years of age. The sample is almost exclusively Caucasian race, of a middle- to upper-middle class background, the majority of whom grew up in a small to midsize rural Midwestern community. The sample is nonrandom and intended for exploratory purposes. Pseudo-names are used in this chapter and all identifying information has been omitted. Data were collected October and November 2012.

2. I fully recognize that there are millions of people for whom techno-sexuality is both irrelevant and absurd. Clearly techno-sexuality is a phenomenon confined to technologically advanced societies and among populations who not only have privileged access but also regularly use those technologies as a routine part of their everyday life. I will occasionally overgeneralize simply for the purpose of clarity rather than repeatedly and awkwardly qualifying statements like these.

3. I should also note that part of Lisa's jolt in receiving an unexpected "dick pic" also owes to how technology allows for jarring shifts in normative sexual scripts. Presumably, Lisa was sending and receiving naughty text messages—*words* that likely included various terms for an *imagined* penis—yet seeing the *actual* penis of the person she was texting with "shocked and weirded" her out presumably because of the medium. This is a good example of how words represent, while images present. But there is more. Within traditional sexual scripts, lovers get to know one another *before* bodies are explored. And, in most cases, genitals are the last part of a person's body that others will get to see or touch—assuming the relationship gets "that far" at all—in fact, the progression is traditionally the other way around; most often lovers touch genitals before they see them. In short, traditional sexual scripts detail not only a progression of sexual activities but also a progression of bodily exposure. The ease by which technology has come to mediate social relationships makes it possible to abruptly change that sexual script such that, in circumstances like Lisa's, she saw an image, the penis of a potential lover, long before she would have normatively, gradually, and consensually became familiar with his physical body otherwise. Since these subtle, taken-for-granted sexual scripts are the principle means by which sexual encounters are made orderly, it is small wonder that Lisa was "shocked and weirded out."

CHAPTER 8

PAINTING DESIRE PINK

Meaning-Making at a Romance Sex Store

Alison Better

In this chapter, I look at how sex stores use symbols to create meaning in the retail environment to sell women sexual pleasure, sexual empowerment, and potential pleasures for their partners as well. In my research, I have found sex stores marketing romance and sexuality to women in ways that mirror socially acceptable femininity and sexuality. Through an examination of a sex store focused on romance and marketing primarily to a female clientele in an upscale urban shopping area, I will shed light on a space of sexual commerce and how this attempts to shape women's sexual understandings and choices. I will do this by exploring the ways these stores construct a set of culturally appropriate sexuality and pleasure norms and aspirations for women, using data collected through fieldwork at a romance sex store and literature on women's sexuality.

Sex stores began to emerge in America in the 1960s, as a result of their legalization through a series of First Amendment cases in the Supreme Court. Early sex stores catered almost entirely to male clientele and often had pornographic video rooms on the premises. Stores were designed without windows so customers would not be seen. These stores have a reputation for being taboo, dirty, and often a menace to the community.[1]

Beginning in the 1970s, sex stores became more common and several new types of sex stores began to open. Some sex stores began to focus on female customers in the market for sexual goods and pleasure devices. Many of these stores were explicitly feminist in their ideals, business strategies, and product selection. In addition to selling sexual goods, these stores focused on women's sexual empowerment, health, and education as well as safety and community needs (Better 2011).

Feminist sex shops began to emerge in America, beginning with Eve's Garden in New York City in 1974 and Good Vibrations in San Francisco in 1977. The establishment of these stores has been growing rapidly since 1991, with stores like Babeland (Seattle and New York City), Smitten Kitten (Minneapolis), and Self Serve (Albuquerque), among others. While there are hundreds of traditional sex shops across the country, there are only 26 feminist sex shops in America.[2]

Also in the 1970s, a new form of sex shop that falls in the middle of the spectrum between traditional and feminist was created. These stores are focused on romance and marketed mainly to women. Often in large retail spaces, which look much like a department store, these stores sell the same goods as traditional stores, but with an ethos of being both woman and couple friendly. In this context, "couple" here seems code for heterosexual couples, with an emphasis on making the woman comfortable. These stores appear aimed at women customers through their décor, staff choices, and product selection. The first and most widely known romance sex store is Adam and Eve, which operates 45 stores in Arkansas, California, Florida, Idaho, Kentucky, Massachusetts, Michigan, Missouri, Montana, Nevada, North Carolina, Ohio, Pennsylvania, South Carolina, Texas, Washington, and Canada as well as a mailed catalog and online store. There are many smaller locally owned romance sex stores, including CS Boutique in Portland, Maine, which has been open since 1992.

These stores sell many of the same products as traditional sex stores, but the owners intentionally shape their store atmosphere to be comfortable for women and couples. Many of these stores market themselves openly as "women and couples friendly." These romance sex stores work to create an environment that is safe, comfortable, and welcoming to women. While many of the products are the same as those sold in traditional stores, the store layout often allows for more interaction with the products. Some romance focused stores model themselves after the look and feel of feminist stores without the politics and empowerment that often mark such spaces.

Romance stores serve as an intermediary category between traditional sex stores and feminist stores. Some romance stores take their business model from traditional stores, working to make a typical sex store's products and environment more welcoming to women. Other romance-focused stores took their cues from feminist stores and are made in their image, though their guiding philosophy differs significantly.

LITERATURE REVIEW

Spaces for Women's Sexuality

Research on potentials for women's intimacy is often focused around particular sites aimed for the procurement of pleasure. Spaces in society that are carved out for the interest of sexual pleasures and sexual play mainly focus on the sexual lives of the marginalized (gay bathhouses, bondage/discipline/domination /submission/sadism/masochism [BDSM] clubs). Women's sexuality has been largely ignored in the creation of sexual spaces. Sexualized spaces are often found in gay communities focusing traditionally on the needs of men (Binnie 1995; Casey 2004:447). Understanding the importance of space aids in the understanding of interactions between identity and institutions (Casey, McLaughlin, and Richardson 2004:388). Spaces for women's sexuality and bodies are uncommon and complicated (Johnston 1998; Nash and Bain 2007).

In an empirical study of a Canadian women's bathhouse, Catherine Jean Nash and Alison Bain explore meanings of sexuality and gender in a women-only sexualized space. This site serves as a meeting place, a site for community building, and a place for sex. Exploring how the bathhouse worked to "queer space," they found that sexual and gender identities were both liberated and constrained in this setting (Nash and Bain 2007:49).

Consumers of Desire and Pleasure

Several researchers in the United Kingdom have taken up the question of women as consumers of sex, pleasure, and sexuality related goods. These studies center notably on examinations of British "fashion and passion" store Ann Summers (Attwood 2005; Storr 2002, 2003). Feona Attwood found that style and fashion were interconnected with women's retail experiences for sexually related merchandise and that sex toys have become so stylish that vibrators are seen as fashion accessories (Attwood 2005:395–396). Merl Storr's ethnographic work focuses on the institution of toy parties, a play on Tupperware parties, where women gather at a host's home and are shown sexually related merchandise, including toys and lingerie available for purchase (Storr 2003). Some of these parties are sponsored by sex stores to increase their clientele and provide women who might not venture into a sex store a venue to purchase its goods.

It is interesting to see also that Feona Attwood's work extends from empirical data analyses about class and status regarding women's pleasure to theory. She finds this new venue for sexuality in women's consumer culture to be an important focus that links her work to the theories of both Giddens and Bourdieu. Attwood (2006) notes "the 'classiness' of female sexual activity is extremely important here both as a way of establishing its legitimacy and of linking sexuality to a range of other contemporary bourgeois concerns such as the development and display of style and taste and the pursuit of self-improvement and self-care" (85). Further research will elaborate these theories in relation to women's sexual pleasure and sex shops.

Attwood also provides us with a framework to think about the sale of women's sexuality and the women as both sexual agents and consumers. According to Attwood (2005), "There is an emphasis on the individual as the creator of her own significance, status, and experience, and on the need to make these culturally visible and meaningful through the manipulation of appropriate consumer goods" (401). Romance sex stores are creating a deliberate environment for women to help develop a particular kind of classy female sexuality, steeped in love, romance, and pleasure for the woman and her partner. These stores go to great lengths to create a narrative for women that is for sale alongside the products.

Methods

The data here come from a larger research study I conducted on sex stores, their patrons, and women's sexual pleasure. As a part of that project, I engaged in extensive qualitative research in a sex shop which I call Flirt.[3] This store advertises itself as a romance focused company. Flirt is located in a high-end shopping district in a large northeastern American city. I conducted 80 hours of observational fieldwork in this store between July and August 2008. Additionally, I interviewed Clare, the 20-year-old employee of Flirt, and Doug, its 32-year-old co-owner as well as several women who had shopped at Flirt.

Atmosphere

Flirt is located in an upscale urban shopping district. The store's sign beckons passersby from the street in large cursive bright pink font. The windows display a variety of sexual goods. Customers enter the store by walking down several stairs to its open glass door. The room is painted in hues of pink, magenta, purple, and yellow, with pink serving as the dominant color. Glass shelves line the upper sections of the walls and black cabinets run below. These shelves display products for sale which have been removed from their packaging.[4] The cabinets below hold the unused packaged items for purchase. Customers can test a variety of lubricants, lotions, creams, and oils. Boxes of tissues line the walls to clean your hands after sampling, and small trash cans are around the room for customers' convenience. Vibrators are displayed on shelves, many leaning on small silver stands. All vibrators have batteries in them and can be tested[5] as well. Next to each product is a tag describing its function, materials, and ingredients. Three large tables are in the middle of the room, holding glass dildos, vibrators, massage lotions, and other goods. In the back of the store, a small section of books is located next to a couch. No pornographic videos are sold here.

Artwork from a local artist is arranged on the walls with tags describing the art. Many of these brightly colored paintings are of nude women. The desk and cash register area is located near the back of the open floor plan. Two computers are located on the desk with two bar stools behind the counter for staff to sit on. Behind the register on the wall in large letters are the satisfaction guarantee and the return policy of the store. This policy is very detailed and customer friendly.

Flirt carries a large variety of products, aimed mostly at women's sexual and erotic pleasure. The front half of the store is filled with candles and lotions to sample. In the back half of the store, the more overtly sexual goods are displayed. This includes vibrators, dildos, sex position furniture, and anal toys and lubricants. On the tables in the center of the store, some of the higher priced vibrators and dildos are displayed. These include Pyrex glass dildos, high-end silicone, and chrome metal vibrators. Goods on the tables cost between $50 and $200.

In the very back of the store are several romantic and erotic books. A few sex kits and couple's erotic games are located on a back table. There are spanking and whipping objects, often untouched by customers. Also, there is a small selection of anal stimulators, specialty anal lubricants, and butt plugs that are not popular items for sale. Several pieces of furniture designed for sexual activity are located in the back of the store. This includes a curved couch which allows for couples to reach many sexual positions. A throw blanket designed to shield expensive linens and couches from sexual fluids and stains is propped on a normal couch in the back. Customers can browse books on the couch if they desire. The final item in the back of the store is a portable stripper pole. Customers do not often find themselves in this area of the store.

The design of the store was developed with the hope of bringing in a female clientele and keeping them comfortable while shopping for sexual goods. The layout of the store contributes to that effort, with lotions and candles in the front section and sex toys in the back half of the space. The employees are seated toward the back as well and often stay behind the desk to keep the patrons more comfortable. The store is located in a luxury shopping district and tries to market sex in a classy way, similar to the findings of Attwood (2005) and Storr (2002, 2003).

CONSTRUCTING A SEX STORE FOR WOMEN

Flirt is owned by two men who worked very hard to try to construct an atmosphere they felt would be welcoming to women shopping for romance and sexual goods. Before they could even get their business off the ground, they first had to find a landlord willing to rent to their business in this visible and high-end retail district. Doug detailed the difficulties to gaining access to space to house the store, despite having a thriving online retail business selling the same goods. While he and his business partner were quite successful online, they did not have an easy time gaining access to the rental market in the neighborhood they wanted to be in. They were committed to running their business in an upscale urban shopping environment, not in an out of the way, possibly dangerous place. They understood their clientele and what their needs would be.

Doug's process of opening Flirt was focused first on the business aspect and gaining respect in the community. Doug has found that people's expectation of what a sex store looks like often does not match up with the higher-end store he created. Though Flirt was a successful and profitable online company for years, Doug was challenged by and remarked about the difficulties in opening a physical store due to people's preconceived notions.

> Had a lot of difficulty opening it. People were, no matter how much we painted the picture of we're gonna open something that's tasteful, that's geared towards women, women with money, it's gonna be those between 25–55, we're not gonna sell pornography, we're not gonna have realistic looking penises in here, we're not gonna have the blacked out windows and the neon lights and the dingy carpet and the crazy typical white lighting and the ceiling, fluorescent lighting, we're gonna do it tasteful. No one was believing us. (Doug, 32, Flirt co-owner)

Though several realtors and landlords seemed to refuse to rent to his business, Doug had luck with one well-established landlord whose colleagues thought that "we were going to open a '70s, '80s style porn shop," but after meeting with Doug, the landlord changed his mind. Since "I met the kid, he came in here with a suit on, he has a multi-million dollar company that he started seven years ago online, I'm willing to take a chance." Doug's skills as a businessman seemed to prevail here, as well as his demeanor and appearance, which seemed to go a long way in getting the landlord to take a chance on his business. Had Doug not come in to the meeting well dressed in a suit, looking like any other business owner, perhaps this deal would have never gotten off the ground.

Doug and his business partner enlisted a woman to design the store, as the two men admitted to not knowing how to create a space that would be welcoming to their female clientele. The female designer they hired painted the store as if Barbie's dream house exploded; shades of pink lined the walls and were accented with darker pink, purple, and yellow. The shelves and cabinets to hold the merchandise were black wood. The feel of the store read clean and modern, very feminine in a cliché sort of way, but safe and comfortable.

Initially, Doug displayed lotions and candles in the windows visible from the street. After having so much trouble renting space on this high-end retail block, he was worried about placing overtly sexual goods in the windows, even though that would help signal to the right kind of potential customers to enter the store. During the early part of my fieldwork, the windows contained massage oils and lubricants but no sex toys. This caused problems in generating the right sort of foot traffic. Later in the year, Doug remarked to me,

> The name Flirt doesn't describe anything. They see these random bottles in the store and it probably like eh, it does nothing to heighten them, it does nothing to entice them to walk in, so basically it's like, so can we put some tasteful things that are vibrators in the window? And will that like at least if not have them walk in, will it do one of two things: either the people who walked in because they didn't know what the balls were and they're freaked out because it's a sex toy store, it would maybe keep them from walking in the first place. Because we don't ever want to put a person in an uncomfortable position, and then or, the people who didn't know what we're about and didn't walk in because we didn't do anything, will seeing that vibrator in the window help them come through the door? So it's more about generating the right foot traffic. Whether that means keeping people that might be offended by our product out, or bringing new people who didn't know what we were before now they do, bringing them in. That is more about having more people walk in but also the right people walk in (Doug, 32, Flirt co-owner)

Doug used the store atmosphere to signify to potential customers that this was a place that they would want to shop, using some of the store's merchandise to signal that this was a space to buy sexual goods and the store's logo and pink colors to help show consumers that this was especially welcoming for female patrons.

The layout and choice of products for the retail store also contributed to an atmosphere of female friendliness and safety for women. Upon walking into the store, it felt like a luxury bath shop. The front section of the store contained candles, lotions, and massage oils. If you didn't know where you were, you would think it was just another high-end soap shop. This was very intentional in the store's design. Doug remarked on this in an interview:

> But I think a lot of people come in, they appreciate the fact; they appreciate the fact that the store is tasteful. Or as tasteful as possible, considering the

nature of the product. Lot of people come in and they say it reminds them of a MAC cosmetic store. They say it reminds them of a Bath and Body Works. That's the sort of feedback we get all the time. People thank us for having a place like that that they don't feel like a creep walking out of. (Doug, 32, Flirt co-owner)

One customer, Tina, contrasting romance focused stores like Flirt with traditional sex shops, emphasized the importance of feeling safe in a sexually oriented establishment:

But the thing I liked about [another romance focused store] was that originally, the original store, way back when it was first opened, was geared towards women. And so it was well lit, the products were well displayed, you didn't get this kind of skeevy feeling and it was really well done, from what I understand. I've been in there a couple of times . . . and I've been in the ones that you walk into and you're kind of, like, okay, I should have worn, you know, [a] chastity belt because I'm sort of afraid of what people are going to try to do to me while I'm in here. (Tina, 27)

The tasteful atmosphere was deliberate and worked to draw in the target female customer and kept her feeling safe as she shopped for sexual goods in public. Another patron, Mindy, favorably compared Flirt to Rocket, a traditional sex store located in the same neighborhood. She noted:

I have just been to [Flirt]. I have been to [Rocket] also and [Rocket] is a little bit sketchy and dirty and I was afraid to get anything there 'cause I was a little afraid of it. And [Flirt] was a lot cleaner and more romantic based and so that was a lot better to go into I think, more inviting. (Mindy, age 20, college student)

Mindy found her experiences at Flirt preferable to those at Rocket. She also noticed Flirt's more romantic focus and its differences from traditional sex stores. These differences made her more likely to return to shop at Flirt over traditional store Rocket. Lisa, another Flirt customer, found her experiences there to be positive as well.

Well, I will definitely say that that [Flirt] was the best experience that I've ever had in one, because it was really classy and just so nice as opposed to some of the other ones that I've been in which are either really trashy, or mixed in with a whole bunch of other things like beer bongs next to vibrators. (Lisa, age 24, graduate student)

Doug's decision about what products to stock was deliberate, to match the clientele of the store and to maintain a respectful and comfortable shopping environment for women seeking sexual goods. He felt that women would not want to be confronted with lifelike penis replicas and pornography, two standard categories of sex store wares, in his upscale boutique atmosphere. Doug focuses primarily on the comfort of his store for its patrons and the goods that can cause joy that he sells in his romance centered store.

In addition to the comfortable retail atmosphere created by product placement and store design, the decision to not carry pornography and lifelike phallic objects helped to contribute to the atmosphere of the space as safer for women. While Flirt carries a large selection of sexual goods on their website, the inventory for the web compared to the physical store is quite different, due to its target market of women. One major difference is that the retail store does not sell or display any pornography. Though this business decision brings in a mass of new customers, some people find this to be problematic.

> Like we don't have porn, so people come in and they're disappointed that we don't have porn and they think that any store in that industry should have porn all over the place. We don't. It's just not what we do. So you have to fight; I've had to fight that a little bit, you know that you are gonna disappoint some people that had these preconceived notions of what a sex shop should be, but we're trying to break that mold. (Doug, age 32, Flirt co-owner)

The decision to not carry pornographic videos or magazines in a sex shop is a very interesting one. Doug made this controversial move for several reasons. First, pornographic images are the only thing sold at sex stores that are age regulated. Not having any pornographic materials means that no patrons need to be asked for identification to enter the store. This changes the atmosphere of a place from one of surveillance to a comfortable shopping environment. Also, Doug seemed to believe the women would be uncomfortable with the addition of pornography and its customers to the store. While women do consume pornography, perhaps Doug believed that these goods would bring in a different customer and change the dynamics of the retail environment he worked so hard to create. Many other sex stores I visited as part of this project were overwhelmingly filled with pornography; with limited retail space, Doug was trying to shape his environment to meet the needs and comfort of his idealized female customer.

In addition to not carrying pornography, Flirt did not sell any lifelike penis replicas. While many vibrators and dildos were for sale, none of them came in natural skin tones. Many vibrators were in the shapes of cute animals, including dolphins, baby bugs, and rabbits. While some dildos were more lifelike in size and shape, none came in realistic colors in the retail store. Flirt carried a variety of flesh tone products online but in the store carried these toys only in clear or bright red. Doug thought that lifelike phallic objects would be off-putting to his female customers.

While the atmosphere at Flirt was very nice and fit in well with the surrounding retail environment, it is interesting to note that the decisions made to shape the store as a safe and comfortable place for women to shop were all made by men. Women did feel safer in Flirt than in other sex shops due to the deliberate framing of this store as safer, using particular signs and symbols, including neighborhood choice, store colors, and products for sale. The intentional creation of these feelings of comfort and safety are important to women as they shop in these spaces and choose which stores to patronize. Additionally, the air of luxury that surrounded the merchandise and the neighborhood contributed positively to women's comfort and reactions to the shopping experience. As Clare, a Flirt employee, noted,

> I feel like people spend longer here [at Flirt]. I think people spend longer amounts of time shopping here because you can turn on the products, you can see how everything works, you can smell everything, you can tell the texture of every liquid product. In [Rocket], what you see is what you get. You kind of just have to look and approximate if you think something is going to be right . . . or not. I've only been in there three times, and I don't remember any of the workers. I remember one guy working there and one girl working there. But I don't remember what they looked like and I don't remember what they sounded like. And that I think is a big difference. When you walk into a store like this it's nice to be welcomed so that you don't feel uncomfortable. I think it's just such a different environment and people respond to it, for sure. I think it's just more fun here. You know there's art, and it's a bright color. You know, the store itself. There's fun music. And I think it's just more fun for people than [Rocket]. I think [Rocket] is much more in your face. There are much more pictures of naked women. There are condoms unrolled, hanging from the walls. Which, I understand, is to show you what they look like, but you could do it in a more tasteful manner. [Rocket] is definitely just less comfortable. It's geared towards really really really horny people, I think. (Clare, 20, Flirt staff)

ANALYSIS

Romance focused sex stores work to produce a version of sexual desire for women that is consumable. These stores try to figure out what women want and develop ways to sell their customers both these products, but they also create an environment, an ethos of romance and pleasure that is framed for women. This view of women's sexuality is laced with notions of a sanitized and demure version of sexual potential. While sex may be complicated, dirty, or messy, romance sex stores sell clean, sweet smelling love with a side of orgasm, wrapped in a beautiful package.

If feminist sex stores are empowering, educational spaces to explore sex and sexuality, romance stores are safe and comfortable places defined by their creators in the image of what they think women want sexually or what they think women would feel safe around. While there is a diversity of sexual experiences that bring us pleasure, the narrative sold at romance sex stores is steeped in a particular kind of heteronormative and normatively gendered female sexuality. It comes from a world of romantic comedies, harlequin novels, and other cultural expectations of female sexuality. The foundation of comfort provided by these stores, coupled with their classy image, provides a space for women to conform to traditional notions of gender and sexuality while seeking consumer goods to enhance their pleasure. Sexual goods are becoming more commonplace, with sex toys being sold in malls and drug stores today. Many brands continue to develop higher end fashionable and trendy sexual goods, and the market for them among modern women will continue to grow.

CONCLUSION

Both the staff at Flirt, as well as the layout and feel of the store, were focused on women's comfort. The owner was aware of issues around gender and power and was very careful to navigate the creation of the store's atmosphere so that the customers would feel comfortable. The placement of the store in an upscale retail neighborhood, the décor, and the products chosen for sale contributed to the store's being a welcoming place for women to explore their sexual needs, desires, and curiosities. This store accomplishes its goals of being a welcome place for women's sexual explorations and a safe and thriving retail environment.

Customers chose to shop at Flirt because they reacted to the signs put out by the owners that marked this space as safe for women, starting from the choice of neighborhood, to the store name and colors used to signify Flirt as a space that is safe and welcoming for women's sexual exploration. Once inside the store, women are welcomed by well-dressed and friendly staff and a clean, well-lit store. The choices of which products are sold (and which are deliberately absent) also contribute to this space that is shaped for women's comfort and safety surrounding their sexual discoveries.

Flirt and other similar stores are part of a larger cultural dialogue around women's sexuality. Women's bodies and sexual choices have always been subject to public scrutiny; sex shops serve as one of many public sites where changing norms around women's sexuality can be consumed and internalized. These stores are part of a larger conversation about what sexual behaviors are acceptable. The mass marketing of devices for women's sexual pleasure as well as objects for particular sex acts and fetishes signals cultural approval for such encounters and behaviors. For these stores to have moved out of the shadows and into upscale retail boulevards signals a cultural shift around sex and sexuality, moving from the margins to a more central and public place in everyday life.

Romance sex stores like Flirt intentionally create a space for women (and couples) to safely explore a particular framework around sexuality that can be purchased and consumed. These stores sell sexual goods, of course, but they also sell an attitude that is created through the atmosphere, choice of products, and tone of the store environment and employees. This sentiment helps to shape conversations and understandings about women's sexuality on a broader scale. Women take home this feeling alongside the products they purchase. This impression, created by the romance sex shop atmosphere, can shape women's understandings of their bodies, relationships, and sexuality.

NOTES

1. In the 1940s after the war, hosiery and lingerie shops popped up for women including Markon in Paterson, New Jersey, Anna Lee and the Corset Bar in Passaic/Hackensack, New Jersey, and Fredericks of Hollywood in New York City and Los Angeles in 1947. They would cater to all women, including prostitutes.

2. However, as an alternative to shopping in stores, women are selling sex toys at parties similar to Tupperware or Mary Kay parties in the privacy of their own homes.

3. This and all names used in this chapter are pseudonyms.

4. Packaging for sex toys often includes pornographic images, usually of nude women. Some of the toys names are also demeaning to women.

5. Testing a vibrator in a sex shop allows a consumer to feel the intensity and speed of the vibrations and the texture of its materials. Customers can hold the product in their hands but cannot use them on the body parts they are intended for.

PART III

NEGOTIATING SEXUAL SELFHOOD

In the next two parts of the book, we deal with one of the most important areas of symbolic interactionist studies: identity. Symbolic interactionists have long been interested in identity processes and identity work. The concern emerges from work in psychology and social psychology, such as that of James (1890) and Cooley (1902) and, later, Mead (1934). The perspective assumes that our selves exist in a reciprocal relationship with society: The self emerges from and in turn shapes the larger society (Stryker 1980).

The chapters in Part III focus on negotiating sexual selves in the context of other—sometimes conflicting—identities. In Chapter 9, J. Edward Sumerau analyzes the identity work of lesbian, gay, bisexual, and transgender (LGBT) Christians as they navigate difficult social terrain. Because gay Christians deviate from what is socially acceptable in both dominant Christian communities *and* normative LGBT communities, many are faced with the need to carve a new space in which to be comfortable as both Christian and queer. Sumerau explores how members of this church do so by distancing themselves equally from "other" Christians and "other" LGBT people.

Jamie Mullaney uncovers a similar process in Chapter 10. Mullaney investigates how members of a straight edge music scene account for their sexuality in a community built around the value of abstinence. Mullaney uncovers the strategies her respondents use in order to make exceptions regarding sexuality consistent with straight edge identity. These strategies hinge on alignment with conservative sexual values of abstention; through the demonization of promiscuous sex rather than *all* sex, members of the scene are able to frame themselves as *relatively* pure.

In Chapter 11, Beverly Thompson deconstructs identity processes among bisexual and multiracial Asian American women. In an illustration of the complexity of intersectional identities, Thompson demonstrates the importance of considering multiple aspects of selfhood in thinking about sexual identity. Thompson illustrates that sexual identity is not best understood as one overarching category that anchors its members to one another. Rather, queer identities are situated within, alongside, and against racial and ethnic identities.

Brandy Simula challenges our beliefs about sexual identities and orientations even more fundamentally, in Chapter 12. Simula tackles the processes by which people choose among multiple potential sexual identities and privilege some over others. By unpacking the narratives of people who choose sexual partners by bondage/discipline/domination/submission/sadism/masochism (BDSM) identity instead of gender, Simula exposes the problems with our assumptions that our erotic interests and attractions are based primarily on gender or biological sex. Like Thompson, Simula calls on us to resist the temptation to dismiss the sexual complexity here by categorizing these respondents as bisexual. Instead, Simula challenges the basic premise that sexual attraction is based on sex and gender.

Each of these chapters deals with how people make sense of identity conflicts. In so doing, they challenge the rigidity of identity categories, and indeed the ways we conceptualize identities, as distinct and separate aspects of self that we must reconcile in order to feel authentic.

Staci Newmahr

CHAPTER 9

"SOMEWHERE BETWEEN EVANGELICAL AND QUEER"

Sexual-Religious Identity Work in a LGBT Christian Church

J. Edward Sumerau

Sitting at a table with a group of lesbian and gay Christians one night before Bible Study, a lesbian Christian woman[1] named Andie (all names contained herein are pseudonyms) walked in visibly disturbed. When a couple of people at the table asked her if she was okay, Andie responded, "I just get so tired of explaining to people that it is possible for me to be a lesbian and a Christian," before taking her seat and grabbing a piece of candy from the jar in the middle of the table. Chuckling in unison with the rest of the table at the latest example of this common topic, a lesbian Christian woman named Carla responded, "It's okay honey, we all get tired of it. This morning Tommy and I, once again, had to explain to the people organizing the Pride Events that yes we are gay and yes we are Christian, but no we are not like 'those' gays or 'those' Christians." Echoing this sentiment, a gay Christian man named Denny added, "Don't let them bother you Sugar, just tell them you live somewhere between Evangelical and Queer and sit back and enjoy their confused reaction." While the laughter around the table increased in volume, a gay Christian man named Barney turned to me, and asked, "Can you explain this, I mean, you study this stuff. Why is it so hard for people to understand us?"

Echoing many conversations I have had with students when they learn of my extensive research into lesbian, gay, bisexual, and transgender (LGBT) Christian groups, this conversation reveals the "queer"[2] social location occupied by religious sexual minorities at the present stage of herstory.[3] Contemporary constructions of normative Christianity, for example, define sexual minorities as sinners, deviants, and abominations in the eyes of God (Wolkomir 2006). In a similar fashion, public officials, citizens, and researchers alike typically define the emergence and expression of the LGBT community as explicitly oppositional to Christianity (Fetner 2008). Although recent decades have witnessed the emergence of explicitly LGBT manifestations of Christian belief and practice (Sumerau 2012) and supposedly more traditional Christian groups that actively seek and support LGBT members (Wilcox 2009), the oppositional construction of normative Christian and LGBT cultures has left many Christian sexual minorities caught between two seemingly incompatible systems of meaning.

Drawing upon insights gained through over three years of ethnographic participation in a southeastern LGBT Christian church, this chapter examines how Christian sexual minorities respond to their precarious position between normative religious and sexual categories by doing "identity work," which refers to "anything people do, individually or collectively, to give meaning to themselves or others" (Schwalbe and Mason-Schrock 1996:115). Specifically, this process involves the work people do to symbolically distinguish themselves from unwanted social labels in order to signify desirable selves. Rather than merely adopting normative depictions of Christian or LGBT cultures, the LGBT Christians at the heart of this study drew upon the symbolic resources at their disposal to fashion sexual-religious selves, and draw distinctions between themselves and normative depictions of Christian and LGBT people.

Importantly, previous research convincingly demonstrates that Christian sexual minorities may experience significant emotional, ideological, and identity-based dilemmas when attempting to resist normative depictions of Christianity. In her examination of lesbian, gay, and straight-but-affirming congregations, for example, McQueeney (2009) found that Christian sexual minorities resisted normative interpretations of homosexual sin by minimizing, normalizing, and moralizing their sexual identities in relation to their religious practices. Similarly, Wolkomir (2006) found that gay Christian men in support groups alleviated feelings of guilt, shame, and fear by reinterpreting scriptural condemnations of homosexuality as the result of human prejudice rather than divine intention. Further, Creek (2013) found that gay, celibate Christians reinterpreted notions of desire in their attempts to integrate their religious and sexual selves. While these studies left unexplored the ways Christian sexual minorities respond to normative depictions of LGBT culture, they revealed that LGBT people could draw upon elements of Christianity to resist condemnation and fashion creditable Christian selves.

Although it is not all that surprising that sexual minorities might face significant challenges within Christian settings, researchers have also shown that these people may face similar dilemmas when seeking shelter within LGBT cultures. Whereas some Queer organizations seek to align with Christian beliefs and practices in hopes of gaining greater social respectability (see Broad, Crawley, and Foley 2004), many other components of LGBT culture explicitly reject the influence, significance, and legitimacy of Christianity (see Warner 1999). In her examination of lesbian, bisexual, and transgender religious women, for example, Wilcox (2009) found that many of these women left explicitly LGBT organizations, religious and secular, in order to escape perceived sexism and the dominance of gay men. Similarly, O'Brien (2004) found that lesbian women and gay men often joined religious organizations as a result of disagreements between their personal values and the sexual and social politics promoted by secular LGBT organizations (see also Creek 2013). Rather than simply avoiding the condemnations of normative Christian groups by aligning themselves with explicitly LGBT groups, many religious sexual minorities, like the ones at the heart of this chapter, thus find themselves outside the normative boundaries of both LGBT and religious cultures and caught in the middle of ongoing sexual and religious conflicts.

To make sense of this phenomenon, I examine how a group of LGBT Christians navigates its position between normative Christian and LGBT cultures. For over three years, I attended and observed a southeastern LGBT Christian church, which I refer to as Shepherd Church. Further, I conducted over 350 informal and life history interviews with prominent members inside and outside of church functions. I began my analysis by analyzing conversations, like the one at the beginning of this chapter, concerning the "queer" social location of the members, and asking members how they explained their sexual and religious identities. After comparing and contrasting their answers as well as informal conversations, three main discourses that the members used to signify sexual-religious selves emerged, which I labeled humorous, emotional, and evangelical.

SEXUAL-RELIGIOUS IDENTITY WORK

What follows is an analysis of how members of Shepherd Church discursively constructed LGBT Christian identities in ways that symbolically distinguished them from normative depictions of Christian and LGBT cultures. First, I show how members mobilized humorous discourses, which defined people that were "too" Christian or too Queer as silly and unworthy of notice. Second, I examine how members mobilized emotional discourses to define themselves as both deeply isolated from and connected to both Christian and LGBT cultures. Third, I analyze how members mobilized evangelical discourses to define themselves as "in, but not of" both Christian and Queer cultures and capable guides for educating both groups.

Humorous

Rather than spontaneous episodes, humorous discourses arise within the context of ongoing social relationships and refer to the shared history of particular groups. Specifically, all groups may develop sets of humorous references known to members, which may be referred to and used to signify shared identities (Fine and DeSoucey 2005). As a result, people may use humorous discourses, or jokes, to signify the types of social beings they believe themselves to be and distance themselves from unwanted social labels. In Shepherd Church, LGBT Christians accomplished both of these goals by "making fun" of normative depictions of Christian and LGBT cultures and symbolically positioning themselves between these two extremes.

While the LGBT Christians I studied did not talk about their humorous discourses as "resistant" to normative depictions of Christian culture per se, they generally defined "normal Christians" by making fun of them. As a lesbian woman named Amy explained in Bible Study,

> I've never been able to relate to most Christians. Before I got involved here, I always felt like Christians took themselves way too seriously, and wasted most of their time worrying about what other people were doing. I mean, you know how they are, the normal Christians, they are always just hooting and hollering over something silly. They just always seem to be carrying on about something crazy, it's hilarious. (Field notes)

By defining "normal Christians" as "crazy" or "hilarious," Amy echoed others who depicted normative Christianity as extremist and difficult to take seriously. Statements like this also implied that Shepherd Church members practiced a different sort of religion. A lesbian woman named Jenny made a similar point when two gay male members came to worship wearing suits:

> Aw, everybody look, we got us some "real" Christians here today. We better be on our best behavior—Patricia cross your legs, Sandy go get the good rainbow flag, and ooh, Michael hide your makeup bag, Sugar. We gonna do us some Bible thumping! (Field notes)

Since Shepherd Church members typically dressed in more casual clothing than normative Christian traditions (see Sumerau and Schrock 2011), Jenny took the entrance of people wearing what could be considered "their Sunday Best" to distinguish between LGBT Christians and normative Christianity. As a gay man named John noted in an interview,

> I think what separates us from the typical Christians, if you can call them that, is that we just have more fun than Christians are supposed to. After all, life is too short to spend all your time yelling like a bunch of fools about every little thing like they do. (Field notes)

Echoing Jenny and other members, John defined "typical Christians" as people that spent all their time "yelling like a bunch of fools" while depicting LGBT Christians as "more fun." In all such cases, Shepherd Church members thus constructed LGBT Christian identities by poking fun at "other" types of Christians.

Whereas Shepherd Church members typically distanced themselves from normative Christian culture by defining themselves as more fun and less serious, they typically took the opposite approach when attempting to distinguish LGBT Christianity from normative depictions of LGBT culture. As a bisexual man named Dana explained following a worship service,

> The problem with the so-called Queers is that they don't take anything seriously. Family, they don't care. God, they don't care. I don't know what they stand for other than simply screwing everything in sight, and trying to make other people feel bad for wanting normal, moral lives. Unfortunately, most people think we're all like that. (Field notes)

By defining the "so-called Queers" as uncaring people that "don't take anything seriously" and waste their lives "screwing everything in sight," Dana symbolically distinguished between "normal, moral" LGBT people and supposedly unsavory others. Echoing these sentiments, a gay man named Micah recalled difficulties he had faced with the local LGBT community:

> I was originally hesitant about coming to a gay church because of how the other gay groups in the area are. Basically, they always seemed like drama factories filled with nothing but sex-obsessed jerks looking to score or party or whatever, and I figured this group would be the same. Luckily, there are actual adults here. Unlike the other gay groups, our church actually takes things seriously and tries, although the other groups make it really hard, to present a more positive image of gay people. (Field notes)

Echoing Dana and others, Tommy defined other LGBT groups as "drama factories" and "sex-obsessed" parties where people did not take life seriously. While each of the illustrations above was met with thunderous laughter, these discursive put-downs relied upon the definition of other LGBT groups as unsavory and ultimately problematic. As a lesbian woman named Saundra noted when discussing PRIDE events, "The good news is we get to show off what the church is doing. The bad news is that we have to put up with the children, and whatever craziness 'those gays' decide to get into" (Field notes). Members thus claimed LGBT Christian selves by putting down other LGBT groups, and defining themselves as "normal" and "moral" sexual minorities.

Overall, Shepherd Church members mobilized humorous discourses to construct LGBT Christian identities and distinguish themselves from normative depictions of LGBT and Christian cultures. Specifically, they used humor to define "normal Christians" as overly serious people incapable of having fun and depict "typical LGBT groups" as people lacking moral fortitude and maturity. While every member did not make these statements, all of the members affirmed those that did and generally responded with rather enthusiastic bursts of laughter. In so doing, they created a shared language whereby members could signify LGBT Christian identities by poking fun at unwanted elements of normative Christian and LGBT experience.

Emotional

Emotions play a primary role in the social construction of identities. Specifically, identities typically contain cultural notions of "appropriate" feelings as well as rules concerning emotional expression and intimacy (Hochschild 1983). In order to signify masculine selves, for example, males typically must learn how to appear emotionally reserved and limit emotional displays in the presence of others (Vaccarro, Schrock, and McCabe 2011). Similarly, male-to-female transsexuals may claim feminine selves by learning how to properly manage and display emotions during interactions with others (Schrock, Holden, and Reid 2004). As a result, people may also talk about emotional experiences in ways that signify identity claims. In the case of Shepherd Church, members signified LGBT Christian identities by mobilizing emotional discourses, which simultaneously expressed their isolation from and connection to both normative Christian and LGBT cultures.

Similar to many other LGBT Christian people (see Wolkomir 2006), Shepherd Church members were intimately familiar with normative Christian condemnations of homosexuality, bisexuality, and transsexuality. A lesbian woman named Shannon, for example, explained how such condemnations left members feeling isolated from other Christians: "Other Christians just make it really clear that we don't belong. It leaves you feeling lost and alone in this world when other faith communities turn their backs on you." Similarly, a gay man named Tommy recalled, "I can't count the number of tears or the times I just felt so alone in other churches. I just felt like I wasn't allowed to be part of the group" (Field notes). Echoing others, Tommy and Shannon recalled feeling isolated from normative Christian groups before coming to Shepherd Church. Rather than forsaking Christian practice, however, members sought to reclaim the positive feelings they experienced attending churches as children. As a bisexual "transwoman" named Alice explained,

I think the main reason for this place is to form an alternative. Many of us, myself included, grew up feeling so loved and so deeply connected to a community of fellow believers that when we lost that later in life we desperately wanted it back. That is what we are going for here. We are building a place outside traditional churches where we can express our connection to God in fellowship with people that love and accept us. (Field notes)

Echoing others, Alice sought to rebuild her "connection to God" and the positive feelings she associated with her religious upbringing by engaging in Christian practice "outside" normative Christian culture. A lesbian woman named Marnie explained: "We are kind of in the middle because we all feel this deep passion for God and for church, but we are also cast out from normal churches" (Field notes). Shepherd Church members thus claimed LGBT Christian identities in order to remain connected to Christianity despite their isolation from normative Christian culture.

Similar to many other sexual minorities (O'Brien 2004), Shepherd Church members initially experienced feelings of relief, exhilaration, and freedom when they came into contact with LGBT cultures. A gay man named Peter, for example, recalled the emotional release he experienced the first time he attended a gay Pride parade:

It was like freedom finally had a name. I just felt automatically connected to these people and our shared struggle. It was kind of like a religious experience for me. I just felt washed over by the love and kindness and affirmation in the crowds and at the booths dotting the street. I wasn't alone anymore, and maybe I didn't have to hide. (Field notes)

Similar to many other members, Peter came from a religious tradition that defined him as inferior or damaged, and as a result, his early experiences with

LGBT groups introduced him to the possibility that he was okay and not "alone anymore." As a lesbian woman named Whitney explained, "It was so strange to feel like I was maybe a good person, and I had walked right by this lesbian bar a hundred times without knowing my people were there" (Field notes). Like Whitney, many members talked about other LGBT people as their "people." While all the members talked about feeling connected to the larger LGBT community and expressed their desire to support other LGBT people, they often felt like normative depictions of LGBT culture did not represent their lives. A gay man named Barney, for example, explained: "I'm all for community, but I sometimes feel left out when other gay men go on and on about sex, sex, sex. I like that I'm accepted, but I just don't quite fit" (Field notes). Similarly, a lesbian woman named Carla explained:

> I think feeling the safety and love I find in other gay groups is priceless, but at the same time it hurts to see the lack of morals and the lack of God in most of the groups. My faith is the most important thing in the world, and I always just felt like there wasn't room for it in the community. Like the speaker we had a couple weeks ago, I just always felt like I was kind of part of the group, but also kind of an outsider. (Field notes)

Echoing many other members, Carla and Barney simultaneously felt like they were members and outsiders within the larger LGBT community. As a gay man named Raymond explained, "I think if you tried to explain what it feels like to be a gay Christian, you could say someone that is not quite stereotypically gay or typically Christian, but maybe the best of both sides" (Field notes).

By constructing LGBT Christianity as an emotional experience of both isolation from and connection to normative Christian and LGBT cultures, Shepherd Church members thus invoked emotion to explain their "queer" social location. Here we see how people can employ their feelings to signify sexual-religious identities that do not align with conventional sexual and religious categories (see also Wolkomir 2006). Sometimes people, like the members of Shepherd Church, do not fit into normative social categories. Rather than defining themselves as Christians that happen to be "queer" or as Queers that happen to practice Christianity, such identity work can powerfully evoke emotional attachments to a group. Overall, through mobilizing emotional discourses, Shepherd Church members made sense of their precarious social locations by constructing specifically LGBT Christian selves.

Evangelical

In our current time period, one major element of normative Christian culture is the evangelical assertion that Christians live *in* this world while not being *of* this world (see Smith et al. 1998). Taken from specific passages in the New Testament, this belief rests upon the idea that while Christian people must inhabit the fallen or natural world for a time, their spiritual essence lies in a higher plane of existence located in God's eternal kingdom. As a result, normative Christian culture preaches that believers should experience social life in between the worlds of nature and God and serve as guides or witnesses for all nonbelievers. While not all the LGBT Christians I studied embraced this particular evangelical idea, all of them were aware that they experienced social life between the Christian and LGBT worlds, and many argued that this position in, but not of, Christian and LGBT cultures made them especially well suited to serve as guides for both of these groups.

Shepherd Church members regularly talked about experiencing life in, but not of, both Christian and LGBT cultures. A lesbian woman named Laney, for example, explained: "We live on the margins of the margins I guess you could say. We are not quite Christians according to most people, but we are not quite the gays either" (Field notes). Similarly, a gay man named Marcus noted, "I think most of us go back and forth if you know what I mean. Sometimes we hang out in the gay crowd, and other times we blend in to the Christian crowd, but in the end we aren't really fully part of either group" (Field notes). In statements like this, Shepherd Church members recognized that they were involved with Christians and LGBT people, but they didn't quite fit in with either. As a lesbian woman named Karen explained, "We tend to take the best of both sides. So I might go to the Evangelical church because they have good music, and then I might go to a lesbian party to meet people, but in the end I come back here where I belong." Similarly, a bisexual man named Dana remarked, "Well it is kind of like you and me being neither gay or straight if you think about it. We fit in well enough with both groups when we want to, but neither group completely understands us" (Field notes). Echoing others, Dana and Karen expressed interests in taking advantage of their position between both cultures in order to acquire offerings from both sides. In so doing, they discursively constructed LGBT Christian experience as a middle ground between normative Christian and LGBT cultures.

Shepherd Church members also interpreted their "in between" status as an opportunity to educate other Christian or LGBT people. A gay man named Tommy, for example, explained the benefits that came from an LGBT Christian perspective:

In some ways, we live what the Evangelicals talk about. We exist in between two worlds that are ultimately opposed to each other, and thus we understand the issues from both sides. As a result, we try to make a space where gay people can learn that Christianity doesn't have to be their enemy, and we go out among the Christians to show them that not all gay people oppose Christian values. So you could say our own lives become a form of Christian testimony capable of broadening God's reach. (Field notes)

Similarly, a lesbian woman named Whitney remarked: "We have an opportunity as people that understand Jesus and gay relationships to educate others, and teach them how to move beyond hate through the love of Jesus." Further, a gay man named Barney noted, "I find it hard to believe that anyone could be more qualified than us to handle the whole religion and homosexuality debate. We understand the issues better than anyone, and it is our job to teach other people a better way" (Field notes). As these illustrations suggest, Shepherd Church members believed their position between normative Christian and LGBT cultures gave them special insight into contemporary debates concerning sexuality and religion. As a result, many of them considered it their Christian and LGBT duty to champion the cause of integration. In so doing, their statements also constructed LGBT Christian identities as social categories situated in but not of normative LGBT and Christian cultures.

Overall, Shepherd Church members used their "queer" social location to define themselves as especially well suited for educating other Christian and LGBT people. In so doing, they echoed Evangelical assertions that Christians must live within worlds where they don't fully belong. It is important to note, however, that not all members invoked this evangelical discourse. Even so, no one ever questioned or challenged the members that did mobilize these discourses. As a result, all members played a part in collectively constructing LGBT Christian identities as in but not of either normative LGBT or Christian cultures, and, as important credentials for witnessing to and guiding other people.

CONCLUSIONS

The members of Shepherd Church found themselves in a "queer" social location between normative Christian and LGBT cultures. Rather than simply adopting either normative Christian or LGBT practices, however, they sought to fashion a symbolic space between these supposedly oppositional cultures. As a result, they collectively drew upon elements of both Christian and LGBT culture to construct LGBT Christian identities. Specifically, they accomplished this by mobilizing humorous, emotional, and evangelical discourses that symbolically positioned LGBT Christianity somewhere between evangelical and Queer cultural norms.

Importantly, the case of Shepherd Church reveals the importance of attending to the interactional construction of sexual and religious identities. Rather than simply picking our sexual or religious identities from some preselected cultural list, we all may, like the members of Shepherd Church, construct and signify the people we believe ourselves to be and actively affirm the religious and sexual identity claims of others. In so doing, we may create new possibilities for both self-expression and social acceptance. In contrast, we may act in ways, regardless of our intentions, that pressure others to conform to socially constructed sexual and religious categories, and in so doing, reproduce meaning systems where many people feel left out or unwanted. Like the members of Shepherd Church, we may thus all construct and affirm systems of social meaning in the course of our everyday social interactions. As a result, we all possess the power to either create room for people who find themselves lost between seemingly oppositional identity categories, or, reproduce patterns of interaction that celebrate some while isolating and marginalizing others.

NOTES

1. Although it has become common practice among researchers to signify gay people as "men" and other sexual minorities by referring only to their sexual identities (e.g., bisexuals or lesbians) without reference to sex and gender terms, in this chapter I clearly identify the ways (e.g., lesbian, Christian woman, gay Christian man, bisexual Christian man) my respondents signified themselves as sexual, religious, and gendered beings, and in so doing, attempt to clearly articulate the complexity of sexual, gender, religious identities. Importantly, I do this to remain true to the people I studied and to avoid the oversimplification noted above, which ignores the existence of sexual and gendered beings that lie beyond "normative categories" including, but not limited to, gay women, lesbian men, lesbian genderqueers, bisexual androgynous people, and bisexual male-bodied women. Although each of the respondents noted in this chapter identified in relatively normative ways, I adopt this practice to avoid contemporary patterns of sexual and gender oversimplification that facilitate the ongoing invisibility and marginalization of non-normative gender and sexual self-presentations and identities.

2. Following other Queer scholars (see Warner 1999), I employ the term *queer* in two ways in this chapter. First, I utilize the term "queer" in quotation marks to refer to any social location or practice that lies beyond or between normative, binary categories including but not limited to, for example, moral/immoral, male/female, homosexual/heterosexual, woman/man, or black/white. In so doing, I seek to draw attention to the multitude of social locations (e.g., somewhat moral, intersexual, bisexual, transgender, or multiracial) that lie between and beyond the binaries promoted in our current society. Following from this insight, I also use the term *Queer* without quotation marks and capitalized to refer to the Queer

Movement, which arose in the 1980s as a branch of activism, scholarship, and practice that promotes the deconstruction of existing binary categories in the pursuit of greater social equality among all types of biosocial beings. Since the Queer Movement is the branch of LGBT culture furthest from normative Christian ideals (according to scholarship and my respondents), I employ this usage to demonstrate the extremes of the continuum within which LGBT Christians seek to carve out identities.

3. Although typically represented as "history," I employ the term *herstory* to draw attention to the social construction of language, and the tendency for supposedly "official" language to contain male and normative bias.

CHAPTER 10

NEGOTIATING PROMISCUITY

Straight Edge (sXe), Sex, and the Self

Jamie L. Mullaney

Anyone familiar with the straight edge music scene (from here on, sXe) knows that claiming sXe means more than just being a consumer of hardcore music; participants construct a self by abstaining from a variety of practices. Although individual straight edgers (sXers) vary as to whether they include veganism, vegetarianism, and/or abstinence from caffeine and over-the-counter drugs as part of their "edge," almost all agree at least on a baseline of not smoking, not using alcohol and illegal drugs, and avoiding promiscuous sex. When asked to describe the origin of this commonality, sXers often point to Minor Threat's early 1980s song "Out of Step." Although their song "Straight Edge" predates "Out of Step," it is in the latter where the lyrics thought to plant the seeds of the movement—"(I) don't smoke, (I) don't drink, (I) don't fuck; At least I can fucking think"—appear.

Almost immediately following the song's release, lead singer Ian MacKaye came on the defensive, suggesting that he did not intend to start a movement or set a mandate; in fact, this emphatic stance on the matter led the band to rerecord the song in 1983 with an explanation from MacKaye that stated, "Listen, this is no set of rules. I'm not telling you what to do." By this point, however, other bands were actively promoting sXe, and kids were "X'ing up" the backs of their hands (using a marker to place the X, shorthand for the XXX triad of abstinence) before going to hardcore shows (in Azerrad 2001:140).

Despite the controversy surrounding the scene's origin three decades ago, sXers continue to invoke variations on these lyrics when talking about how they "do" sXe in the present. Straight edgers go beyond cigarettes and alcohol by including illegal drugs in their abstinence from substances, an addition that seems consistent with their emphasis on clean living (Haenfler 2006:43). In contrast to these absolute abstinences, the one related to sex has never been as cut-and-dried in its execution. MacKaye insisted that the "don't fuck" line was not a charge to maintain one's virginity but instead referred to a disdain for "conquestual" sex, where "all other issues, everything else that's important, like friendships or other people's feelings, are secondary" (in Azerrad 2001:139).

While researchers of sXe have focused on the scene's situation among youth and music subcultures as a substance-free scene (Haenfler 2004b, 2006; Wood 2006), its gendered and masculine dynamics (Haenfler 2004a, 2006; Mullaney 2007) and issues of authenticity (Mullaney 2012; Williams 2006; Williams and Copes 2005), no one has grappled seriously with this element of promiscuous sex. Furthermore, when talking to sXers themselves, they, too, do not appear to have much to say about this particular abstinence.[1] Still, sXers' discourse surrounding promiscuity serves as a gateway into potentially rich insights into the meaning-making practices of sex as they relate to the sXe self. Unlike in the cases of substances, which entail total abstinence, sXers must navigate and negotiate the fuzzy boundaries of promiscuity. Although sXers insist that their decisions as to how to define and practice abstinence from promiscuity are personal in nature, they recognize that they do not exercise complete control in setting the parameters; they must give convincing social performances even in the face of loose and ambiguous guidelines.

In this chapter, I use the framework of a symbolic interactionist (SI) understanding of meaning-making as it relates to the self. Starting from the position that "the key to comprehending a social world is to understand it from the perspective of the people actively engaged in it" (Schweingruber and Berns 2011:306), I rely on the firsthand accounts of 47 sXers in 2003 to untangle some of the issues surrounding constructing a self largely based on abstinence when one of the abstinences itself appears somewhat "out of step." After an overview of the theoretical background, I explore how sXers create meaning out of the fuzzy concept of promiscuity and how they evaluate these practices in the context of the scene. I then discuss the longer-term advantages of these constructions of promiscuity, in particular, how they allow for a flexible yet convincing sXe self over time.

CREATING A MEANINGFUL SELF

Coined by Herbert Blumer and rooted largely in the writings of his mentor, George Herbert Mead, symbolic interactionism takes on the task of understanding how individuals create meaning as social actors. According to Blumer (1969), symbolic interactionism rests on three interrelated premises:

[First], human beings act toward things on the basis of the meanings that the things have for them. . . . [Second], the meaning of such things is derived from, or arises out of, social interaction that one has with one's fellows. [Third], these meanings are handled in, and modified through, an interpretative process used by the person in dealing with the things he encounters. (2)

These premises extend to the concept of the self, regarded as an object created and understood in a social context. Departing from theoretical perspectives that conceptualize the self as an already-present structure, symbolic interactionists insist that the self gets established through interaction (Blumer 1969; Jenkins 1996; Mead 1934; Sandstrom, Martin, and Fine 2010). In fact, "It is the social process itself that is responsible for the appearance of the self; it is not there as a self apart from this type of experience" (Mead 1934:142).

Reflexivity also plays a key role in this process, as the final stage in the self's development occurs when individuals find themselves able to take the attitude of the other. The ability to see oneself as others do, to develop what Cooley calls a "looking-glass self," occurs not in isolation as a philosophical exercise but in "the real social world of interacting individuals" (Adams and Sydie 2002:312). Far from being inconsequential, this process whereby "people come to see themselves as they think others see them" (Gecas and Burke 1995:51) solidifies a sense of self and highlights the interconnectedness between self and others. As Cooley sums up, "the imaginations which people have of one another are the *solid facts* of society" (in Adams and Sydie 2002:312). The self, then, remains "something that has to be routinely created and sustained in the reflexive activities of the individual" (Giddens, 1991:52). For Mead (1934), it is language that ultimately anchors the self in this process; as he insists, "I know of no other form of behavior than the linguistic in which the individual is an object to himself, and, so far as I can see, the individual is not a self in the reflexive sense unless he is an object to himself" (142).

Both classic and contemporary strands of symbolic interactionism appear when thinking about straight edgers' construction and performance of the self. First, sXers insist that their sXe identity does not just "happen" but arises through a series of intentional choices. As Patrick insists,

> You can't happen to be straight edge. I don't think anybody's born straight edge. Just because you're born, you haven't drank [sic] and you haven't smoked, you haven't done any drugs, you haven't had any promiscuous sex. It doesn't mean you're straight edge. There's plenty of people who do that and they're not straight edge. (Interview transcripts)

Patrick's quote illustrates a central point from my earlier work on abstinence (Mullaney 2006), that is, that not doing something alone does not qualify as abstinence; the behaviors have to be deliberately incorporated into the self.

Second, this group-level understanding of sXe surfaces in the intentional use of language and symbols. Not just anyone calls him- or herself sXe; when identifying as such, the accompanying abstinent practices are not random but instead hinge around the triad reflected in the XXX symbol. Interestingly, many sXers like to frame their abstinence choices as personal, believing that they exercise great agency in constructing their sXe identity. Patrick continues,

> I have always believed that they're not rules. A rule's made to be broken, pretty much. Like if there was no breaking a rule, then it wouldn't be in existence. And I don't really believe that these are rules because they are something I would never break. And also there have been times when I would change something, like I considered something a part of straight edge, and then I'd be able to change it later on, as my perception of whatever was changing, you know? (Interview transcripts)

Despite this claim that how one performs sXe is a personal decision, the practices of sXe cluster around the triad of abstinence (alcohol and drugs; cigarettes; promiscuous sex). Although many sXers cling to the idea of sXe's personal element, their general definitions of edge closely mirror those of others in the scene, and their individual practices fall very close in line with these definitions, especially in relation to drugs, alcohol, and cigarettes. In fact, every single interviewee included strict abstinence from these substances in the general definition of *edge* as well as their personal practice of it. For these reasons, other sXers scoff at the idea that sXe is personal. With a hint of exasperation in his voice, Donnie says,

> What [sXe] means to me? I don't know if I can answer as much as what it means to me as to what I think it IS. Like I feel really weird when people say over and over again that it's a personal choice. I don't know what the fuck that means. If there's not some sort of structure to it, you can keep adapting it any way you want. (Interview transcripts)

Straight edgers reinforce a third and final connection to symbolic interactionism, reflexivity, in their discussions of potentially shifting practices related to edge. Straight edgers recognize that, while they might shift to vegetarianism or eliminate caffeine or over-the-counter drugs, they cannot easily alter the core abstinences of sXe if they wish to be recognized as such. Although straight edgers make space for a personal past in which individuals may have engaged in some of these acts, they take an especially rigid view not only on what one does in the present (gauged by the popular saying in the scene

"If you're not now, you never were") but also on what one will do in the future. For sXers, in order to be deemed authentic by others in the scene, edge must be a permanent and consistent part of one's identity. In the language of Goffman (1967), in order to give a convincing performance of the self, individuals must become self-regulating, recognizing that "some situations and acts and persons will have to be avoided" (43). In the context of sXe, this means no alcohol, no drugs, and no cigarettes now or ever, moving forward.

DEFINING AND MANAGING PROMISCUITY

The question remains as to how abstinence from promiscuous sex fits into this conceptualization of sXe. For a group that promotes such a rigid understanding of the self and total abstinence from substances, what does it mean to incorporate an abstinence that is so fuzzy and ambiguous? How can reflexivity occur when the practice of one X of the XXX may vary from sXer to sXer?

In order to begin to answer these questions, it is important to understand how sXers make meaning out of the blurry concept of promiscuity. Popular conceptualizations of abstinence frame it in cut-and-dried, black-and-white terms with a clear line separating the doing from not doing. Although sXers adopt this type of thinking in regard to substance use, the wide range in quantitative and qualitative understandings of promiscuous sex suggests that they understand this abstinence to be more of a negotiable zone than a defined point between not doing something and doing it one time (Mullaney 2006:108–112). To be sure, sXers' understandings of what counts as sexual abstinence in the first place appear far less cohesive than in the case of substances. Although two informants (both men) include total sexual abstinence in their definition of sXe, most sXers, like Cindy, believe that such views reflect more "hard-line" and militant views of the scene rather than those of everyday sXers. Indeed, 39 of the 47 sXers (26 men, 13 women) interviewed frame edge as including abstinence from promiscuous sex. The remaining six (five men, one woman) who fall outside of these two categories claim that they do not include sex as part of their edge at all. (It is also important to note that two of these six are married and see promiscuous sex as irrelevant to their lives.)

So what exactly is abstinence from promiscuous sex? As Karl notes, the "whole sex thing gets blurry." While variation in personal understanding exists, sXers are not at complete liberty to define promiscuity if they expect others to recognize their abstinence from it. Below, I include a sampling of the axes along which sXers define promiscuous sex both as a practice of edge and how it applies to their own lives.

Some Highlight the Type and Commitment of Relationship:

"[Promiscuous sex refers to] any sexual relationships outside of a closed, caring relationship." (Rick)

"Many feel that sex for the sake of sex, without commitment to your partner, is also not part of the movement." (Xavier)

Others press the notion of commitment one step further by adding the emotional tie of love for one's partner:

"I will never have sex with another girl without meaning. I think sex is something sacred that should have love attached to it." (Eric)

"Sex should be kept for relationships where you love the person and have intent to marry them." (Anne)

"[Avoiding promiscuous sex means] not having like sex with just like any random person. Like for me it was like, if you want to have sex, have sex with somebody you love." (Tony)

For others, motivations also matter in addition to relational ties:

"I don't consider that being edge, like just going around just seeing who you can sleep with. I see kids that will see a girl and will just be like, 'I'll get her in two weeks.'" (Russ)

"With the sex thing, I do my best to have sex only in a relationship. I am not the town whore, but I am by no means a choirboy. I just don't let my actions and my motive be determined by lust." (Simon)

An exchange between Donnie and his fellow band members highlights the nonmutually exclusive quality of these definitions of promiscuity while further revealing the difficulty of agreeing on its parameters:

Donnie: It's kind of tough to nail down the definition. I would say that I have a problem with people who kind of uh—how can I say this—like someone who actually says, "Man, tonight I'm going to get laid" or "Tonight I'm going to go out and try to get laid."

Jay: It just seems like it takes love out of the equation.

Donnie: I can even accept love not being in the equation, but I can't like, I don't know. It can't be a game or . . . just be for your, I don't know. It's a weird area; it's not as clear-cut. And I just don't know what it is. I haven't figured it out.

JM (to Tucker): Do you want to add anything?

Tucker: I'll put it in the best word that I can, like it shouldn't be something like it's a hobby or something that they do for the pleasure of feeling good. And it shouldn't be something where you should do it for the gratification and feeling of, "I'm a big man 'cause I got laid last night" and like shit like that.

It is important to note, however, that this amorphous and variable character of promiscuous sex precludes neither the presence of boundaries nor the serious nature of transgressing them. After all, in a very social and public scene, sXers know that their claims to edge matter little should their actions not pass the scrutiny of their peers.

DOING EDGE, BREAKING EDGE

In addition to not always defining abstinence in uniform ways, individuals also adopt different strategies for "doing" abstinence. When examining abstinence from a more generic approach—including individuals who avoided practices ranging from diet to sex to technology—I identified two general strategies of abstinence, ones I termed "fence building" and "fire walking." Fence building describes how most people likely think about abstinence, that is, as a commitment to never engaging in the act one claims to not do. But fence building entails one additional element: It involves adding a layer of insulation or protection around one's abstinence. For example, someone who fence builds might not only avoid intercourse but also any acts that could be seen as leading up to intercourse, such as oral sex. Fire walking, however, takes an altogether different approach to abstinence. When individuals fire walk, they test how close to the fire they can get without getting burned. Taking that same example of sexual abstinence, someone who fire walks would perhaps engage in physically intimate acts while avoiding intercourse. Rather than regarding these practices as hypocritical, individuals who fire walk propose that toeing the line of abstinence (but not crossing it) serves as an identity-affirming act, and *not* one that discredits or disconfirms their abstinence.

Outsiders to the scene might expect the variability in definitions within the scene to manifest in fire walking when it comes to sexual abstinence. However, just because the zone that lies between promiscuous and nonpromiscuous sex may appear a somewhat gray area does not mean that sXers practice this abstinence loosely. In fact, precisely because of this ambiguity, many sXers engage in acts of fence building as a way of adding an additional guarantee that they will not cross the line from acceptable sex to promiscuity, however defined. For Eric, fence building means dating largely within the scene. He says, "I have dated girls that were not [sXe], and my character and their characters would conflict greatly. I will never knowingly date another girl that partakes in any form of drinking, drugs, or promiscuous sex again." Quinn, too, discusses how his practices changed over time as he became more committed to his current girlfriend:

> When I was at the age when I knew I could hang out with a lot of girls and go to shows and hang out with girls from shows afterwards, I was in love with this girl, so I knew that I was in love with this girl and I wasn't going to jeopardize that by, you know, doing something stupid just for the satisfaction of one day or a one night stand or whatever. . . . I never look at girls on the street and say, "Oh, I wonder what it would be like to be with someone else?" I find it in my heart not to think that way, so I'm not tempted really. (Interview transcripts)

Although sXers express confidence in their own methods of avoiding promiscuity and what would violate their abstinence, consensus disappears when attempting to generalize to the scene.

Discrepancies arise when trying to delineate what would count as a transgression of those boundaries. When asked what would disqualify someone from convincingly claiming edge, the blurriness resurfaces. Smith grapples with this dilemma when he says,

> Who's to say that I broke edge because I'm having sex with this girl? Like nobody knows for sure if I'm in love with her. It's always that extremely grey area. Then, you know, it's like, "Well what counts as sex? And what counts as fucking?" And then you get into this whole big thing. (Interview transcripts)

To be sure, all sXers who include avoidance of promiscuous sex in their understanding of edge state that engaging in such acts would disqualify edge, yet there is no clear definition of what that means. Whereas sXers apply what could be thought of as an identity performance version of the one-drop rule of substances (that is, by suggesting that one cigarette, drink, or illegal substance would destroy one's claim to edge), they do not offer any comparable quantitative parameters of promiscuous sex (number of encounters, number of partners). When asked what would disqualify someone from claiming edge, the short answer for almost every sXer hinges on drinking, smoking, using drugs, or engaging in promiscuous sex. The more revealing data, however, appear in the elaborations (and nonelaborations) of the short answer.

When sXers talk about breaking edge in the interviews, they experience no shortage of real-life examples. Almost every sXer reflects on someone who broke edge and what behaviors constituted that fall. Although sXers claim that participating in any of the abstinences violates edge, their examples suggest that all abstinences do not fare equally in their ability to break edge. Again, drinking, smoking, and using drugs *even one time* can nullify one's edge, but sXers remain conspicuously silent on whether one sexual act can make someone promiscuous. Instead, in the rare moments when sXers discuss breaking edge through a violation of sexual abstinence alone, they present them in extremely egregious forms. Jenna describes with distaste "a kid that wouldn't do drink or do drugs and considered himself straight edge but yet had sex with different girls every night. I hate that." While this kid did abstain from substances, the repeated, excessive actions ("every night") disqualified his edge in her mind.

More commonly, sXers do not discuss sexual transgressions alone but instead couch them among other ways of breaking edge (e.g., getting drunk). In these examples as well, sXers characterize a fall from edge as entailing a spiral into excess. Dylan, for example, says,

> I had two friends that were both straight edge at one time that when they sold out, went on this mad binge; they'd get drunk all the time and they were both into coke for a little while. They both got gonorrhea from this one girl. I like to make fun of them for it all the time because it's like if you were so serious, it never would have happened, you know. (Interview transcripts)

While Luke speaks at the hypothetical level, he offers a similar example:

> I mean, if, if someone came up to me and said, "Oh, I'm straight edge." You know, and I said, "Oh, okay. Cool." And then a friend of theirs comes up and says, "So how was the drunken frat orgy that you had, you know, each night for the past three weeks?" or something like that, I would just be like, "Hmmm, wait a second." (Interview transcripts)

Straight edgers may limit their examples of breaking edge through sex to situations of excess and/or in conjunction with other violations of edge for several reasons. First, due to the more private nature of sex, a sexual transgression of edge may simply be less visible and more difficult to "see" than the more public acts of drinking and smoking. Second, as Haenfler (2006) suggests, perhaps "the movement's 'rule' against promiscuous sex is more difficult for members to enforce" precisely because "there is greater variation in belief regarding sex than substance use" (45). Finally, and not unrelated to the first two explanations, by opening the door to looser and more personal interpretations of the range of acceptable sexual practices, sXers simply cannot rely on a standard measuring rod to evaluate violations; instead, to use the old cliché applied to pornography, they believe that they will know it when they see it. Due to the porous understandings of promiscuity, violations of other abstinences—ones that do have agreed-upon parameters—can more swiftly discredit one's edge, especially when paired with questionable sex practices.

"I've Got the Straight Edge" (But Can It Change?).

Given that sXers exhibit less consistency as a scene as to whether abstinence from sex (promiscuous or otherwise) is a primary tenet of edge, interpret the parameters of sexual abstinence in different ways, and evaluate violations of sexual abstinence on a case-by-case basis, the importance of this abstinence comes into question. In this final section, I suggest that, even when varied and contested, definitions of promiscuity matter greatly in creating and providing meaning to the sXe self, not only on the level of the individual but also on the larger scale of the scene.

For women in the scene, the avoidance of promiscuous sex carves out a legitimate space for them in a hypermasculine, male-dominated scene. Many women discuss the double standard applied to them, evidenced by charges that sXe women participate in the scene only because of men. Not only do women endure the ironic charges of being sluts, they hear also the label "coat rack" hurled at them, an implication that women serve an incidental and passive role while men actively participate. Jenna describes this struggle:

> When I was starting to do shows, it was very hard for me to get respect. I was often treated like I must be some band member's girlfriend. To get respect in [the hardcore] community is hard enough and then be straight edge, you're saying blatantly, "No, I'm not gonna drink with you; I'm not gonna have sex with you. I'm not here for that. I'm here for something more." [As a form of protest], women make shirts that say "Coat Rack Attack." (Interview transcripts)

In addition to the benefits for women in combating sexism, abstinence from promiscuous sex offers a less recognized benefit for all sXers: the possibility of a flexible self over time. On the one hand, the notion of a flexible self runs counter to how sXers regard their edge. In fact, most sXers view their edge as fixed, permanent, and unchanging moving forward. As Donnie suggests,

> Straight edge is not just the ACT of not drinking and not smoking and not having promiscuous sex. It's the act of saying, "I am NEVER going to drink; I am NEVER going to do drugs; I am NEVER going to have promiscuous sex." It's not just the physical not doing it; it's the mental saying, "I'm NEVER going to do this. This is something that I reject so wholeheartedly that there's no chance that I'm ever going to do this again." (Interview transcripts)

Still, when young kids claim edge, they often do so without imagining the self through time. Donnie continues,

> That's why I feel like it's such a mishandled term because I really feel that there are people who say that they're straight edge who really haven't thought about the future of their life and who really haven't thought about what their life is going to be like when they're 30 or 40 or 50 years old. Can they still maintain these ideals and objectives? I don't think they can. (Interview transcripts)

Young kids break edge frequently in part because they do not foresee life changes ahead of them. Many older edgers lament that kids claim at such a young age before fully understanding the gravity of pronouncements. But kids also break edge because the strict parameters surrounding substances force them out should they experiment or choose to drink or smoke on occasion. However, Kier illustrates how abstinence from promiscuous sex—precisely in its fuzziness—allows for change over time in a way that the other abstinences associated with edge do not. He says,

> I think that straight edge has a very rigid definition itself, but my interpretation of what is and what isn't is somewhat flexible and fluid. And, it's something that I'm still trying to explore and figure out what is permissible and what isn't. [For example], if I don't agree with the institution of marriage, then what is promiscuous sex within a straight edge rubric? And so, you know, if I don't believe that in order, if I don't believe in church-sanctioned sexual activity, then what is the moment in my life in which I can say, "This is fine and not promiscuous?" So it opens up a lot of really heavy problems to kind of work through and I don't know if straight edge has successfully resolved them. (Interview transcripts)

This is not to say that sXers frame the sexual abstinence component in loose terms because they intend to act promiscuously in the future. Nonetheless, conceptualizing abstinence in such a manner allows for behavioral change over time in ways that the rigid framing of abstinence from alcohol and substances does not.

Most sXers would vehemently oppose the notion that one can use drugs or alcohol in moderate ways (or even one time) because partaking in them violates the clean living principle of the movement. However, their insistence of avoiding promiscuous sex (and not sex entirely) suggests that certain behaviors are not inherently dirty or tainting in and of themselves. As sXers themselves make clear, in the case of sex, the act itself does not threaten to contaminate or discredit one's edge, but *how* one participates in the act may. Rather than being static, the meaning of these behaviors is one that sXers must navigate and negotiate as situations arise and life circumstances change.

CONCLUSION

Contemporary theorizing suggests that identities that are more group-based (versus role- or person-based) in nature assume more uniformity of perception (Burke and Stets 2009:119), and, "because the meanings (responses) to the objects and categories are shared, they also form the basis of expectations for the behavior of others" (15–16). As a result, issues of authenticity, a focus "on the motivational implications of beliefs about self with regard to what is real and what is false" (Gecas 1991:177), frequently surround group identities. In its contested and varied meanings, the tenet of avoiding sexual promiscuity presents a challenge for sXers as they try to make sense of and assess their decisions and practices surrounding sex (as well as those of others) as they relate to edge. Unlike the clarity in relation to drugs and alcohol, evaluating sexual practices presents murky terrain in trying to determine who is "truly" sXe and who is not.

Although sXers and researchers alike remain fairly silent on the avoidance of promiscuity, this abstinence provides rich insight into the sociological and social phenomenon of meaning-making as it relates to the self. While many sXers like to insist that their interpretative understandings of sex are personal in nature, sXers must ultimately concede that, in practice, their actions must withstand the scrutiny of their peers in the scene. As Goffman (1967) notes, while "the general capacity to be bound by moral rules may well belong to the individual, [the] particular set of rules which transforms him . . . derives from requirements established in the ritual organization of social encounters" (45).

Even with room for personal variation, then, sXers quickly learn to see themselves as other sXers do, recognizing the limits on their actions if they desire others to see them as credible and authentic.

The constraints on their ability to freely improvise on the sexual dimension of their edge notwithstanding, sXers collectively challenge popular notions that "real" abstinence demands a complete refusal to engage in a given act but instead demonstrate that individuals can engage in sex in a manner deemed appropriate. In doing so, sXers model how flexibility and fluidity do not preclude the creation and experiencing of a self that is both meaningful and adaptable to change over time. Despite the unwillingness (or perhaps) inability of many younger sXers to acknowledge it, interviews with older sXers reveal that edge *does* change over time (Haenfler 2006; Torkelson 2010) in both practice and meaning. Burke and Stets (2009) insist that individuals must be able to imagine the self in the future in order to move it effectively from point A to point B in time (20). Rather than complicating or discrediting their edge, the fluid nature of promiscuity affords sXers the opportunities to negotiate and modify the meanings of their edge rather than forcing them to leave it behind.

NOTE

1. In the present study, this shortage of commentary may have to do with the fact that the interview guide centered largely around gender relations within the scene. Nonetheless, even though it was not the focus of the interviews, sXers do have a lot to say about not smoking, drinking, and using drugs, especially in proportion to their discussions of sex.

CHAPTER 11

THE CHALLENGES OF IDENTITY FORMATION FOR BISEXUAL-MULTIRACIAL WOMEN OF ASIAN/WHITE DESCENT

Beverly Yuen Thompson

When I asked my mother if she was a lesbian, she always avoided the question, saying it did not make sense to her. Interestingly for me, she never said, "yes" or "no." I persisted. "Is Rita my step-parent?" I would probe, teasingly. She and Rita would laugh at me and then revert back to their conversation in Chinese. I was, once again, shut out. I had been raised in a historically all-White hometown: Spokane, Washington. After marrying my White father and giving birth to me, my mother ended up living in cultural isolation from her Hong Kong roots. She downplayed all aspects of her heritage and raised me to be a White American—there was just one problem—I didn't pass. And if I wasn't White, then what was I? I was not Chinese, like my mother. By the time I was a teenager, questioning my own sexuality, she and my father had divorced. My mother had moved back in with her college roommate, Rita, also from Hong Kong. This was no ordinary female friendship; it was far more emotionally and physically intimate. They shared a bedroom in their four-bedroom house, with couplelike pictures of them together on the wall: mom sitting on Rita's lap. My father told the story of Rita yelling at him in the hallway of the college where they all met—in a jealous rage—when it became apparent that he and my mother were moving forward in their relationship, leaving Rita behind. Perhaps my mother was bisexual, like I suspected I was. But when I asked her this, she didn't understand the concept. Perhaps her closeness with Rita was a cultural difference that I did not understand, just like my blossoming bisexual identity was a concept she did not understand.

When I asked my mom what race I was supposed to check on the forms at school as a child, she responded, "Amerasian." I knew better than to ask this of my father, who was completely baffled by the question, lacking even the unsophisticated racial understanding of my immigrant mother, who was forced to confront the issue by being a person of color in the United States. But Amerasian was not an option on the forms. "Which one?" I asked, parroting the confines of the forms. "White *or* Asian?" For women like myself, those of "multiple identities" forced into the confines of mono-identity boxes, our self-understanding does not align with the larger cultural definitions. Our self-understanding, and how we explain ourselves to others (sometimes differently), still resonates with the double consciousness that W.E.B. Du Bois ([1903] 1994) describes in *The Souls of Black Folks*. He states: "It is a peculiar sensation, this double-consciousness, this sense of always looking at one's self through the eyes of others, of measuring one's soul by the tape of a world that looks on in amused contempt and pity" (1994:3).

In this chapter, I will examine the ways in which bisexual and multiracial Asian American women construct their concepts of identity and community differently from those who identify as "only" lesbian or gay or Asian American. When positioning these participants in the center of identity theorizing, different ideas emerge. This chapter contrasts the participants' self-understanding of their overlapping identities, against that of the mainstream singular identity model. Already involved in complex relationships with racial and ethnic communities to which they "belong," the participants later interact with lesbian, gay, bisexual, and transgender (LGBT) communities. While ethnic communities may be homophobic, LGBT communities are often predominantly White and, thus, uncomfortable. Ultimately, participants must navigate these complex alliances to find a place for themselves.

METHODOLOGY AND PARTICIPANT DEMOGRAPHICS

As the recruitment process for this study began, I cast a nationwide net in order to attract diverse participants. I advertised with political organizations based on race and sexual identity. Because of this, participants were overwhelmingly politically active individuals. From these postings, and through the snowballing technique (word-of-mouth), I was able to attract nine participants. Two participants resided in the Los Angeles area; therefore, face-to-face interviews were conducted in their homes, as I was then living in San Diego. The remaining interviews were conducted over the telephone, ranging from one to two hours in length. Interviews were conducted in 1999. The geographical locations of these participants were California, New York City, Boston, Hawaii, and Washington State. For the interviews, participants created names for themselves.

Most (but not all) of these women have lived in international settings and came from privileged backgrounds. Several of them had lived in other countries or had gone for extended visits, most often to their parents' home country. Others had lived and traveled all across the United States. Thus, they were sophisticated in their outlook and social understanding of identity, as it was informed from multiple, international perspectives. The racial heritages of the interviewees were diverse and thoroughly mixed, and the participants had a fairly detailed understanding of their various White, Asian, and Latino lineages on both sides. Linguistic identity also provided insight into the participants' identities, as it expresses their relationship to their parents, culture, and history. Their relationship to the languages of their parents' native lands fits within the larger global picture of colonialization, immigration, and assimilation. Most of the participants did not learn their parents' languages, other than English. This represents a distancing between themselves and their parents' ethnic cultures. It is as important to understand the loss of language as it is to understand how individuals acquire language. This loss of language was the strongest characterization of their linguistic identity and relationship to their parents' native tongue. Sometimes, parents want their children to learn their native tongue; other times, parents want their children to assimilate and "become American." While it is very typical for second-generation children to learn only English, it can still present a sense of shame or failure on the individual's part. For example, when I go to a Chinese restaurant with my mother where our server is Chinese, he speaks to my mother in Cantonese, and within a few sentences, mom always turns to me and says, "I told him you are my daughter, but no, you don't speak Chinese." The waiter shakes his head, says, "such a shame; you should learn." Cultural competency tests are a frequent stumbling block for second-generation children, where they are asked to prove that they are *really* of their ethnicity by their familiarity with language, cultural facts, food, and so on.

RACIAL AND SEXUAL IDENTITY INTERPLAY

> Well, my gender is a little queer, my sexuality is a little queer, and my race is a little queer, and I guess I'm just a little queer!

Eve playfully brings her multiple identities to the center of analysis. She argues that she is outside of identity boxes, that her identity is based on undefined categories: She is queer and mixed. Her use of the term *queer* is playful and brings out parallels of racial and sexual identities. *Queer* means both eccentric and unconventional; in addition, it's a more recently adopted umbrella term for people who identify as gay, lesbian, bisexual, or questioning, and it includes a further assortment of sexual identities that fall along the spectrum of sexuality, from heterosexual to homosexual. One may be queer if she or he does not identify as straight. *Genderqueer* is a newly created term for those who do not easily identify with a masculine or feminine gender expression; they are somewhere along the continuum, having a blend of masculine and feminine attributes. Eve's sexuality is queer because she is not heterosexual; yet she is not a lesbian, either, but somewhere in the middle. And she extends this use of queer to signify her racial identity, which is also along a continuum.

This section analyzes the ways that the participants understand the interplay of their sexual and ethnic identities. Three general themes emerged. First, some of the women recounted that the processes of developing their identities were powerfully integrated: Questioning their racial identity made them question all aspects of their lives, including their sexuality. Second, other women felt that the process of understanding their sexual and racial identities was parallel and similar, yet not necessarily integrated. Third, some felt that these two processes were very different and did not necessarily overlap in process.

The first theme is expressed by participants who feel that the development of their racial and sexual identities was intertwined to the point that their racial identities led them to question their sexual identities. Their understanding of racial diversity and their mixed race status made them aware that individuals do not necessarily fit into established categories. Experiencing diversity in their surroundings made participants less rigid in developing an understanding of the world around them. Sharon explains how her family influenced her non-dichotomous mentality:

> My family never saw that there was any conflict with my being strongly identified as American and with being Filipino. So for me, there was never any reason to draw lines. I think that is very different from a lot of people who are mixed race and then raised to try and pass as one or the other. Those people tend to have a much more boxed-in take on the world. When I first started to figure out that I was bi, it was like, "oh, okay, this makes sense." You know, it was not like, "on my god, I can only be one thing." I have never been only one thing. So I think family had a huge influence on my understanding. (Interview transcripts)

From early on in her childhood, Sharon was taught to be inclusive of her diverse history; therefore, she was not exposed to the conflicted loyalties that some multiracials face. She did not "draw lines" between her different heritages. When she came out as bisexual, she recognized the similarity to her racial identity and did not perceive a conflict necessitating a choice between the two.

The second theme is exemplified by participants whose identity formation processes were parallel, but not as integrated. Puanani discusses how being multiracial in Hawaii made her open to diverse people:

> When I was a kid I faced more discrimination because I was also White, rather than Hawaiian. . . . It opened my mind. People weren't just one thing. And it's the same nationality wise. . . . I realized that everything's not always one way. I knew gay people, and I had no judgment against them. Being a different sexuality could be totally similar to being a different race. And I just didn't filter out anybody or anything regardless of race, sexuality, religion, or anything. (Interview transcripts)

Because of her experiences of racial discrimination growing up, Puanani did not discriminate against others. She developed pride in her diverse ethnic heritage and compared this to sexuality, religion, or other identity categories. Another participant, Lani, also experienced different processes of dealing with her sexual and racial identity and believes that her racial identity made her open-minded to diversity. Her racial identity changed throughout her lifetime. As a child she was proud and pro-active about celebrating her diverse Hawaiian heritages. Yet, as she grew older, it became less central in her life "because I pass for White," and therefore, "my sexual identity got me politicized in a personal way, way more that if I didn't pass [as White], because racism then would have been much more in my face as an issue." Race was not a central issue in her life postchildhood. Instead, she displaced her ethnic identity upon her mother and sister, neither of whom passed for White: "I distanced myself from my mother and my sister, I started to hear what I was saying, my *mother* is Hawaiian, or my *sister* this, and when did I let go of that? Cause I use to be really proud growing up." However, she does feel that her mixed heritage gave her the ability to see complexity:

> I think my mixed heritage and being raised with so many different cultures, Hawaiian, Japanese, Irish, helped me see the world in a very complex, diverse way. In some ways, I think it allowed me to be more open to the complexities of everything, including sexuality. . . . But it was the sexual identity and gender, being a woman, that I got radicalized with feminism. And the racism piece came later. I thought I was going to write a piece on lesbian chauvinism and I wrote instead about (racially) passing. That's what came up and I had no idea that was going to happen. (Interview transcripts)

Sexual identity opened the door for Lani to once again reexamine her racial identity. Indeed, while writing about bisexuality, she instead explored her mixed heritage. Her sexual identity opened her perspective about her ethnic heritage.

The third theme demonstrates how some interviewees processed sexual and racial identities separately, without overlap. Lucki's racial identity was a family process. She and her parents spent time with extended family in Chile and with Chinese family members in California, and during the visits, they learned some Spanish and Chinese through various family members. Her sexual identity, on the other hand was a personal process:

> They were pretty different processes for me. The racial thing had a lot to do with my family, and was much more a group process in terms of coming to terms with what we are. It was very much me, and my sister, and even my mom to some degree, because she didn't really recognize herself as Asian. . . . My sexuality was definitely more of a personal process. I came to them from really different places. (Interview transcripts)

Regardless of whether their racial and sexual identity formation processes were similar or different, all of the participants understood or defined themselves in terms of all of their identities (though one may be prioritized in certain settings or times). While all understood their bisexual and biracial-multiracial identities as compatible, complementary, and/or overlapping, they felt that they were confusing, or "problematized," by outsiders (Dajenya 1995:236).

The participants find their identities compatible and integrated. They define themselves in relation to their position outside narrow categories. They use terms such as "hodge podge," "mixed," and "queer" to describe their complexity. They have difficulties with other people's perceptions of them, their misunderstandings, and their demands for simplification or explanation. While participants most often see themselves within the context of all of their overlapping identities, the larger culture is focused on singular identities. We now turn to see the ways in which these singular identities are constructed and how participants' self-understanding is contextualized against this backdrop.

MULTIRACIAL IDENTITY

Multiracial individuals have a diverse array of appearances, some of which are not easily identifiable as a particular ethnicity; thus, they often encounter the question, "What are you?" Some may pass as White. Others may appear to be a member of an ethnic group of which they may or may not be a member. If their appearance does not match their racial identity, they may encounter conflict when they express their identity to others (e.g., "But you're a White girl, why are you trying to say you're Asian?"). Because of this diversity, they may describe their racial identity differently in different contexts. For example, Wendy Thompson self-identifies as "undercover Asian American" because, she states, "to many people, I look 'just black'" (2001:202). Mixed race individuals often have difficulty expressing a racial understanding that does not correlate with their physical appearance and the mainstream interpretation of it. Therefore, there is a situational element to multiraciality similar to that of bisexuality. Others may focus on whatever is most obvious and make blanket assumptions based on their perceptions: if one appears Asian, or if one appears holding her girlfriend's hand. The geographical location and its ethnic context can bias people's understanding of the mixed-race individual's ethnicity. For example, when I lived in Albuquerque, New Mexico, some locals assumed I was Native American, rather than Chinese, because that was the dominant ethnicity in the area and reflected the observer's reference point. The participants realize that their understanding of their racial identities, like their bisexual identities, may not be understood or accepted by outsiders; therefore, they alter their story based upon the expectations of others. Karin operates from the assumption that others would not understand her identity:

> Sometimes I'll say that I'm Asian, it depends on the context and whom I'm talking to. It depends on how specific I have to be. Usually I'll say South Asian. If I say Sri Lankan, half the people don't even know where that is. They'll think I'm from Africa. So I'll say South Asian, and then they think that means Vietnamese or Laotian, or South East Asian. So people get confused. (Interview transcripts)

She, however, understands herself as "half Sri Lankan and half White." Many participants described their racial identities as situational, depending on "who is asking."

Some participants explain that their racial identity was a family process, which differentiated it from their sexual identity. Parents and family members have an important influence on their racial self-understanding. Parents may tell their children how they should identify, how parents themselves identify, and whether their given name reflects their multiracial heritage. Karin discusses how she experienced her racial identity process with her mother and sister:

> [Her mother] will say she's American first, in terms of the order of identities, and then she's Sri Lankan. . . . When my sister and I took an

Asian American studies class together, it all came together. We had to do a research project on an Asian immigrant, so we did a paper on my mom. It was the first time we really sat down and grilled her about her life. . . . After that, she started being more open. When I would come over and visit, she would take out treasures she had from Sri Lanka and talk about them. So I think in a lot of ways, the same way we got into our Sri Lankan identity, she got back in touch with it too. No one really wanted to know anything about it until we did. No one ever really cared or was interested. (Interview transcripts)

The participants differed in how their parents influenced their self-concept, with some parents encouraging their children to appreciate their complete heritage, while others tell their children they are "American" or, in some cases, "White." Steph describes an instance when she and her mom went to get Steph's military ID, and she witnessed her mother checking "White" on her form:

That was when I saw my mom put on the application that I'm White. I said, "Mom, I'm not White." And she said, "Yes, you are. My father, my biological father, is Irish American; therefore, you are White." I said, "Okay, alright." I went home and told my sisters, and we had a big discussion about it. I remember it caused somewhat of a commotion. My sister K is darker than all of us, so she had a real problem with it. (Interview transcripts)

Steph shows how differences of racial identity within the family setting can occur. Siblings may have different racial appearances and, therefore, different racial identities. Lucki describes the differences between herself and her sisters: "I look really Asian, then the next one down looks really mixed, otherwise she could look more Latina. And then the youngest one could go either way—she looks Asian or Latina." (Interview transcripts)

All of the participants have a shifting relationship to their racial heritage and how they understand it. For some, this has come through their politicization around identity issues in general; for others, the importance of their racial identity has become less pronounced over time. Lucki describes such a shift:

I think it's very fluid. There are day[s] I definitely feel South American. And there are other times I feel Asian American. I definitely have become much more Asian American in the past couple of years. In college, I was really trying to figure out what race meant to me. But it doesn't hold the same kind of importance that it once did. I just feel comfortable with who I am. I don't really agonize about it anymore. I usually describe my family history more than any racial identity. I don't really have a really politicized racial identity in the same way that I do sexual. (Interview transcripts)

These examples show how racial identity can be situational and changing. The influences of parents, geographic location, and physical appearance can shift the participants' self-understanding or presentation to others. Most monoracial individuals possess a single label for their identity that is culturally understood (e.g., White or African American). Standing outside of accepted racial categorizations can be difficult. It can give one a sense of freedom to define one's self uniquely. Or it can make individuals feel marginalized, misunderstood, or invisible.

BISEXUALITY IN A (WHITE) GAY AND LESBIAN WORLD

Sexuality is impacted by culture. Particular countries, ethnicities, and regions have different beliefs about appropriate sexual behavior. For those who are second generation in immigrant households, their parents' views of sexuality can be different than that of the dominant White American culture in the United States. Tolerance toward homosexuality varies between cultures, individuals, and generations. This provides a complex social context that the mixed-race, bisexual women must negotiate. For the heterosexual women participants in Pyke and Johnson's (2003) "Asian American Women and Racialized Femininities" study "reaffirmed the ideological constructions of the white-dominated society by casting ethnic and [White] mainstream worlds as monolithic opposites" (42). Indeed, Sumie Okazaki (2002) finds that the more exposure to American culture, the more Asian American youth began to "act out" sexually (35). Even still, Asian Americans have the lowest rates of sexual activity, teen pregnancy, and sexually transmitted infections (STIs) out of all racial groups in the United States, including Whites.

With different cultural norms and perspectives regarding sexuality, I can imagine that bisexual Asian American women might seek out the gay and lesbian community to support their sexual identity development over the assumed intolerance of ethnic Asian communities (Blasingame 1992:50; Mao, McCormick, and Van de Ven 2002:426; Okazaki 2002:39). However, (White) bisexuals "have long emphasized the marginality and the resentment" that they have experienced within the gay and lesbian community (Garber 1995:39; Shokeid 2001:64; Wosick-Correa 2007). They have been accused of being promiscuous, spreading disease between straight and gay communities, and being uncommitted to a binary sexual identity (i.e., one is either gay or straight, bisexuality does not exist). Bisexual and transgender identities have only recently been included within the LGBT community. Transgender individuals have gender-identities that are not in-line with their bodies; therefore, they attempt to transition to be accepted as the opposite sex (or, e.g., at a different place on the gender continuum, some may be "genderqueer"). Often, transgender people will attempt to alter their appearance and sex through clothing, hormones, or surgery, although not all follow these paths. Some people within the LGBT community do not feel that transgender individuals should be included in the LGBT umbrella term, as theirs is one of gender-identity, not sexual identity, necessarily, although they can also be queer. (For example, a male-to-female transgendered individual who is attracted to women was assumed to be a heterosexual male before the gender transition and, afterward, considers herself a lesbian.) Often, bisexual and transgender organizations are formed to provide a more nuanced sense of community for those that feel marginalized within lesbian and gay organizations. Kassia Wosick-Correa (2007) finds that bisexual women often "mask and shift" their identities to fit into lesbian spaces and that polyamorous spaces also provide a potentially safe space where relationships can take on different forms. Polyamory is the concept that one can have relationships with different people at the same time, often fully communicating with their partners about each other. As polyamorous people face great stigma for their transgression of monogamy from mainstream society, organizations based on these relationships can also be places in which bisexuals can be understood and accepted. However, Wosick-Correa's participants are racially unmarked within the article; their sexuality provides the only conflicting identity within a lesbian context. It may be different for mixed-race women to find acceptance in lesbian spaces than for White bisexual women.

For bisexuals of color, their inclusion and comfort within the LGBT community is often problematic. Subtle and implicit racism has been reported (Blasingame 1992:50–1; Duvauchelle et al. 1994:90; Mao et al. 2002:427). Additionally, the LGBT identity is firmly rooted in Western discourse, which does not easily translate into an Asian cultural understanding (McLelland 2000). Instead of reinscribing the dominant LGBT stages of identity development (i.e., coming out to oneself, then coming out to family and friends), theorists Kaufman and Johnson (2004) propose that researchers use symbolic interaction theories to get at the nuances of identity development, especially for those outside the White gay and lesbian models. Not everyone has the same understanding of what their gay or bisexual identity means. Kaufman and Johnson point to a crucial aspect of identity negotiation: "creating self-affirming spaces where individuals selectively associate with friends and family and choose to congregate in 'safe'" communities (822). This process of interaction with accepting family and friends is closer to the story of how bisexual-multiracial participants came to express their identities.

> Usually I would call myself queer, over bisexual. I think identity is something that's much more complex than anything that can be summarized in one word. And I think identity politics are a political tool and nothing more. I try and keep it really separate from my personal life. I like "queer" because it doesn't really say a whole lot about your sexuality, except that it's not straight. In terms of bisexuality . . . it doesn't have a lot of meaning for me personally. (Lucki, Interview transcripts)

Many of the participants expressed caution using the term *bisexual,* and several of them rejected this term and adopted others. When I asked Lucki whether she identified as bisexual, her first response was, "It depends on who's asking." All the interviewees held this sentiment: The labels and definitions they used to describe themselves shift in relation to the questioner. They viewed identity as fluid, changeable, and multiple, while the language of established labels tended to narrow and solidify the understanding.

The interviewees face misunderstandings of, and challenges toward, their sexual identity, from several different directions. Since these pressures come from both lesbians and heterosexuals, the interviewees use caution with all sides. Although they express a clear understanding of their own sexuality and its fluid nature, they face difficulty when they have to express this to others. The participants face the challenge of constructing a positive self-understanding, in a potentially hostile, gay-or-straight-only context.

CONCLUSION

How these bisexual-multiracial participants construct their own identities can provide alternative examples for understanding identity. Binary thinking rests on the foundation of inequality and singularity (Garber 1995:89). You can be only one or the other, and one side is more powerful and socially accepted. For queer Asian American women, their identities form a "dynamic relationship, one whose dialectic combination often yields unrecognized, unacknowledged, and understudied configurations" (Eng and Hom 1998:12). Looking at identity politics from a complex perspective provides us with new insights and opportunities to reconsider categories.

> I do not have to be one or the other. I think that the way I'm made, whoever made me, they didn't intend for me to have to be one or the other. (Steph, Interview transcripts)

This chapter has looked at the concepts that the bisexual-multiracial women use to understand their sexual and racial identities. The participants have constructed alternate views of identity based upon their own subject positions, ones that integrate fluid, nonstatic, and evolutionary processes. This has infused many aspects of their lives, including the ways that they understand identity, their use of labels, and their perspectives on social groups.

The interviewees perceive themselves as remaining outside of established parameters of accepted identity categories. This gives them the freedom to define themselves based on their own understanding. Yet the ability to remain "outside of the box" was also accompanied by other people's misunderstandings. Opinions that categorized bisexual or multiracial identity as "deviant" or unacceptable deeply affected all participants. As they described themselves, they would discuss how outsiders perceived them as well. All of the interviewees viewed their identities as complementary, overlapping, and integrated to the point where some identified as much with their position of being "outside the box." Such insights can create an opening for new perspectives. Sabrina discusses the need for such visibility:

> We just really need to be visible. Whether that is in writing, or through speaking, so that people start realizing that there are other groups out there besides just lesbian and straight, or Chinese and White. There are mixes in between, not just one definition of what multiracial means, or what multiracial people look like. When people think of a multiracial person, they might think of just a half and half person. And sexuality also needs to be seen as more fluid, it can't just be categorized as gay or straight. It's very important for us to be really visible, so that people can see that we exist. And that's the last thing that I want to mention. (Interview transcripts)

This fluidity of identity, of getting outside of Western identity categories, can help me understand my mother as well. Why was I so adamant to put her in a lesbian or bisexual box, while I went through my own process of identity formation? Was this the only way in which to identify? Even after years of pestering her, my mother never admitted to being bisexual or lesbian. But she had established a long-term committed relationship with Rita, which has included buying houses and cars together, working the same jobs on occasion, and spending about seventeen years together—the same amount of time that my parents were married. Which relationship was more authentic? In the end, my mother had committed, long-term relationships with both a man and a woman. Does that make her a lesbian or bisexual? Not according to her. Part of understanding my own fluid identity is to give her the respect and openness of not imposing my learned categories onto her own reality. That is the beauty of fluid identities: the freedom to not flatten one's self, and others, into socially constructed categories that do not encompass one's full, lived experience.

CHAPTER 12

"GIVE ME A DOMINANT OF ANY GENDER OVER ANY KIND OF NON-DOMINANT"

Sexual Orientation Beyond Gender

Brandy L. Simula

> If I had a choice between being shipwrecked on a desert island with
> a vanilla lesbian and a hot male masochist, I'd pick the boy.
>
> – Pat Califia, *Public Sex*

How do preferences based on factors other than gender influence our sexual orientations and decisions about the partners with whom we engage in sexual activities? Can the traditional concept of sexual orientation, which elevates gender above all other preferences in defining and structuring sexual desires, attractions, and experiences, adequately explain the sexual orientations of *all* individuals? Or are there some people for whom different models of sexual orientation are needed to fully understand their sexualities? I investigate these questions by analyzing the experiences of bondage/discipline/domination/submission/sadism/masochism (BDSM) participants—people who participate in consensual activities that involve power exchange and/or pain. BDSM is an umbrella term that encompasses a variety of consensual activities and relationship dynamics that frequently but do not always have sexual meanings for participants—a point to which I return later. Activities and relationship dynamics that fall under the BDSM umbrella include but are not limited to leather, kink, sadomasochism (SM), dominance and submission (D/s), master/slave (M/s) relationships, power exchange (and variations including erotic power exchange and Total Power Exchange), bondage, and discipline. I explore the comparative importance of gender and BDSM role (such as dominant and submissive) in participants' understandings of their sexual orientations and selections of partners and identify the complex patterns that emerge in how BDSM participants conceptualize their own sexual orientations.

SEXUALITY, SEXUAL ORIENTATION, AND THE SYMBOLIC INTERACTIONIST PERSPECTIVE

Because I am interested in how participants perceive and assign meaning to BDSM experiences, the symbolic-interactionist (SI) perspective is particularly useful. The SI framework emphasizes that identities, experiences, and meanings are interactionally created through negotiation with others and that meanings vary across settings as well as individual actors within a given setting (Blumer 1969; Goffman 1967; Mead 1934). This allows me to explore the variety of meanings that BDSM has for those who participate in it, rather than assuming a stable, fixed meaning across all participants. The SI approach demonstrates that meanings do not inhere in activities or objects themselves but are "social products" created through interactions with others (Blumer 1969; Goffman 1967; Mead 1934). BDSM participants themselves make explicit use of this reality, often using BDSM interactions to explore ways of creating non-normative meanings; as Mike, for example, explains, "Feeding coins to a vending machine is usually less sexy than using a spoon to feed cum to a bound slave, but everything depends on what is going on in the minds of the people involved." The notion that what happens in the minds of participants is of significant importance in the creation of meaning is a theme that occurs repeatedly in my data.

Symbolic interactionists conceptualize sexuality as a process rather than an inherent, stable, individual characteristic (e.g., Gecas and Libby 1976; Jackson 2007; Longmore 1998; Plummer 2002). The components that make up an individual's sexualities—and one can have different sexualities at different times and in different social settings—include one's self, identity, orientation, desires, fantasies, attitudes, and behaviors (e.g., Kimmel 2007; Plante 2007; Rye and Meaney 2007; Valocchi 2005). Sexuality is situationally variable. The sexuality one enacts in one social situation may not necessarily be the same as the sexuality one enacts in another social setting. The sexuality one performs while discussing sexual health with one's doctor during an office visit, for instance, may be different from the sexuality one performs while engaging in sexual activity with one's partner(s).

Sexual Orientation

Sexual orientation is a concept that refers to the kinds of people to whom we are attracted. The concept has been traditionally been used to identify gender-based orientations, such as bisexual, lesbian, gay, pansexual, and heterosexual. More than a decade ago, Kinsey and colleagues shifted how we think about sexual orientation and attraction away from a binary (homo/ heterosexual) model to a continuum (Kinsey, Pomeroy, and Martin 1948, 1953). At one end of the continuum (0) is exclusively heterosexual; at the other (6) is exclusively homosexual. Points in between include categories, such as predominantly homosexual and incidentally heterosexual, equally homosexual and heterosexual (bisexual), predominantly heterosexual and more than incidentally homosexual, et cetera. Kinsey and colleagues found that very few people are exclusively homosexual or exclusively heterosexual; instead, most people fall at other points along the continuum, findings that have been replicated repeatedly in the decades since, including in a recent large-scale survey (Epstein et al. 2012).

In addition to demonstrating that sexual orientations exist along a continuum rather than as a dichotomy, sexuality research has also demonstrated that sexual orientation is fluid and can shift over time (Chung and Katayama 1996; Diamond 2008; Epstein et al. 2012; Rosario et al. 2006). An individual's orientation might be heterosexual at one point in her/his/"zir"[1] life, bisexual at another point, gay at another point, and heterosexual again at yet another point. The existence of multiple orientations at different points in the life course does not mean that an orientation at a particular point is "truer" or more "real" than an orientation that exists at another point.

In recent decades, the categories of gender-based sexual orientations have expanded significantly beyond heterosexual (attracted to people of a different sex/gender) and homosexual (attracted to people of a similar sex/gender). It is worth noting that while categories such as bisexual, queer, and pansexual share in common a resistance to the normative homo/hetero binary and are frequently used interchangeably, they carry different meanings and histories. "Bisexual" has historically been used to refer to people whose sexual orientation includes attraction to both men and women. "Queer" is often used as an inclusive term for lesbian and gay identified people, but it has evolved to include people with a variety of nonconforming sexualities and sexual orientations, including those whose sexual orientations do not map neatly onto traditional sex and/or gender categories. "Pansexual" refers to people who are attracted to individuals of a wide variety of genders beyond traditional masculine or feminine categories, including, for example, transgendered people, genderqueers, and gender nonconformists.

Using the classic example "gentlemen prefer blondes," Bem (1996) points out the implicit assumption of a gender-based orientation; gentlemen don't prefer *all* blondes, they prefer *women* blondes. We tend to treat gender-based sexual orientation as the single most important factor in our selection of sexual partners, nesting other factors *within* our gender preferences. We also tend to think of gender as the overarching, most significant component of how people choose partners. But are there other sexual preferences that are as significant as gender in the selection and evaluation of sexual partners for some individuals? Crocket (2010), for example, finds that some gay men have racial sexual preferences that are as important as their gender preferences. Crocket also finds that gay men with racial sexual preferences often developed those preferences simultaneously with—or even *before* their gender preferences. Following Bem (1996), Crocket argues that individuals have a more difficult time recognizing their racial preferences than their gender preferences because there is little ideological structure to support the concept of racial sexual preferences or orientations. In this chapter, I extend this work to a different context to explore the relative importance of gender and BDSM role in BDSM participants' selection and evaluation of partners.

BDSM

While the extremely diverse array of activities that are encompassed by the term BDSM makes it difficult to identify common features, several decades of research have led BDSM scholars to agree to a significant extent on definition criteria including consensuality, mutual definition of the situation, some form of power exchange, and a frequent but not necessary sexual context or meaning (Langdridge and Barker 2007; Moser and Kleinplatz 2006; Taylor and Ussher 2001; Weinberg, Williams, and Moser 1984; Weinberg 2006). The last criterion, that BDSM frequently but not necessarily involves a sexual context or meaning, is the most controversial among BDSM scholars. Research on BDSM often begins from the premise that BDSM is a type of sexuality and/or sexual practice or that it is an activity that takes place only in a sexual context and always has a sexual meaning (e.g., Deckha 2011; Langdridge 2005; Langdridge 2006a; Langdridge 2006b; Richters et al. 2008; Santtila et al. 2002; Taylor and Ussher 2001; Weinberg, Williams and Moser 1984; Weinberg 2006). Recently, however, Newmahr (2010a; 2010b; 2011) challenged the widespread tendency to frame BDSM as necessarily sexual. Newmahr (2010b) argues, for example,

Although many SM participants do frame their "play" as having an erotic aspect, the conceptualization of SM as "kinky sex" has obscured a more nuanced understanding of this community and their activities. . . . The perspective that SM is "about sex" persists despite widespread acknowledgement that at least some SM community members reject this framing. Research reveals that many participants do not understand their activities as an alternative or a prelude to, sexual interaction (Dancer, Kleinplatz, and Moser 2006; and Weiss 2006 cited in Newmahr 2010b:314–316).

The present study lends additional support to the recognition of Newmahr; Weiss; and Dancer, Kleinplatz, and Moser and others that BDSM is not always nor for all participants a sexual experience. The vast majority of participants in the present study, including 87% (n=26) of my interview partners,[2] perceive BDSM as not always nor necessarily sexual. Most participants do not use the presence or absence of traditional markers of sexual experience (e.g., genital contact, orgasm) in assigning sexual or nonsexual meanings to specific activities or even to scenes more generally. Instead, for the majority of participants in this study who perceive BDSM as an experience that *can* but does not *have to* involve a sexual meaning, the particular interactions to which they assign sexual meanings vary not according to the particular activity but instead according to a variety of interactional factors, such as the particular partner(s) present, what other kinds of activities are taking place, the overall definition of the scene or set of interactions, and whether or not participants intend the scene or play to be sexual.

BDSM Activities and Identities

The various categories subsumed under the umbrella term BDSM are interrelated but not synonymous. *Kink* is a general term for non-normative sexuality. Like BDSM, it is often used as an umbrella term, but kink is a much broader category than BDSM and includes sexual interests like fetishes, cross-dressing, strap-on sex, voyeurism, et cetera. *Leather* is a term that originated in gay male communities in the 1960s and subsequently spread to lesbian s/m communities in the 1970s (Rubin 1994). Leather retains a strong association with gay and lesbian BDSM but is also used as a synonym for BDSM regardless of sexual orientation (Moser and Kleinplatz 2006; Rubin 1994). *Dominance and submission* (D/s) refers to practices involving exchanges of power and/or to a Dominant/submissive relationship. *Sadomasochism* (S/m, s/m, s&m, SM) refers to practices that involve pain and/or to a sadist/masochist relationship.

Master/slave (M/s) refers to a Master/slave relationship—a relationship in which the participants have agreed that one person will control the other either for a given period of time or indefinitely. For some, this control is limited to BDSM interactions, while for others it includes all interactions between the participants; the latter is known as 24/7 and/or Total Power Exchange (TPE). *Bondage* (including bondage and discipline—B&D) refers to practices that involve physical and/or mental restraint, such as rope bondage and the use of restraint cuffs to limit movement.

The variation in uses and meanings of BDSM terminology extends to the roles participants take, or with which they identify. Terms that are used to describe roles or identities are sometimes used synonymously yet are often used to mark significant differences. *Top, dominant, master,* and *sadist,* for example, can have significantly different meanings for some participants and in some contexts, yet, are often also used interchangeably, as are the corresponding terms *bottom, submissive, slave*, and *masochist.* When distinctions among these roles exist in a given community or for a specific participant, they are often critically important. For example, someone might identify as a submissive (someone who enjoys consensual submission and power exchange) but not as a masochist (someone who enjoys receiving pain).

The BDSM Population

Previous estimates of the size of the BDSM population range from 5% to 25% of the U.S. population (Janus and Janus 1993; Michael et al. 1994; Rubin 1994; Scott 1993). How one defines the "BDSM population" itself factors significantly into the estimation process. Will someone be counted as a member of the population if ze, that is, she or he, attends BDSM events? Purchases BDSM paraphernalia? Views BDSM pornography? Or only if ze reports having BDSM experiences? If so, which experiences will count—specific practices, specific kinds of interactions? Will cyber interactions count—or only face-to-face interactions? And what about people who engage in practices or relationships that would generally be recognized as BDSM but who do not themselves identify in terms of BDSM? These questions are related to larger questions being debated in the field of sexuality studies about sexual identities and have led many sex researchers to abandon identity categories (e.g., gay) and instead focus on practices (e.g., men who have sex with men—MSM). However, as discussed above, because BDSM involves a variety of aspects of sexuality, including both identities and practices, that strategy is not viable for this project. For the purposes of this project, I therefore define the BDSM population as including anyone who identifies with and/or has experiences with any of the aspects of BDSM described above.

Methodology

This study relies on a variety of qualitative data including 32 semistructured, in-depth interviews with self-identified BDSM participants (conducted between 2010 and 2011); thousands of pages of discussion board data collected (2010–2011) from Bondage.com, one of the largest BDSM community websites in the world with over one million members; and over a decade of informal conversations with BDSM participants and observations in public physical and cyber BDSM communities in the Southeast and West Coast. The interview sample was divided evenly in thirds across general BDSM role preferences: dominant, submissive, and switch, with considerable variation across specific roles within these general categories. Approximate length of time participating in BDSM ranged from less than one year to more than 20 years. Most (60%) had participated in BDSM for ten or more years at the time of our interview. Participants ranged in age from early 20s to early 70s; most participants were between 30 and 50 years old. Most (78%) of my interview partners reported white and/or Caucasian as their race or ethnicity. While my interview partners reported complex, often fluid gender expressions in the course of the interview conversation, when asked "How would you describe your gender or genders?" in demographic questions at the conclusion of the interview, most participants (94%; n=30) responded with normative sex categories (i.e., male, female); one participant described zir gender as trans and one as non-gendered.

In responding to the open-ended question, "How would you describe your sexual orientation?," 38% of my interview sample identified as heterosexual, 10% identified as heteroflexible, 3% identified as primarily heterosexual with some bicurious tendencies, 21% identified as bisexual, 7% as pansexual, 3% as queer, 14% as gay, and 3% responded, "I like everybody." Lesbian-identified participants are missing from my interview sample but are included among the discussion board participants. Yet for at least two important reasons, the gender-based sexual orientations participants reported in demographic questions at the end of the interview do not fully capture the often complex sexual orientations and experiences participants reported during the course of interviews. First, many participants reported engaging in what they defined as sexual BDSM with partners of any gender, despite reporting monosexual orientations (orientations limited to people of one gender, such as heterosexual and gay) when asked demographic questions. Second, many participants also reported that their BDSM orientation (e.g., dominant, submissive) was more important to them than their gendered sexual orientation. This apparent conflict between the normative sexual orientations reported in response to standard demographic questions and the more complex, often non-gender-based orientations that participants described in the course of the interview suggests that standard demographic questions about sexual orientations may not adequately capture the complexity of individuals' sexual orientations.

Rethinking the Concept of Sexual Orientation

On a 2004 discussion thread titled "Gender or D/s role—which trumps the other?" participants explicitly debate the relative importance of gender and BDSM role in the selection of BDSM partners. Perhaps referencing Califia's (2000) infamous assertion "if I had a choice between being shipwrecked on a desert island with a vanilla lesbian and a hot male masochist, I'd pick the boy" (159), as the initial poster asks,

> My mostly straight master once made the casual comment that he'd rather be stranded on a desert island with a male submissive than a female non-submissive, and that's where the idea came from. If you could only have one erotic partner for the rest of your life, would you prefer one who was compatible in terms of D/s role or in terms of gender?[3] When does gender trump D/s role? When does D/s role trump gender? For example, would you prefer to be stranded on a desert island with a member of your less-preferred gender but more-preferred BDSM role or vice versa? For example: for straightish dommes, would you prefer a submissive female, or a non-submissive male?

This question gets to the heart of the complexity of sexual orientation among BDSM participants, highlighting the importance of both BDSM role and gender in participants' selection of partners.

It is important to note that while the participants in the present study were more likely to report engaging in BDSM with partners of a variety of genders (60% of the interview sample) than to report gender limitations on their choice of partners (40% of the interview sample), these results cannot be understood as a simple case of using versus rejecting gender as a criterion for selecting partners. Even for those who engage in BDSM with partners of a variety of genders, gender often plays a significant role in their choice of partners, as the following sections show. Importantly, as discussed earlier in the chapter, not all participants view all BDSM activities as sexual. Some participants engage in BDSM with partners of a variety of genders, but they define only the interactions that occur with individuals of their preferred gender as sexual. In this chapter, I focus specifically on interactions, experiences, and preferences that participants frame as sexual.

In this section of the chapter, I identify and analyze two types of sexual orientation reported by BDSM participants that are not adequately accounted for in the current gender-centric model of sexual orientation. Unsurprisingly, for some participants, gender is the most important component of their sexual orientations as well as the most important criterion for selecting partners; because these participants' experiences can be analyzed through the traditional concept of gender-based sexual orientation, I do not focus on these participants in this chapter. However, for many participants, gender and BDSM role are equally important components of their sexual orientations and are equally important criteria in the selection of partners. Further, for the majority of participants in this study, BDSM role is more important than gender as a component of sexual orientation and is a more important criterion in the selection of partners. For these participants, the relationship between gender, BDSM role, and sexual orientation is complex and not adequately captured by the traditional gendered concept of sexual orientation.

Expanding the Concept of Sexual Orientation Beyond Gender

Among participants who engage in BDSM with partners of a variety of genders—the majority of participants in this sample (60%; n=19 in the interview sample)—the importance of gender varies, as do the specific ways participants use gender when making decisions about and interacting with BDSM partners. Among these participants, two main patterns related to the use of gender in the selection of and interaction with partners emerged. In the first pattern, BDSM role and gender are equally important component of participants' sexual orientations. In the second pattern, BDSM role is *more important* than gender as a component of participants' sexual orientations. Significantly, this is the most frequent pattern in my data, suggesting that for BDSM participants in particular, the traditional gender-based model of sexual orientation may not adequately reflect their sexual desires, attractions, and/or identifications. These two patterns suggest that the traditional gender-based model of sexual orientation may not completely or accurately reflect individuals' sexual orientations.

A Blended BDSM Role/Gender Orientation

In the blended orientation model, BDSM role and gender are equally important components of participants' sexual orientations. In response to the question about gender and BDSM role "trumping" each other, for example, one participant writes,

> I wouldn't be sexually compatible with a dominant woman, because I'm straight; I wouldn't be sexually compatible with a 'nilla man, because I'm kinky. So the desert island thing is kind of a wash, in that regard. I would not be erotically interested in either a dominant woman or a 'nilla male (on or off the island); the former would be incompatible due to gender, the latter due to lack of kink. No trump.

One of the most interesting patterns that emerges among many of those with this blended orientation who identify as switches is a preference for bottoming to people of one gender and topping people of another. For example, another participant who responds to the question about "trumping" explains, "I'm sub to women, and I like topping men very much." Similarly, Chris, who identifies as a switch, told me,

> I've always felt more how should I say—more—I felt safe being a little more sexually aggressive with women. And then more sexually or sensually submissive with other men. So even through college, when I think of that, when I had a boyfriend, he was always on top, he was always the top, I was always bottom.

Similarly, on a 2005 thread titled "Switching based on gender," posters describe an interaction between BDSM role preference and gender preference. Like Chris, the initial poster describes submitting to men and dominating women, writing, "I am a switch who is submissive with males and top with females. I don't really try to understand it, it's just how it is, but I do wonder how many others are out there like me who are gender-specific switches." Another writes, "I am a definite sub bottom with men, but when I have fantasies of women, I'd want them as my slaves. I'm not sure why but it's true." Yet another explains, "I am sub to male top to female." For participants such as these, there is an interaction between their gender preference and their BDSM role preference. Which specific role they prefer to enact at a particular time influences the gender of the partner(s) they choose to interact with.

A Non-Gendered BDSM Role Orientation

In the final and most frequent orientation reported by participants in this study, BDSM role plays a much more significant role in sexual orientation than does gender, and many participants report not using gender at all when selecting BDSM partners for what they define as sexual play. For instance, Alex says,

It's not whether I'm gay or straight. And with Christina, she's a female. She was a straight woman. And she was the one that first started me in this. I had no problem submitting to her any more than I do with Sir [Alex's current, gay male-identified dominant]. Because it's more about the connection than the gender of who it is.

Likewise, when asked, "Does gender matter when you are considering a potential BDSM partner?" Pat says, "It isn't really much difference. . . . So I play with women and men." Similarly, Cody says,

I really don't think that gender had anything or has anything to do with what I do because I play with men and women. So I really don't think gender would have anything to do with it. At all. Because I've played with some really rugged lesbians and some straight men have bottomed to me. And gay men as well. I'm a gay male. I've actually owned a female slave. You know. So gender doesn't have anything to do with it at all.

For Cody, gender is irrelevant to zir choice of BDSM partners. Cody emphasizes having "actually owned a female slave," indicating that Cody's indifference to the gender of BDSM partners is not restricted to casual or time-limited scenes but extends to long-term relationships as well.

Harper also explains viewing gender as irrelevant in the selection of BDSM partners:

To me gender has no relevance in who I'm attracted to. The best way I can describe it is I see gender simply as an issue of plumbing. And I don't understand why that would affect why you care for somebody or how you care for somebody or whether or not you're attracted to them. That just really makes no sense to me. . . . I enjoy playing with male, female, TG [transgender], TS [transsexual], and everything in between. It really makes no difference to me. To me the importance is the mental connection. And enjoying the play. And plumbing's really not an issue to me. So what gender I play with is not an issue at all.

For Harper, BDSM is about the mental connection with another person—a connection that can exist with partners regardless of gender. Similarly, Shawn, who identifies as a top, says, "I'll play with a guy as much as I'll play with a girl. . . . For me it doesn't matter if you're a female or male or something in between, making your transition."

This non-gendered BDSM role orientation is also reflected by many of the participants who responded to the discussion board question about gender and BDSM role trumping one another in participants' preferences for partners. One participant, for example, responds,

> I wasn't going to answer this question because I'm a bisexual without any particular preference for one gender or the other. Then I remembered that the *reason* that I don't particularly have a gender preference is because, for me, D/s compatibility almost always trumps gender completely. So give me a good dominant of either gender over any kind of non-dominant.

The next participant agrees with "what she said." The following poster agrees as well: "I'd rather have a submissive male than a nonsubmissive female. I agree . . . it's all about the D/s compatibility vs. gender. ALWAYS." And another writes, "It would have to be Dom—male or female for me." Similarly, a different poster writes, "In my case, I'd pick D/s over gender." For these participants, BDSM role trumps gender when it comes to selecting BDSM partners. For these participants, the traditional gender-based model of sexual orientation cannot adequately capture their process of selecting partners, since gender is significantly *less* important than BDSM role among these participants. Rather than simply extending the traditional gendered model of sexual orientation to also include BDSM role preference, the orientations and methods of selecting partners reported by these participants suggest the need to develop models of sexual orientation that are not based primarily on gender.

COMPARISONS BETWEEN BDSM AND LGBT ORIENTATIONS

Without prompting, seven interviewees drew comparisons between LGBT and BDSM orientations and experiences, focusing on similarities in stigmatization, coming-out processes, and the notion of an "innate" or "hardwired" sexual orientation, further emphasizing many participants' understanding of BDSM as a sexual orientation in its own right. Aubrey, for instance, said of identifying as a submissive,

> It's actually been something that has been part of me for like a really long time. Like an analogy like I make when I explain it to people that I talk to about it's like I think sort of like for a person who becomes aware of their sexual orientation much later in life. But then when they look back on it they see that they always were. . . . And I sort of realized that was my sexual orientation.

Similarly, Shannon identifies as a dominant: "It's who I am. It would be like being homosexual. It's part of who I am and it just is. And you can't just make it stop. It's just how I'm wired." Dominique, who also identifies as a dominant, echoes this account, saying, "I think that's just something that is naturally part of who I am. It's kind of like if you're gay you're gay. You don't really decide to be gay. You just are." And Jordan, who identifies as a slave wife, says,

> You know what if this person was a lesbian and they came out to their parents and you know they were cool with it. A person that's a slave and that's kinky and submissive, you know she should feel she should be able that side of her should be able to come out you know as far as serving her master. . . . It's not like you can turn off that part of your personality. . . . You know if the person's gay or lesbian and if the person's like I am—a slavewife—it's not like they can turn that off. It's an extension of your body and of yourself. It's your personality and all that.

Drawing on discourses of gender-based sexual orientation as a matter of "wiring" and a "natural" part of the self that can't simply be "turned off," participants such as Aubrey, Shannon, and Dominique use comparisons with LGBT orientations to frame BDSM as a natural, hard-wired sexual orientation similar to gender-based sexual orientations.

DISCUSSION

While the move away from identity-based to practice-based research designs has significantly improved the accuracy of sexuality research, this study suggests the need for further refinement of our approach to sexualities. The findings of this study suggest that individuals may not include their non-normative or alternative sexual experiences, such as BDSM experiences, when responding to questions about their sexual practices unless specifically asked to do so. Additionally, the surprising finding that some individuals who perceive BDSM as sexual and engage in BDSM with partners of a variety of genders self-identify with monosexual orientations (e.g., gay, heterosexual) suggests that "sexual orientation" may have previously under-recognized limitations as a conceptual tool. Individuals may consider only their mainstream or normatively recognized sexual experiences when identifying their sexual orientations, for example.

Sexual orientation may also be of limited value as a conceptual tool when working with individuals whose sexual identities or orientations are based on social categories and identities other than gender—such as dominant and submissive, in the case of BDSM. This suggests that sexuality research must be conscious of identities, practices, and orientations relevant to specific kinds of sexual practices and interactions. It also lends additional support to Yost's (2007) argument that "meaningful identities, beyond gender and beyond sexual orientation, must be incorporated into research designs whenever possible, in order to avoid imposing larger cultural norms on subcultures that conceptualize gender and sexuality in more complicated ways" (152). Rather than eliminating sexual orientation as a conceptual tool when working with individuals whose sexualities are not based significantly on the gender(s) of their partners, we might usefully extend the concept of sexual orientation to include non-gendered orientations.

These findings of this study have both methodological and conceptual implications. Methodologically, they suggest that relying on demographic questions about sexual orientation may not accurately capture the gender(s) of BDSM participants' partners. More participants reported engaging in sexual BDSM with partners of a variety of genders than reported polysexual orientations in response to demographic questions. This suggests that people who participate in alternative sexualities—including but not limited to BDSM—may not always include their alternative sexuality practices when responding to standard demographic questions. More research is needed to better understand *which* types of experiences people are most likely to rely on when asked to identify their sexual orientations. Conceptually, these findings suggest that "sexual orientation" may be too narrow a concept to adequately reflect the criteria people rely on to make decisions about which individuals they will engage in sexual activities with. Further, these findings suggest that there are some practices, such as BDSM, for which the traditional gendered concept of sexual orientation is an inadequate conceptual category. These findings also suggest that the ways in which individuals use gender in selecting sexual partners vary across particular kinds of sexual contexts or activities (e.g., BDSM compared with "vanilla" sexual activities).

Developing models of sexual experiences and orientations that can illuminate non-genitally centered sexual orientations is likely to be of significant benefit in our continually evolving understanding of sexualities and sexual experiences. Because our present models of sexuality are built around homo/ hetero binary understandings of sexual experiences that rely on sex category and gender, these models cannot account for desires and experiences *not* organized primarily according to genitals, sex category, or gender. As Weiss (2006) explains, "unintelligible desires" (Valentine 2003:123, quoted in Weiss 2006:230)—desires that fall outside hetero/homo logics of identity—have received little scholarly attention (Crawley, Foley, and Sheehan 2008). Developing models of sexuality that do not assume that sexual experiences are genitally centered or organized through the logics of sex category and gender can help us develop a more accurate understanding of the range of sexual experiences, identifications, and orientations that exist in the empirical world.

NOTES

1. "Zir" is a gender-neutral pronoun that replaces his/her; "ze" replaces she/he. Both because participants described gender identities and expressions that do not always correspond with dichotomized masculine/feminine categories and because many participants described different gender identifications and/or performances in different settings, I assigned gender-neutral pseudonyms to interviewees and refer to interviewees by these gender-neutral pronouns.

2. The responses of two participants with whom I conducted a joint interview were inaudible during the sexuality section of the interview tape and are excluded from this analysis.

3. The first part of the question was added by the initial poster after the thread had received several dozen responses.

PART IV

SEX, EMOTION, AND IDENTITY

The sociology of emotions, though not the domain of symbolic interactionism, is an important and rapidly expanding direction for interactionist research. In particular, symbolic interactionists are concerned with how emotional experience and understandings shape social life and, in this case, sexualities. This section deals also with sexual identity, but it focuses primarily on the role of emotions and emotional experience in identity construction and negotiation.

Chapter 13 lays the groundwork for thinking about the centrality of emotion in sexual identities (broadly defined). In this chapter, Clare Forstie illustrates the connection between talking about feelings (what she calls "discursive emotional labor") about a lesbian social space and lesbian identity more broadly. Forstie's analysis uncovers the extent to which people rely on emotional expression to understand ourselves and our social spaces. It also demonstrates the symbolic value of emotional expression in social interaction. Using Forstie's model of "emotion flows," we can think more deeply about how people *use* emotion in constructing, resisting, and otherwise navigating sexual identities.

From a symbolic interactionist perspective, the study of emotion is crucial to a fuller sociological understanding of sexuality. The social control of sexuality (recall, for example, Chapter 3 by Luminais) has drawn on essentialist assumptions about sexual behavior and emotions—particularly love and intimacy. In other words, our beliefs about what sex *means* to people has impacted our sexual choices and behaviors. This has been especially constraining for women. The social control of sexuality has translated to the social control of women. This control is tethered to essentialist assumptions about the relationships between sex and emotion. It is only relatively recently that scholars are beginning to draw deliberate theoretical distinctions between sexual behaviors, desires, and arousals from eroticism, love, and intimacy (Kipnis 2004; Newmahr 2011; Shilling and Mellor 2010). A symbolic interactionist perspective of emotion highlights emotion as a form of communication between people, through which we both reflect and create social meaning. A social constructionist approach to emotion takes this a bit further, exploring how emotions come to be felt and interpreted the way that they are.

The notion of "intimacy," for example, has a long history in sociology. Studies of sexuality have frequently assumed that sexual contact—and particularly sexual intercourse—was intimate, that people (again, especially women) felt emotionally connected during sexual acts. This continues to reinforce the sexual "double standard," in which casual sex for women is far more stigmatized than casual sex for men—particularly with multiple partners. Emotion, then, is both a source and explanation of social control, for it is the assumption that we know how women do feel about sex, coupled with how we think women should feel about sex, which results in the marginalization of people who deviate from sexual norms. Emotion is also, of course, a means of social control, for the stigmas themselves operate on the level of emotion. In seeking to control people's sexual desires, behaviors, or arousals, we shame them—by, for example, calling them sluts, fags, or perverts. It is the *goal* to make them ashamed of their sexual selves. These stigmatic labels function as emotional weaponry: a primary means of informally controlling sexual behavior. The study of what people say they feel—and when and why they say they feel it, and the relationship of the saying to the feeling—is therefore central to understanding sexual experience in a social context.

These values need to be understood as part of an ideology of lifelong dyadic monogamy that underpins our social system. People are increasingly rejecting the monogamous dyad as the model for lives and for families, and researchers challenge the assumptions that monogamy is natural (Anapol 1997, 2012; Heckert 2010; Ryan and Jetha 2010; Sheff 2005). Elisabeth Sheff's chapter discusses the ways in which polyamorous people understand the ends of their relationships. Like Chapter 13, this chapter (14) explores the way in which people use emotional discourses in their identity projects. In addition, Sheff's work demonstrates that polyamory is based on the construction of sexual meanings in opposition to mainstream meanings about sexual monogamy and love. The standard scripts around relationships that "work" and relationships that "fail" understand failure as cessation and success as continuation, regardless of the experiences of people in these relationships. When people doubt that poly relationships "work," what they are really asking is whether sexual nonmonogamy is feasible over time. This question is built on the idea that monogamy—and the accompanying ideas of sexual ownership and jealousy—is natural to human beings. The rapidly increasing challenges to this assumption contribute to new and changing sexual meanings. Polyamorous relationships challenge the idea that the best measure of a sexual relationship "working" is the continuation of the sex and that romantic love and sexuality are inherently intertwined.

However, as sex becomes less private over time, the picture changes, as does what we experience as "intimate." We see increasing evidence of non-intimate sexual encounters, and of nonsexual intimacies. The centrality of the "bromance" in contemporary cinema is one example of our current understanding of nonsexual intimacies. Other examples include nonsexual sadomasochistic play (Newmahr 2010a, 2010b, 2011), erotic pedagogical relationships (Rowe 2012), and romantic asexual relationships (Cole 1993; Przybylo 2011; Scherrer 2008). This understanding of intimacy as an emotional experience is at the heart of Chapter 15. Scott and Dawson and I explore asexuality as it pertains to experiences of intimacy, desires for intimacy, and conceptualizations of the intimate self. Forstie's "emotion flows" (Chapter 13) can be used to think about the way that these understandings of intimacy are used in constructing asexual identity and self-concepts. Finally, in illustrating the social embeddedness of the process of becoming asexual, Scott and Dawson and I problematize our understandings of intimate experience and intimate relationships.

Overall, this section illuminates intersections of the study of sexuality with the study of emotion, from a symbolic interactionist perspective. By treating the often-overlapping areas of inquiry as distinct from one another, we can more clearly understand the multiple and proliferating contemporary challenges to heterosexual, monogamous, dyadic sexuality.

Staci Newmahr

CHAPTER 13

"BITTERSWEET" EMOTIONS, IDENTITIES, AND SEXUALITIES

Insights From a Lesbian Community Space

Clare Forstie

In 1995, Ann[1] and her sister opened Sisters, a Maine lesbian bar, in a transitional Portland neighborhood between tourist, industrial, and postindustrial spaces. From 1995 until 2005, Sisters was known locally as Portland's only lesbian bar, one that catered, as Ann explained, to the needs of women and, in particular, to the Portland lesbian community. While the physical space of Sisters has disappeared from this urban landscape, emotionally ambivalent stories about the bar continue to circulate in queer communities in and around Portland. Talking about Sisters's final night, Nicki, one of Sisters's regulars, recalls,

> I hate country music, and I remember they played, "I Love This Bar, I Love That Bar," or whatever that song is, and I saw [Ann, the bar owner] sitting up in the little lounge area. It looked like she might be crying, and I look around, and all the regulars are kind of, you know, misting up too, and . . . Almost surreal, almost surreal that last night, um, and maybe I was drinking too much, but it was awesome and awful, all at the same time—in the same wave, like, you knew it was done, but here it was, like you've always known it kind-of-thing and how you wanted to remember it. It was a good last night. [It was a] sad February . . . Yeah. (Interview transcripts)

Nicki's recollection represents the kind of emotionally ambivalent comments former patrons frequently made in my interviews; in other words, her emotions seem contradictory, and she expresses loathing of country music, love for the bar expressed by a popular country song, crying, senses of awesomeness and awfulness, the good and the sad. Patrons expressed this kind of intense, emotional ambivalence by describing Sisters's final night as "bittersweet," a word they used to describe the embodied feeling of closing Sisters.

Patrons' affective[2] narratives about lesbian and transgender identities and related community membership and alienation at Sisters point toward the lingering power of emotions to define identities, communities, and the tenuous spaces they inhabit. Patronizing a lesbian bar, in other words, offered opportunities for acceptance, alienation, and loss, and reading patrons' stories with an eye toward emotion suggests that lesbian, gay, bisexual, transgender, and queer (LGBTQ) identities are perpetually changing. Identities, in other words, are not static, and they must be renegotiated as individuals interact with each other and as communities face internal and external social pressures (Burke and Stets 2009). I suggest that what I call "emotional flows" demonstrate this process of identity change. Furthermore, emotional flows are central to the ways in which queer, transgender, and lesbian identities are negotiated and fundamentally change over time.

In the process of identity change, emotional flows operate in two key ways: First, emotional flows are observable at the level of discourse (that is, in conversation) and, second, emotional flows involve labor. Emotions, in other words, are not exclusively or simply naturally occurring; as Arlie Hochschild (1979) has noted, individuals perform some amount of *work* to align their innermost feelings with what they think they *should* feel. In this chapter, I explore how discursive emotional labor relates to the process of identity change by investigating the case of Sisters. Key research questions include how do patrons' discursive use of emotions both shape and result from identity change in lesbian communities? How do ambivalent emotions (in particular, feelings of both support and betrayal) construct shifting queer identities in historically and geographically located spaces? What do we learn about identities by focusing on their emotional discursive production? What is the role of (changing) space in the production of identities as remembered and constructed in an ongoing way? Finally, how do communities use emotion to construct the past, present, and future of identities? I propose, in brief, that the case of Sisters illustrates, first, how emotions are discursively produced within a community. Second, patrons' experiences at Sisters show how emotions both create and result from the process of identity change. For lesbians, these identity shifts have been tightly connected to community understandings of gender, particularly as patrons claimed and rejected a lesbian identity. A model of emotions that emphasizes how they "flow" through this identity change process reveals the complexities of identity change in local spaces. Finally, exploring these questions not only illuminates the process of identity change but also forces us to grapple with the loss of place as a possible or desirable outcome of community-based identity change.

IDENTITY FORMATION AND CHANGES: LESBIAN BARS IN THE UNITED STATES

Many scholars have written extensively about the role of informal "third places"[3] like bars (Oldenburg 1999) in building gay and lesbian communities and identities (Chauncey 1995; D'Emilio 1998; Kennedy and Davis 1994; Stein 1997). Lesbian and gay bars in America emerged as a concrete "homosexual" identity that was being articulated and disciplined by medical and legal establishments. Bars provided an opportunity for gays and lesbians to exercise agency in forming a shared identity against a backdrop of medical narratives of "inversion" and "deviance" and legal proscriptions against gender nonconformity (Chauncey 1995). Bars provided a safe haven and political rallying point for gays, lesbians, and transgender community members, as the resistance to the 1969 police raid at the Greenwich Village gay bar, the Stonewall Inn, demonstrates. Beginning in the 1930s, lesbian bars functioned as safe environments for lesbians to enjoy each other's company and create community; however, even as they offered some protection, bars were also sites of significant financial and physical risk for some lesbians (Kennedy and Davis 1994). This dual role of lesbian bars, in terms of safety (of community) and danger (of exposure) persisted in tandem with national legal, political, and cultural trends (Donnelly 1989; Nestle 1997) as, post-Stonewall, gays and lesbians became increasingly (but not exclusively) socially accepted:

> Beginning in the 1990s, the lesbian bar was undergoing a process of change, mirroring changes in the broader lesbian community. Women of color and radical queers began to challenge the limited boundaries of lesbian identity, and lesbian communities stretched into new geographic and corporeal territories. Arlene Stein argues that, in the early 1990s, "There was no longer any hegemonic logic or center; lesbian culture seemed *place-less*. It had become more and more difficult to speak of 'lesbian' identity, community, culture, politics, or even sexuality in singular terms." (Stein 1997:185)

In the face of these broad changes, explicitly lesbian spaces faced the need to change or risk disappearing. While Sisters might appear to be a straightforward example of this diffusion phenomenon, I argue that understanding the role emotions play in a local case like Sisters should give us pause in considering an overarching narrative of increasing differentiation in lesbian communities. While Stein's assessment of lesbian identity in the 1990s as "tolerat[ing] inconsistency and ambiguity" (1997:200) sounds promising, the experience of Sisters's patrons challenges a simplistic evolutionary LGBTQ narrative: that is, an assumption of linear history in which identities move from separate (lesbian separatism, gay) to multiple (queer). The evidence that Sisters continued to be salient for bar patrons suggests that *lesbian* identity carries the weight of meaning, buoyed by emotions, even after the bar closed. Patrons' narratives offer some explanation about how lesbian placelessness occurs and what this process means for lesbian identities in a local context.

HOW EMOTIONS WORK: A MODEL FOR INTEGRATING EMOTIONS IN STUDIES OF IDENTITY CHANGE

If we understand lesbian identity as constantly changing, emotions are both the motor and the signpost of these shifts. Here, I propose a model that enables researchers to think through how emotions work, through discourse, to produce identity change. I bring together three somewhat disparate sociological theories to develop a modified model for how emotion works in and through identity change: Arlie Hochschild's (1979, 2003) work on "emotion management," Randall Collins' (2004) concept of "emotional energy" in interaction rituals, and Deborah Gould's (2009) focus on power and visibility in political activism. From Hochschild I emphasize the idea of "emotion work" as "the act of trying to change in degree or quality an emotion or feeling" (1979:561), which may take the form of either emotional evocation or suppression. Hochschild also proposes the concept of "feeling rules" as delineating which feelings are appropriate in a given situation, and she explains that feeling rules are tenuous, shifting as ideologies shift (more rapidly or slowly depending on the historical context). Finally, Hochschild focuses on places where emotion work must be done to bring feelings in line with feeling rules. I add that emotion work is being done even in places where a match between feelings and feeling rules seems to exist.

Collins posits the micro-level mechanism of the "interaction ritual" (or, to be more precise, the interaction ritual chain) as the machinery that dynamically converts group interactions into shared cultural symbols. Individuals engage in everyday interactions, these interactions involve meaningful rituals, and the "emotional energy" created through these repeated rituals is the "glue" that binds groups and communities together (Collins 2004). While this industrial imagery is compelling, if we extend this mechanistic metaphor, what happens to the shell of the building once the raw materials of the factory physically disappear or are transformed? In the case of Sisters, all visible markers of the site as a former lesbian bar have been erased, and it now exists exclusively in memory and narrative. In writing about the political trajectory of the AIDS activist network, ACT UP, in the 80s and early 90s, Gould's goal is not unlike Collins's in that she articulates the mechanisms through which political strategies are continually remade. I use the term *emotions* to mean observable expressions of feeling, rather than what patrons "truly" felt, and I suggest that what is important in the way that emotion "works" in a particular social context is more about the narratives people tell about emotions than what is true or not true about a particular feeling. Also, like Hochschild, Gould emphasizes the *practice* of emotions, that is, the idea that emotions *do work* to reinforce or alter affective states. Gould describes the power of emotions to produce specific effects that either reproduce or challenge the existing economic, political, social, or moral order.

Rather than viewing emotion as a machine used by particular operators to stamp out uniform, or uniformly new, cultural or political contexts, I suggest that emotion "flows"[4] in community spaces like Sisters. In proposing this more fluid metaphor for how emotion works in social contexts—in particular, in the ongoing, everyday process of identity construction, negotiation, and change—I identify a set of dimensions along which we might consider specific examples (Figure 13.1). The first dimension is the *level* at which discursive emotion work occurs, from the everyday interactional level to institutional and structural levels (Collins 2004). That is, emotion may flow at a trickle in interaction rituals but may flood a community, causing and responding to significant social change. The second dimension is the *location* of emotions as affective or social (Gould 2009). While emotions may be seen as individual and psychological in origin, their meanings may be understood at a community or social level. That is, emotions may be experienced individually in an embodied way (what Gould calls the *affective* dimension of emotions), but their meaning is interpreted within particular social, historical, and political contexts like bars, along with homes, churches, workplaces, and other public and private spaces. The third dimension is the *function* of emotions as, at one extreme, normative and, at another extreme, deviant (Hochschild 1979, 2003). Depending on the context, emotions may work to align us with others or distinguish our group from the mainstream. The fourth dimension is the relative *visibility* of emotions; here, I point to the role of narrative in the way emotion flows, because it is in telling our stories about emotion that meaning is articulated, translated, and transmitted (Gould 2009). The fifth dimension is emotional *power*, as it wells up around particular issues and may be channeled in specific directions, depending on who may access the resources to shape action at a given moment (Gould 2009). The sixth dimension is the *contingent* nature of emotions. In other words, there is nothing inevitable about the way emotions flow. Small and large changes alter the path of emotions and their relative impact on individuals, identities, and communities (Hochschild 1979, 2003). A final dimension is the *quality* of emotions as they are framed by community members as, on the one hand, exceptional and, on the other hand, ordinary. While critical to identity change in specific communities, emotions are both mundane and remarkable aspects of everyday social life. In what follows, I employ these dimensions of emotional flow to show how emotions and identities are related within community spaces. At Sisters, emotions flowed in particular ways, creating solidarity in shared lesbian-ness for some, alienation around gender expressions for others, and a still-persistent sense of community loss for former patrons more generally.

BITTERSWEET EMOTIONS AT SISTERS

Sisters was, in Ann's words, a "women's bar," popularly known as a lesbian bar, that operated between 1995 and 2005 near Portland, Maine's, downtown tourist hub and the working waterfront. I interviewed one former owner, along

Figure 13.1   Seven Dimensions of Emotional Flows

1. Level: interactional ↔ structural/institutional

2. Location: affective ↔ social

3. Function: normative ↔ deviant

4. Visibility (in narratives): less ↔ more

5. Power: resources to shape action

6. Contingency: depends on context

7. Quality: exceptional ↔ ordinary

with 14 of Sisters's staff and patrons in the spring of 2009. I obtained interview contacts through individual e-mail and phone communications with community members and postings on the Maine Family Affairs Newsletter (FAN) e-mail listserv and Facebook. My goal was not to contact a representative sample of lesbians in the greater Portland area. Rather, I see Sisters as a cultural "text" that has been—and continues to be—"read" by patrons in particular ways, for particular reasons. It is the ways in which Sisters has been read and the questions that those "readings" raise about lesbian, transgender, and queer identities that interest me. The discursive use of emotions (as expressive, to some degree, of the *felt* or *embodied* aspects of emotions) represents one observable way in which the relationship between emotions and identities can be explored.

To begin, then, how does the discursive use of emotions both shape and result from identity change? In other words, how does emotion "flow"? What kind of work is it doing, and how is it shaped by community-based shifts in identity? In the case of Sisters, I propose that emotion flowed in four intersecting and overlapping ways: first, in the construction of safety and family in relation to a perceived external threat; second, in the negotiation of insider/outsider boundaries within the self-identified lesbian community, primarily organized around gender; third, in the ultimate loss of a community space to lesbians and trans-identified patrons alike; and, finally, in the construction of future lesbian, transgender, and queer identities.

The Need for Safety: Lesbian Bars as Safe Spaces

First, Sisters patrons used emotion-laden language as a way to articulate and construct a sense of safety and community in the face of external hostility. Robin, for example, recalled,

> That little fear is in the back of our minds, because we grew up in the era where people got beat up on a regular basis—I'm one of them, I got beat up a lot. . . . Yeah, it was rough, it was pretty rough, and even later on, growing up, moving to Portland, people would chase, people would spit, people would throw things, people would bash into your car. I mean, it happened, and it happened, you know, not infrequently, not every day, but not infrequently. It was a constant battle to not hide; because you want to hide, your instinct is to protect yourself. (Interview transcripts)

Robin's quote highlights the ways in which emotions work to both emphasize the affective experience of marginalization and make this marginalization more visible. Emotions, in this case, help normalize the experience of a marginalized group. Robin uses the second-person "you" to help her audience locate herself in the affective experience of being a marginalized lesbian in Maine's most urban environments. Ann and her sister initially decided to open Sisters against this hostile backdrop. When I asked Ann about what made Sisters different from other bars, she stated,

> My perspective is that it's a women's bar and so that makes it wonderful and that makes it different. And when I go into another type of bar—it doesn't cater to women, it's just. I don't know how to explain it, it just, it's just different . . . I think women are the nurturers and the carers and all of that is brought together in this type of [bar] situation, and so you immediately feel it—it's just like going home, you know, to mom. You feel it. (Interview transcripts)

Ann's quote reveals how emotions flow from the affective to the social; that is, her quote connects the embodied feeling of "going home" to a social need: the need for the bar. In both of these stories, it is the affective, or "felt," experiences of claiming membership in a marginalized group, facing hostilities from others in the urban community, and creating safe, "home"-like spaces that solidify a sense of lesbian community and identity. In these discourses, emotions flow as a unifying force, and both Robin and Ann employ narratives rife with emotionality to connect with a perceived audience: a "you" who experiences a sense of "going home . . . to mom" by visiting the local lesbian bar. However, lesbians' emotional experience of lesbian community within the bar varied, and these variations reflected and contributed to shifts in identity within the LGBTQ community in Portland. Patrons' emotional, embodied experiences at Sisters revolved around the axis of gender, in particular, through butch and femme identities and emerging transgender identities.

Insiders and Outsiders: Butch and Femme Identities at Sisters

As significant elements of lesbian identity, gender and sexuality have historically been performed[5] in multiple, changing ways in lesbian bars like Sisters. In spaces specifically marked as "lesbian," patrons employed clothing, language, gestures, and music to perform gender or sexual identity. A butch-femme system functioned as a central organizing principle of gender expression for lesbians in lesbian bars beginning in the 1930s (Kennedy and Davis 1994; Nestle 1997) simultaneously, this butch-femme aesthetic was itself historically and geographically located. In the 1940s and 50s the butch-femme system offered a range of gendered and sexual styles for lesbians to construct, perform, and reconstruct.

In the 60s and 70s, some lesbians rejected the butch-femme system as an expression of society's sexism, an analysis that was itself seen as a product of middle-class lesbian academic institutions. However, while the butch-femme aesthetic has been criticized and denigrated in spaces outside lesbian bars, it has continued to function as a useful, flexible, and risky system of gender and sexual expression.[6] At Sisters, manifestations of the butch-femme aesthetic heavily leaned toward the butch end of the spectrum with a notable absence of visibly femme-identified lesbians. Interviewees read Sisters's patrons as primarily butch, "soft butch," or "androgynous." Clothing, hair, and music marked patrons of different classes and different generations as butch. The butch-femme aesthetic pervaded interviewees' narratives about gender expression at Sisters, but this system, rather than being singularly perpetuated at Sisters, was challenged by bar patrons. These challenges illustrate the *level, location, function,* and *contingency* of emotions as they continually recreate identity. Meg described her first visit to Sisters and the absence of butch-femme couples there:

> I didn't see a single butch-femme couple at the bar my first time. . . . It was never a problem to just assume that someone was butch or someone was femme in the Midwest. But what I quickly learned in Portland is that when you made that assumption, it was met with a really big correction, um and a lot of feeling, "I am not butch! I am not femme!" whereas in the Midwest like it was like, "Of course I'm butch. Yeah, I'm femme." (Interview transcripts)

Despite the fact that Sisters's patrons challenged the butch-femme aesthetic, this system of gender expression was still clearly used as a framework that interviewees used to understand the primarily butch gender landscape In other words, to some patrons, lesbian identity was visibly connected to a butch or mostly butch aesthetic in the space of Sisters.

Femme-identified interviewees remarked on the absence of visibly feminine lesbians at Sisters, and, given the lack of other lesbian bars in the area, this sense of exclusion was particularly acute for femme-identified lesbians. Lyn stated that "When feminine-identified women would come in, there were often comments about how, like, 'Does her boyfriend know she's here?' And stuff like that." Jamie told me that "when I first started working at Sisters, everybody called me the 'straight girl.'" Casey expressed frustration that "there were definitely times . . . where I would be one of the only two or three people in the bar in a dress, and that was so often remarked upon." In yet another example, Alli described the experience of a friend, a Sisters regular:

> I have a friend who was like, "I go there all the time, but I never get dressed up to go anymore. I don't want to get dressed up." And I said, "Why not?" And she said, "You know, every time I get dressed up and go, people just give me the stink eye all night long, and I'm tired of getting looked up and down. I'm tired of people rolling their eyes" (Interview transcripts)

Finally, Meg described the experience of being a femme-identified lesbian at Sisters as "being femme, I felt a little lonely. . . . I didn't see a lot of people who I perceived to be like me, visibly at Sisters, or visibly around the community in Portland" (Interview transcript). While Sisters was open, the authentic or permissible lesbian gender expression was perceived as butch, while a narrative of femme invisibility or oppression weaves through the stories of currently self-identified femmes.

Stein's assertion that the 1990s brought a rise in younger lesbians' ability to "tolerate inconsistency and ambiguity" is complicated in the space of Sisters, given that femme-identified lesbians at best felt "isolated or misunderstood" (Alli) or at worst "marginalized" (Meg). As Alli stated, "I felt like this was my community. I didn't always know that my community recognized me." Claiming membership by visibly declaring a butch identity allowed bar patrons to be recognized as lesbians, and it also reinforced the association between butch gender expression and lesbian identity at Sisters.

Femme patrons expressed an emotionally ambivalent sense of home-ness at Sisters. First, the emotional sense of alienation was experienced at the interactional level, as femmes responded to experiences of loneliness and criticism and, in some cases, rejection from a more butch-friendly bar clientele. Second, femmes' experience was *located* both affectively and socially, as femmes felt an embodied sense of rejection but attributed this sense to patrons' interpretation of their gender expression as femme lesbians. Third, emotions mark femmes' experience of *deviance* in terms of gender expression and attempted to reconcile this deviance with their simultaneous feeling that Sisters represented "their community." Finally, femmes' emotional expressions highlighted contingency in the way that identity itself was similarly contingent: subject to both "eye-rolling" and protection. In brief, femmes' emotional experience of lesbian identity at Sisters illustrates the first four elements of emotional flows: level, location, function, and contingency. Among femmes, emotions reflect and re-create ambivalent experiences of lesbian identity in a local lesbian bar.

What Is a Lesbian? The Role of Transgender Identities

Both femmes and transgender patrons expressed a sense of emotional contingency at Sisters. As transgender (or trans) individuals have fought for visibility within and beyond lesbian and gay communities, employing a more explicit transgender politics, the effect on gender and sexual expression in third places like lesbian bars remains unclear and unarticulated. The role of transgender individuals and transgender identities in the systems of gender expression in lesbian bars is a heretofore underexplored topic, and trans and queer patrons' existence and persistence calls into question the very legitimacy and authenticity of the concept of a "lesbian bar." For if gender itself is called into serious question, what, really, is a lesbian? Transgender and queer identities changed substantially between the years Sisters opened and closed and played a significant role in the kind of identity created therein.

In fact, many interviewees perceived the rise in transgender identities as contributing to or directly causing Sisters's demise, for better or worse. All but one of the interviewees described either obliquely or directly the increasing number of trans men (female-to-male transgender individuals) in the lesbian community (and the bar owner's and staff members' responses) as contributing to Sisters's closing. For some patrons, trans men chose to leave the Sisters community, and they believed that trans men's refusal to patronize Sisters was an individual, personal decision. Casey suggested that trans men would decide to patronize or avoid Sisters "depending on what your personality was that determined how comfortable you felt or how accepted you felt," but she admitted that for individuals who were new to Portland or questioning their gender identity, "it could feel really threatening." Max, who self-identified as trans, actively avoided Sisters, particularly on the last night it was open:

> My presence there—and transgendered people's presence there in general—would add to—and put salt on an open wound. Because . . . I think there are several people who blame the trans community and people going from lesbians to . . . trans men—that that somehow was a huge contributory factor into Sisters closing. (Interview transcripts)

For some Sisters's patrons, then, trans men chose not to patronize the bar, believing that it wasn't a place of comfort or a place that fit their changing gender identities.

Other patrons explained that trans men had little choice in being excluded from the lesbian community defined by Sisters. They placed responsibility primarily on older lesbians for not responding to the changing needs of transgendered patrons. Lyn suggested that "towards the end . . . that that's why they started losing business, actually, because the community was changing in a certain way, and the owners and the managers I suspect were having a hard time changing as well." Max explained negotiating entrance into Sisters during "ladies' night" as a loss of safety and membership in lesbian community after he began to identify as "gender-queer":

I remember the first time going back to Sisters after like a 3-month hiatus, and kind of identifying as gender-queer, and changing my pronouns, and . . . it was, like, ladies' night, or women's night only, or something like that, and another trans guy got a bunch of us together to go, and quote-unquote protest—a.k.a., see if we can get in and just do what we did every single fuckin' Friday night before we came out as trans—and [the bouncer] stopped us at the door and was like, "you know, this is a lesbian bar, it's a women's-only space, it's a women-only night" and [the manager] was like—you know, they had to have a big talk, and . . . I remember we got in. And I just—I didn't have anything to drink, and I just shook the whole night, like, I couldn't calm my hands from shaking, and the whole day I didn't drink anything 'cause I didn't want to have to go to the bathroom, because the end-all and be-all compromise part of it was, "well, you still have to use the women's restroom, you can't use the men's restroom." . . . But, even now, talking about it, my heart races—because it's not so much that I didn't feel safe; but the people making me feel unsafe, like, 3 months ago, were people that I would feel safer with than my family or cops or, you know, the Army or whatever, you know? And now, all of a sudden, they were against us; but they were us at the same time. (Interview transcripts)

He expressed his frustration at being excluded from the lesbian identity "team": "It was like, [cisgender[7] lesbians were saying] 'wait a second—you're supposed to be on our team!' And then you had the team saying, 'We are on your team, we're just switching up the uniforms.'" Both trans and cisgender interviewees recognized the explicit and implicit ways in which trans individuals were refused access to a previously "safe" lesbian space and, by extension, lesbian family and identity.

The emotionally ambivalent stories both by and about trans men's alienated experiences at Sisters illustrate the ways in which identities seen as deviant *within* lesbian spaces are normalized through the discursive use of emotions. Emotionality—that is, the relative visibility and intensity of trans men's experiences—actively constructs understandings about Sisters and ambivalences about lesbian community. Hurt and anger offer claims to legitimacy and *potential* access to power, although, as Alex (an employee at Sisters) noted, it may have been "too little, too late." Narratives by and about trans men's emotional experiences illustrate the visibility, power-laden, and contingent qualities of emotional flows. Emotions, then, flow through negotiations of lesbian community boundaries and through work that re-creates or challenges those boundaries across time, in ways that *may* make community members feel welcome.

The End of Sisters: Loss of Community Space

Both those who felt alienated *and* those who felt welcomed at Sisters remarked on the sense of loss of Sisters as a community space, however. On the one hand, bar employees and regulars felt betrayed because they perceived lesbians *choosing* not to support Sisters for myriad reasons. In response to the question about whether she hesitated to respond to the interview call, Alex stated,

> My hesitation was only, the part of the bittersweet factor, the bitter part of that bittersweet ending that we had of that generation not speaking up and saying, "This is what I want, this is what it would take for me to come in as many times as you need me to come in to make you go for another 10 years." I think part of—I will always have a part of me that says, "Somewhere, my community failed me." It's part of times changing, but it doesn't take away the hurt, it doesn't take away the disappointment of what you thought was a fight that others didn't think was a fight any more. So that would be where my pouring-salt-in-an-old-wound feeling comes from. (Interview transcripts)

Notably, these bittersweet, affective feelings (oriented toward the bodily experience of taste) are directed primarily internally toward members of one's own community, not outwardly at a perceived onslaught of straight folks. As in Max's comment above, too, emotions flow or work through these narratives in ways that highlight contingency, multiple interpretations, and the fractured nature of identity. Even in this community space, these narratives reveal that identity was fractured all along.

On the other hand, marginalized patrons who ultimately felt alienated at Sisters also keenly felt the loss of the space or, more specifically, what the space of Sisters *represented* to lesbian and queer community in Portland and in Maine more broadly. Logan, who explained in his interview his recollection that "that place sucked!" also described Sisters as "a queer space," one of few spaces available for "running into [queer] people" in the late 90s and early 2000s. Max, whose quote above suggests his own emotional ambivalence about Sisters, explained:

> You know the story of King Solomon? The, you know, the woman has the baby, and the other woman steals it and says, "well, it's my baby," and King Solomon says, "okay, I'll just cut the baby in half, and you can have half, and you can have half." And the real mother says, "don't cut the baby in half. She can have the baby." [But] nobody came together, it was split. And then what we both ended up with was nothing: the trans community ended up with dialogue, but no physical place to meet to reinvent our community; and the lesbian community has no bar and no softball team from that bar. (chuckles) . . . It just really sucks. It was the end of an era. (Interview transcripts)

What is crucial in these comments is the simultaneous unity and fracture that they highlight: that Sisters felt "lost" both to regulars and to those who felt alienated from the bar when it closed but that some meaningful aspect of idealized common identity was also lost *during* the time Sisters was open.

A final way in which emotions flow in patrons' narratives is oriented toward how patrons constructed the future of sexually marginalized identities. In discussing her decision to close Sisters, Ann remarked,

> I was seeing an era come to an end, and I knew there were gonna be people that didn't understand what it meant. And I felt kind of bad that way because I couldn't explain to them what it's going to mean, you know. They thought, "Oh well. It's just, you know, it's just closing. We'll all still be together. We'll all still be, you know, the best of buds," and all that, and I said "You don't understand what a difference it's gonna make." (Interview transcripts)

Ann's quote offers evidence of the kind of emotional exceptionalism patrons used to remind me and each other that things have changed. Sisters, while it was open, offered a space that was *different* from what is available now, and, by extension, the *meaning* of lesbian identity had changed with the closing of the space. However, a final quote by Max highlights again the contingency of emotional flows and suggests that lesbian identities might morph into a newly diverse vision of community. He asserts,

> Sisters will come back once we get through this friggin' economic crisis. It will come back, *somebody* will have it, but I think it's like—it's like Moses wandering through the desert—we need another couple forty years to forget what Sisters was like, so we can reinvent what it should be like. (Interview transcripts)

Max is hopeful that "we" can re-create a newly unified sense of identity around a community space. However, that space remains elusive to Maine lesbians and transgender and queer folks alike.

CONCLUSION: EMOTIONS AND THE FUTURE OF LESBIAN IDENTITY AND PLACE

While the physical space of Sisters transitioned into a hip-looking gastropub that retained no visible evidence of its former life as a lesbian bar, emotionally ambivalent stories about the bar still circulate among its patrons. Emotions both reflect and structure how patrons negotiated lesbian identity at Sisters and in the larger Maine LGBTQ community. I have argued that we might conceive of emotion labor using the metaphor of emotion that *flows* in multiple ways across multiple dimensions in processes of identity change. In focusing on the seven dimensions of emotional flow (level, source, function, visibility, power, contingency, and quality), the work emotions do within changing identities becomes evident. In the case of Sisters, four types of this discursive work emerge: constructions of safety and family; boundary negotiations around butch, femme, and trans gender expressions; management of community loss; and constructions of transgender, lesbian, and queer identities. However, these types of discursive work may not be directly applicable or generalizable to other kinds of discourses around the loss of lesbian, gay, transgender, or queer spaces, given the small group of interviews conducted for this study. I have attempted to illustrate one application of the dimensions of emotional flows, one that reveals *how* patrons' emotional discourses about Sisters create, challenge, and re-create concepts of identity and community that are meaningful within a particular historic, geographic, and small-scale urban context.

In constructing this model, I have added to Hochschild's theory the assertion that emotional labor is ambivalent, that is, enacted simultaneously in multiple dimensions and in multiple directions. To Collins's work I have added that "emotional energy" is not simply shared effervescence but emotion that flows in situations of community loss as well. Finally, to Gould's assertions, I have added that emotion work is enacted in both taken-for-granted, everyday kinds of ways and in what I think of as "small-p" political contexts. In fact, Sisters employees were very clear that Sisters was intended to be an *apolitical* space and, while I propose that really any social space is politically fraught in some sense; certainly the function of Sisters as a gathering—rather than an organizing—place makes it a less obvious site to study.

Thinking about emotions as flows reminds us that social change is neither linear nor persistently progressive and that identities are neither clear-cut nor permanent. Furthermore, emotions play a complex role in actively structuring conceptions of the past and past spaces, identities, and communities. What is crucial for the construction of identities—both as experienced in interactions and as remembered—is the *affective* (embodied and felt) and *discursive* (in narrative and conversation) use of emotions. Remaining attentive to the role emotions play in individual and community negotiations of identity changes allows us to understand *how* and *why* these changes occur.

Sisters ultimately joined the ranks of other lesbian bars across the United States, closing its doors in 2005. Given the experiences of Sisters's patrons, theorists of queer place are faced with an awkward question: Are lesbian, gay, or queer third places desirable, necessary, or viable as identity-building locales? As the case of Sisters suggests, gender expression was and is central to lesbian and queer boundary making both within and outside of the space of the bar, and how community members manage emotion-laden conflicts around gender both constitute and are constituted by these kinds of everyday spaces. In the post-Sisters era, some manifestation of lesbian community persists in Portland, although a physical locale is notably missing. We might ask whether third places like lesbian bars are simply outmoded relics. Patrons might answer that lesbian bars and lesbian places have always been contested, if not outmoded, and lesbian spaces always reside in a tenuous position. Identity boundaries are drawn and redrawn in ways that either retain or limit the possibilities for such spaces to exist.

NOTES

1. All interviewees' names are pseudonyms.

2. Here I use "affective" to mean an embodied sense of emotion, that is, an emotional experience that is *felt* in the body. The term "bittersweet" suggests an

ambivalent, felt emotional experience, one that is simultaneously painful (bitter) and joyful (sweet).

3. Unlike the first and second places of home and work, "third places" are informal, everyday, community-based spaces like bars and coffee shops (Oldenburg 1999).

4. My concept of a sociological model of how emotions flow within and through social life is conceptually quite distinct from the social psychological concept of "flow" (Csikszentmihalyi 1997), which refers to an intensity of individual focus.

5. Here I am indebted to Judith Butler's explanation of gender as performative, as mutually constitutive/constructive and as impossible to escape, that is, bounded by the threats of punishment if the "performance" steps out of the "normal" (Butler 1993).

6. Writing about the butch-femme dynamic in the 1950s and 60s, Smith notes that "butch-femme was a way for lesbians to express aspects of their sexuality to one another. It should not be assumed, however, that the roles were all-defining, that everyone who used them gave them the same meanings, or that they worked equally well for everyone" (1989:399–400).

7. "Cisgender" is the term used to describe individuals whose gender expression matches the gender they were assigned at birth.

CHAPTER 14

NOT NECESSARILY BROKEN

Redefining Success When Polyamorous Relationships End

Elisabeth Sheff

Relationships in the United States at the beginning of the 21st century exist in a bewildering state in which couples routinely promise to stay together "until death do we part" in their marriage vows, even though most people are painfully aware that roughly half of all marriages end in divorce (Cherlin 2010, 405). Although most families have divorced members in their kinship networks, conventional wisdom still defines a marriage or long-term relationship that ends in any other outcome besides death as a *failure*. Children of divorce are said to come from "broken homes" (Fagan 1999), and their parents have "failed marriages" which mark them as personal, relational, and often financial failures (Elmaci 2006). These cultural norms define "successful" relationships as monogamous and permanent in that the two people involved remain together at all costs. In this worldview, sexual fidelity is fundamental to the successful relationship and functions as both a cause and a symptom of relationship success.

Polyamorists, in contrast, define the ends of their relationships in a number of ways in addition to success or failure. *Polyamory* is a form of non-monogamy in which people openly maintain (or wish to establish) multiple sexually and emotionally intimate relationships. With its emphasis on long-term, emotionally intimate relationships, polyamory is different from *swinging*, which focuses more on sexual variety and often discourages emotional intimacy outside of the core couple relationship. Polyamory also differs from *adultery* because poly relationships are openly conducted, so (at least ideally) everyone knows about all of the poly relationships. Some polys are married, and others either cannot marry their partners (bigamy is illegal) or do not want a marital-type relationship with their partners, which distinguishes polyamory from *polygamy* in which people are married in groups larger than two. An even more important distinction between polyamory and polygamy is that both men *and women* have access to multiple partners in polyamorous relationships, which is generally not the case in polygamy. Historically and cross-culturally, polygamy is usually practiced as *polygyny* in which one man has multiple wives, and the wives are "monogamous" with the husband in that they are sexually exclusive with him though he is not sexually exclusive with them. *Polyandry*, or one woman with multiple husbands, is quite rare and frequently involves a woman marrying a small group of brothers or other men who already know each other (Levine and Silk 1997).

Polyamorists use the term *poly* as a noun (a person who engages in polyamorous relationships is a poly), an adjective (to describe something or someone that has polyamorous qualities), and an umbrella term that includes "polyfidelity," or relationships based on both sexual and emotional exclusivity among a group larger than two. Following the polyamorous community habit of making up words to describe things that conventional English does not contain (Ritchie and Barker 2006), I coined the term "polyaffective" to describe nonsexual or affectionate relationships among people in poly families.

Respondents in my research emphasized the importance of choice as a guiding principle for their lives and relationships. Focusing on the utility and health of their relationships, respondents reported that if their relationships became intolerable, violated boundaries, or no longer met the participants' needs, then the correct response was to modify or end the relationship. Tacit, a man in his 40s and an information technology (IT) professional, opined,

> If you are in a relationship or several relationships then you *choose* to do that, every day, whether you recognize it or not. You can stay because you consciously make that decision or you can just stay because you are on automatic pilot, but that is a choice too. (Interview transcripts)

This consciously engaged choice means that polyamorous people acknowledge their own responsibility for their relationships, with little or no social pressure (from the polyamorous paradigm at least) to either stay together or break up. As a result, poly people ultimately define their relationships as both voluntary and utilitarian, in that they are designed to meet participants' needs. Clearly, this self-responsibility is easier to espouse when the people in question are financially self-supporting and do not have children whose lives would be affected by parental separation. Given the framework of those familial and macrosocial constraints, poly people attach diverse meanings to the ends or transitional points of relationships. In this chapter, I first detail the research methods I used in the study and then discuss those meanings that poly people apply to the ends of their relationships. I conclude by examining the social implications of redefining the ends of or transitions in relationships.

METHOD

This chapter is part of a larger project based on three waves of qualitative data collected between 1996 and 2012 through participant observation, content analysis, Internet research, and in-depth interviews. Over those 15 years, I chatted with and observed about 500 people at a variety of poly gatherings (support groups, movie nights, dinner parties, etc.), and interviewed another 131 people (109 adults, 22 children). Like many other researchers who have studied polyamorous populations (Sheff and Hammers 2011), I found that most of the people I interviewed or saw at community events were white, highly educated, middle or upper-middle class people in professional jobs who lived in urban or suburban areas.

Interviews usually lasted about an hour and half and were *semistructured*, meaning that they began with a simple set of questions about why and how respondents got involved in polyamory and their past and current relationships and then focused on whatever the respondent decided was important. I had permission only to speak to adults for the first two waves of data collection,[1] so I spoke to children only in the third wave of data collection and included the children's important adults. Interviews with children were shorter, with simpler language and less intensive probing. I used inductive data gathering methods (Lofland and Lofland 1995) and constant comparative methods (Glaser and Strauss 1967) to analyze interview data and field notes by reading the transcripts over and over and carefully noting what people said, looking for trends, patterns, and variation in what people told me and what I observed. Finally, I let respondents read rough drafts of my writing to make sure I was quoting them correctly and to allow them to further comment if they wanted.[2]

POLYAMOROUS MEANINGS FOR ENDS AND TRANSITIONS

Respondents held three primary definitions of the ends of their relationships: success or failure, shifting interests and needs, and change or transition. While each category is distinct, they are not mutually exclusive in that they often overlap, and respondents' categorization of the same relationship often changed over time. Fewer respondents defined their relationship ends in terms of failure, and many more emphasized their shifting needs and interests, and especially the fluid nature of relationships over time.

It Is Really Over: Success and Failure

Some polyamorous relationships last until one of the partners dies, and in that sense, they meet the conventional definition of "success" because the family members did not separate from each other during life. The Wyss "moresome" (polyamorous group of five or more), a poly family in the California Bay Area, began as a sextet of three couples and evolved significantly over time, losing partners to death and divorce. The original sextet was composed of three legally married couples—Loretta and Albert, Kiyowara and Patrick, and Margret and Tim—who conglomerated into a cohabitational family with children from previous or extant relationships. After 2 years of love, fighting, and conciliation, Margret divorced the entire family, including legally divorcing Tim. The resultant group had only just restabilized when Tim was killed in an automobile accident. Even though the surviving "spice" (the plural of spouse) lost their husband to death, they did not frame it as a "successful" end. Instead of using a success or failure characterization, the Wyss "quad" emphasized the joy they'd had with Tim when he was alive, the pain they felt at his death, and how the relative invisibility of their poly widowhood compounded their sense of loss because the monogamous culture at large did not define them as widowers.

About the same time Tim was killed in the accident, Kiyowara became pregnant with Albert's child and bore the quad's daughter Kethry. Fourteen very full years later, the Wyss quad became the Wyss "triad" when Patrick divorced Kiyowara (legally), Albert, and Loretta (socially). Kiyowara characterized the relationship as a success even though it ended.

> I am glad we are co-parenting and not married. . . . I certainly can't call it a failure; it was a 20-year marriage. And I am glad his current choices are not my problem. Any time a relationship ends there is a tendency to view it as a failure. I was very clear that a relationship that had good times and lasted 20 years was not a failure, it just ended. End does not mean fail. That totally invalidates anything good that came out of it. I had a lot of people remind me that it is not a personal failure just because something had run a full cycle and come to its end. (Interview transcripts)

Kiyowara redefined the end of the relationship with Patrick from failure to relief from dealing with his choices and continued contact as co-parents.

Friends in her poly community "reminded" her that it was not failure but rather the end of a cycle, supporting her redefinition. Such reinforcement allowed these alternate meanings to take on more social gravity and ultimately become solidified as poly social norms that accept the ends of relationships and encourage former lovers to remain friends.

For others, the end of a poly relationship retained the taint of failure in the conventional sense. Although poly community norms encourage people to remain friends with former lovers, some relationships end with such acrimony that remaining friends is neither desirable nor feasible. Respondents in this category were more likely to see the end of the relationship as a failure, both in the conventional sense of ending sexual and intimate relations, and as a *poly* failure in that they broke community norms dictating continued friendly contact with former lovers as friends. Jessica, a 43-year-old woman and registered nurse, had been in a triad when she was in her mid 30s with Mira and James, a married couple with two young children. For about a year and a half, the triad spent five to seven nights a week together, often at the couple's home engaged in family activities like making dinner, doing dishes, and bathing and putting the children to bed. When the triad broke up, Jessica reported feeling like they had failed because

> at the beginning we said that if we were going to be like a family then I would stay connected to the girls, no matter what happened with us [the adults]. And for that time I was definitely, not quite a second mom, but at least an auntie who was around all the time. . . . But then when we broke up, I just realized they [Mira and James] were not who I wanted to spend time with and it was awkward to call them or try to talk to the girls. Mira was especially weird on the phone and . . . eventually I just kind of stopped calling, and now it has been years since I have seen them. So I guess in that way it feels like a failure, because we didn't stay connected like we had planned to. (Interview transcripts)

In Jessica's view, the end of the triad was a failure not only because the adults stopped interacting but also because she lost contact with the children she had lovingly cared for, for over a year and a half.

Because poly relationships can have multiple adults involved, the relationship between or among some members can end while it continues between or among others. In these cases, some may define it as a failure but others may not. Morgan and Clark's family was characteristic of this tendency for some adults to maintain contact even though others stop seeing each other. Morgan and Clark met in college and married in their mid 20s.

After several years of contented marriage and the birth of their daughter, they attempted to form a quad with another female-male couple. Six months later, it was clear to everyone that the quad was not working, and while they no longer stayed in contact, Morgan reported that "I learned a lot from that initial experience so I don't think of it as a failure—it was a learning experience."

Later, when Morgan was pregnant with their second child, she and Clark established another quad with Ted and Melissa, a couple who had been married for almost 10 years. Melissa and Ted's marriage had been in crisis before, and they had separated for almost six months several years earlier but had reunited prior to meeting Morgan and Clark. Ted and Morgan fell in love, and Clark and Melissa investigated a relationship but realized, as Clark reported, "We did not have the right chemistry." Melissa was sometimes close to Morgan and Clark and at other times quite distant, but Morgan, Clark, and Ted established an intimate emotional connection. For 5 years Ted, Morgan, Clark, and their two children spent three to six days per week together and shared many family events.

Eventually, Ted and Morgan's relationship soured and, with hurt feelings on both sides, they stopped seeing each other. Clark, however, reported that he and Ted maintained friendly relations:

> Oh yeah, we get to see him all the time. Either we drive down to [a town about 45 minutes away] or he comes up here. Actually, usually we go down there, probably every other week or so. I actually get along with Ted better than Morgan does right now, so it makes sense for me to take [the kids] down to see him. I know the kids miss him a lot so I definitely put effort in to getting them together. I still like him, too, so it is nice for me to see him, though I don't think I would do it nearly as much if it weren't for the kids. (Interview transcripts)

While Morgan and Ted's relationship fit one definition of failure because they no longer saw each other, the rest of the family maintained a successful relationship with Ted, if success is defined as remaining in contact. This flexible definition allows for polyaffective relationships in which children can stay in contact with adults who are important to them, even if the adults are no longer in sexually intimate relationships with their parents. In that sense, this expansion of options that allows polys to define the relationships as successful (even though they have "failed") also sustains family connections.

MOVING APART: DIVERGENT INTERESTS AND NEEDS

Some respondents like Angela, a 32-year old woman in the IT industry, emphasized the idea that they were no longer relating to former partners the same way (or possibly at all), but rather

> moving apart without blame—people change over time and what worked before no longer does, or what was once interesting to everyone is now boring to some of us who are now interested in this new thing. Like [my ex-husband] Mike with his whole anime thing, that holds no interest for me, absolutely none . . . and he has no interest in crafting, which has become really important to me and takes up a lot of my time. There is no judgment or shame for changing from the people we were when we met at SCA[3] all those years ago, we're just not who we used to be and don't fit together as well anymore. (Interview transcripts)

Like Angela, respondents in this category emphasized divergent interests and decreasing time spent with partners who had formerly shared more interests as the key factors that influenced how they defined their shifting relationships. Poly people tend to have full lives and hectic schedules, so time is at a premium, and how people "spend" it frequently indicates their relational allegiances. If partners spend a lot of time doing different things, then they may develop divergent social lives, resulting in less overlap in social circles and decreasing importance for some relationships as others increase in intimacy and time together. This shift is not necessarily failure; for some, it is simply change.

Some respondents discussed the shifting definitions of relationships as they ended or changed once they were no longer meeting participants' needs. If communication and renegotiation did not address the lack, and the relationship remained unsatisfying or defective despite attempts to address the problems, then poly people either reconfigured their expectations or ended the relationship in that form. Jared, a 46-year-old divorced father of two and health care professional, linked his recent break up with a girlfriend to the fact that the relationship was no longer meeting needs for either of them.

> When I first started dating Janice we were pretty much on the same page with our needs. She has a primary who is out of town a lot and wanted a close secondary, and I am not ready for a primary but wanted a close secondary, so it was great that way for a while. Then she started dating Erika and Mark and began spending more and more time with them to the

point that I only got to see her, from two or three nights a week sometimes down to every other week or something. That just wasn't enough for me—I didn't need to move in with her or anything, but twice a month? I mean, come on. So when it became clear that she needed more freedom and I needed more intimacy, we split. (Interview transcripts)

Characteristic of the many respondents who identified the ability for multiple relationships to meet a variety of needs as a primary motivating factor for becoming polyamorous, Jared and Janice had begun dating to meet their needs for companionship and sex. When the amount or kind of companionship— or any other basic motivator for the specific relationship—no longer met participants' needs, respondents like Jared reported "moving on to other relationships that will meet my needs better, at least I hope." Here respondents usually did see the relationship as ending or at least changing dramatically to something far less than it had been previously. Even so, it was not a failure as conventionally defined—rather acceptance that people change and no one need be at fault.

Not Really the End: Changes and Continuity

For some respondents, simply no longer having sex did not signal the end of a relationship, but rather a shift to a new phase. In these cases, the emphasis of the relationship changed to a nonsexual interaction, but the emotional and social connections remained continuous. JP—a 68-year-old mother of five children with eight grandchildren and one great-grandchild—had been married eight times, four of them to her first husband Richard, with whom she retained an emotionally intimate, nonsexual relationship. Reflecting on her long and varied relationship with Richard, which began in high school when they "got pregnant and got married immediately—both of us were virgins and we got pregnant on our first time, imagine that!" JP reported:

We have a tremendous closeness. We've always been able to talk. Intellectual connection, spiritual connection. Just a very intimate relationship. We've got all of this history together, grandkids, a great-grandchild even! I went to Houston not too long ago, and we celebrated the 50th anniversary of our wedding. We got to celebrate all of it! (Interview transcripts)

While JP harbored no illusions that Richard was perfect, stating that he has a "multi-faceted personality, a wonderful person on one hand, and a male chauvinist controlling jerk on the other," she was able to retain the positive aspects of the relationship and celebrate a 50th wedding anniversary with her longtime companion, even though they had both been married to other people over the years. Their relationship overflowed the boundaries of conventional marriage, and their emotional continuity overshadowed the fact that they no longer had sex.

True to form in poly communities who shape language to reflect their relationships (Ritchie and Barker 2006), some polys reject or redefine the concept of the "ex." Laszlo, a man in his mid 30s, commented that

> the notion of ex is ill-defined unless you have a social context, like (serial) monogamy where at least some "privileged" relationship statuses are single-person-only exclusive. That is, if you don't *have* to "break up" to be with someone else, then attempting to categorize *all* of the people from your past relationships as "ex-" pick-relationship-label is kinda goofy/ nonsensical . . . I can see using the "ex" label structure for relationships that were abusive and continued contact would be unhealthy, but if instead they're still-or-once-again a friend, why focus on what they aren't-anymore instead of what they are-right-now? (Interview transcripts)

While Goddess of Java, a woman in her mid 40s, was clear that "I am not best buddies with all of my exes, not by any stretch" she nonetheless asserted that

> I have other former lovers that I suppose ex would be "a" term for. But, I don't think of them as exes. We were lovers and now we're friends, and ex just seems kind of a weird way to think of someone I'm close to and care about. The real difference here, I think, is that the changes in relationship tended to have a much more gentle evolution rather than "official" breakups. (Interview transcripts)

Rather than an "official breakup," the relationship went through a transition and entered a new phase. Emphasizing the present and continuing existence of the relationship, Goddess of Java defined her former lover as her friend with whom she remained close and caring.

As in most relationship styles, this varies by relationship and depends on how people handle transitions. Sorcia, a woman in her mid 30s, commented that

> of course, it depends on the person. Of my former triad—one parent is . . . not even on the remotest of friendly terms with the other two of us. On the other hand, my ex-wife and I are still good friends. We do the holidays

together with the kids, get together regularly for dinner and generally weather our ups and downs. We consider each other to be family. She moved in with a boyfriend last fall and one of her pre-reqs was being OK with our familial connection. It's turned out much better than I ever expected and it's pretty cool. (Interview transcripts)

Thus, people in poly relationships have a range of relationship outcomes and a wide array of meanings from which to select. Some follow a conventional pattern of alienation when a sexual relationship ends, while others forge views that define former partners as continued intimates, or "chosen family" (Weston 1991).

Shifting the crux of the relationship from sexuality to emotional intimacy can foster more connected and cooperative co-parenting, because it allows for continued and cooperative relationships among adults. While Michael and his co-parent divorced 15 years ago, they continued to cohabit for 6 years afterward, and

we have stayed in frequent contact, taking vacations together (sometimes with our other lovers), continuing to raise our kids in close concert, and recently undertook a major multi-year project together (though we were on opposite coasts). She recently told me that she was thinking about her best friends in the whole world, and of the four people she identified, one was me and another was my long-term nesting partner. (Interview transcripts)

Michael reported that his nonsexual relationships had been crucial to his life and well-being and that being in poly relationships allowed him the unique opportunity to remain not only emotionally intimate in a cooperative co-parenting relationship but also "free 'not' to have sex with your intimate partner(s)."

I have these amazing relationships that were once sexual, and in the monogamous world, if I stayed as close as I am with these women, it would be likely to cause substantial stress, or at least some negative social pressure. And each of my emotionally intimate relationships can be sexual or not, sometimes shifting one way or another, without damaging our basic relationship. In a monogamous world, if I stopped being sexual with my primary partner, this would either be a major source of distress, or might end the relationship entirely. As a poly person, I don't feel uniquely responsible to meet my partner's sexual needs. If it best serves our intimacy not to be sexual, either temporarily or permanently, then we can do that without any other "necessary" consequences. (Interview transcripts)

Michael emphasized the changing nature of relationships over time, as sexual interest waxed and waned due to the vigor of youth, having children, shifting circumstances, and passage along the life course.

Over the years, I've had two lovers, both previously "very" sexually assertive, who found that menopause made sex less interesting and less enjoyable for them. They suspect that this may change back at some point, when their hormones settle down, but in the meantime, sex is pretty much off the table for them with all their lovers. This didn't change our connection at all, though. We still sleep (sleep!) together from time to time, do naked cuddling, and have intense, intimate conversations. We just don't have sex, as it is usually conceived of. (Interview transcripts)

Regardless of whether this relationship phase was truly the end of their sexual connection or simply a hiatus, Michael's long-term relationships with his partners continued despite changing sexual and relational circumstances.

CONCLUSIONS

My data indicate that poly relationships may not last in the traditional sense of permanently retaining the same form. Instead, some poly relationships appear to last more durably than many monogamous relationships because they can flex to meet different needs over time in a way that monogamous relationships— with their abundant norms and requirements of sexual fidelity—find more challenging. While the familiar and well-explored structure that monogamy provides can foster a comforting predictability, it can also constrain the meanings available to people who engage in monogamous relationships. This is not to say that there are no relationship innovators among heterosexual, "vanilla" monogamous people—feminists and others have a long history of creating alternative definitions that provide meanings outside of a patriarchal framework. But the scarcity of these role models frees people in polyamorous relationships to create new meanings and innovate alternative roles that better suit their unique lives. A polyamorous identity framework provides the flexible and abundant relationship choices that a conventional monogamous identity, with its firmly defined roles and well-explored models, cannot.

Such persistent polyamorous emphasis on fluidity and choice has several ramifications for the multitude of ways in which people can define the ends of or changes in their relationships. The most flamboyant version of poly identity is explicitly sexual in that it centers on being open to multiple sexual partners. A quieter version of poly identity, polyaffectivity appears to be more durable and flexible—able to supersede, coexist with, and outlast sexual interaction. Relationships that have such a multitude of options for interaction and define emotional intimacy as more significant than sexual intimacy provide poly people with a wide selection of possible outcomes.

This expanded choice has two primary implications for poly relationships: graceful endings and extended connections between adults. Once a relationship can end without someone being at fault, the social mandate for couples to stay together and fixed in exactly the same way at all costs can relax. As stigma subsides, the subsequent drop in shame and blame simultaneously decreases the need for previous lovers to stay together until they have exhausted their patience and sympathy for each other, and possibly lied to or betrayed each other in the process. Once it becomes clear that the relationship no longer meets participants' needs nor works for people who have grown apart, accepting the change and shifting to accommodate new realities can contribute to more graceful endings and transitions. When people are able to amicably end one phase of their relationship, it increases the chances that they will be able to make the transition to a new phase characterized by continued connection, communication, and cooperation. As one respondent stated, "Don't drag it out until the bitter end, disemboweling each other along the way. Split up while you can still be friends, *before* anybody does something they will regret later" (Interview transcripts).

Dethroning sexuality as the hallmark of "real" intimacy is key to this redefinition. If sexuality can be shared among more than two people and emotional intimacy can outlast or supersede sexual intimacy, then nonsexual relationships can take on the degree of importance usually reserved for sexual or mated relationships. That is, friends and chosen family members can be as *or more* important than a spouse or sexual mate. People who used to be a spouse or mate and remain platonic emotional intimates don't have to be "exes," or ex-relationships, forever defined by what they used to be. They can be friends, co-parents, and kin. This extrasexual allegiance is fundamental to my concept of *polyaffectivity*, or emotional intimacy among nonsexual participants linked by poly relationships.

Expanding important adult relationships beyond sexual confines, whether they be former sexual partners or polyaffective partners who don't have sex, provides people with more templates for interaction and choices in how to define relationships. Such choice becomes increasingly important as the limited range of conventional templates prove unworkable or inadequate for many contemporary relationships. People live a lot longer now than they used to, and these longer life spans include more time to change and potentially grow apart. If they are to remain in relationship, some of these long-lived people require the room to shift and expand over time, outside the narrow confines of previously entrenched social scripts. Others might be wiser to avoid organizing their lives around marriage and instead invest their emotional and material resources in something more durable than romantic love, crafting relationships that provide reciprocal care and support with siblings, friends, or other chosen family members. This need not mean an end to sexual relationships or childbearing, simply a shift in which relationship(s) take on practical and emotional (if not sexual) primacy.

Serial monogamy—the pattern in which two people couple in sexually exclusive relationships for a time, break up, and recouple exclusively with someone else—has replaced classical monogamy in which young people marry as virgins, remain sexually exclusive for their entire lives, and become celibate after their spouse's death. As a social pattern, serial monogamy inevitably creates some families with multiple parents related to children through various legal, biological, and emotional connections. Parents who used to be romantic partners often end up trying to figure out how to create a workable co-parental relationship when they were unable to create or sustain a spousal relationship. For the many people in this situation, remaining on positive terms with a former partner–current co-parent makes the transition less painful for children and more cooperative for adults (Sheff 2013). Crafting relationships able to transition from a romantic phase to a platonic co-parental phase can be challenging. Polyaffectivity provides a pathway to continuity and a way to remain connected across time, even through a breakup and beyond. In an era when conventional stability appears to be difficult for many to sustain, this new form of stability can prove quite useful.

NOTES

1. In many nations, research conducted at universities is overseen by a committee called the Institutional Research Board (IRB) that previews all of the research methods to make sure they will not hurt any of the people who volunteer for the research (called subjects, respondents, or participants). In my case, the IRBs at two different universities were very cautious about my research, and it took a long time for me to get permission to talk to children.

2. For a more complete discussion of my research methods, please see my previous publications in which I go into greater methodological detail (Sheff 2005, 2007, 2013).

3. The Society for Creative Anachronism is an "international organization dedicated to researching and recreating the arts and skills of pre-17th century Europe" that hosts gatherings across the United States (http://www.sca.org/ [accessed October 24, 2012]).

CHAPTER 15

A SYMBOLIC INTERACTIONIST APPROACH TO ASEXUALITY

Susie Scott

Matt Dawson

Staci Newmahr

A few years ago, one major website (Asexual Visibility & Education Network [AVEN]) comprised the online asexual community. As of this writing, although AVEN remains the largest and best known, there are at least three different significant asexual gathering sites, as well as dozens of influential asexuality blogs (*Asexual Experiences*, *The Asexual Agenda,* and *Asexy Beast*, to name a few). Although a lack of sexual desire or attraction is of course not new, asexuality as an identity is a newly emerging phenomenon. Its visibility, in both academia and popular media, is quickly increasing. Like homosexuality in the 18th century, asexuality has become a new "problem" to be explained. Previously, people practiced asexual relations but did not define themselves, and were not defined, in these terms. The most prominent example of this is the *Boston marriages* of the late 19th century (Rothblum and Brehony 1993), in which women cohabited (without sexual relationships) for the sake of emotional intimacy and companionship.

Asexuality has attracted a good deal of scholarly attention in recent years (see Bogaert 2004, 2006, 2012a, 2012b; Carrigan 2011, 2012; Chasin 2011; Przybolo 2011; Scherrer 2008, 2010a, 2010b). Within this body of work, however, asexual identity projects are neglected (Scherrer 2008 and Carrigan 2012 being exceptions). A symbolic interactionist account of asexuality shifts the focus even further toward asexual identities. This can help illustrate how changes in meaning-making around sex, romance, and intimacy give rise to asexuality as a social phenomenon. Further, a symbolic interactionist approach to asexuality allows us to interrogate cultural assumptions around sexuality, intimacy, and romantic love and helps to illustrate the profound changes that are occurring in these meanings. Based on a review and reflection of pioneering studies in asexuality identity, augmented by qualitative research by one of us (Newmahr) on Internet asexuality communities and over a dozen asexuality blogs, we offer a framework for an interactionist approach to asexuality.

Like any other kind of social identity, asexual identities are *relational*: created out of perceived similarities or differences from other groups or categories (Williams 2000). In this case, being asexual involves positioning oneself as relevantly different from cultural norms around romance and sexuality. Scherrer (2008) discusses how asexual people partly come to identify as such by first grasping the meaning of "sexual" from dominant discourses of essentialism: They seek to understand themselves by drawing on the categories, labels, and identifiers that abound in these debates. They also compare themselves to normative cultural representations of romantic relationships, which may be perceived as inclusive or exclusive depending on whether romance is associated with sexual desire. Consequently, asexuals can develop complex forms of identifications, such as "demi-sapiocentered-heteroromantic," which means that the self-identified asexual person is "sometimes-sexual-but-only-when-I-have-an-intellectual-and-emotional-connection-to-a-person-of-the-opposite-sex." In other words, people define themselves sexually not just according to the object, or lack thereof, of romantic attraction (e.g., bi-romantic or a-romantic) but also according to the existence (or not) of context-dependent sexual attraction. Asexual identities therefore include people who feel sexual attraction only in specific circumstances (e.g., only once a relationship has developed); "gray-A" or "demisexual" asexuals fall under this umbrella.

SYMBOLIC INTERACTIONISM AND ASEXUAL IDENTITY

Symbolic interactionists view social identities as meaningful phenomena, in and of themselves. The meanings of identities are shared, defined, and negotiated through interaction (Blumer 1969). Interactionists study the diversity and mutability of these meanings and the social processes of their creation. We propose an interactionist approach to thinking about asexual identities along three different dimensions: meanings, selfhood, and negotiation.

Meanings

The multiple identification labels in the online asexual community testify to the wide range of meanings of the term *asexual*. Some asexuals come to the identity through feeling and/or being less sexual than most people appear to be. For others, this may manifest itself in an "antisex" identity where sex is not merely uninteresting but also something they feel repelled by. However, this does not necessarily imply a political stance of countercultural rebellion or deliberate transgression—not all asexual people are involved in activism and consciousness-raising—but rather a more private sense of difference or exclusion from mainstream cultural norms. Przybolo's notion of the "sexusociety" (2011:447) as "a massive conglomerate of tangentially repeated sexual language, deeds, desires and thoughts" may help us understand how some asexual people view dominant society as obsessed with the sexual. Still others identify as asexual because they are not *always* interested in sex; the identity is not fixed but situational, and contingent on circumstances. The meanings of asexual identity, then, differ considerably and in important ways. What unifies many asexual people is their consideration of themselves, their experiences and situations, as differing from dominant, normative framings of sexuality.

Each asexual story is unique since people have different constellations of experiences, relationships, and interactional contexts to navigate. Within, for example, the subgroup of asexuals who identify as "antisexual" or "sex-averse," the meaning of the same identity may be quite different for a 16-year-old boy who has never experienced sexual desire, compared to a 60-year-old woman who has lost that desire through a "disenchanted" long-term relationship and "drifts" into asexuality as a new identity (see Matza 1964). Similarly, the interactional process of "coming out" as asexual may be a very different identity process for the 16-year-old, for whom masculinity, youth, and expectations of sexual desire are differently intertwined than for his older female counterpart.

Selfhood

The interactionist perspective is concerned with the *social* self, embedded in the interaction order and linking mind to society (Mead 1934). The self is not an objective, fixed private thing but a social object, whose form and meaning emerge out of interaction as a "co-operative process" (Mead 1934:194). This takes place in both the immediate contexts of situated encounters, with their dramaturgical significance (Goffman 1959) and over time as experiences develop into patterns of interaction (Becker 1963). Actors orient their social action toward each other, taking into account the meanings they interpret from the "conversation of gestures" (Mead 1934) between self and other, gradually converging upon a set of working definitions to understand and frame their experiences.

This makes identity an inevitably relational process, whereby actors develop selfhood not only as an individual "I" (subjective thoughts and feelings) but also as a social "Me" (an image of oneself through the eyes of the generalized other). My understanding of who I am is dependent on who others believe Me to be, and how I imagine myself from their perspective:

> It is only as the individual finds himself *[sic.]* acting with reference to himself as he acts toward others, that he becomes a subject of himself rather than an object, and only as he is affected by his social conduct in the manner in which he is affected by that of others, that he becomes an object to his own social conduct. (Mead [1913] 1964:143)

Asexual identities exist partly in relation to sexual identities. They are defined by comparison with other forms of sexual identity—as indeed are all sexual orientations. These relational identities render possible a multiplicity of asexual identities. The gray-A self, for example, is thus about moderation in relation to perceived extremes; the identity signifies to others that it is "in the gray area" between other forms of sexual desire and/or behavior.

Negotiation

Meanings that are attached to a particular identity, such as asexuality, will be important not only to the individual so defined but also to significant others (Mead 1934) who surround him or her and whose attitudes constitute their lifeworld. "Identity," in this view, is not a final state to be achieved, but rather a process of *identification* (Williams 2000) through which individuals associate or dissociate with different possible identities and navigate the boundaries in between. Identity projects are therefore "negotiated in, and emergent from" everyday activities which make us aware of our own and others' "gendered and social lives" (Jackson and Scott 2010a:91). A poster on AVEN likens sexual behavior for asexuals to an adolescent trying her first cigarette, indicating that disliking the cigarette is not a reason to stop; she still smokes it and pretends to like it because everyone else seems to. Here, peers are invoked as reference points through which she comes to identify as asexual; this can also be true of intimate others. An individual's understanding of her- or himself as asexual can emerge and change during intimate relationships as the meanings of being asexual and in a relationship are negotiated. Indeed, the meaning of "being asexual" may change from something that had been thought of as purely a personal matter to something that suddenly has implications for others, such as a partner. These partners, who research indicates are unlikely to identify as asexual themselves (Carrigan 2012), will have to adapt to this asexual identity and consider how it will affect their intimate relationship. Consider the role of identity in the following story:

> I am 29 and I have been married for 1 year. We love each other unconditionally but the one thing we have always struggled with is our sex life. My husband wants one and I could care less [sic]. It's for years been a very stressful topic upsetting us both emotionally. Him thinking he was undesirable me thinking I was broken because I lacked desire. Lots of tears, and shouting, and confusion and resentment. But we muscle through it and work together. About a week ago I discovered the vocabulary I needed to discuss the issue at hand. I was Asexual. We have been talking about [it] incessantly. It suddenly makes everything so much clearer. We are a little scared and there is a little mourning involved and confusion for sure. But we are also deeply relieved. The blame and resentment can fade and we can begin to grow. We have a long road ahead of us and will probably need some guidance and a friend on occasion. But already we feel closer than ever and empowered with our new knowledge. (Pan'sShadow 2013)

This story illustrates the power of the adoption of an identity in the negotiation of the poster's relationship. Viewing the identity as an explanation of her situation, the identity project lifts a burden; it provides her with a vocabulary and a community to help her navigate social and sexual waters. The emergence of asexual spaces, including online communities, has created additional forums for identity negotiations.

Symbolic interactionists view identities as fluid: constantly unfolding and perpetually unfinished, subject to continuous reflection and revision. Asexual identities are socially mediated experiences of *becoming*, rather than fixed states of *being*. Whether and to what extent individuals come to identify as asexual is just one of many paths that their life course may take, affected and shaped by their experiences of interaction.

Identities emerge as this open-ended process begins to consolidate and converge toward an integrated set of meanings, especially when these can be linked to a particularly dominant master status (Hughes 1945). Certain role performances may become more salient than others and lead to greater levels of commitment (Stone 1962). Where this is met with social reactions of disapproval, the individual may encounter deviant or stigmatizing labels that may prove to be "sticky" or fateful for interaction (Goffman 1967). This in turn will inform the biographical identity work actors do to make sense of their lives retrospectively and the way they narrate these experiences through (a)sexual stories (Plummer 1995). However, every narrative is only a snapshot, a situated performance (Denzin 1989), and an individual may tell several asexual stories over their life course. An AVEN discussion about the "ace" identity (a positive representation of asexuality as liberating and authentic) demonstrated the fluidity of the asexual identity. One poster, for example, reported finding the label limiting and was therefore abandoning it, while another expressed that identifying as ace at present did not preclude adopting other sexual identities in future.

An interactionist understanding of asexual identity involves complex processes of differential meaning, social selfhood, negotiation, and the development of an identity trajectory. All of these theoretical concerns place the understanding of asexuality within a social context. Symbolic interactionism can achieve a more sophisticated understanding of how individuals both *become* and *be* asexual. Since this is a profoundly relational process, it also raises questions about intimate others.

SYMBOLIC INTERACTIONISM AND ASEXUAL INTIMACY

Generally, symbolic interactionists reject the common conceptualization of "intimacy" as a characteristic of a relationship that resides in relationship structures, designations, or other conditions. Instead, interactionists call for a view of intimacy "as a social situation, with a focus on the moments in, through, and by which people construct intimate experience, regardless of the nature of the relationship, or of the emotional experience of the intimacy" (Newmahr 2011:169). This understands intimacy as emerging from and produced within particular interactions and meaning-making practices. Scholars have argued that as meanings and practices of sexuality have changed, intimate life has also changed (Giddens 1992), but interactionists are interested in what, precisely, intimacy *is*: what we mean when we talk about intimacy, what it looks and feels like to people, and how it is created and experienced through social interaction.

An interactionist investigation of asexual intimacy might therefore explore the same dimensions we have used to discuss asexual identity: meanings, negotiation, and social selfhood.

Meanings

Much of the research on romantic intimacy presumes that sexual and romantic desires are intrinsically linked, with those in relationships seeking both. Social representations of romantic intimacy either subsume sexual attraction within romance (Jackson 1993) or see lust as central to modern ideas of romantic love (Evans 2003). One crucial interactionist question, then, is, given that hegemonic notions of intimacy are conflated with sex, what does intimacy mean to people who reject this association within their own relationships? To understand this, we can look at the processes of entering, maintaining, and leaving intimate relationships. It has been suggested that asexuals engage in "ongoing and creative" attempts to develop alternative practices of intimacy (Carrigan 2012:14). Other studies demonstrate that people construct intimate experiences through the transgression of interpersonal boundaries—whatever those boundaries are (Katz 1988; Laurendeau 2008; Newmahr 2011). Georg Simmel surmised that "intimacy exists . . . if its whole affective structure is based on what each of the two participants gives or shows only to the one other person and to nobody else" (1950:126–27). Following Simmel, Newmahr argues that

> what is experienced as intimacy is what is understood as somehow *distinguishing the relationship from others*. As ideas about what is protected and private change, the experience—and quest—for intimacy also changes. The (potential) transformation of intimacy lies not in the places where intimacy newly appears, but in the processes through which it is created. It lies not necessarily in marriage, disclosure, or sex, but anywhere that people experience each other *differently enough* than other people experience them (2011:172).

Hence, blogger Semiel, who identifies as "aromantic," in a post about what he terms the "intimacy crisis," muses:

> A lot of my treasured moments with people have to do with sharing some special level of intimacy with them. For instance, I've been casually involved with a certain girl for several months, and the most meaningful moment in that relationship so far is when I was allowed to be there during a family crisis. The level of vulnerability and connection shared there was way more important than any of the sexual things we've done. . . . If we decouple intimacy, sex, and romance, then we have so

many more ways we can make our relationships work for us. Why not have a straight guy and an asexual guy as primary partners, with the straight guy having sex with women on the side? Why not have a triad where only one of the relationships is sexual? If we break down the assumption that we have to sleep with people we're intimate with, we can start to solve our intimacy problem. (Semiel, 2011)

For Semiel, being present during his friend's family crisis provided a stronger sense of privileged access to her life, or her emotions, or perhaps her personhood, than sex would have. A discussion of intimacy must take into account what exactly intimacy means and for whom, in order to explore how those meanings come to be.

Negotiation

Other core questions for an interactionist framework for studying asexual intimacy concern the ways in which relationships are negotiated in this context. We use cultural scripts for navigating social situations—that is, learned and patterned ways of feeling, responding, communicating, and behaving within social situations. Given that "intimate" relationships are normatively expected to be sexual, how do people negotiate *asexually* intimate relationships? What does this mean for them, and how do they accommodate their different needs and establish the grounds of the relationship within the contextual and contingent elements of intimacy (Jackson and Scott 2010a:69–71)?

Asexual identities are complex and involve many different factors, including the presence or absence of romantic attraction and, if relevant, the objects of attraction. Therefore, intimate relationships involving one or more people who identify as asexual[1] take multiple forms. People in asexual intimate relationships, lacking any established cultural scripts, need to engage in "life experiments" (Weeks, Heaphy and Donovan 2001) concerning the nature of intimacy within the relationship.

Consequently, the study of intimate relationships involving one or more asexual individuals is inevitably a study of *negotiation* of the behaviors that develop and maintain the practices of intimacy. Since asexuals often enter into intimate relationships with "sexuals," the role of sex in such a relationship must be established via negotiation. Intimacy can be "framed" differently by actors (Morgan 2011), but whatever definitions they agree on will shape the course of the relationship and determine its parameters. The varying and carefully differentiated nature of intimate practices are suggested by Scherrer's participants, one of whom claimed, "I enjoy cuddling, and kissing and even pleasing my wife, but I don't desire sexual intercourse" while another said, "I am sexually attracted to men but have no desire or need to engage in sexual or even non-sexual activity (cuddling, hand-holding, etc.) with them" (Scherrer 2008:627). In a guest post on the blog *Shades of Gray*, C advises sexuals dating asexuals as follows:

> Don't make any assumptions about subtle or non-verbal gestures with regards to sex. Clearly ask questions before any sort of sexual thing happens, since the asexual person might not be okay with things that are sexual in nature. (Elizabeth [The Gray Lady], February 3, 2012)

Lacking a cultural script for these kinds of asexual relationships, asexual intimacy is newly negotiated in these situations. These negotiations vary across these "asexy" relationships and are constituted within their relational contexts.

Selfhood

The asexual self, like any social self, emerges out of relationships. It is at once situated, performed, and presented. Dramaturgically speaking, partners constitute a performance team (Goffman 1959), who construct frameworks of definition and meaning around the relationship and the parts they will play in it. As teammates, their collaborative practices of intimacy serve to uphold this reality through "reciprocal familiarity" (Goffman 1959:88) and make the relationship "work" pragmatically on a day-to-day basis. The participants' understandings of themselves are shaped by their experience of the relationship, which takes on its own identity as a reified social object. In negotiating their roles and repertoires of action, each person must take into account not just what they each desire (or not) individually but also what the *relationship* "needs" to survive:

> I am a sexual female. I have been married to my asexual husband for over 16 years.[...]He was interested in sex before we got married, but it turned off like a switch during the honeymoon and has been that way ever since. He has no explanation for why this happened. I find I sometimes feel so resentful and deceived. It's so hard to deal with. I used to always think my husband just wasn't into me or that I was unattractive, but a few years ago I started looking for a "cause," so to speak. Eventually found this site, pretty much when I was at the point I felt like I couldn't take it anymore and might jump on some random strange man walking down the street. Then I started getting depressed again and had to stop thinking about it and had to take a break from reading online and AVEN, and now I've

started thinking about it again and decided to reconnect with AVEN. It's really helpful for me to talk with people in the same situation. I had talked to my husband a lot after finding AVEN, and he agreed that he is asexual (had never heard of it before). I'm so conflicted . . . feel like I can't keep living like this but don't want to put my kids through a divorce, so I live in limbo. Unfortunately on top of no sex we have absolutely no intimacy or affection of any kind. My husband pretty much doesn't talk to me. [....] I've been trying to throw myself into activities and am planning to go back to college in the next year or so for a career change, but still, there is such emptiness in my life that I don't think will ever be filled. (Tapestry 2010)

In the above story, the asexual husband experienced a shift in selfhood, facilitated by the sexual wife's discovery of the asexual identity and subsequent proposition to her husband that he "is" asexual. According to the poster, the husband had never heard of this identity before but "agreed" that he is asexual. Her own search for a "cause" might be read as a selfhood project, in response to her husband's disinclination toward sexual behavior. Clearly, the poster views *both* of their selves as being intertwined not only with one another but also with the information she has learned in the AVEN community.

Moreover, her comment that there is no intimacy or affection suggests that the collaboration is not a successful team performance; they do not appear to share the same goals regarding intimacy, in whatever form it might take. Nonetheless, the poster suggests that her participation in AVEN has been helpful in coping with being a sexual person in an asexual relationship.

From a symbolic interactionist perspective, what actually happened between this couple is less relevant than the story being told. The story reveals intersections of selfhood and relationships and the role of interactions outside the relationship in mediating, perhaps even constituting, these intersections.

An interactionist approach encourages a pragmatic focus on the negotiated and contingent nature of intimacy as a set of cooperative practices. "Practices of intimacy" (Jamieson 2005) emerge from the conditions of the relationship as a unit, rather than from individual decisions. Additionally, an interactionist framework recognizes that asexuality exists only (that is, comes to be socially visible) in the context of sexuality. It is defined as something "other" than the normative forms, expressions, or intensities of sexual desire that asexuals may feel are assumed by mainstream culture. The forms of intimacy this can create will manifest differently within different relationships. The symbolic interactionist perspective precludes us from viewing the life experiments such a situation engenders as inherently desirable or undesirable. Instead, it compels us to view them simply as interactive ways of being, which are designed pragmatically by asexual people to navigate their way around a sexualized cultural context. Asexual intimacy is a contingent, collaborative practice, emerging from everyday forms of negotiation and meaningful attachments of becoming and being sexual.

CONCLUSION

Like early studies of many social identities, research on asexuality originated in psychology and sexology. These clinical approaches depicted "the asexual" as a particular type of person, whose absence of sexual desire required explanation. This is problematic for two reasons. First, it unquestioningly accepts the idea of a unilaterally understood experience of "sexual desire" as natural. Second, it limits the analysis to the level of individual thoughts, decisions, and behaviors, neglecting to consider the social interaction context in which these are created, experienced, and negotiated. Symbolic interactionists challenge us to move away from essentialist conceptualizing, in order to understand the social conditions that inform and give rise to these identities. Independently, two of us (Newmahr 2008, 2011 and Scott 2007) have made similar critiques of essentialist theories that tend to view other "deviant" identities as fixed personality traits, genetic temperament, or pathologies. Scott (2007) proposed a symbolic interactionist theory of shyness as a role identity that arises out of situations of dramaturgical stress and perceived relative incompetence. Its meaning, development, and consolidation are negotiated through interaction and contingent upon the (real or anticipated) reactions of others to norm-breaking behavior. Newmahr (2008, 2011) used the case of sadomasochism to offer an interactionist theory of intimacy, arguing that intimate experiences are constructed through joint boundary transgression. Taken together, these works suggest that asexual identities might be regarded as deviant or challenging because of the way they transgress some of its taken-for-granted assumptions and deeply held boundaries (between, in this case, platonic intimacies and romantic partnerships). However, actors are skilled and pragmatic in the way that they navigate this cultural terrain and resolve its uncomfortable tensions at the micro-social level, by redefining and renegotiating the meanings of intimacy in their encounters.

A symbolic interactionist analysis of asexuality helps to better understand two key elements of asexual experience: identity and intimacy. We see three key research questions as central to a symbolic interactionist view of asexuality.[2] First, what are the key processes involved in *becoming* asexual? This might involve the study of how interactions lead (some) people toward "coming out" as asexual and the biographical identity work they use to make sense of this trajectory. By seeing asexual identity as a process of negotiation rather than a state to be achieved, we can achieve a greater understanding of how asexuality is experienced and practiced.

Second, how do asexual people's identities shape, and get shaped by, their different understandings of intimacy in relationships? What are the meanings attached to being asexually intimate, and how are these negotiated in everyday interaction?

Finally, what can asexuality teach us about intimacy? How can we use asexuality as a case to interrogate other assumptions about sexuality, love, and intimacy more broadly? By studying what Goffman termed the "limits" of intimate relationships, where asexual and sexual definitions clash and must be reconciled, we can reach a deeper understanding of the unique ways in which actors navigate their way through this rocky terrain. The presence of asexual life experiments may challenge or subvert conventional myths and idealistic representations of love, such as romantic heteronormative scripts (Jackson 1993) or the magical uniqueness of exclusive insularity (Simmel 1950). Examples of this can be found in the claim that asexual relationships, by "blurring" the lines of romantic and friendship relationships, may "rewrite language" to better describe these relationships (Schrerrer 2010b) or even to transform the discourses of love (Carrigan 2012:16) by presenting alternative definitions of it. For example, consider the case of a newlywed couple who used their honeymoon suite to play Scrabble with their friends (Cox 2008), demonstrating different meaning-making around intimacy and arguably the emergence of new intimacy rituals. Asexual relationships thereby help to illustrate the range of "practices of intimacy" (Jamieson 2005).

All of these questions are united by the wish to appreciate, to paraphrase Plummer (1995), asexual stories. Viewing asexual identification and intimacy as embedded within meaningful social practices adds a uniquely sociological perspective to the understanding of asexuality. Asexuality is seen not just as a state of being achieved through individual reflexivity but also as a process of lifelong *becoming*, developed via the meanings attached to forms of social negotiation.

NOTES

1. We avoid speaking of asexual "couples" since research suggests polyamory is a trend in asexual intimate relationships (Scherrer 2010a).

2. These mirror the research questions for a project that two of us (Scott and Dawson) are currently working on, with Dr. Liz McDonnell at the University of Sussex, UK. The project is called A Qualitative Exploration of Asexual Identity and Practices of Intimacy and is funded by the Leverhulme Trust (grant code RPG-2012-575).

PART V

SEXUAL STORIES

In addition to the academic papers appearing in this book, we have also included several sexual stories or "narratives." All but one of these are first person accounts written by nonsocial scientists about their personal experiences. We include these narratives for two reasons. First, they illustrate one of the core interests of symbolic interactionists, how people make sense of their behaviors and selves and their relationship to others as they progress through what sociologists have variously called "careers" (Becker 1963) or "moral careers" (Goffman 1961a). More importantly, however, we wish to provide students with an empathetic understanding of how people, who may feel stigmatized, cope with their situation. This is what Cooley (1909) called "sympathetic introspection." The modern social psychologist, says Cooley, comes to understand people, "largely by what may be called *sympathetic introspection,* putting himself into intimate contact with various sorts of persons and allowing them to awake in himself a life similar to their own, which he afterwards, to the best of his ability, recalls and describes. In this way he is more or less able to understand—always by introspection—children, idiots, criminals, rich and poor, conservative and radical—any phase of human nature not wholly alien to his own" (Cooley 1909:7).

In *Telling Sexual Stories: Power, Change and Social Worlds* (1995), Ken Plummer notes that the writing of stories involves interaction between the "producer," or storyteller, and the "consumer," or reader. "The meanings of stories are never fixed," he writes, "but emerge out of a ceaselessly changing stream of interaction between producers and readers in shifting *contexts.* . . . Stories get told and read in different ways in different contexts" (Plummer 1995:22). That is, how you, as a reader, interpret and understand these stories depends in large part on your own experiences, sense of self, and, consequently, the meanings you bring with you as a consumer. Your responses to these stories are, in turn, shaped by your own biographies and cultural contexts.

By shifting the focus of study from what people are doing to what people are *saying* about what they are doing, Plummer follows what has been called "the postmodern turn" in thinking about social life, shaped profoundly by Michel Foucault's work (1978) on sexuality. Plummer urges us to understand people's sexual stories as revelatory about society at large, to uncover the cultural narratives that give rise to the sexual stories being told at a given moment in history. In this way, symbolic interaction is uniquely positioned for C. Wright Mills's sociological imagination, bridging the gap between individual biographies and larger society. As you read these stories, ask yourself how they relate to the society in which they were produced. Could they have been written the same way in another country, 100 years ago or 100 years from now? What can these stories teach us about our views of sexuality?

SELF, IDENTITY, AND CAREERS

While the stories in this section appear to be very different, all of them deal in one way or another with issues of self, identity, and careers. For symbolic interactionists, the concept of "careers" is an analytical tool used to understand how behavior and social changes are patterned over time (Hewitt and Shulman 2011). Howard S. Becker (1963) adopted this concept from the sociology of occupations and used it in the development of what he called a "sequential model" of deviance. Included in this model is the idea of "career contingencies," factors that "include both objective facts of social structure and changes in the perspectives, motivations and desires of the individual" (Becker 1963:24). These contingencies affect whether or not and how a person moves from one stage to another in a (deviant) career. The concept of "deviance" is fraught with problems, and we would not frame all of the narratives in this section as deviance. However, sexuality on the whole is marginalized. In everyday life, we police and regulate conversations about sex and sexual behaviors themselves. We enforce cultural notions about appropriate sexual behaviors, disclosures, and values, and we gawk at situations that challenge these ideas. For this reason, Becker's work can be useful in understanding the stories in the pages that follow. (Drawing on Plummer, for example, we might view the telling of sexual stories in a reader as deviant in and of itself and view the willingness of contributors to tell their stories, and of the editors to showcase them here, as aspects of deviant careers.)

Becker identified the sequence of stages in deviant careers as, first, "the commission of a nonconforming act, an act that breaks some particular set of rules"

(1963:24). This breach may be either intentional or unintentional. The second step in the career is "the development of deviant motives and interests. . . . Many kinds of deviance spring from motives which are socially learned" (30). The third step in developing a stable pattern of deviant behavior is "the experience of being caught and publicly labeled as a deviant" (31). This, writes Becker, is one of the most crucial events in the deviant career. Once labeled, there is a critical change in one's public identity. One acquires a new, deviant master status and public identity and inherits the negative auxiliary status traits seen by others as belonging to it. (Interestingly, several of our contributors use pseudonyms in this section. Whether one tells one's sexual stories under an assumed name likely has something to do with the credibility afforded them— or not—by their other statuses. D. J. Williams, for example, is a university professor.) In Goffman's (1963) terms, when one is labeled as deviant the person is "thus reduced in our minds from a whole and usual person to a tainted, discounted one" (3). In a word, he becomes *stigmatized*. For Goffman, a stigma is not an attribute but rather a relationship between a person's virtual social identity (what we believe him to be) and his actual social identity (what he could be shown to be if we possessed all the facts about him). When we find out that someone is not what we thought he was, and, when what he really was all along is socially undesirable, he has a stigma.

The fourth step, according to Becker, is joining a subcultural group of like-minded people. Within this group, "the individual learns, in short, to participate in a subculture organized around the particular deviant activity" (Becker 1963:31). These subcultural groups serve two important functions for deviants: First, they provide the justifications, rationales, explanations, and neutralizations that allow their members to feel all right about who and what they are and what they do, and second, they facilitate this behavior and enable individuals to carry out their deviance and avoid detection. As part of this process, individuals may engage in secondary deviance, which may help cover or facilitate their initial deviance (Lemert 1967). In his model Becker presents only one possible sequence of events. There are, of course, other possibilities. The individual may successfully conceal his or her deviance and never be discovered. Sociologist Erving Goffman (1963) terms individuals whose deviance is hidden as "discreditable." That is, they are always in a situation in which they are vulnerable to discovery and stigmatization. Their problem, says Goffman, is to control information about who they really are. People whose deviance is known, the "discredited," have a different set of problems, managing tension in interaction with others.

Throughout the processes described by Becker and Goffman, people are continually engaged in sense-making. They may or may not make a connection between their behavior, which sociologist David Matza (1969) calls "doing," and their sense of self ("being"). For many people, this journey of self-discovery and self-labeling is traumatic, and they struggle with it. For others, it is a smooth transition, and for still others, it never happens. There are, for example, heterosexually self-identified men who have sex with other men and never consider the implications of this behavior for their sexual identities. The writers in this section illustrate a variety of adjustments to issues of identity, self-realization, and revelation. In presenting these very personal stories, we hope that students will learn to use sympathetic introspection to gain important insights into the minds and lives of others whose orientations may be different from their own.

Thomas S. Weinberg

CHAPTER 16

THE UNFORTUNATE ADVENTURES OF A GIRL IN THE KNOW

Stella Meningkat

EDITORS' NOTES: *A fundamental question, which feminist writers have debated about sex work in general and prostitution in particular, is whether sex workers are entrepreneurs or victims. Writers who hold the first position often identify as "sex-positive feminists" and see sex-related decisions as at least potentially unproblematic, making sex work "an occupational choice among other gendered and discriminated forms of work available to women"(Kissil and Davey 2010:6). Sex-positive feminists may object to the problematizing of prostitution, because it emerges from antisex morality that has functioned to regulate and control women's bodies. Many sex-positive feminists view traditional thinking about prostitution as part of a larger process of controlling people (often especially women) through demanding particular relationships to, and feelings about, sexual acts.*

The other position is that entering into prostitution is always ultimately nonconsensual, the result of social inequality and a devaluing of women's nonsexual worth that leaves women no other choice. There is no doubt that sex workers, especially those who work the streets, are sometimes victimized by customers ("johns"), their pimps, and police, yet the majority of sex workers do not report having been victims of violence (O'Doherty 2011). In fact, some sex workers, characterized by Williamson and Baker (2009) as "outlaws," saw their customers as legitimate objects for exploitation. At their poles, both positions overstate their case, since prostitution is a complex and varied phenomenon (see, for example, Kissil and Davey 2010; O'Doherty 2011; Vanwesenbeeck 2013). How sex workers see themselves and their occupation is probably related to their position in the prostitution hierarchy. Autobiographies of call girls and madams present themselves as business women and entrepreneurs, in control of their own situation (e.g., Barrows 1986; Davis 2009; Fleiss 2002; Hollander 1972).

In the following chapter, Stella Meningkat writes about her time as a sex worker. This experience was temporary, engaged in as a lark, and as a way of making money. She does not convert doing into being, resisting commitment to the identity of prostitute. Stella avoids the process of self-labeling through the mechanism of what Goffman (1961b) calls "social distance." Social distance is a way in which someone attempts to avoid negative labeling by withdrawing emotionally from the role in which he or she is engaging. Stella tells us how she psychologically separated herself from the commercial sex act, thus avoiding its implications for her self-identity: "I had mastered the art of detaching myself from my body while I performed," she writes, "being able to see, objectively, what was happening." She struggled with her feminist sensibility and how her occupation relates to it, illustrating the psychological state of cognitive dissonance, an uncomfortable situation in which an individual holds conflicting attitudes or beliefs. Stella tried to answer a fundamental question: Is she in control of the situation, or is it the customer who is using her? As you read Stella's story, pay attention to her description of her interaction with her johns. How does she feel about them and her sex work? What meanings do she and they bring to the situation? Do these meanings change during their interaction? If they do, in what ways do they change? Does she feel stigmatized because of her sex work? Where would you locate her in the range of feminist positions on sex work? What does Stella's story reveal about our contemporary values and perspectives regarding sex, money, gender, and power?

憇扌

When I was eighteen, I decided to give prostitution a whirl. I was working at a stuffy sticky Dairy Queen for minimum wage, where the incentive of the sound of people's change clinking into our overused plastic lid of a tip jar and my ten minute cigarette and slushy break were the only things that prevented me from dipping my hand into the too-hot fudge dispenser as soon as I arrived. I had moved out of my parents' house a few months earlier and was living with my girlfriend in a bright and smoky one bedroom apartment above a children's entertainment company/stripper-for-rent agency. Rumor had it that the boss would fuck you in the Barney costume before adding your snapshots to a book full of anonymous sets of tits and ass. Customers would gawk at the pictures when they came into the office, hoping to find the one that would add the right kind of spice to their party. I could never track down any proof to confirm the rumors though, and the girls weren't talking. I worked long shifts at DQ and always managed to have just enough money to pay my rent and stay properly hydrated with any college student's essential liquid diet combination of Red Bull, Steele Reserve and orange juice in order to survive. But I wanted more.

More came in the form of my girlfriend's bright idea to re-hatch her Yahoo account and Craigslist alter ego and go fishing for poor suckers who we would suck off to make some cash—we could even buy Newports if we worked hard enough, she said. She had done it in the past and said that she could make at least $100 per trick for an hour's work. Sometimes, in a good week, she could make over $500 from doing full service jobs for just a handful of guys and still pick up an extra $50 or so by hanging around the porn theatre. She would masturbate in front of an audience who would give her a standing ovation at the peak of her orgasm, pushing her over the edge through the bottom of their wallets under a storm of raining dollar bills and liquid DNA. She always told me that they were more afraid of "us" than we were of "them" and that we had the distinct advantage of being able to search them out online long before they could climb the dusty stairs to our love nest-turned-carnal home office. We always performed together, which made us more money and turned me on to the tricks of the trade. We always had the last word in who the lucky winner would be for the day, but that didn't stop us from having to feign intimacy with hairy old veterans and "business professionals." We thought that if our male dominated society was going to make its profits by selling sexual imagery, stripping women down past their bare skin, we were merely collecting on the indentured profits of that sick system. Taking back some of what was originally ours: the authority to capitalize on our own bodies on our own terms. How fucking radical is that, dude?

Each and every time a trick came over I would lock myself in the bathroom, breathing heavily while I applied my mask of makeup, cheap perfume and lipstick the color of menstrual blood, transforming myself into the person who would perform this circus act. Each time praying for a quick end to this masochistic show so that I could again wash off the paint, hide the admission fees and slip into the security of my Tegan and Sara t-shirt as I sank deep into the womb of my twenty-five year old mattress and trendy sheets. Each time my girlfriend would coax me out of my secure cell while reassuring the Trick on our couch that I was just a little shy, reminding them not to be fooled, that I was a nasty little freak who would be begging for their cock once my pussy was wet enough. That I loved this shit, that I didn't want to be anywhere else in the world at that moment. That their "manly man" manliness and crazy huge cocks (*"She's never had one that big before, you know"*) were what I dreamed about every night. My dreams of becoming a professor someday were merely a front for my true passion, the opportunity of a lifetime: that chance to experience their prodigal sexual prowess.

During that summer I raked in roughly five hundred dollars by fucking, teasing, sucking, riding, and flirting with Santa Claus, our mailman, a fat and boring corner store owner, a married man and his married friends, as well as a few others who were far too drab to leave any lasting impression. By the end I had experienced and survived my fill of cum and empowerment. I longed for the normalcy of the sticky floors of Dairy Queen and the tedium of my idiotic peers at school. I felt comforted knowing the white goo on my arm at night was definitely vanilla syrup and was relieved that my conversations were again filled with genuine human emotion rather than high pitched, sarcastic mocking of dick inflating banter. I was sick of hearing the guttural moans of the Goddess inside me trying to inch her way out to bash me over the head and flee me for disrespecting her so. My body, which once belonged to me, had been transformed into an olive-toned depository for other people's shameful secrets and sweaty slimy secretions devoid of emotion and wrapped in twenty dollar bills during an Academy Award worthy performance of mocked human intimacy. I had mastered the art of detaching myself from my body while I performed, being able to see, objectively, what was happening. I could watch myself on all fours (or on my back, or upside down, or whatever the contortion *de jour* happened to be) while whoever was renting me at the time would grunt and sweat and push and hiss through his teeth. He would call me his baby, or his little slut, or his master, until he would distort his face into hideous shapes, grab onto my raven black hair like his life depended on it, shouting, "This is it, this is it." At that point I would up the ante of panting and pretending, directing him to release his demons onto my breasts because my head was filled with too many dark shadows already for him to shoot his cum into the back of my skull like he really wanted to. Afterwards I would moan and thank him for his sacred offering upon my temple of worship, and he would laugh and make an awkward excuse or departure. "I have to get back to work, I should let you clean up, got to get back to the wife, well I'm beat now, ha ha . . .". . . and more predictably. . . . "Hey we should do this again sometime. So you're a student? Women's Studies? Oh that's so cute, here's an extra $10. I heard textbooks are expensive these days." They would leave and I would retreat back into my oversized bathroom, walls plastered with the pictures of fictitiously beautiful women; the mermaids, and the pin-up models; we were now, all of us, one and the same. Turning on the lava jets, I would soak underneath the power of their intense molten heat, hoping that I could sweat out the poison of the person who was just inside and return my body back to the bright young woman who previously resided there. I had to be more than this, I thought, but why did any of that matter when I could make more money with a mouth full of cock instead of my head full of ideas? I was sixteen all over again, except this time the men were paying for the show and not stealing it on the exotic kitchen floor.

The summer came and went and life moved on. I spent the next year having sex for money on and off, sometimes feeling like I was in charge and other times resisting the urge to see what shiny metal rectangles dancing down my arms would feel like. I was certain that the oozing that followed would be well worth it, but unsure that the expelled red mess would truly belong to me.

I remember once letting a trick who was there for a thirty dollar blow job fuck me on the dusty living room floor because he said he would give me an extra forty if I did. He had driven such a far way on his lunch break and could have chosen any other girl's ad online, so why the fuck did I think I was so special? He said I was so irresistible he might not be able to restrain himself if I said no. I looked and saw his clear blue eyes dilate; fixing them onto mine so that I knew that he meant what he said. If I said no he was just going to do it anyway so I may as well recite my lines that had become etched into my skull's squishy grey matter and put on a tip-worthy performance. I lay down on my back, my eyes closed hard, as he jammed himself inside and fucked me and fucked me until he pulled himself upward, breaching like a whale and grunted loudly, "That's a good little whore, you take that." I did. I was, and he never paid me that extra forty dollars.

⚜

The debate among feminists regarding sex work and pornography is a long and circular one. Many sex-positive feminists argue that the key to true female liberation and equality lies in the sexual liberation of women from the constraints of patriarchal ideas of sexuality and sexual norms. Part of this sexual liberation would be to destigmatize any and all sexual acts between two consenting adults. To them, it is most important that we as a society understand that women can, and do, feel a sense of empowerment in each and every sexual choice they make throughout their lives. Moreover, some sex-positive feminists believe that there is nothing inherently oppressive about prostitution and pornography, that many women who choose the field of sex work do so knowingly, and, do indeed enjoy their work. Radical feminists, on the other hand, believe that prostitution and pornography stem from patriarchy itself and that any manifestation of these activities is inherently harmful to women and an act of violence.

Sexuality can be a wonderful thing. Sex can, and does, mean so many different things to different individuals, different cultures, and different societies. Sex can be pleasurable and fun. Sex can be transformative. Sex can be scary. Most importantly, sex should be a positive experience each and every time one engages in it. Sex should not be something that is forced upon someone, whether that force is applied in the form of physical violence, emotional pressure, or economic necessity. If we, as a society and as a global community, can dig ourselves out of the mucky swamp that we fuck in daily and make a clearer path for ourselves, then sex and the context in which it exists can be positive for every human on this planet, all the time. Sex is not a shameful thing. The fact that any woman in any part of the world at any point in history has had the last resort option to sell her body to pay her rent, or buy a loaf of bread, or get her next fix or pay for her next textbook is what is shameful. This is what we should be working to change, and it is possible.

CHAPTER 17
BACKROOM "DANCE"
Ruby Pearson

*E*DITORS' NOTES: *Ruby Pearson's story about her experience as a stripper is similar to Stella's. Like Stella, she, too, is a feminist, and she has to deal with a conflict between her occupation and her feminist beliefs. This tension has been richly explored by symbolic interactionists and ethnographers, including Carol Rambo Ronai (1998), Danielle Egan (2006), and Katherine Frank (2002). Ronai and Ellis (1989) frame stripping as a manipulation via "interactional strategies" or what Pasko (2002) later calls a confidence game, in which "strippers manipulate symbolic communication and create emotional control over their patrons" (50). The men, however, "still possess a pervasive power: the sex-object role dancers must assume and perform is defined and managed by men and their desires" (50). The setting, itself, is defined and controlled through interactions between stripper, customer, and club staff. Part of what strippers do is "counterfeit intimacy" (Enck and Preston 1988; Ronai and Ellis 1989). As Pasko (2002) notes, "Strippers use different masks and guises, falsify social relationships and vary social roles for monetary gain. They are experienced emotion managers and excellent scholars of human nature" (53). The novice stripper learns this through socialization by more experienced strippers and staff (Mestemacher and Roberti, 2004; Morrow 2012).*

Like Stella, Ruby had an alternative status outside her occupation, one which conferred a certain amount of prestige: She was a college student. This enabled her to escape taking on the stripper identity as a permanent part of her sense of self. Trautner and Collett (2010), in their study "Students Who Strip," similarly point out that the college student status serves these strippers by providing an alternative (and higher status) self-identity, enabling them to see their work as transient and enhancing their interactions with customers to whom they reveal themselves, "allow[ing] these women to maintain a positive sense of self" (275).

Ruby's introduction to her story illustrates the feminist tension around dancing for men. The questions she poses are entry points into thinking about gender, power, and sexuality from a feminist-interactionist perspective.

CB EO

Despite all of my time spent insisting, debating and representing the idea that women could choose to, love to and be empowered by stripping my experience provided information difficult to align with my beliefs. I always believed women could be in charge as strippers, they did not have to dance for or talk to anyone they did not want; they had control over their schedules and skimmed off the paychecks of men without having to buy the idea that men controlled them. Plenty of clubs are women run and many dancers tout their independence, schedule flexibility and high pay as something they have chosen and love. Of course there are women who feel stripping or sex work is their only option, of course there are women whose poor financial situation may choose stripping for them; I never denied that. What I deny is that no woman can truly elect to be a stripper and be empowered by it. I reject the idea that the world we live in makes it impossible for women to be in control of themselves as strippers and sex workers simply because, looking in, it seems they are being controlled by men. You may be ogling my crotch while I lie half naked on display; but I do not have to be here, I do not have to talk to you, dance for you or pretend to like you, I can put my top back on and I am taking your money.

I didn't think about the men so much, just my love of being naked and my lack of dancing ability. When I did think about the men, Julia Query's (2002) thoughts on stripping always provided an answer saying, "It's like they figured out what to do about patriarchy: Take their money" (Query 2002). I read every website and book about stripping and how to be a stripper I could find, and was convinced it could be an empowering job.

In the beginning I felt that I especially would be in control of my experience, given my long term lesbian partnership and full time job outside the club. I was not in it for the money, and what did I care if the men found me sexy or not, I had a honey at home. Easier said than done; everyone likes to be the popular flush girl. I was shaving my legs, waxing my pubes, wearing more makeup and perfume and trying, ineffectively, to be coy and flirtatious. I was submitting to the male ideal, and it did not matter one bit that I claimed not to "like" (read: "want to fuck") men. I was right; you can wear whatever you want, be as hairy as you want, talk to or ignore whoever you want, dance how you want and generally be anybody you want. But newsflash, feminist: you simply cannot make money in a strip club without embracing and becoming the male ideal. It does not matter if you have a full time job because when you are spending six hours of your life walking around a dance club in painful heels and underwear it is simply a waste of time if you do not rake in at least double the hourly wage at your day job. Regarding my image, I did not find that my sexual preference affected my want to be desired by men, and I certainly wanted to be up to par with the other dancers. In the United States, women are all raised in a society that teaches them, and taught me, to seek the affection of men and compete with women. The strip club extracts these features of society and magnifies them. But the ultimate feminist question for me is: does this environment further the degradation of women, or does it allow women an opportunity to profit from the treatment they face from men every day in any profession?

Stripping takes advantage of a system that takes advantage of women. If strangers are going to call me "baby," look me up and down before they can return my hello, and make every friendly conversation about my relationship status anyway, then why not do it half-naked in a strip club while making tips? A stripper is not empowered without making money, and making money means submission to the male ideal of women that feeds the patriarchy. How about the idea that women fulfill a facet of their own sexual expression as strippers? Should that expression be discounted simply because it falls within the parameters of a patriarchal sexual environment? What if the extracurricular excitement isn't just for the boys?

◌⃝℘

I laughed in my head as he pinned me against the wooden divider between the corner backroom booths. My sparkling high-heeled feet and bare legs were too far in front of me, and his hand on my neck was the only thing keeping me balanced. He was saying gruffly how he'd like to fuck me hard when the bouncer entered the space. Noticing the other dancers neglecting their customers to stare at me, I smiled enthusiastically and gave a thumbs-up to the bouncer. He slowly backed out through the hanging beads. The pushy customer didn't miss a beat. He swung me around by the waist and flung me headfirst toward the cushioned booth. I braced myself with my arms as he humped away behind me fully clothed and talked incessantly about my nice ass and the hard fuck he would give me. I thought he was a hoot.

The dance was over in a whirlwind; the song ended before I had taken my top off. The bouncers had mentioned the customer was rough when he bought the dance. He assured me that the man would tip, which he didn't. Passing him as I headed back onto the floor, he advised me to "just push him around and demand your tip next time."

Feeling somehow off balance, I continued back onto the floor. I caught sight of Jezebel sitting at the stage with a man. Longingly, I ran my hand across her bare shoulders.

"Talk about being a rag doll," I whispered in her ear.

Nudity has always been something of a passion for me. In my high school dormitory, there were days I didn't even wait to get to my room before I started ripping off the confines of my uniform. Eventually, the freshmen were no longer shocked, and my general lack of clothing in the halls and my room was widely accepted. It became understood even by adults in the dorm that when entering Ruby's room, "come in" never meant "I'm decent."

My nudity wasn't about being sexy or getting attention. It was about personal comfort, and I'd be damned if people couldn't learn to deal with that. By the time senior year rolled around, I was running dorm meetings in my underwear, and my friends had started a running joke in anticipation of the shock of my college roommates. In our last year of high school, we were all cautioned that defining oneself in a college essay demanded creativity and introspection. This would be the only glimpse of personality for those scary college admissions officers who, we were reminded, were infinitely bored with generic essays about hard workers and sports lovers. I wrote my college essay about being naked, and I received no letters of decline.

When I started dancing, the owner's son, who was the manager of the club, the ex-dancer-turned-bartender, and the DJ all warned us not to let the "other girls scare us away." In contrast, I found them to be quite friendly. Being on stage was the most nerve-racking, and it was always a relief when another dancer came up to tip me and say hello. Jezebel and I used to dance extensively for each other at the edge of the stage just to kill time during the set, complimenting each other on the recency of our pubic shaves and other nonsense. Onstage during one of my first sets, a polished, slim brown dancer approached the stage. She had flawless skin surrounded by shoulder length wavy hair; she smiled as I gracelessly walked over to her and knelt down.

"Ruby's your name, right?" she asked. "This your first time dancing? I figured. Look, honey, you're fucking beautiful and I think you're gonna make a lotta money; but you need to take the price sticker off the bottom of your shoe. These men, they notice the details, and you need to *smile*. Also, let's think about your name. You chose Ruby 'cus of your hair, right? How about Velvet? I like that better, give it some thought."

She slid a bill under my thong and was gone. I didn't change my name, and it wasn't the first time I was reminded to smile, but I did take the price sticker off my heel.

Being onstage is similar to so many things. It's dancing in front of the bathroom mirror naked to your favorite song . . . with your dad's friends watching. It's when you're drunk, and you're the center of attention at a dance party. If the club is really quiet, it's like a sleepover with your friends where you practice dancing so you can look cool at the next party. Dancing onstage always brought together my feelings of power and glamour with those of self-conscious nervousness in a way that made me dread my turn in the rotation.

As a new dancer, my legs were jelly by the second song. Dying to get off stage, I would will my thighs to push me back up from every booty pop. Often, I let the DJ pick my music: nothing too fast or I would tire out, nothing too slow, or I would end up pretending to masturbate far too much. It was a delicate game. Customers would come to the stage so they were even with the dancers' feet to get a show up close, and tip. This was always the toughest part about dancing. I never mastered the trick of spreading my legs and shaking my pelvis in their faces without looking ridiculous or of putting my heeled shoes next to their drinks and making small talk while they ogled my crotch. I liked watching myself in the mirror covered walls, pretending I was in the kind of music videos that as a feminist I hated but as a dancer I watched for ideas. Even when my wife was also at the stage, I wanted the approval and attention of the male customers, so that it would be mine to thwart or exploit. I could feel myself working for that attention while I danced. It added an element of confusion to my experiences onstage as I fought not to blur the line between my "act" and my true emotions.

Even though every stripper how-to warns against the habit of drinking on the job, I found it immensely helpful, sometimes even necessary. Talking to customers was easier, and I liked more people. I felt my dancing was smoother, just as long as I managed to stay sober enough to transition between the two poles without stumbling. We tried never to buy our own drinks, as there was usually someone at the bar we could coax into paying, but once in a while, especially at the beginning of a shift, we would end up buying for ourselves.

In the position of paying for a first round one night, a young man, no older than thirty five, stepped in to foot the bill, a gin and tonic for Jezebel and a cranberry vodka for me—our usual. He was well kept and a little chubby, with a round face and an easygoing demeanor. He said he'd had a rough workday, so we chatted about his job and then my freshman status at the club. On a quick sneak to the back room, an experienced dancer told me if he stuck around he was a "nice guy." I was intrigued and almost stopped caring if I made much money; he was so considerate, we could have been on a date. The older customers liked to grab girls by the waist and shake them around some when they talked to us, but Mike didn't lift a finger. He just kept buying me drinks, saying he was here to spend money and I was here to make it. Fantastic.

We were sitting at the stage when I asked him for a backroom dance. To my surprise, he declined. "Not yet," he said. Then, he pulled a twenty out of his pocket and tipped me a twenty to keep me around. A few more drinks, more small talk, more tipping the dancers onstage, and we finally made it to the backroom; he bought three songs up front, the most I had ever sold at once. I was nervous about disappointing, still being only about a week into conquering the art of lap dancing, which played to my benefit as he guided me to do what he wanted. I knelt on the cushioned booth, one leg on each side of him as we pressed our hips together. The distance I usually kept during my dances disappeared; the game of touching the customer enough to be pleasing but not more than necessary was not being played. I could feel him watching me as our hips worked together in pattern. I let him look me in the eyes.

"How could you be new at this? Do you feel this?" he asked squeezing my butt. I did. With his hands on my hips, he pushed me upward, so I was standing on the cushion, afraid my heels would poke through the leather, my knees bent so my cunt was inches from his face. I imagined he could smell me, and I didn't mind. Maybe that was his intention. The three songs passed, and I leaned back in his lap as he sturdily held me up with his hands on the small of my back, our hips never stopping. I had to be sure he would pay for additional songs if we stayed, even though I could feel a twinge of guilt at interrupting our good time. "I don't care, I don't want it to end," he said, and so we continued for two more songs, entering back into the real world of the club with an after-sex-like stupor and contentment, his arm comfortably around me. He told me then that his real name was Dave but he felt safer using a fake, like we did, and he mentioned the local bar he claimed I could frequently find him at if I wanted to hang out. Our fun ended then, with his disclosure and suggestion. We were back in the real world, on the main floor with dancers and shot girls circulating between the customers and the DJ calling out dancers for their set. Our recent intimacies quickly faded as my focus turned back to the club where a close friend was sitting at the bar. As I approached to join his exclusive party, he was having a $400 bottle of champagne taken off display, a sign that the night was only beginning.

CHAPTER 18
A CONFLICTED MIND
John P.

*E*DITORS' NOTES: *John P.'s story about his struggle with his sexual identity is a common one (see Plummer 1995; Weinberg 1983). Succinctly titled, "A Conflicted Mind," his narrative perfectly illustrates the problems many gay men have in converting doing into being. John, like Stella and Ruby, suffered from cognitive dissonance, although the sources of his discomfort are different. "I didn't want to be gay," he writes. "I wouldn't allow myself to be gay. I could change this. I was just going through a phase. 'It'll pass,' I kept telling myself." His feelings are similar to those of "Thomas," a college student quoted by Savin-Williams (2005), who fluctuated between seeing himself as straight, bisexual, and gay: "I wanted desperately to be straight, and the label implied some level of commitment. I dated females and realized that I was attracted to females and so I thought of myself as straight . . . and then in . . . my sophomore year I realized that my feelings for guys must mean something, and it must mean that I'm bisexual" (206). Being discreditable, John's biggest fear was that "the guys" would reject him if they found out he was gay. He kept his feelings to himself and engaged in information management (Goffman 1963; Orne 2011), all the while praying that he would be able to control his feelings. Like the LGBT youth studied by McDermott, Roen, and Scourfield (2008), who tried to cope with homophobia by engaging in self-destructive behavior, John tried to resolve his cognitive dissonance by heavy alcohol consumption, and even made suicide attempts, but that didn't work. Neither did excessive eating. He was able to eliminate it only by coming to terms with his sexuality and coming out to others.*

John was selective in coming out, using some of the strategies identified by Orne (2011). At first, he practiced concealment. Then, he engaged in what Orne calls "clues" (690): "I phoned a few friends from home," John writes, "and told them that I had a three-way with a girl and guy. It was my way of easing into the subject to see what their reaction would be." Finally, John engaged in what Orne terms "classic 'direct disclosure'" (689). In doing this, he follows the pattern noted by Grierson and Smith (2005), typical of gays born after 1969, which they label "Post-AIDs." In contrast with earlier cohorts of gays ("Pre-AIDs," born 1953–1962 and "Peri-AIDs," born 1963–1969), who come out only after establishing themselves within the gay world, men like John reveal themselves to others before entering fully into the gay community. For this group, the first people to whom they come out are friends and then siblings and finally, parents. The way in which one comes out depends on a number of factors, including the social context, "mediated by personal and micro-social factors" (Grierson and Smith 2005:56. See also, Orne 2011). An important issue for John in his coming to accept himself was shame, which he eventually replaced with pride in who he really is as a gay man (see McDermott, Roen, and Scourfield 2008 for similar stories from their respondents).

What are the meanings that John P. places on his feelings and behavior? How and why do these meanings change? How are they affected by his interaction with other people? When you read John P.'s story, it is important that you try to empathize with his situation by taking the role of the other in order to understand it emotionally as well as intellectually. Can you extrapolate a personal experience to help you feel what he feels? Have you ever, for example, had a secret that you were afraid to reveal because you thought others would not understand? If so, how have you dealt with it?

ೞ೮ಐ

I don't know when it began. I don't know when I realized I was gay. I suppose I have always known. I never thought, however, that I was necessarily born gay. I have, until recently, believed, or better said, persuaded myself to believe, that I was born with a predisposition to homosexuality. I rationalized that homosexuals were born with a genetic predisposition, and subsequently, my notion was that homosexual tendencies would either be triggered or not with the onset of puberty. I refused to believe, as many homosexuals do, that same-sex attraction had always existed in my life. However, after coming out to my parents, and within the next few weeks, I began to suddenly awaken from a dead sleep, time after time, with vivid childhood memories; all these resurfaced memories would have the same undercurrent of a theme, that is, occurrences of same-sex attraction at an early age. It seemed as if the different layers of my consciousness were trying to unite in the acceptance and understanding of my own sexuality. One memory, the first to resurface, but long forgotten, or maybe repressed, was of homoerotic feelings toward my father when we went harmlessly into a restroom on a family road trip. I do not remember the age I was, maybe 4, maybe younger, but as I laid in my bed, drenched in sweat, having long forgotten this memory, my mind for the first time in my life felt at ease. In my mind, I came to terms with an inner turmoil that had inflicted me as far back as I could remember. It was in that very moment that I finally rationalized that I was indeed born gay and no matter how hard I tried to change my lustful longings I wouldn't be able to do so. Everything in my life, good and bad, I realized then, had been impacted by my sexuality or lack of acknowledgment of it, but nothing seemed as clear as the impact it had upon my young adulthood and the decisions I made.

Adolescence is for many a very tumultuous time. For me, however, my adolescence was a time of experimentation, depression, chaos, and utter numbness. At the start of high school, I was just a typical freshman—still losing that last bit of baby fat, distraught at the slightest emergence of an unsightly pimple, and wearing gawkily coordinated clothing as I searched for my style. I was well liked, although I never felt fully accepted. I can say with certainty that I knew back then that I was gay—and in hindsight, I guess I knew I was different at even an earlier age—for I remember being extremely turned on by the sight of my classmates changing in the locker rooms after swimming lessons during middle school. However, it wouldn't be until high school that the stigma of being "gay" really resonated with me. I didn't want to be gay. I wouldn't allow myself to be gay. I could change this. I was just going through a phase. "It'll pass," I kept telling myself. I dreaded being associated with Scott, the only openly flamboyant boy I knew, who hung around with a swarm of girls and sometimes even wore a pocketbook. That wasn't me; I was one of the guys—the kind of guy who would spend all summer long with the guys playing football at the park, jumping off the rope swing at the local lake, loitering outside the deli, chugging down some energy drinks, as we figured out whose house we would be spending the night at. I was the kind of guy who enjoyed sitting around my friends' bedroom after a sun-filled day, all of us shirtless and in our boxers, playing video games and just swapping stories of what girl had the biggest tits or nicest ass. Although I never really participated in the conversation, I felt oddly accepted. You see, I felt part of the group. This is what guys do. And I was a guy. I felt if they found out I was gay, this dynamic would change, and I would be excluded from much of this male bonding time and become an outcast from the guys I considered my best friends.

Coming from a deeply religious Irish and Italian upbringing, I thought that I could curtail such homoerotic feelings and rectify my homosexual tendencies to the point where I contemplated enrolling in Exodus International. Through prayer, refraining from thinking impurely, and a steadfast determination to find women attractive, I knew it would not be long before I found myself attracted to the right sex. "God grant me the serenity to accept the things I cannot change; the courage to change the things I can; and the wisdom to know the difference," I would recite every time I found myself sexually excited at the sight of a cute guy. However, such self-conditioning would soon become a recipe for self-hatred and self-destruction that would consume much of my life.

Those of you who come from an Irish background will understand when I say that if Irish people have one thing in common, it's their stubbornly obsessive sense of pride. Nothing, and I mean nothing, will knock down a son of Eire more quickly than making him feel embarrassed or ashamed for something. Oddly enough, the Irish are masterminds at making others feel ashamed for *their* behaviors and attitudes.

Years before I knew what being gay was, my sister came across some gay pornography I had unknowingly saved on my computer. After coming across it, my sister, who was in high school, pulled me aside and scolded me, telling me how disgusting I was and how much mom and dad would be embarrassed if she told them. I remember being scared out of my mind that she would tell on me; I was frozen in a moment of pure and utter numbness. Nothing ever came from that episode. Truth be told, we never spoke about the issues after that night. Not ever. But the thought of her having this information and being able to expose me at any moment of her choosing scared me night and day.

I may not have known it at that moment in time, but that encounter with my sister and the looming fear of being outed would set in motion one of the most crippling of human emotions to take hold of my life for years to come—shame. It was shame of not being "normal" that propelled me to keep these unnatural longings in the deepest, darkest corner of my mind. It was self-inflicted shame that would cause me to live a dual life—one in which my sexuality would become a deviancy—a debilitating stigma that if exposed would cast a dooming shadow on my character and credibility as a genuine, affable, and candid guy. I was an actor fooling the world and, in so doing, trying to fool myself.

As time went on, I began to numb feelings of isolation by growing extremely close to certain friends. They, in turn, would become my best friends, and I would fall in love with them, want to be with them all the time, and deeply I knew I wanted something more to happen. But they were always completely straight and unaware of my sexual as well as emotional desire to be with them. I would be jealous, envious, and saddened when they would tell me about their sexual encounters with women. We would always get into little tiffs, and I would be pissed off at them, but they could never figure out why. I suppose they might have thought I was bipolar. But truth be told, I was just crazy in love.

I suppose in many ways, this subconscious awareness of never being desired by these friends pushed me to become a victim of a deepening depression that spanned years. During the early part of my sophomore year of high school, I stopped eating. I had always had a weight problem, and I blamed my weight on the reason I couldn't get a girlfriend. The only time I ate was at dinner, when I would consume just enough food to keep my parents in the dark, but at 3 a.m., I would get up and stick those fingers down my throat. I was slimming down, and people were complimenting me, but I was becoming more and more uneasy and unhappy. Little changed my depression or feelings of loneliness, the way, as I would soon find out, that alcohol and other experimental drugs did.

I started drinking in large quantities because, frankly, for the first time in my life, I found a method which helped me feel comfortable in my own skin. Alcohol became a means of finding happiness in my life. I had a water bottle filled with vodka stored in my locker that I would take a swig of every time a class ended. However, as with abusing any type of drug, more problems would soon emerge. Suffice it to say, I was the "party-kid." I had a zillion friends, as evident from my student council wins, and won election as the class superlative of "Mr. Most Likely to Brighten up a Bad Day," but I was the kid who had all these friends but not a single good friend, no one to turn to when things got tough, no one to understand me. I attempted suicide on more than one occasion, clearly unsuccessfully, and no one seemed to care. I was deeply tormented but always had a painted smile on my face.

At one party, I met this kid, Joe, who slept over my house after the party. We soon became sort of friends, and in time, due to his insinuation, we started to become sexually active. He was the first guy I was ever with. However, we never told anyone, and as far as I know, we were the only two to know we were doing such things. It was all very secretive, in parking lots, in my car, late at night, when parents weren't home, things like that. In school, we barely spoke, but outside of school, we were having fun. Although secret, for a short while, I felt rather complete and began to feel better about myself. I stopped drinking as heavily as I once did but when that affair ended because, once again, I found myself growing attached to someone unwilling to show me the love I sought, I went back to the bottle. It was during this time that I began to move away from drinking and start dabbling with drugs—in particular, pain killers. At a homecoming game, high on a mixture of booze and drugs, I decided it was wise to leap from the bleachers and dance with the cheerleaders. In such a crazed stupor after landing on the track, a busted leg throbbing, I still managed to get up and give my adoring audience a little dance. After breaking my leg, a dear friend of mine, who I had once had a crush on, told me, "I want to see you at graduation but at this rate I'm scared you won't be alive in another couple months." He was a good friend, and I pushed him away after that comment, and sadly, those were probably the last things he ever said to me.

That winter, I went to a Catholic Youth Conference, which was more of a weekend away with friends than a religious retreat. I had the intention of ending my life once and for all in the backwoods of this deserted Catskill resort. However, before we were allowed "free time," we were required to take part in a confessional. As I sat in a darkened room with a priest, he stared at me in a manner that made me terribly uncomfortable. I may have been able to fool the world, but could I truly fool this old man who sat before me? Could he see the fraudulent person that I truly am? He must have sensed the tension that I was enduring, because a required 5 minute confession turned into an hour long discussion of drinking, drugs, depression, the loss of friends, and relations with my father, which had become tremendously strained during this time. However, never once did I tell him about my sexuality, because my sexuality wasn't really a matter of concern to me at that time. I had created a myriad of outwardly self-destructive layers that securely guarded the deep-seated turmoil of being a sexual deviant.

The priest, having sympathy for me, gave me a dose of reality and told me that I needed to distance myself from everyone I had become accustomed to calling friends. I needed to break free from the chains of my former self and begin to create a new identity. Feeling refreshed and determined after this emotionally moving moment in my life, and knowing that I would soon be graduating high school, I took the old man's advice to heart and began to transition away from the substances I was so heavily dependent on, for practically the last four years of my life.

When I graduated from high school and [when I] began college the following fall, I was determined to push myself hard. I rarely went out. Instead, I studied. Every time I had the urge to go out, I would remind myself that I didn't want to regress into my old high school ways. But looking back on it, I think a lot of it had to do with my still latent sexuality and fear that in a drunken stupor I would expose my true nature.

After my first year of college, a few friends and I went up to Montreal to celebrate my birthday. As the night dragged on and the shots continually poured, I found myself growing increasingly interested in this fair skinned, blond haired Kevin Bacon look-a-like sitting in the corner of the bar. In time, I would introduce myself. Following him into the restroom on one occasion and standing next to him by the urinals, I made some passing lewd remarks. He asked me if I was gay, and I responded back no, but that I would be willing to suck him off if he wanted. I reached over and grabbed his dick. Clearly excited, he said, "Not here" and led me out of the bar and into a maze of dark, foreign alleyways that make up the underground world of Montreal. We stopped at this one location, which seemed to be blocks from the bar, and in the not so far distance, I could see another guy standing up against the wall having his junk played with. It was here, in this dark unknown alleyway with a complete and utter stranger, I performed oral sex and received a forceful unprotected penetration. When the act was over, we discovered we had been away from the bar for over an hour. How was I to explain such a disappearance to my friends; the guy I had just had sex with was walking side-by-side with me and insisted that I just tell them because after all we'd just had sex and I had to be gay. I remember stopping him in his tracks and looking him deep in his eyes and saying, "Listen, I'm not gay. Here is $40; take it, walk in the other direction and never talk about this again." He easily complied with my offer. Walking back to the bar alone, my mind was racing, I'd just had unprotected sex with a complete stranger, and although the fear of having just contracted an STD or worse should have been the most pressing issue, the fear of having to face my friends with a believable story that protected me from having to expose my sexuality to them was more of a concern. After they scolded me in front of the bar about disappearing in a strange country, I told them that I had gone out and smoked a blunt.

By the time I returned to the states, I had decided to leave my hometown for a while. I needed to run away from the messy situation in which I had recently found myself. Having almost been caught was too close a call for my comfort, so I returned to Buffalo and refused to come home for over a year. During this time, I felt very alone and still depressed. Although I no longer consciously sought to kill myself, I had resorted to another means of self-destruction: food. Food became a much needed comfort for feelings of isolation and loneliness. I would scarf down whole pies of pizza and a gallon of coke in single sitting. After 2 years of being in college, I had gained over 100 pounds, so at age 19, and standing only 5 feet 9 inches, I weighed an astounding 268 pounds and had over a 47-inch waist. I didn't care about myself. I never bought new clothes. I didn't bother about my appearance. Who was I trying to impress anyway?

By the end of my junior year of college, having been sexually dormant since the Montreal incident, I went out to a party with a group of college friends. As the night dragged on, I once again found myself growing attached to a good looking fellow. However, this time I knew him by association and also knew he was gay. Suffice it to say, the following morning, I woke up and rolled over to find him and myself lying naked on my bed. I knew at this very moment, as I began to panic, that I couldn't hide it anymore. I couldn't hide this one. I couldn't hide it from myself nor could I hide it from anyone else. I couldn't lie my way out of this one like I had in the past. People were bound to have witnessed us going at it. People knew I was gay. And I had to begin to accept it. However, in those early morning moments, as I watched this beautiful man sleeping soundly next to me, I felt at ease, and as I settled myself back down next to him, I closed my eyes and started to envision how to come to terms with being gay. For the first time in my life, I knew I had to make changes. However, I knew that coming out at this point in my life was not the right move. I still had a year of college left. I was extremely overweight, and I still wasn't completely confident that I was, in fact, gay. For the first time, though, I was seriously questioning it. It was days after this incident that I phoned a few friends from home and told them that I had a three-way with a girl and guy. It was my way of easing into the subject to see what their reaction would be. It would be a little over a year later, having dropped over 80 pounds, recently graduated from college, and having met a new gay guy at work whom I fell madly in love with, that I decided to start coming out to friends and siblings. It would be several months later that I finally came out to my parents.

You see, coming out is not simply telling the world that you're gay; it's about overcoming shame and the power it holds over an individual. Coming out is coming to terms with one's sexuality and putting an end to the shame that stems from self-inflicted hatred and external stressors. It is a process of healing and rebirth, but mostly, it's the process of going from being ashamed of who you are to being proud of who you are.

The process is long and at times difficult; however, I consider myself much better off today than I was merely a year ago when I first came out. Yet, looking back on my life, I consider myself a completely different person today than I was prior to coming out. Today, I've lost over 115 pounds all on my own. I'm an active graduate student seeking a career path in mental health counseling, and the lonesome void in my life has now been filled with promising first dates and hopes of a future filled with love and family—a life only a few short years ago I could never have imagined.

CHAPTER 19

ON CONFESSING ONE'S KINK IN A SEXUALITY TEXTBOOK

Tanya Bezreh

*E*DITORS' NOTES: *There is very little scientific literature on spanking. One important study was done by Rebecca Plante (2006), who combined observations of spanking parties and individual couple's private interactions with formal and informal interviews. She noted the importance of relationships and social context for the construction of self by spanking aficionados: "So for those interested in sexual spanking, the construction of the self relies on cultural contexts and recognition of the reality of stigma" (66). As a subculture, erotic spanking enthusiasts develop strategies to minimize stigma and proclaim the normalcy of their interests by finding, collecting, and sharing examples of spanking in popular culture, maintaining a belief that most people are interested in spanking but are unaware of this interest and differentiating themselves from sadomasochism (SM) practitioners. Importantly, Plante concludes that "it is safe to say that sexualities are enormously complex. The sexual self is clearly fluid, variable, and is simultaneously individually and culturally contextualized" (77).*

Tanya Bezreh's rather poetic narrative is unique among the stories in this section; she is coming out to the reader as she writes it. She lets the reader into her heart and mind, opening up her innermost feelings as she reveals her sexual interest. She does this with some trepidation; how will she be perceived? Can the readers of her story really understand what she is telling them? Or is her experience too foreign to you, the reader, for you to comprehend? Now that Tanya is "discredited," she has the task of breaking down readers' preconceptions, so they will continue to read, and so she can effectively communicate her experiences and feelings. One of the important points Tanya makes is that her interest in being spanked is not about pain; it is erotic and also about feeling loved: "If it's working, it's an internal journey. It feels like liquid, serious truth.

The experience is a trance, a delivery, a return, a safety, a feeling loved, a feeling safe, a feeling held, a journey together, an experiment, a step forward, a heart-glow, a warmth, a safety." Similarly, Plante (2006) reports that the women whom she studied "did not link spanking with masochism, pain or SM. . . . In other words, the women's desire to be spanked was seen as an emotionally laden activity within a caring context, not as a desire for pain or humiliation" (71).

Tanya is careful to make clear that her experiences are hers alone and do not represent the experiences of other people interested in erotic spanking. Her narrative makes explicit, more than any other chapters in this section, the interactional nature of sexual stories (Plummer 1995). How can we understand Tanya's story in the context of contemporary culture? Think about this narrative in relation to Chapter 2, on cultural constructions of the erotic. What is it about contemporary Western societies that might give rise to the eroticism Tanya describes? What do you make of the importance of cultural media (pop music, television shows, books, and websites) in her story? What does this consumption have to do with sexual identities?

CB&O

If we were lovers, there might be reason to confide. It's obvious why people disclose their sexual interests to lovers; the promise of sexual fulfillment is, every once in a while, more powerful than shame, reticence, or self-protection. The reasons people disclose their kinks to friends or family are different. To feel known? To be honest? To live loud and proud? Because their sex is noisy and could be misunderstood? Because someone suspects something anyway, that is, to clarify? But what reason is there to proclaim it to the world at large, or, more specifically, to you? When I first went public, my primary motivation was to stare down my worst fear. I wanted to make art and create outreach but was limited by the terror of telling my truth. So I deliberately came out on a very large scale, trying to get so much toothpaste out of the tube that it could never be scooped back in there. But I think it's a particular, peculiar choice, and I want to unmake it all the time.

I'm not sure the public arena is an appropriate place for this discussion. If we were having a conversation, we could negotiate what you want to hear, and I could stop talking if I felt uncomfortable. Like, I nudge toward some vulnerabilities, and then, you cue, by encouraging me or perhaps by sharing your vulnerabilities, that you want to continue the exchange. I know calculating appropriateness is a major part of any disclosure decision.

For me *appropriateness* is tied to questions of *effectiveness* and *persuasiveness*. In the wake of my "coming out," I have addressed kink in art and projects, with a goal of lifting stigma. But how do you lift stigma? By nudging gently? By marching in the streets? How do you create a new place in people's brains that isn't polluted by judgments and inherited phobias? Which words create understanding rather than uncomfortable tittering or polarization? Stigma is a vast sticky thing, and every once in a while, I take a vacation from my efforts by deciding that stigma around kink is impossibly entrenched; if this stigma is "un-budge-able," I don't have to bother trying to budge it. I was on such a hiatus when the editors of this textbook invited me to share my kink story. It's as close as it comes to an "appropriate" venue.

But is it a good idea to share my story? I've seen the discomfort on people's faces when I tell them the focus of my work. Even when I received an award for my graduate work on the subject, the president of the prize-giving institution used distancing language, something like, *people at Name of College do work in all sorts of different areas.* When my dad proudly announced my thesis work to our tablemates at his friend's 80th birthday, everyone stared, and no one spoke. In the buffet line afterward, he marveled, "That went over like a lead balloon!" I've lectured on my research and have heard the questions that come up, questions that assume kink is bad, wrong, or sad. And I have had the feeling of being misunderstood when I made personal artwork about this stuff; memories of my oversharing or overexposure come in terrors of regret when I'm down and out about something else. Why open myself to more of that?

The energy it takes for me to overcome these misgivings creates a logistical problem: On the one hand, my artist side takes heaps of pride in my ability to "take emotional risks," but once I'm doing that, it's not my sexuality that is on the page but an act of self-exploitation, a "Ta da! Look what I can do. I can tell perfect strangers all about myself." That's not sexy to me. "Ta da! Look what I can do" is ignoring boundaries and railroading fears, and that is the opposite of the patience and allowing that holds space for tendernesses to unfurl, if they will, in an intimate moment.

And then God forbid, you think I'm *brave.* I mean, some part of me wants to feel terribly brave for writing this, but the idea that speaking about kink is brave massively feeds the taboo, so please don't think me brave. Have you ever run across an article in a local alternative paper, for example, about some kink event or film or whatever where you get the impression that the reporter is so proud that they are open-minded enough to cover this "wacky" subculture? Oh, Lord. Kink is just another thing—with good parts and bad parts and annoying parts and people you end up loving and people you end up having chemistry with, and maybe the only difference is the porn sites you default to.

And it's scary to be the token voice. I haven't thought too much about textbooks or how sexuality is taught and codified. But I'm pretty sure that it's dangerous ground, this theory battling that theory. This or that piece of what I am about to share is getting glommed on to, excerpted, misinterpreted. No chance to clarify or correct myself, no chance to update and evolve.

So here it goes. With these and other concerns in tow, [come] the workings of my inner sancta:

OK, so let's say I describe myself as kinky. Now, I'd love feedback. Does this strike you as, "who isn't?" Does it strike you as "sick"? Does it remind you of a former lover who maybe wanted something you didn't want to do, and you fear this essay will be an indictment of you? Are you hopeful that you have found a kindred spirit and you're now reading to see if our kinks are similar or complementary, and how disappointed will you be when they diverge? Does the confession bore you to pieces? Have each of your friends done a one-woman show about their sexual identities, and you're just about ready to watch *Matlock*? Are you armed with a *DSM* disorder or some psychoanalytic theory? Or are you tasked with a thesis to write or a paper to find quotes for, and you are fishing here for an example, a representative, a pattern, something to analyze? I will do my best to give you some details, but please don't round me up to be representative of anything. You may not chalk my musings and anecdotes up to data, neither about kinksters nor spankos. No, no, no. Bad scientist!

If I'm throwing around jargon, don't worry. Nobody knows exactly what "kink" is, it's a wonky construct. But in my experience, people use the word to mean something in the power-exchange or sensation-play domain (if you're needing some clarity, maybe try the Wikipedia page on "sadomasochism"). Anyway, I use the word *kink* as a hedge. It tells you nothing about my interests. In fact, even if I say I'm into "spanking," it tells you almost nothing about my interests. *Spanking* gets you to the continent. You need more parameters to get to the country. I'm trying to think of what you might have seen that makes you think you know what I mean when I say "spanking." So, just taking videos on something like spankingtube.com, you can eliminate the following: I detest sensationalization like the spanking machine on the Howard Stern Show. Abandon scenes with mean or dull people. I don't like spankings for reasons (like doing something wrong). I prefer nonsense reasons, but this is very rare in porn. The actual impact can easily be too hard or too slow. I like light stuff: no marks beyond a rosy glow, no crying, nothing that looks even temporarily damaging. I prefer scenes where the sexuality of spanking is unacknowledged but present, nothing lascivious. (Overtly sexual can be OK, but that's a vacation home in another country.) I have to trust that both models are making the video for reasons I can accept and enjoy. I have gender and physical preferences. Let's say you knew all that; I would say it gets you to serviceable porn and to the regional level of understanding. Maybe then, if all the politics, languages, demographics, and sapiosexual stuff align, you get to the greater metro area. And then, congratulations, you're looking for a partner like anyone else: one with chemistry, one with compatible life goals, one with a compatible work schedule. What I'm trying to convey is that just because you know someone's label doesn't mean you know what or whom they are into.

I should probably reiterate that I am not representative of any group; there are many ways to be into spanking differently. Some people are into being punished or corrected. Some people are submissive, which I am not. Some people allow their partners to live out their topping fantasies; I'm mainly interested in everything happening more or less when I want, how I want, with space for play and surprise within a clear range of parameters. My interests have all sorts of lingo attached to them in the spanking scene, but I've not gotten into that lingo. (I have mostly dated people who don't have spanking fetishes of their own, and so I just tell them what I want using conventional terminology.) Regardless, I cannot say it enough; you are hearing a story about *me*, not a tribe of people or a movement or a species, just me. Just me.

I think some people at this point might be looking at my "pleasure in spanking" confession and wondering how this qualifies me as kinky at all. A spank here and there is so common, you see it in couples walking arm and arm; you see it in the choreography of high school dance troupes. It's a common naughty or cheeky gesture. I've seen enough "normal" porn to be convinced that a little spanking is a pretty common part of a sexual repertoire. It's suggested in the *Kama Sutra*. I think that one could enjoy spanking and not label it anything, and comfortably not label it "kink." But for one, I didn't know when I was discovering my interest that it *is* fairly common. And for another thing, I assumed from my devotion to fantasies of being spanked that I had a "fetish." I feel more comfortable aligning with kink via the fetishistic nature of my interest than via the idea that spanking necessarily be unusual. Fetish in the classical sense refers to requiring the fetish object to experience sexual gratification. So high heel fetishists "need" to be around or thinking about high heels to come. Fantasizing about spanking was my go-to fantasy from childhood through my early 30s.

When I was little, I fantasized that God spanked me. God's spanks fell like force fields onto my bed. I figured if a layer was even, like a blanket, that would nullify the spank, but if I pushed my pajamas down, my un-pajamaed bottom "felt" the slaps. It's not that God was angry or anything—I remember no major emotions related to God. I felt safe and happy, if also excited. I had never actually been spanked, but I thought about the phenomenon all the time. Sometimes, I tried out chopping boards or fly swatters on myself, curious about the sting. My only actual experience was very occasionally being play-punished during a phase where my cousins and I were inspired by a TV show we had seen where a girl steals a wallet and her teacher canes her.

There was no awareness then of sex qua sex. And there was a purely physical sexuality I was discovering, and I don't remember if there were fantasies associated with it or not. I had a way of masturbating (not that I knew there was such a word or concept) by propping my hips up in the air like a yoga inversion (*sarvangasana*), leaning my legs back (toward the floor away from the head). Orgasm made me tumble over. Eventually, I worked out a way of lifting my legs while lying on my belly; that way I didn't fall. Once, when my parents were out, I got the idea to do it in every room of the house, thinking the house would take off into outer space. There was an intuitive aversion to doing it in my parents' bedrooms, though, so the experiment remains unproven.

There was some disadvantage to having no words for any of it. The aforementioned childhood play, for example, ended in a moment of feeling utterly misunderstood. My grandmother came into the kitchen one day as I was aiming a fly swatter at a bent-over cousin, and gave a quick disapproving frown. Immediately, I had a defense in my brain that would take years to find words: *I know I look like a sadist, but I have no sexual interest in sadism. I am* being *asked* to do this. It is consensual. Not only that, my play partner doesn't even want to feel any pain at all; I'm *pretending to strike. I don't even want to be the one hitting! But I can't always lobby to play the character that gets punished, because I don't want to seem too obvious or pushy! I probably do feel some sense of shame that I enjoy being on the receiving end, even craving the sensation and excitement of this play. Is that wrong? Is this play wrong specifically because it is wrong to play at hitting people? Or is it wrong because I have funny stirrings? Are the stirrings themselves wrong? Or is it wrong to get the stirrings from activities that involve other people who may not be interested or consenting to the stirrings, in other words, the secrecy part?*

I think that play phase was around age six. It wasn't until college that spanking play came back into my life. In sixth grade I learned that the yoga pose I'd been doing was masturbation. I liked doing it much better before I knew that. Also in sixth grade, I learned in a bizarre snippet of conversation that "some people like to be spanked." That went through me like a shudder; I could barely process the horror. *Was I one of those people?!* I spent many years worried I was crazy.

When my family first got cable, we briefly got Playboy TV. When I first witnessed sex, I came standing in front of the television, remote in hand. So it's not that I had never found sex sexy, it's just that I exclusively fantasized about spanking. Presumably, puberty is terrifying even when growing into a "normal" sexuality. But I can imagine that, however ridiculous or poisonous, the sexual imagery floating around in the 1980s helped adolescents feel a sense of permission about their emerging sexuality and created a cultural context and language within which to position sexual ideas.

Here was my cultural landscape: John Cougar Mellencamp's "Hurts so Good." And, somewhat more ambiguously, the Eurythmics singing, "Some of them want to abuse you; some of them want to be abused." (Couldn't George Michael have sung something like, "Sex is natural, sex is good, and this stuff that you're into, Tanya, that's great, too!") Eventually, I learned the word *masochism,* and that at least felt like a plausible home. But this was the 1980s. Rihanna was not yet singing "S&M," Madonna's "Human Nature" was not yet all over MTV. When I learned about the phenomenon of masochism, I understood from the general silence that the subject was taboo and that I should keep still about it, too.

The silence became an integral part of my sex life. At some point, I started rolling through teen relationships. The conventional physical milestones gave me thrills, but I was wishing, wishing, wishing for something that was never going to happen. In writing this now, it occurs to me that the idea of directly asking for what I wanted never occurred to me then. That fantasy was deeply hidden. Attempts to provoke anger or machismo from my boyfriends were met with confusion, and I always felt insulted that my partner wouldn't realize I was play-acting annoying, *not actually annoying!* I pretty much assumed that I was completely alone in liking something like this.

For my sweet sixteen, a friend gave me a pornographic book. It chronicled the corruption of a girl named Angel by a guy named Rod and his sister (except not really!), Rose. And, miraculously, there were scenes with spankings! Angel gets spanked by the pool! Angel gets spanked in the pool house! The day I read this book, I came 14 times. I have to say, for me to come 14 times is not just about being turned on. It is about some profound hope of maybe not being alone in this world. The Angel spankings were not clearly erotic, but since it was a dirty book, one could infer a relationship. My friend deserves a medal of honor for smuggling this precious comfort into my hands.

In college, I finally stammered into the ear of someone I was in love with that I thought spanking was hot, and one day against my pleading protestations (I was soooo scared), he flipped my screaming body over his lap and slapped me like four times, and I came. By chance that same summer, I had bought Anne Rice's *Sleeping Beauty* trilogy (on pure intuition! without having cracked the cover!). Later that summer, he read to me how the prince woke Beauty and took her on his horse and spanked her—*He what?* I thought my boyfriend was kidding, like making fun of my obsession. But no! There it was in black and white. And while Rod, Angel, and Rose had done some spanking, this book was devoted to that sort of thing. This book had a fresh spanking every few paragraphs. Soon thereafter, I figured out things like Shadow Lane and Blue Moon Press. And those were welcome discoveries for someone who had felt isolated since the dawn of her sexual awareness.

The fantasy of finding someone whose kink matched mine was my dream of true love in my 20s. I think there were probably many possible people out there who would have fit my formula; but to meet people with a specific kink, it helps to be able to admit your specific kink. After dating a few guys who weren't into spanking, and weren't into even exploring it for my sake, or judged me for it, I felt like I had to start dating in the kink scene. I'd stand around kink events not wearing latex, not wearing leather, and have fun conversations and fascinating experiences, but no luck finding a fetish match. One of my deepest conversations was with a burly firefighter dressed in a tutu, but we were the same, not complements. I knew about far-away spanking parties, but was too terrified to go. So I pined. I read. I got overly excited about allusions. I fantasized. It was a waste of a twenty-something. And I had heard fetishes don't leave people, so I occasionally dutifully tried again.

I went to a few meetings of young kinky people called New York TNG. One evening, someone in the room confessed compatible interests during introductions and afterward came out to dinner. Our eyes locked in a deep trance. A few days later, we had a first date. A few days later, he spanked me. I was scared of him, scared of his messy room, scared of ways he seemed lonely. The spanking was fantastic. I *loved* it. Both of us could come from spanking alone, and that compatibility felt so sweet. But I didn't love him. That's how dating goes, right? Via a Shadow Lane ad, I eventually met a few other men who were identified spankos. I dated one of them. I was spanked and stung and thrilled and made to squeal; it was like a kid finally getting to eat all the cotton candy she wanted. But I didn't fall in love with him. I fell in love with boys for whom this was not a priority or interest. Sometimes, the kink would sit on the shelf for a while, sometimes be accommodated. For me, the big questions were, *How important is a kink match? And is a boyfriend willing to indulge my interest enough, or do I keep the quest for my reciprocal alive?*

How are you doing? Let me take a step back. Some people are unaccustomed to considering spanking or impact play in a consensual way. During lectures on my research, sometimes people ask why they should care about the disclosure needs of people who want to hurt people. It becomes clear that their brain resets consensual impact play to "violence." I encourage them to think of a sword fight at the theater. The words kinky people say to each other before and after (and with meta-level talk during) a scene is like the stage and the curtains. I met someone at a party once who staged her own abduction, because she fantasized about struggling for her life. She arranged for her friends to break into her apartment and drag her to a car; I can't remember what else. She was very happy with how it went. She chose friends who were comfortable with a lot of kicking and fighting back. Some of the friends were at the party where she was telling me this story. So you get the consensuality and the *pretend* part, right?

I've also had someone ask, "If it's crazy to have these fantasies in the first place, how is it OK to indulge what a crazy person is asking for?" I don't really know how to respond to that because it brings you right up to how do you define "crazy"? It's a shifting cultural construct. And, from a personal note, I can say that I've spent a good chunk of my life worried that I was crazy to enjoy this and that did not do anything for me except create alienation and self-doubt, and that alienation and self-doubt are way worse than having an orgasm from someone slapping your bum. (For a thorough argument about how people into SM are no more crazy than any other group of people, see Moser and Kleinplatz's [2005] article, "DSM-IV-TR and the Paraphilias: An Argument for Removal".)

Of course, you may not vibe with any of this. Some of these ideas might disgust you or leave you cold. That is totally fine! I don't force myself to vibe with people I don't vibe with, or to do things that gross me out, or freak me out, or bore me. I might try things out of curiosity; they might be nice, they might leave me cold. That's life. I did talk to an amazing person once who was a professional dominant who had cultivated an ability in himself to, as he called it, "resonate" with all different sorts of fantasies. Some people have really really unusual fantasies, he said, and it was a huge gift to them for him to be able to catch the vibe and, yes, *resonate* with what was hot for them. I think that's a really lovely thing to be able to do. But that's not for everyone. It's OK to like what you like, and if possible stretch a bit to see if you can vibe with what your partner likes.

Even if their physical desires perplex you, one way to connect with a kinky person is to figure out what emotions and needs are elicited or met by the kinky fantasy or behavior. My fantasies often evoke a feeling of being seen through and, thus, deeply known. That's the feeling of the *Oh my gosh is he going to spank me?* part of the excitement. On the flip side, another kind of scene that has really worked for me is an idea that someone "has to" spank me, usually for a ridiculous reason (like, it's Tuesday). So he doesn't *want* to do it, he *has to*. This is somehow about the helplessness and indignity of *not* being seen, of not being able to fight against systems, cultures, larger forces, and thoughtless compliance. I don't know why exactly those feelings are so relaxing and erotic to me, but I guess they meet some needs of my psyche?

Also, my fantasies are not generally about eons of spanking; they are about the idea of being spanked *at all*. And they replay the excitement of that very first moment: the heartbeat in the throat. I can come from threat alone. Of course, I've enjoyed actual spanking, too, though writing about it in physical terms seems vulgar, maybe because "sting" or "leather" is not how it feels. If it's working, it's an internal journey. It feels like liquid, serious truth. The experience is a trance, a delivery, a return, a safety, a feeling loved, a feeling safe, a feeling held, a journey together, an experiment, a step forward, a heart-glow, a warmth, a safety. I can't say safety enough. That's how it feels. I go into a nest and feel so safe. Sometimes inside that nest, I turn into a banshee and want to have sex like [in] a bad 80s movie. That's how it works for me.

A meditation teacher of mine once suggested that all the things we lust after are things that have brought us into that present moment and that we get attached to the strategies that brought us there, even though that "present moment" state is inside of us. I remember learning how to meditate and arriving at the present moment in meditation for the first time. And realizing that I'd been there a thousand times before in moments of surrender at climax. Seen that way, my sexuality seems like a flavor burst on the way to something eternal and utterly universal. I hope that we can resonate in that peace at the center, if not in the specifics of the periphery.

It's actually a wonderful sexuality, seen on its own terms. So rarely do I see it that way: such a harmless, incredibly sweet, and straightforward way to surrender control. Or at least I *feel* a pretend surrender of control. It takes the smallest suggestion of spanking (in the right context) for me to gush love—so sweet, really. But look at the literature. Look at the parade of people who pathologize this sexuality—or analyze it: who think it impugns my mental health or who would put it in a flower arrangement with the other peculiarities of my mental health to draw conclusions and suggest causations: crappy, crappy scientists.

Just one example from a thrift-store-find lying on my desk: In *Everything You Always Wanted to Know About Sex (But Were Afraid to Ask),* Dr. David Reuben calls people who combine sadism, masochism, and homosexuality "among the cruelest people who walk this earth. In ancient times they found employment as professional torturers and executioners. More recently they filled the ranks of Hitler's Gestapo and SS." This was a best-selling book in the 1960s. It was translated into 54 languages!

Or another example: Freud and his idea that masochism is sadism turned against the self. I mean, it's a fine idea for a poem or something. But how much of my life am I supposed to spend trying on this theory before I'm allowed to set it aside and be like, *I don't think that feels useful to me.* And up until *DSM-III*, masochism was called a "sexual disorder." How was I supposed to know in my 20s years that the *DSM* is more of a battleground than a description of reality? Yanking out the purity of your own experience from under a heap of labeling and judgments is tough work.

When you make a sexuality invisible or couch it entirely in judgments or psychological theories, a festering breeding ground is created for shame. Even just the sense of being different has massive effects. Really, the idea of "normal" needs to be banished from the earth. Then, we could show sex ed students a massive chart of all known sexual behaviors and say, *Everyone has a nuanced, complicated sexual landscape and certain things feel better to them than others; everyone has a vocabulary; everyone has a scope; and everyone has some work to do to decide how much effort to put into finding a compatible match. Even within common activities, everyone's sexuality is unique. Some want to do 100 different things. Some want to do one thing. Some want to experiment. Some will hand you a script. Some want to gaze into your eyes and let it evolve from there. Some want to drag you to a tantric temple. Find someone whose sexuality you can live with.*

I wonder if this glimpse into my kink has given you anything useful. I hope that it has. There is much more to explain, really. Mainly, I want to cast a protective spell over you to make sure *your* sexuality isn't beset by any of the same judgmental nonsense mine has been tangled in—and that you're aware enough to shoo the judgments away when they try to land on you. For example, years ago on an airplane, I got into a conversation with a therapist who, after hearing my confessions, gave her opinion that she thought bondage was probably fine but that she worried about an interest in the pain of spanking. "I don't usually give any advice," she said, "but I would tell you to learn how to nurture yourself." I was very offended at that last part. I wanted to say that I *did* know how to nurture myself. But as I aged, I learned how to be kinder to myself, take better care, and be clearer about asking for support—a lovely part of growing older. I began to appreciate that therapist's advice. But not until writing this essay did I remember and zoom in on her offhand little analysis of bondage: OK, spanking not so much. That part I had simply accepted. Like, I was so ground down by my own and others' pathologizing of spanking that I wasn't even outraged.

Being thorough about flicking away all the judgment that gets lobbed at one is tricky. There's a part in a 1996 *New Yorker* essay by Daphne Merkin in which the therapist to whom she has confessed an interest in spanking says "violence isn't foreplay." She writes, "He's right, of course, but, as I tried to explain to him, a certain amount of violence lubricates my mind and—strangely—releases me, if only for a moment, from my vigilant distrust of men" (98). This essay is like the mother of spanking confessional essays; Daphne Merkin is a hero, and I'm not being critical of her when I say she needed to kick her therapist's facile dismissal so much further into the stratosphere. Whether violence is ever foreplay is not relevant because consensual spanking is not violence. And as for her response that spanking is "strangely" liberating, why label it strange when it is biologically true? Then, she brings up her distrust of men which makes me question: Is it a worse distrust of men than anyone else's distrust of anyone else? I'm so familiar with this pattern: agreeing to the assumption that there must be something wrong with liking spanking and then feeling the need to confess personal limitations that may be feeding into the supposed pathology. I spent years positing etiological hypotheses that take for granted that "there is something wrong with liking this." I auditioned every personal tragedy, relationship, every playful spanking moment as possible cause or reason. Someday, one of these essays will say, *Yay! I was born with a gene that makes me respond very happily to spanking play, and this gives me an awesome form of sexual gratification that involves no risk of STDs. Yippee!*

It's not just theoretical judgments, either. There are legal problems in the United States for people who like to be spanked; their lovers can be prosecuted. And it doesn't have to be that way. In Germany, for example, it is illegal to spank a child. And it *is* legal for adults to consent to BDSM play as long as that play is relatively safe and stoppable by a safe word. I would say that's pretty fantastic, and both points make the United States look barbarous by contrast.

So I would be wary of what you internalize from this environment. Even stuff that's not necessarily judgmental may be just plain wrong. When I was learning about SM, I read everywhere that a fetish is static, never changing, and permanent. That idea of permanence massively influenced my decision to go public. If this thing was a permanent part of me, then it seemed worth "owning it" and getting over the anxiety of who might find out about it. But my fetish has not been static. Weirdly, after my first big art project that revealed my interest, I started having sexual fantasies about a guy repairing my garage door. I was like, *Oh, shit, I just came out in a really big way, and now this fetish thing is changing?!* And it did. In my 30s, the number of things that reliably turned me on expanded many fold. Now, I like tantric stuff, soft stuff, overtly sexual stuff that used to feel too overwhelming. I still think spanking is hot, but it's no longer the only way in. Which, technically, kicks me out of the label "fetish." Which I guess (since having a fetish was my primary way of identifying as kinky) kicks me out of the label "kink." Which disqualifies this essay for the "token kink person" spot! (I'm being somewhat facetious, obviously, but these considerations are what labels are made of!)

I do think that there are other people who could give you a better view into kink life. I have done lots of thinking about kink in culture, but my life is not some phantasmagoric blossoming of my fantasies. Every once in a while, I see people who appear massively kink-confident and self-actualized, and I imagine them living out their fantasies vehemently, not hesitating to ask for what they want and making it happen. I've talked to people who grew up with "out" kinky peers who always felt supported or at least not judged and with people who live their lives in peer groups selected for kink-supportiveness. I think my anxieties to some degree have to do with using my personal experience as a point of activism to push this subject into public dialogue and into the scope of public health. I'm focusing on getting people to care about humans experiencing stigma, and that creates an anhedonic bias. So take even this essay with plenty of salt. Don't let my bitterness getcha!

The fear that I have herein embodied all sorts of self-loathing and self-ghettoization or other by-products of stigma or concretized stigma by naming it is the final misgiving I'll mention about this essay. You must vow to me that you will give primacy to your own experience. Your body/soul matter way more than any theory or concept. And, as much as you can, create a community that somehow posits a world where stigma never happened. If that community includes a way for people to connect on similar interests without feeling the rest of their life like they're wearing an indelible label, I want to live there with you.

CHAPTER 20

INTERSECTIONS OF VAMPIRISM AND SEXUALITY

A Narrative Description of a Vampire Feeding

D J Williams

*E*DITORS' NOTES: *D J Williams is the only professional sociologist, researcher, and writer included in this section. While his narrative describes the interaction of two other people, Dr. Williams is not an entirely objective observer. He reveals his feelings about what he is observing and his interaction with the participants before and after the scene. He actually does have a role in the scene. "Dr. Deviant," as the vampire calls him, takes the role of professional voyeur. Fortunately, for sociologists who study sexuality, the voyeur role is often a legitimated and sometimes an integral part of some sex scenes. For some participants, exhibitionism is part of what turns them on. However, this does not seem to be the case in this very private interaction; Dr. Williams was afforded a very special courtesy by the women he observed. What is interesting about the story is his own sense making of the interaction, which goes beyond a purely scientific description of his observations. He describes his own feelings: "I was excited to be here"; he felt "a mild uneasiness inside me"; "a chill runs down my spine"; and "a highly deviant act somehow feels overwhelmingly spiritual." For Dr. Williams, his sense making of this scene was not only on an intellectual level but on an emotional plane as well.*

INTRODUCTION

As a social scientist with a background in sociology, criminology, social work, and leisure sciences, I have been privileged to get to know many interesting people within a broad range of social spaces. I have worked with several populations that are commonly viewed as deviant, including prisoners, sex workers, radical body modifiers, and bondage/discipline/dominance/submission/sadism/masochism (BDSM) practitioners. However, perhaps none of these groups is as controversial and least understood within the mainstream as the diverse, international community of self-identified vampires.

I have worked with people who secretly identify as vampires for the past several years in an effort to better understand this hidden community and the practices of its members. In this chapter, I will situate the topic of vampire sexualities by introducing the widespread popularity of vampires, including the increased sexualization of these monsters. I will then introduce readers to different vampire identities and discuss how these identities remain connected to broader understandings of sexuality as suggested by the World Health Organization (WHO 2006). However, a vampire identity does add a fascinating new dimension to understanding one's unique sexuality. Finally, I will also discuss some potential sexual practices that are enjoyed by vampires as an expression of their vampirism.

Contemporary Vampire Popularity: Mythological Roots and Increased Sexualization

The word *vampire* evokes strong images and emotions for many people. Vampire myths have been present for thousands of years across numerous cultures and geographic locations. Beliefs of vampire beings were present among the ancient Sumerians and Assyrians, and various vampire monsters were present in early cultures throughout Europe, Mexico, Puerto Rico, Brazil, Iceland, Malaysia, Scandinavia, South Africa, and the Philippines (Curran 2005; Melton 1999). More recently, narratives of vampires, including Bram Stoker's classic *Dracula* (1897), have blended early lore with historical reports of actual people, such as Vlad Tepes, the vicious Romanian ruler during the 1400s who viciously tortured and impaled his enemies, and Erzebet Bathory (1560–1614), the Hungarian countess who creatively tortured and killed hundreds of young women before bathing in their blood. Forensic behavioral scientists commonly report that some extremely violent crimes, including numerous past and present instances of serial murder, seem to be highly motivated by sexuality, particularly extreme sadism. Vlad Tepes and Erzebet Bathory both seemed to be motivated to a large degree by fusions of sex and power in their murderous acts. Curiously, Picart and Greek (2003) reported that serial killers and vampires are our two primary monstrous figures and that these figures blend together and reflect our deepest fears and taboos, yet also our most repressed fantasies and desires.

Since the time of Stoker's *Dracula*, popular culture has increasingly portrayed vampires as being more physically attractive and sexual. For example, Ann Rice's highly popular *Vampire Chronicles* (1976–2003) and, more recently, Stephanie Meyers's *Twilight* series (2005–2008) sexualize vampires much more so than earlier portrayals. Researchers have found that vampires are the most popular and appealing monster in movies and easily outdistance competitors (Fischoff et al. 2002/2003). Vampires are intelligent, strong, assertive, mysterious, erotic, and seductive, yet also abhorrent and frightening. It is precisely such a curious mix of attributes that is responsible for such widespread fascination with vampires. We highly value and promote positive traits of the vampire, yet beneath a polished exterior that we present to others (sociologically, social desirability bias), human beings have various imperfections and character flaws. Human history has shown repeatedly that under certain circumstances sometimes "good" people can commit unthinkable atrocities. Vampires, then, are reflections of us as human beings.

Of course, sexuality is also a powerful aspect of us as human beings. We must remember that sexuality is socially constructed and involves many contextual factors and that individual sexuality varies, often considerably, from person to person. The WHO (2006) position is that sexuality is shaped by interactions of biological, psychological, cultural, social, economic, political, legal, ethical, historical, and religious and spiritual factors. Therefore, every person, including each vampire, can be understood as having a unique sexuality. People's sexual preferences (as expressions of unique sexualities), including preferences among vampires, can also vary considerably.

Despite the massive literature (both scholarly and otherwise) dealing with vampire beliefs, legends, folklore, and fiction, very few scholars have had the opportunity to explore people who secretly, in one form or another, self-identify as vampires. Many self-identified vampires rightfully seem to be distrustful of scholars and professionals for fear of being labeled as delusional and/or dangerous (see Williams 2008). Nevertheless, several years ago, Gunn (1999) pointed out the need for scholars to engage ethnographically with subcultures (he specifically addressed Goths) in order to understand them, rather than relying on "experts," usually from law enforcement, who have never actually spent time with members of such communities.

In light of the above background, the personal narrative below is based on an experience observing what vampires call a "feeding" (taking of human energy) that involved both blood drinking and sexual behavior. In order to protect the identities and confidentiality of participants, the names (specifically vampire "night names"), various features, and details have been changed. My purpose is to give readers a flavorful taste of a particular erotic and powerful subjective experience involving a female vampire and her donor. Readers should note that vampire practices can vary considerably. Therefore, this account is not generalizable. With that in mind, let us begin . . .

It is after 11:00 p.m., but I am wide awake as I look around the small hotel room. The room is dark with its lights turned off, but several small candles placed strategically around the room provide ample light to see basic features of my surroundings. It is a nice but fairly typical hotel room. I notice a large mirror on the west wall across from the king sized bed where I patiently wait. I can see my form in the mirror, but the darkness in the room hides details of my face and its slightly anxious expression. There is a painting of several small white boats docked at a quiet harbor that hangs on the wall above where I sit. As I stare at the painting, I can't make out all the details of the boats or the harbor, either. To pass the few minutes of waiting, I move closer to the top of the bed and the painting. My new position provides a much clearer view of the painting. I notice that the lower sides of the boats have different designs painted on them with different colors. Each boat is different, I observe. I look away from the painting and back toward the front of the room. The shadows from the candlelight produce mysterious forms on the walls behind them. My mind quickly remembers scenes from Dracula, *along with bits and pieces of various other vampire movies and stories that saturate our culture. I am excited to be here, yet reminders of pop culture villains also seem to simultaneously inject a mild uneasiness inside me.*

"Have you been to our city before?" Dot, the pleasant 33-year-old woman sitting in the corner asks, breaking the silence. She has already taken off her clothes down to her bra and snug-fitting panties.

"A few times," I warmly smile. "I always enjoy visiting the Northwest." Still, I wonder what it would be like to live day in and day out with frequent rain.

Dot smiles back as she, too, waits with eager anticipation. She has done this before, numerous times, though intimately giving her energy to her vampire partner in a hotel room is a rare treat. Dot has high cheekbones and a cheery smile. My eyes glance across her petite form including small breasts hiding beneath her bra, but I am careful not to stare. I am a guest, and I want to be as respectful as possible to this fascinating couple. Despite meeting me only a few hours earlier, Dot seems plenty comfortable. She works during the day as a human relations specialist for a local manufacturing company and is active in her community. She appears normal by any measure; surely, none of her neighbors or coworkers would ever suspect she is a donor in a vampire relationship. Her partner—a vampire—and I have known each other for several months.

"I am ready." Lady Nightstryke suddenly appears. "Are you ready for this, Dr. Deviant? And are you ready, my precious Dot?"

I sit up straight, and my heart beats faster as my eyes seem to focus naturally on blood-red lipstick and beautiful long black hair. Lady Nightstryke is a little taller than I realized. I see that she is seductive and powerful in her black lingerie with its red lace across the top; her power and mystique are undoubtedly amplified in my mind by the burning candles and room's ambience. Her slender legs move up from the floor to slightly wider than average hips. As she moves closer toward the candlelight, however, clues of her ordinary humanness become more visible. Like most adults, including myself, she is a little heavier around her torso than she probably once was. And, although she maintains her beauty extremely well for being 54 years old, there are a few subtle signs that she is gradually aging.

"Thank you again for inviting me to watch your feeding ritual," I gratefully acknowledge. I nod and look at Lady Nightstryke then at Dot.

Dot smiles wide and nods back. I notice her eyes sparkle in the candlelight.

"No problem, Dr. Deviant!" replies Lady Nightstryke. She arranges a few necessary items on the nightstand next to the bed. "I am pleased that there are researchers like you who truly want to understand who we (real vampires) are. To most people we must be psychopaths. They don't understand that we do not choose this condition, but we are born with it."

Dot smiles, too, and her eyes quickly meet mine. I sense that she is perfectly content with me watching a most intimate practice that she and Lady Nightstryke usually perform with no one else present. As the two women move toward the large bed, I quickly scoot to the chair in the corner where Dot had been sitting. I want to make sure that I am not in their way. Lady Nightstryke opens a small container on the nightstand near the bed and carefully pulls out a shiny silver scalpel along with Band-Aids and some alcohol prep pads. Her eyes quickly scan the room, seemingly a final check before the feeding session begins.

"Dr. Deviant, please remain quiet until we are finished." The vampire's piercing eyes are riveted upon me from across the shadow-filled room.

"Of course," I acknowledge, fully aware that I am fortunate to have such a rare opportunity to observe.

My mind wanders back to my previous interactions with Lady Nightstryke. She is highly educated and works a day job as a business consultant. She travels frequently for work, but always keeps her vampire identity and practices private and secretive. Lady Nightstryke had learned over a year ago that I have research interests on topics that might be understood as deviant leisure, including BDSM and vampirism. She seemed intrigued with my work and later contacted me. Several times, we have discussed sociological and psychological perspectives on various unconventional leisure practices and mainstream interpretations of such practices. I enjoy visiting with her, and she seems to trust me. Occasionally, she worries that her vampirism with Dot may be discovered by outsiders. "Sure, people are more accepting than they used to be about a lesbian couple," Lady Nightstryke once said, though she technically identifies herself as pansexual and Dot as bisexual, "but Dot and I would lose our jobs if people knew that our relationship involves vampirism. Both our lives would be ruined."

Although Lady Nightstryke often wears dark clothing and has some interest in vampire myths and imagery, she strongly identifies as a real vampire and not a "lifestyler." Curiously, she reports taking subtle human energy through both drinking blood and sex. Apparently, sometimes her feeding sessions with Dot involve only blood drinking; other times, she can feed during sex. However, on occasions when Lady Nightstryke desires what she describes as a "full feeding," she will feed with Dot via blood and sex within the same intimate session. I am about to witness such a full feeding now. The room is quiet and peaceful. I look across at the two women near the edge of the bed. The women lovingly gaze into each other's eyes for several seconds. I notice that I can hear my own breathing.

"My precious Dot, please take off the rest of your clothing," Lady Nightstryke finally instructs. Her words are spoken with gentleness and compassion, but also firmness.

Dot quickly slips out of her panties and unhooks her bra. Lady Nightstryke carefully surveys Dot's slender body up and down before smiling with satisfaction and placing a single kiss on her lips. While there soon will be some sexual activity to the degree they are comfortable with me being present, this intimate experience is primarily a feeding session. It involves an expression of an unusual identity.

"Now lie back and relax," Lady Nightstryke again instructs her donor. Soon Dot is lying on the bed, her back slightly arched, with the vampire directly over her feet. Dot takes several slow, deep breaths.

Lady Nightstryke playfully kisses each of Dot's toes one by one, before gradually kissing and licking her way up the donor's smooth legs. Both women are completely absorbed in the experience, and neither says a single word. The vampire takes her time and inhales deeply several times along the way, before stopping at the sexual zone where Dot's legs meet. Dot's breathing gets faster and heavier. The vampire quickly changes position and straddles her donor. They are now face to face, vampire and donor, gazing intensely into each other's eyes. I sit on the edge of my chair with my own eyes wide open and trying not to miss any detail. To them, however, I am miles away. They are completely focused on each other, and right now nothing else exists.

Several seconds pass in silence. Lady Nightstryke inhales deeply and powerfully in a perfect rhythm as her donor exhales. I notice Dot's hands clench hard onto the hands of her partner for a few tense moments before relaxing again. Inhale slowly, exhale slowly. Inhale slowly, exhale slowly. I notice the women's bodies seem to be in subtle rhythm moving together as they breathe, and their artful synchronicity casts beautiful shadows on the curtains behind them. The dark hotel room is now electrified. An occasional sensual moan from Dot interrupts the silence in the room. Time seems to have stopped.

"I love you, Dot." Lady Nightstryke yanks the hair of her donor, causing Dot's head to snap back. The vampire finds the lips of her partner and begins kissing them softly at first, but the kisses very quickly turn much more passionate. As the vampire kisses, I notice her eyes inspecting Dot's neck. Soon the kisses move lower to the donor's neck, and Dot turns her head slightly to give her vampire better access to this new anatomical target. I quietly shift my position on the chair, trying not to make a sound, so that I can get a better view. The vampire begins to bite, softly at first but then harder. The groans from Dot's open mouth grow louder and more frequent, and her small body occasionally bucks and shakes from the harder bites. Both seem to enjoy this intensity and intimacy.

Suddenly, the calculating vampire jumps back to her previous position so that her face is positioned directly above the most sensual junction of Dot's shaking legs. Lady Nightstryke deliberately licks slowly and carefully around the donor's pleasure zone as Dot spreads her legs wider to invite more delightful inspection from her partner. For several seconds, the vampire teases her donor with her tongue, and once again Dot's moans grow continually louder. Eventually, the vampire's skilful tongue zeros in on a specific sexual target, and I watch as the back of the vampire's head vigorously moves up and down in a predictable motion between her donor's throbbing legs. At a point of apparent climax, Dot's ravished body shakes violently with pleasure. The vampire stops her motion, quickly leans back, licks her lips, and savors the sexual aroma from above her target. As the vampire deeply inhales, she seems to become more alert and focused. At the same time, Dot's body dissipates into a state of intense release.

"You need to stay with me now, my beautiful and precious Dot!" Lady Nightstryke directs. "We are not quite finished. Just stay where you are and lie still."

The vampire straightens up and reaches toward the nightstand where she opens what appears to be a small alcohol prep pad, the same type that a nurse would use just before administering an injection to a patient. The vampire locates a precise space on her donor's body, high on the upper part of the chest and just below the clavicle, where she intently scrubs in preparation to make a tiny incision. Soon the shiny scalpel is nestled in the vampire's right hand. She leans over her donor with the silver instrument poised tightly in her long, bony fingers.

"Take a big breath in, precious," Lady Nightstryke calmly commands.

Dot's eyes glance down at the shiny medical instrument, and she takes a breath in as instructed, though this breath is not particularly deep. She knows what is coming, and it does not bother her in the least. At Dot's exhale, the vampire's fingers work their magic and the scalpel moves a tiny distance across Dot's upper chest. Immediately, bright red blood oozes from Dot's skin and forms a line behind the scalpel before quickly transforming into a tiny puddle. As freshly oxygenated blood still oozes, the vampire carefully sets the scalpel back on the nightstand and begins to lick the tiny red puddle above Dot's exposed breast. She playfully licks at the tiny wound before sucking forcefully for several seconds. Dot's body is perfectly still, energy spent, and her eyes are not quite closed.

Lady Nightstryke leans over her resting partner with the donor's own fresh blood still dripping from her vampire smiling lips. "I love you, my precious Dot," the vampire whispers and gently kisses her donor. "Thank you, my love. I am forever with you, and now I am renewed once again."

Dot acknowledges her partner's gratitude with a small smile as her eyes close. Her spent body still does not move. The vampire kisses her donor one more time and gently pulls up the soft covers of the bed to keep her partner comfortable and warm. I can feel the intense chemistry between them. A chill runs down my spine as it occurs to me that this may be perhaps the most intense display of intimacy I have ever witnessed! Strangely, my initial uneasiness has been transformed into a state of extreme gratitude to this unusual couple, and a highly deviant act somehow feels overwhelmingly spiritual!

Lady Nightstryke gets up from the bed and walks confidently toward me. Human blood smattered around her devious smile becomes brighter and slightly eerie to my consciousness as she approaches the candles near where I sit.

"Well, now Dr. Deviant has witnessed a real vampire feeding." Lady Nightstryke's eyes meet mine. I see that she is very satisfied with the feeding. "So what are your thoughts about it?"

"It was intense, very arousing, and powerful," I stammer. "I could really sense the trust and intimacy between you and Dot."

Lady Nightstryke nods in agreement and disappears around the corner into the bathroom. Soon, we will talk further. I still have many questions and much more to learn.

CONCLUSION

Vampires continue to be appealing and fascinating to the general population. They reflect common aspects of our humanness, along with our deepest fears and insecurities. Vampires in popular culture have become increasingly sexualized. At the same time, there appear to be thousands of people internationally who self-identify as vampires, either through relating to the persona of the vampire (lifestylers) or personally feeling a chronic need to take in extra energy from time to time (real vampire).

Despite an unusual self-identity, vampires seem to be diverse and rather normal in other aspects of their lives. The unique sexualities of people seem to be shaped by multiple forces, which also shape common identities within each person. For vampires, their vampire identity seems to be a salient part of their overall sense of self. As such, it combines with other aspects of self to reflect a unique sexuality for the particular vampire. In other words, it is simply a piece, though an important piece, of the overall unique puzzle of sexuality. Furthermore, vampire sexuality seems to reflect the vampire identity via selected sexual practices and personal interpretations and meanings of those practices.

Finally, we must remember that what is often understood to be "normal" or acceptable sexual behavior is socially constructed and reflects dominant dimensions of sexuality. In other words, historically in Western society, socially accepted sexual behaviors that predictably reside within the "charmed circle," using Rubin's (1993) framework, are categorized as such due to privileged positions of the masses—those who are White, male, upper- or middle class, Judeo-Christian, and heterosexual. Sometimes, we forget that it is sexual diversity, especially looking across history and culture, which is the norm (see Popovic 2006).

There seems to be nothing inherently wrong, psychopathological, or dangerous with claiming a vampire identity. Furthermore, we should expect that sexualities and sexual preferences would reflect important aspects of people's identities, including those of vampires. Simple social convention is far from adequate in determining acceptable from unacceptable identity, sexuality, and/or sexual practice. What should be carefully assessed across all forms of sexual expression are questions concerning diverse needs of human beings, ethics and risks of specific sexual practices, and respect, communication, and mutual consent of all involved.

CHAPTER 21

ADJUSTING THE INNER FACE

Giselle Ridgeway

*E*DITORS' NOTES: *Giselle Ridgeway's story is complex. Born a genetic male, her gender identity is as a woman. Like John P., Giselle tried to deal with her feelings by using alcohol. She had a difficult time in transforming what she felt inside (a variant of "doing") into her being. "I tried for many years to live as a 'normal' heterosexual man. . . . I did anything I could to try and obliterate the person I knew I was but was afraid to become," she writes. As Giselle puts it, "I saw how trans people were treated in society and even by some of the people I called friends. . . . I had learned by this time that I could have a list of stigmatizing conditions as long as my arm, but none of them carries a greater stigma than being transgendered." The negative effect of feeling stigmatized for transgender people was noted by Bockting et al. (2013). In their study of over 1,000 transgender people, they found that "in comparison with norms for nontransgender men and women, our transgender sample had disproportionately high rates of depression, anxiety, somatization [e.g., physical symptoms of stress such as nausea, upset stomach, etc.], and overall psychological distress . . . associated with enacted and felt stigma" (e6).*

One thing in Giselle's story that may be puzzling to the reader is that at first, she identified herself as a lesbian. Yet later in her story, she describes another sort of "coming out," the realization that she may also be attracted to men. This, however, is not unusual. As Zimman (2009) points out, "transgender people—just like anyone else—may be attracted to any combination of genders" (57–58). Giselle is what is termed bisexual or, in her case, more accurately, ambisexual, since she is unequally attracted to both sexes. In fact, physical sex (or genetic sex, whether one is born with the male XY chromosomal configuration or female XX chromosomes) is separate from one's gender identity (the sex with which one identifies), and both of these identities are separate from sexual orientation (the sexes to which we are attracted). Sexual identity (the acknowledgment of one's attractions as defining who one is; the "being") is a separate issue from sexual orientation. For example, there are men who are attracted to and have sex with other males but never develop a gay self-identity. These four aspects of our self—physical self, gender identity, sexual orientation, and sexual identity—interact in a variety of ways. They are not fixed but can flow and change over time, as Giselle's story illustrates.

Giselle describes the reactions she faces as someone who lives as a trans-person and is therefore discredited in the eyes of some people. Not surprisingly, in a national probability sample of adults in the United States, Norton and Herek (2013) found that attitudes toward transgender people were significantly less favorable than attitudes toward lesbians, gay men, and bisexuals and that heterosexual men were more negative than heterosexual women. Additionally, Giselle faces criticism from other trans-people for "not being trans enough, whatever that really means," illustrating Rubington and Weinberg's (2008) observation that "social control operates in deviant ways of life just as it does in the conventional world" (253), and she also deals with non-transgendered friends and strangers whose perceptions often unintentionally hurt her feelings. In addition, Giselle receives hostility, which "keeps a constant undercurrent of fear in my life." This fear is not without a basis in fact; in their review of the literature, Bockting et al. (2013) cite a recent study in which over half of the more than 400 transgendered people studied reported being verbally harassed and almost one fifth said that they had been victims of physical violence.

How does Giselle's story illustrate the fluidity of sexual orientation and sexual identity? Contrast Giselle's coming out with John P.'s. How are they the same? How do they differ? How is she affected by the perceptions of other people, both transgender and nontransgender? How does she deal with stigma? What conclusions might you draw about a culture in which excessive alcohol consumption is more socially acceptable than gender bending?

ॐ

Knowing since childhood that something was off about my gender, I seemed to understand instinctually that gender was much more fluid than was taught to me. I tried for many years to live as a "normal" heterosexual man. I even had a 7-year relationship with someone who is still a dear friend. However, this led me down a path of self-destruction. Drugs and alcohol took over my life. I did anything I could to try and obliterate the person I knew I was but was afraid to become. I saw how "trans" people were treated in society and even by some of the people I called friends. I still find it strange how being a drug addict or alcoholic is still more socially acceptable than being transgendered. In fact, it is less uncomfortable for others to hear my stories of excessive drinking than it is when I talk about normal relationship issues. The topic of sex just amplifies the discomfort, but I talk about what interests me and sex definitely has my interest. Trans-sexuality on its own is taboo enough. When you add in things like same-sex relationships, multiple partners, or my previous occupation as an escort, the conversations can get quite interesting to say the least.

Sexuality always seemed quite rigid to me. I had no real evidence to question that assumption until one morning at the tender age of 32, I was having coffee with some new friends, and one of them made a comment on how everyone thought this one guy was cute. Naturally, being the good lesbian that I am, I looked at him to refute this statement and found myself thinking that this guy was hot. I was shocked at first! I had to leave and call a friend of mine and ask if I were still sane. My friend asked me one simple question, "Do you think there is something wrong with that?" I had learned by this time that I could have a list of stigmatizing conditions as long as my arm, but none of them carries a greater stigma than being transgendered, so realizing that I was also attracted to some men was not very hard to digest, just surprising as I had never had such feelings before.

Luckily for me, I have many supportive and loving friends. Unfortunately, as I learned firsthand, perceptions can be deceiving and, for some, love and support has limits. My first relationship as a woman was with a close friend who I had fallen hard for not long after we started hanging out. It was after 2 years of spending much time together that the relationship moved into the romantic realm.

Almost immediately, all was not well. When by ourselves at my apartment, she was incredibly loving and passionate; it was a different story in public. She asked me not to make our relationship publicly known except to very close friends. I knew deep down that she was somehow embarrassed to be with me, but I rationalized away these feelings of doubt and insecurity. I had an inkling that the same social expectations of what passes for normal that led me to self-destruction were tearing at her, and I would be proven right when speaking to her months after our breakup.

The drive to be societally normal is hard to ignore. It is just as difficult to ignore the ideas of what is normal in the marginal group to which I now belonged. I have been accused by other trans-people of not being trans enough, whatever that really means. I can say, however, that I have never been accused of being a female stereotype. I can laugh today at how similar people's problems are regardless of social group. This was not the case when I was trying to find my own identity. When this person broke it off with me in order to try to be heteronormative, it felt as if my core identity was under attack.

Anyway, there are a number of issues which arise when it comes to my romantic life. I am openly transgendered. I do not try to be "stealthy," which I interpret as trying to blend in completely with regular society, nor do I try to conform to traditional gender stereotypes in a number of ways. My presentation though is entirely female. I am comfortable in my own skin today but since I do not hide behind my gender identity in the binary sense of male or female, my dating pool is decreased significantly from its already low starting point. Unfortunately for me, lesbian women are not particularly interested in women with penises.

This brings me to the biggest issue I face, the perceptions other people have about gender. For insurance purposes, I maintain a diagnosis of gender identity disorder, but, the disorder is not mine. I am quite sure of my gender identity. Other people, including some of my closest friends, have a much more difficult time grasping my gender. Even people who never knew me prior to transition struggle with the littlest things, like using the proper pronouns. It hurts the most in intimate situations when I am referred to as a man. Other people's perceptions hurt me sexually too. A few of the men I have found attractive have come right out and said that they are not gay. I did not realize that a man sleeping with a woman made someone gay. Strangers are even worse. I received this message on a social networking site a day ago, "How can u be out of the closet as a lesbian when Ur a fucking dude not a fucking chick?" This type of hostility is much more common than I would like to admit. It also keeps a constant undercurrent of fear in my life that at times can prevent me from doing things I want to do socially.

I have yet to find a good place to be a pre-op transgendered mostly lesbian woman (92–98% lesbian on any given day), especially when it comes to romance. I state this with a sad acceptance that opportunities for quality relationships are few and far between. When I first came out, my mother told me it would be a difficult and lonely road because of how much I love women. Although she was correct in many ways, I do not regret my decision as the alternative was to kill myself.

So where then do I go to meet people who may be interested in me? Since I do not drink anymore, I have no interest in hanging around bars. Besides, straight bars are just dangerous, and gay bars are not the place I am looking for dates, and at lesbian bars, I am viewed mostly with indifference and a few times with loathing. The word imposter was floated at me a few times. I can still feel the sting of those words sometimes when I hit an emotional low point.

Online dating sites have proved less than promising, even specialty sites that cater to trans people. I tend to get single guys looking for a booty call who obviously did not read my profile; otherwise, they would not have contacted me in the first place. While I am not averse to being with a man, he must come as part of a couple and meet a number of specific requirements. I am incredibly picky. I refuse to lower my standards in order to feel loved, even though a good friend of mine jokingly says that is the key to a successful relationship.

My next approach was to see if there were any local groups who shared similar interests and started attending their functions. This proved to be the most fruitful avenue for meeting people, although it still took a while to build connections within the group. Despite being very open about all aspects of my life, I am quite cautious about who I am willing to have intercourse with. I tend to negotiate boundaries extensively with partners. I enjoy getting to know people, warts and all. Despite my lifestyle, I have not had many sexual relationships. Even when I was escorting, I did not have intercourse with any of my clients. Most of them just wanted to be smacked around, which I was happy to get paid to do.

On top of the issues related to being transgendered, I still have to deal with the everyday crap that women and lesbians put up with, such as the heterosexist idea that if I am living as a woman, I must be attracted to all men and that I should be grateful when one of them is actually interested in me. Then, there is the idea that I can be made somehow less attracted to women if I just let whatever random guy have sex with me.

Despite the challenges of finding partners, there is a great amount of freedom in my sexuality. I am not interested in relationships that reinforce traditional gender roles, and the people I date are not interested either. I find myself redefining what it means to be in a relationship all the time. For instance, I am currently part of a polyamorous family in which I play multiple roles, depending on who I am around. Independence thus becomes a much more flexible value where sexuality is concerned. While we treat each other as equals, egalitarianism is freely cast aside in some situations to explore different aspects of our sexual nature. Giving oneself completely to the moment at hand is a spiritual experience for me.

I also like to take advantage of the ability to re-create myself as a sexual being. Things I never thought I would ever do or were even possible for me to do are routinely explored in a safe and loving environment. As an example, being polyamorous was not something I ever thought much about until the last year or so. I was, and still am, comfortable with the idea of being in a monogamous relationship, but it is not a prerequisite for dating someone nowadays. Who knows, I may even decide to get married someday if I meet the right person. Very little in my life is absolute anymore, and I prefer it that way. The road may sometimes be lonely, but it is always interesting.

CONCLUSION

Staci Newmahr

The title of this book, *Selves, Symbols, and Sexualities,* is intended to capture the central concerns of the symbolic interactionist perspective in the study of sexuality. These are not sections unto themselves because interactionists treat them as interrelated. Within each section of this book, our contributors have been dealing with selves and symbols as they relate to sexualities.

We opened this book with the often-taken-for-granted idea of "sexiness." For many students, symbolic interactionism is sexy itself (at least as far as sociological perspectives go). Its microsociological lens invites us to think about ourselves, our everyday lives, our gestures, and our communications, all of which can be especially appealing for students beginning to think critically about the social world. Yet symbolic interactionism does not stay at the microsociological level. It is, like all sociology, about connections between biography and history, private troubles and public issues, the experiences of everyday lives and the world around us. Symbolic interactionists are chiefly concerned with the processes by which things happen in order to understand the larger picture; we generally hold the perspective that we cannot understand the *why* things come to be if we do not understand *how* they come to be. It is a broad umbrella, with its own styles, tastes, and divisions, but interactionists generally agree that "the foundations of society lie in face to face interaction, the institutions that arise from this and the spontaneous order that results" (Dingwall, DeGloma, and Newmahr 2012:5).

We hope that as you have read the work in this book, you have moved with us, away from taking sexiness for granted and toward a deeper questioning of all things "sexual." As a whole, the book is intended to inspire thinking about sexuality theoretically: what it is, and to whom, how it works as social interaction, and ultimately, why it works that way. We hope that it is easier to see some of the connections between lived sexual experiences and the society in which they occur, how "sex" is used as a means of social control, and how our sexuality is not at all the private realm most of us assume it is.

We also hope that the chapters have illuminated some of the myriad ways to think about sexualities. From behaviors to identities, practices to selfhood, communications to laws, excitement to eroticism, the realm of the "sexual" is a confluence of social processes. We hope that it is clearer that the sexual does not simply reside within bodies but comprises modes of communications between people that teach us how to be sexual, how to "do" sexuality, how to define and experience situations as sexual, how to regard ourselves as sexual— and how not to.

In much of Western discourse, the "sexual" is regarded as a particular and distinct kind, or mode, of experience. Sexuality is bracketed off, compartmentalized, bound by moral legacy, and unbound by cultural challenges to those histories. On the ground, though, our sexualities infiltrate, characterize, enrich, texturize, and flavor everyday life. Far from being relegated to a separate section of experience, the sexual infiltrates every other aspect of our identities. Regardless of the intensity of our individual libidos, the quantity or quality of our erotic experiences, the importance we accord to sex or sexuality, all of us negotiate it. We navigate our feelings, our families, our friendships, our communications, our spaces, and situations in relation to cultural values and social forces around sexuality.

In sum, we aim for this book not only to model a symbolic interactionist approach to sexuality but also to highlight the importance of both symbolic interactionism and the study of sexuality in understanding social life. From our perspective, the management of our sexualities is uniquely human and inextricably social. The study of sexualities, as we experience, interpret, understand, and represent them, is crucial to understanding human society.

Glossary

anhedonic is the inability to experience pleasure.

BDSM is an umbrella term that encompasses a variety of terms often used interchangeably both in the literature and by participants to refer to a range of consensual activities including but not limited to leather, kink, sadomasochism (SM), dominance and submission (D/s), master/slave (M/s) relationships, power exchange (and variations including erotic power exchange and total power exchange), bondage, and discipline. (definition provided by Brandy Simula)

dry humping is a practice in which a clothed couple rub their groins against each other, often to the point of orgasm. It was a common practice among teenagers in the 1950s and early 60s.

DSM is the *Diagnostic and Statistical Manual of Mental Disorders* of the American Psychiatric Association. It has gone through several editions. The current edition is the *DSM–5*.

gastropub is a high end restaurant, bar, bistro, or tavern that serves high quality meals.

genderqueer refers to identities outside the gender binary of man and woman. It can include the transgendered, people who claim no genders, and people shifting between genders.

Gramscian is derived from the name of Antonio Gramsci (1891–1937), an Italian philosopher and sociologist who developed the theory of cultural hegemony, in which he explained how the upper classes (bourgeoisie) controlled society.

heavy petting covers a number of sexual acts short of actual sexual intercourse or oral or anal sex. It often involves (mutual) masturbation.

heteronormative is the belief system in which all behaviors and social institutions are seen through a heterosexual point of view as the only valid perspective.

intrapsychic refers to an individual's internal psychological processes.

LGBT stands for lesbian, gay, bisexual, and transgendered; it is now often also written as LGBTQ, where the Q stands for "queer."

ludic refers to playfulness. In the digital age, a ludic interface is a type of playful interface in interaction between humans and computers.

macrosociological perspectives focus on large scale systems, societies, and social institutions and on their interrelationships and effect on social actors. Examples of macrosociological theories include structural functionalism and Marxian and conflict theories.

master status was first coined by sociologist Everett C. Hughes to refer to that position in society that individuals use to locate an individual within the social structure. For Americans, especially males, one's occupation is a master status. Asking about one's occupation gives others additional information about one's education, income, lifestyle and, perhaps, even one's beliefs. A deviant label often becomes a master status.

microsociological theories examine everyday life, including interaction between and among individuals and objects, how people construct, interpret, and manage meaning, and how they act in terms of these meanings. Examples of microsociological theories include symbolic interaction, exchange theories, and behavioral sociology, ethnomethodology, and phenomenological sociology.

outed or **being outed** is a process by which one's sexual activities and/or identity are (is) revealed to others, especially to those who do not share them.

panopticon refers to a type of building in which all of its parts are visible from one place. This design was originally developed for prisons. Michel Foucault's use of it (1975) as a metaphor for the regulation of people's lives within a society has led to the common usage of the term to refer to modern disciplinary power, from which citizens are increasingly "visible" to the state and each other.

poststructuralism is an intellectual movement based on understanding social reality apart from the binary structure that structuralism emphasized. Again inspired partly by Foucault, poststructuralist understandings require study of both the object itself and the systems of knowledge that produced the object. Because it views all intellectual inquiry as shaped by discursive and interpretative practices, poststructuralist analyses tend, like symbolic interaction, to be concerned with language, symbols, and meanings.

reflexivity refers to the mutual relationship between cause and effect, with each affecting the other.

sapiosexual is being sexually attracted to or aroused by intelligence.

structural functionalism is a macrosociological theory, first appearing in the writings of Auguste Comte and, later, Emile Durkheim and developed in the mid-20th century by sociologist Talcott Parsons and his student Robert K. Merton. Structural functionalism focuses on social systems and their relations to one another. They use a biological analogy, seeing social systems as analogous to biological systems. For structural functionalists, social systems (like, for example, societies) are in a state of equilibrium, in which subsystems are mutually supportive and each of which contributes certain functions to maintain the larger system.

vanilla is a term used by kinky people, sometimes deprecatingly, to refer to non-kinky people, activities, or spaces.

REFERENCES

Adams, Bert N. and R. A. Sydie. 2002. *Classical Sociological Theory*. Thousand Oaks, CA: Pine Forge Press.

Ahmed, Sara. 2006. *Queer Phenomenology: Orientations, Objects, Others*. Durham, NC: Duke University Press.

Alpert, Emily. 2013. "Eating Disorders Plague Teenage Boys, Too." *The Buffalo News,* June 23, F3.

Anapol, D. 1997. *Polyamory: The New Love Without Limits*. San Rafael, CA: IntiNet ResourceCentre.

———. 2012. *Polyamory in the Twenty-first Century: Love and Intimacy with Multiple Partners*. New York: Rowman & Littlefield.

Ashford, C. 2012. "Heterosexuality, Public Places and Policing." Pp. 41–53 in *Policing Sex,* edited by P. Johnson and D. Dalton. Abingdon, VA: Routledge.

Attwood, Feona. 2005. "Fashion and Passion: Marketing Sex to Women" *Sexualities* 8(4):392–406.

———. 2006. "Sexed Up: Theorizing the Sexualization of Culture." *Sexualities* 9(1):77–94.

Azerrad, Michael. 2001. *Our Band Could Be Your Life: Scenes From the American Indie Underground: 1981–1991*. Boston, MA: Little, Brown and Company.

Barrows, Sydney Biddle. 1986. *Mayflower Madam: The Secret Life of Sydney Biddle Barrows*. New York: Arbor House.

Bartoli, A. and M. D. Clark. 2006. "The Dating Game: Similarities and Differences in Dating Scripts Among College Students." *Sexuality and Culture* 10(4):54–80.

Bataille, Georges. 1984. *Death and Sensuality*. New York: Walker and Company.

Becker, Ernest. 2010. *The Birth and Death of Meaning*. 2nd ed. New York: The Free Press.

Becker, Howard S. 1963. *Outsiders: Studies in the Sociology of Deviance*. New York: Macmillan.

Beckerman, Bernard. 1976. "Definitions—Theater." In *Drama in Life: The Uses of Communication in Society,* edited by James E. Combs and Michael W. Mansfield, Pp. 4-7. New York: Hastings House.

Bell, D. 2006. "Bodies, Technologies, Spaces: On 'Dogging.'" *Sexualities* 9(4):387–407.

Bem, Daryl. 1996. "Exotic Becomes Erotic: A Developmental Theory of Sexual Orientation." *Psychological Review* 103(2):320–335.

Bennett, Alan. 1981. "Cold Sweat." *London Review of Books* 3(19), October 15, 12–13.

Bergdall, Anna, Joan Kraft, Karen Andes, Marion Carter, Kendar Hatfield-Timajchy, and Linda Hock-Long. 2012. "Love and Hooking Up in the New Millennium: Communication Technology and Relationships Among Urban African and Puerto Rican Young Adults." *Journal of Sex Research* 49(6):570–582.

Berger, P. and T. Luckmann. 1969. *The Social Construction of Reality: A Treatise on the Sociology of Knowledge*. London, UK: Allen Lane.

Berger, Peter. 1967. *The Sacred Canopy. Elements of a Sociological Theory of Religion*. New York: Anchor Books.

Berger, Peter. 1984. *Invitation to Sociology*. New York: Anchor Doubleday.

Bettelheim, Bruno. 1976. *The Uses of Enchantment: The Meaning and Importance of Fairy Tales*. New York: Random House.

Better, Alison. 2011. "Pleasure for Sale: Feminist Sex Stores." Pp. 348–354 in *Introducing the New Sexuality Studies,* edited by Steven Seidman, Nancy Fischer, and Chet Meeks. 2nd ed. London, UK: Routledge.

Binney, Jon. 1995. "Trading Places: Consumption, Sexuality and the Production of QueerSpace." Pp.182–199 In *Mapping Desire: Geographies of Sexualities,* edited by David Bell and Gill Valentine. London, UK: Routledge.

Blasingame, Brenda Marie. 1992. "The Roots of Biphobia: Racism and Internalized Hetrosexism." Pp. 47–53 in *Closer to Home: Bisexuality & Feminism,* edited by Elizabeth Reba Weise. Toronto, ON: Seal Press.

Blumer, Herbert. 1937. *"Social Psychology."* Pp. 144–198 in *Man and Society,* edited by Emerson P. Schmidt. New York: Prentice Hall.

———. 1969. *Symbolic Interaction, Perspective and Method.* Englewood Cliffs, NJ: Prentice-Hall.

Blunt, Alison. 1999. "Imperial Geographies of Home: British Domesticity in India, 1886–1925." *Transactions of the Institute of British Geographers* 24(4):421–440.

Bockting, Walter O., Michael H. Miner, Rebecca E. Swinburne Romine, Autumn Hamilton, and Eli Coleman. "Stigma, Mental Health, and Resilience in an Online Sample of the US Transgender Population." *American Journal of Public Health.* Published electronically March 14, 2013:e1–e9. doi: 10.2105/AJPH.2013.301241.

Bogaert, A. 2004. "Asexuality: Prevalence and Associated Factors in a National Probability Sample." *Sex Research* 41(3):279–287.

———. 2006. "Towards a Conceptual Understanding of Asexuality." *Review of General Psychology,* 10(3):241–250.

———. 2012a. *Understanding Asexuality.* Plymouth, MA: Rowman and Littlefield Publishers.

———. 2012b. "Asexuality and Autochorissexualism (Identity-Less Sexuality)." *Archives of Sexual Behavior* 41(6):1513–1514.

Bolter, Jay and Richard Grusin. 2000. *Remediation: Understanding New Media.* Cambridge, MA: MIT Press.

Bourdieu, Pierre. 1983. "Erving Goffman: Discoverer of the Infinitely Small." *Theory, Culture and Society* 2(1):112.

Brickell, C. 2006. "A Symbolic Interactionist History of Sexuality?" *Rethinking History* 10(3):415–432.

Brissett, Dennis and Charles Edgley. 2006. *Life as Theater: A Dramaturgical Sourcebook.* New Brunswick, NJ: Rutgers/Transaction.

Broad, K. L., Sara L. Crawley, and Lara Foley. 2004. "'Doing Real Family Values': The Interpretative Practice of Families in the GLBT Movement." *Sociological Quarterly* 45:509–527.

Brown, G. 2008. "Ceramics, Clothing and Other Bodies: Affective Geographies of Homoerotic Cruising Encounters." *Social and Cultural Geographies* 9(8):915–932.

Broyard, Anatole. 1997. *Kafka Was the Rage: A Memoir of Greenwich Village.* New York: Vintage Paperbacks.

Burke, Kenneth. 1969. *A Grammar of Motives.* Berkeley: University of California Press.

Burke, Peter J. and Jan E. Stets. 2009. *Identity Theory.* New York: Oxford University Press.

Butler, Judith. 1993. "Imitation and Gender Insubordination." Pp. 307–36 in *The Lesbian and Gay Studies Reader,* edited by Henry Abelove, Michèle Aina Barale, and David M. Halperin. Florence, KY: Psychology Press.

Califia, Pat. 2000. *Public Sex: The Culture of Radical Sex.* San Francisco, CA: Cleis Press.

Camus, Albert. 1991. *The Myth of Sisyphus.* New York: Vintage. First published 1942.

Carrigan, M. 2011. "There's More to Life than Sex? Difference and Commonality within the Asexual Community." *Sexualities* 14(4):462–478.

———. 2012. "'How Do You Know You Don't Like It If You Haven't Tried It?' Asexual Agency and the Sexual Assumption." Pp. 3–20 in *Sexual Minority Research in the New Millennium,* edited by T. G. Morrison, M. A. Morrison, M. A. Carrigan, and D. T. McDermott). New York: Nova Science.

Casey, Mark. 2004. "De-dyking Queer Space(s): Heterosexual Female Visibility in Gay and Lesbian Spaces." *Sexualities* 7(4):446–461.

Casey, Mark, Janice McLaughlin, and Diane Richardson. 2004. "Locating Sexualities:

Politics, Identities, and Space" *Sexualities* 7(4):387–390.

Cerankowski, K. J. and M. Milks. 2010. "New Orientations: Asexuality and Its Implications for Theory and Practice." *Feminist Studies,* 36(3):650–664.

Chan, A H-n. 2008. "Talking About Good Sex: Hong Kong Women's Sexuality in the 21st Century." Pp. 195–215 in *East Asian Sexualities: Modernity, Gender and New Sexual Cultures,* edited by S. Jackson, Liu Jieyu, and Woo Juhyun. London, UK: Zed Books.

Chasin, C. J. 2011. "Theoretical Issues in the Study of Asexuality." *Archives of Sexual Behavior,* 40(4):713–723.

Chauncey, George. 1995. *Gay New York: Gender, Urban Culture, and the Making of the Gay Male World, 1890–1940.* New York: Basic Books.

Cherlin, Andrew. 2010. Demographic Trends in the United States: A Review of Research in the 2000s. *Journal of Marriage and Family* 72:403–419.

Chung, Y. B. and M. Katayama. 1996. "Assessment of Sexual Orientation in Lesbian/Gay/Bisexual Studies." *Journal of Homosexuality* 30(4):49–62.

Cole, E. 1993. "Is Sex a Natural Function: Implications for Sex Therapy." Pp. 187–193 in *Boston Marriages: Romantic but Asexual Relationships Among Contemporary Lesbians,* edited by E. D. Rothblum and K. A. Brehony. Amherst, MA: The University of Massachusetts Press.

Collins, Randall. 2004. *Interaction Ritual Chains.* Princeton, NJ: Princeton University Press.

Connell, Catherine and Sinikka Elliott. 2009. Beyond the Birds and the Bees: Learning Inequality Through Sexuality Education. *American Journal of Sexuality Education* 4(2):83–102.

Cooley, Charles Horton. 1902. *Human Nature and the Social Order.* New York: Charles Scribners and Sons.

———. 1908. *Human Nature and the Social Order.* New York: Charles Scribners and Sons.

———. 1909. *Social Organization.* New York: Charles Scribners and Sons.

Cox, P. 2008. "First Person: We're Married, We Just Don't Have Sex." *The Guardian.* Retrieved September 8, 2008. (http://www.guardian.co.uk/lifeandstyle/2008/sep/08/relationships.healthandwellbeing?INTCMP=SRCH).

Craib, I. 1984. *Modern Social Theory.* Brighton, MA: Wheatsheaf.

———. 1994. *The Importance of Disappointment.* London, UK: Routledge.

Crawley, Sara, Lara Foley, and Constance Shehan. 2008. *Gendering Bodies.* Lanham, MD: Rowman and Littlefield.

Creek, S. J. 2013. "'Not Getting Any Because of Jesus': The Centrality of Desire Management to the Identity Work of Gay, Celibate Christians." *Symbolic Interaction* 36(2):119–136.

Crockett, Jason. "Narratives of Racial Sexual Preference in Gay Male Subculture." PhD dissertation, University of Arizona, 2010.

Csikszentmihalyi, Mihaly. 1997. *Creativity: Flow and the Psychology of Discovery and Invention.* New York: Harper Perennial.

Curnutt, Hugh. 2012. "Flashing Your Phone: Sexting and the Remediation of Teen Sexuality." *Communication Quarterly* 60(3):353–369.

Curran, B. 2005. *Vampires: A Field Guide to the Creatures That Stalk the Night.* Franklin Lakes, NJ: Career Press.

Dajenya. 1995. "Which Part of Me Deserves to Be Free?" Pp. 235–236 in *Bisexual Politics: Theories, Queries, & Visions,* edited by Naomi Tucker. New York: Harrington Park Press.

Davis, Kristen. 2009. *The Manhattan Madam: Sex, Drugs, Scandal & Greed. Inside America's Most Successful Prostitution Ring.* Beverly, MA: Hollan Publishing, Inc.

Davis, Murray S. 1983. *Smut: Erotic Reality/Obscene Ideology.* Chicago, IL: University of Chicago Press.

Deckha, Maneesha. 2011. "Pain as Culture: A Postcolonial Feminist Approach to S/M and Women's Agency." *Sexualities* 14(2):129–150.

Delphy, C. 1993. "Rethinking Sex and Gender." *Women's Studies International Forum* 16(1):1–9.

D'Emilio, John. 1998. *Sexual Politics, Sexual Communities: The Making of a Homosexual Minority in the United States, 1940–1970.* Chicago, IL: University of Chicago Press.

Denzin, N. K. 1989. *Interpretive Biography.* Newbury Park, CA: Sage.

Diamond, L. M. 2008. *Sexual Fluidity: Understanding Women's Love and Desire.* Cambridge, MA: Harvard University Press.

Dingwall, R., T. T. DeGloma, and S. Newmahr. 2012. "Editors' Introduction: Symbolic Interaction—Serving the Whole Interactionist Family." *Symbolic Interaction.* 35(1):1–5.

Donnelly, Nisa. 1989. *The Bar Stories: A Novel After All.* New York: St. Martin's Griffin.

Du Bois, W. E. B. 1994. *The Souls of Black Folk.* Avenel, NJ: Gramercy Books. First published 1903.

Duvauchelle, Zelie, J. Kehaulani Kauanui, M. Leolani, and Desiree Thompson. 1994. "Tita Talk: A Cross-Talk with Zelie Duvauchelle, J. Kehaulani Kauanui, M. Leolani, and Desiree Thompson." Pp. 85–108 in *The Very Inside: An Anthology of Writing by Asian and Pacific Islander Lesbian and Bisexual Women,* edited by Sharon Lim-Hing. Toronto, ON: Sister Vision Press.

Egan, Danielle. 2006. *Dancing for Dollars and Paying for Love: The Relationships between Exotic Dancers and Their Regulars.* Basingstoke, UK: Palgrave Macmillan.

Edgley, Charles. 2013. *The Drama of Social Life: A Dramaturgical Handbook.* Surrey, UK: Ashgate Publishing Company.

Edgley, Charles and Kenneth Kiser. 1982. "Polaroid Sex: Deviant Possibilities in a Technological Age." *Journal of American Culture* 5(1):59–64.

Elizabeth (The Gray Lady). February 3, 2012. *Shades of Gray* "Guest Post: Why Date An Asexual? An Interview with C" [Online forum post]. Retrieved from http://grasexu ality.wordpress.com/2012/02/03/guest -post-why-date-an-asexual-an-interview- with-c/

Ellenberger, Allan R., and Edoardo Ballerini. 2005. *The Valentino Mystique: The Death and Afterlife of the Silent Film Idol.* Jefferson, NC: McFarland.

Elliott, Sinikka. 2012. *Not My Kid: What Parents Believe About the Sex Lives of Their Teenagers.* New York: New York University Press.

Elliott, Sinikka and Elyshia Aseltine. 2012/2013. "Raising Teenagers in Hostile Environments: How Race, Class, and Gender Matter for Mothers' Protective Carework." *Journal of Family Issues* 34(June):719–744. (http://jfi .sagepub.com/content/early/2012/07/09/01 92513X12452253).

Elmaci, F. (2006). "The Role of Social Support on Depression and Adjustment levels of Adolescents Having Broken and Unbroken Families." *Educational Sciences: Theory & Practice* 6(2): 421–431.

Emerson, Joan. 1970. "Behavior in Private Places: Sustaining Definitions of Reality in Gynecological Examinations." Pp. 74–97 in *Recent Sociology No. 2,* edited by Peter Drietzel. New York: Macmillan.

Enck, Craves E. and James D. Preston. 1988. "Counterfeit Intimacy: A Dramaturgical Analysis of an Erotic Performance." *Deviant Behavior* 9(4):369–381.

Eng, David and Alice Y. Hom. 1998. "Introduction: Q&A: Notes on a Queer Asian America." Pp. 1–21 in *Queer in Asian America,* edited by David L. Eng and Alice Y. Hom. Philadelphia, PA: Temple University Press.

Epstein, Robert, Paul McKinney, Shannon Fox, and Carlos Garcia. 2012. "Support for a Fluid-Continuum Model of Sexual Orientation: A Large-Scale Internet Study." *Journal of Homosexuality* 59(10):1356–1381.

Evans, M. 2003. *Love: An Unromantic Discussion.* Cambridge, MA: Polity Press.

Fagan, P. F. (1999). "How Broken Families Rob Children of Their Chances for Future Prosperity." *Backgrounder* (1283).

Family Planning Association of Hong Kong, The. 2009. *Report of Youth Sexuality Study 2006.* Hong Kong: FPAHK.

Farrer, J., G. Suo, and H. Tsuchiya. 2012. "Re-embedding Sexual Meanings: A Qualitative Comparison of the Premarital Sexual Scripts of Chinese and Japanese Young Adults." *Sexuality and Culture* 16(3):263–286.

Fetner, Tina. 2008. *How the Religious Right Shaped Lesbian and Gay Activism*. Minneapolis, MN: The University of Minnesota Press.

Fields, Jessica. 2008. *Risky Lessons: Sex Education and Social Inequality*. New Brunswick, NJ: Rutgers University Press.

Fine, Gary Allan and Michaela De Soucey. 2005. "Joking Cultures: Humor Themes as Social Regulation in Group Life." *Humor* 18:1–22.

Fine, Michelle and Sara I. McClelland. 2006. "Sexuality Education and Desire: Still Missing After All These Years." *Harvard Educational Review* 76(3):297–337.

Fischoff, S., A. Dimopoulos, F. Nguyen, and R. Gordon. 2002/2003. "Favorite Movie Monsters and Their Psychological Appeal." *Imagination, Cognition and Personality* 22:401–426.

Fleiss, Heidi. 2002. *Pandering*. Los Angeles, CA: One Hour Entertainment.

Foucault, M. 1981. *The History of Sexuality Volume One*. London, UK: Pelican.

Frank, Katherine. 2002. *G-Strings and Sympathy: Strip Club Regulars and Male Desire*. Durham, NC: Duke University Press.

Frith, H. and C. Kitzinger. 2001. "Reformulating Sexual Script Theory: Developing a Discursive Psychology of Sexual Negotiation." *Theory and Psychology* 11(2):209–232.

Fuss, Diana. 1995. *Identification Papers: Readings on Psychoanalysis, Sexuality, and Culture*. London, UK: Routledge.

Gagnon, J. 2004. *An Interpretation of Desire*. Chicago, IL: University of Chicago Press.

Gagnon, J. and W. Simon. 1973. *Sexual Conduct: The Social Sources of Human Sexuality*. Chicago, IL: Aldine.

———. 1974. *Sexual Conduct*. London, UK: Hutchinson.

———. 2004. *Sexual Conduct*. 2nd ed. New Brunswick, NJ: Aldine/Transaction.

———. 2005. *Sexual Conduct*, 2nd ed. Hawthorne, NY: Aldine Publishing Co.

Garber, Marjorie. 1995. *Bisexuality*. New York: Touchstone, Simon & Schuster.

Garcia, Lorena. 2009. "'Now Why Do You Want to Know About That?': Heteronormativity, Sexism, and Racism in the Sexual (Mis)education of Latina Youth. "*Gender & Society* 23:520–541.

Garlick, Steve. 2011. "A New Sexual Revolution? Critical Theory, Pornography, and the Internet." *Canadian Review of Sociology* 48(3):221–239.

Gecas, Viktor. 1991. "The Self-concept as a Basis for a Theory of Motivation." Pp. 171–187 in *The Self-Society Dynamic: Cognition, Emotion, and Action*, edited by J. Howard and P. Callero. Cambridge, MA: Cambridge University Press.

Gecas, Viktor and Peter J. Burke. 1995. "Self and Identity." Pp. 41–67 in *Sociological Perspectives on Social Psychology*, edited by K. S. Cook, G. A. Fine, and J. S. House. Boston, MA: Allyn and Bacon.

Gecas, Viktor and Roger Libby. 1976. "Sexual Behavior as Symbolic Interaction." *The Journal of Sex Research* 12(1):33–49.

Giddens, Anthony. 1991. *Modernity and Self-identity: Self and Society in the Late Modern Age*. Palo Alto, CA: Stanford University Press.

———. 1992. *The Transformation of Intimacy: Sexuality, Love, and Eroticism in Modern Societies*. Stanford, CA: Stanford University Press.

Glaser, B. G., and A. L. Strauss. 1967. *Status Passage*. London, UK: Routledge & Kegan Paul.

Goffman, Erving. 1959. *The Presentation of Self in Everyday Life*. Garden City, NY: Doubleday Anchor Books.

———. 1961a. *Asylums: Essays on the Social Situation of Mental Patients and Other Inmates*. New York: Anchor Books.

———. 1961b. *Encounters: Two Studies in the Sociology of Interaction*. Indianapolis, IN: Bobbs-Merrill.

———. 1963. *Stigma: Notes on the Management of Spoiled Identity*. Englewood Cliffs, NJ: Prentice Hall.

———. 1967. *Interaction Ritual: Essays on Face-to-Face Behavior*. Garden City, NY: Doubleday Anchor Books.

———. 1971. *Relations in Public: Microstudies of the Public Order*. New York: The Free Press.

———. 1983. "The Interaction Order." *American Sociological Review* 48(1):1–17.

Gorman-Murray, Andrew. 2007. "Sexy Stories: Using Autobiography in Geographies of Sexuality." *Qualitative Research Journal* 7(1):3–25.

Gould, Deborah B. 2009. *Moving Politics: Emotion and ACT UP's Fight against AIDS*. Chicago, IL: University Of Chicago Press.

Grierson, Jeffrey and Anthony M. A. Smith. 2005. "In From the Outer: Generational Differences in Coming Out and Gay Identity Formation." *Journal of Homosexuality* 50(1):53–70.

Gullage, Amy. 2010. "An Uncomfortable Fit: Fatness, Femininity and the University." *Atlantis* 34(2):66–76.

Gunn, J. 1999. "Marilyn Manson Is Not Goth: Memorial Struggle and the Rhetoric of Subcultural identity." *Journal of Communication Inquiry* 23:408–431.

Guttmacher Institute. 2012. State Policies in Brief: Sex and HIV Education. Washington, DC: Guttmacher Institute. (http://www.guttmacher.org/statecenter/spibs/spib_SE.pdf).

Haenfler, Ross. 2004a. "Manhood in Contradiction: The Two Faces of Straight Edge." *Men and Masculinities* 7:77–99.

———. 2004b. "Rethinking Subcultural Resistance: Core Values of the Straight Edge Movement." *Journal of Contemporary Ethnography* 33:406–436.

———. 2006. *Straight Edge: Hardcore Punk, Clean Living, and Social Change*. New Brunswick, NJ: Rutgers University Press.

Haughton, Neil. (2004). "Perceptions of Beauty in Renaissance Art." *Journal of Cosmetic Dermatology* 3:229–233.

Haviland, William A., Harald E. L. Prins, Dana Walrath, and Bunny McBride. 2008. *Anthropology: The Human Challenge*. Belmont, CA: Wadsworth Thomson Learning.

Heap, C. 2003. "The City as a Sexual Laboratory: The Queer Heritage of the Chicago School." *Qualitative Sociology* 26(4):457–487.

Heckert, J. 2010. "Love Without Borders? Intimacy, Identity and the State of Compulsory Monogamy." Pp. 255–266 in *Understanding Non-Monogamies*, edited by M. Barker and D. Langdridge. New York: Routledge.

Herdt, Gilbert. 1981. *Guardians of the Flutes*. New York: McGraw-Hill.

———. 1993. *Ritualized Homosexuality in Melanesia*. Berkeley, CA: University of California Press.

Hewitt, John P. 2013. "Dramaturgy and Motivation: Motive Talk, Accounts, and Disclaimers." Chapter 7 in *The Drama of Social Life: A Dramaturgical Handbook*, edited by Edgley. Surrey, UK: Ashgate Publishing Co.

Hewitt, John P., and David Shulman. 2011. *Self and Society*, 11th ed. Boston, MA: Allyn & Bacon.

Hochschild, Arlie Russell. 1979. "Emotion Work, Feeling Rules, and Social Structure." *American Journal of Sociology* 85(3):551–575.

———. 1983. *The Managed Heart: Commercialization of Human Feeling*. Berkeley: University of California Press.

———. 2003. *The Managed Heart: Commercialization of Human Feeling, Twentieth Anniversary Edition, with a New Afterword*. Berkeley, CA: University of California Press.

Hogbin, Ian. 1996. *The Island of Menstruating Men: Religion in Wogeo, New Guinea*. Long Grove, IL: Waveland Press. First published 1970.

Hollander, Xaviera. 1972. *The Happy Hooker: My Own Story*. New York: Dell Publishing Company.

Hooper, Kay. 2012. *Shades of Gray*. New York: Bantam Books.

Houlberg, Rick. 1991. "The Magazine of a Sadomasochistic Club. The Tie That Binds." *Journal of Homosexuality* 21(1/2):167–183.

Hughes, E. C. 1945. "Dilemmas and Contradictions of Status." *American Journal of Sociology* 50(5):353–359.

Ingraham, C. 2008. *White Weddings: Romancing Heterosexuality in Popular Culture.* New York: Routledge.

Irvine, Janice. 2002. *Talk About Sex: The Battles Over Sex Education in the United States.* Berkeley, CA: University of California Press.

Jackson, Stevi. 1993. "Even Sociologists Fall in Love: An Exploration in the Sociology of Emotions." *Sociology* 27(2):201–220.

Jackson, Stevi. 2007. "The Sexual Self in Late Modernity." Pp. 3–15 in *The Sexual Self: The Construction of Sexual Scripts,* edited by Michael Kimmel. Nasvhille, TN: Vanderbilt University Press.

Jackson, S. and S. Scott. 2010a. *Theorizing Sexuality.* Milton Keynes, UK: Open University Press.

———. 2010b. "Rehabilitating Interactionism for a Feminist Sociology of Sexuality." *Sociology,* 44(5):811–826.

Jackson, S., Petula Sik Ying Ho, and Jin Nye Na. 2013. "Reshaping Tradition? Women Negotiating the Boundaries of Tradition and Modernity in Hong Kong and British Families." *Sociological Review.* Forthcoming.

James, W. 1890. *The Principles of Psychology.* New York: Henry Holt and Company.

Jamieson, L. 2005. "Boundaries of Intimacy." Pp. 189–206 in *Families in Society: Boundaries and Relationships,* edited by L. McKie and S. Cunningham-Burley. S. Bristol, UK: Policy Press.

Janus, Samuel and Cynthia Janus. 1993. *The Janus Report on Sexual Behavior.* New York: John Wiley and Sons.

Jenkins, Richard. 1996. *Social Identity.* New York: Routledge.

Johnston, Lynda. 1998. "Reading the Sexed Bodies and the Spaces of Gyms." Pp. 182–196 in *Places Through the Body,* edited by Heidi J. Nast and Steve Pile. London, UK: Routledge.

Katz, Jack. 1988. *Seductions of Crime: Moral and Sensual Attractions in Doing Evil.* New York: Basic Books.

Kaufman, Joanne M. and Cathryn Johnson. 2004. "Stigmatized Individuals and the Process of Identity." *The Sociological Quarterly* 45(4):807–833.

Kennedy, Elizabeth Lapovsky and Madeline D. Davis. 1994. *Boots of Leather, Slippers of Gold: The History of a Lesbian Community.* New York: Penguin (Non-Classics).

Keys, D. 2002. "Instrumental Sexual Scripting: An Examination of Gender-Role Fluidity in the Correctional Institution." *Journal of Contemporary Criminal Justice* 18(3):258–278.

Kimmel, Michael. 2007. *The Sexual Self: The Construction of Sexual Scripts.* Nashville, TN: Vanderbilt University Press.

Kinsey, A. C., W. B. Pomeroy, and C. E. Martin. 1948. *Sexual Behavior in the Human Male.* Philadelphia, PA: W.B. Saunders.

———. 1953. *Sexual Behavior in the Human Female.* Philadelphia, PA: W.B. Saunders.

Kipnis, Laura. 1998. *Bound and Gagged: Pornography and the Politics of Fantasy in America.* Durham, NC: Duke University Press.

———. 2004. *Against Love: A Polemic.* New York: Pantheon.

Kirby, Douglas. 2002. "Do Abstinence-Only Programs Delay the Initiation of Sex Among Young People and Reduce Teen Pregnancy?" Washington, DC: The National Campaign to Prevent Teen Pregnancy. (http://www.teenpregnancy.org/resources/data/pdf/abstinence_eval.pdf).

Kissil, Karni and Maureen Davey. 2010. "The Prostitution Debate in Feminism: Current Trends, Policy and Clinical Issues Facing an Invisible Population." *Journal of Feminist Family Therapy* 22:1–21.

Klein, Marty and Charles Moser. 2006. "S/M (Sadomasochistic) Interests as an Issue in a Child Custody Proceeding." *Journal of Homosexuality* 50(2/3):233–242.

Klesse, C. 2006. "Polyamory and its 'Others': Contesting the Terms of Non-Monogamy." *Sexualities* 9(5):565–583.

Kulick, Don 1992. *Language Shift and Cultural Reproduction: Socialization, Self, and Syncretism in a Papua New Guinean Village.* Cambridge, MA: Cambridge University Press.

———. 1993. "Heroes from Hell: Representations of 'Rascals' in a Papua New Guinean Village." *Anthropology Today* 9(3):9–14.

Lane, Fredrick. 2001. *Obscene Profits: The Entrepreneurs of Pornography in the Cyber Age.* New York: Routledge.

Laner, M. and N. Ventrone. 2000. "Dating Scripts Revisited." *Journal of Family Issues* 21(4):488–500.

Langdridge, Darren. 2005. "Actively Dividing Selves: S/M and the Thrill of Disintegration." *Lesbian and Gay Psychology Review* 6(3):198–208.

———. 2006a. "The Time of the Sadomasochist: Hunting With(in) the 'Tribus.'" Pp. 280–287 in *Handbook of the New Sexuality Studies,* edited by Steven Seidman, Nancy Fischer, and Chet Meeks. New York: Routledge.

———. 2006b. "Voices From the Margins: Sadomasochism and Sexual Citizenship." *Citizenship Studies* 10(4):373–389.

Langdridge, Darren and Meg Barker. 2007. "Situating Sadomasochism." Pp. 3–9 in *Safe, Sane, and Consensual: Contemporary Perspectives on Sadomasochism,* edited by Darren Langdridge and Meg Barker. New York: Palgrave MacMillan.

Laumann, E. O., J. H. Gagnon, R. T. Michael, and S. Michaels. 1994. *The Social Organization of Sexuality: Sexual Practices in the United States.* Chicago, IL: University of Chicago Press.

Laurendeau, Jason. 2008. "Gendered Risk Regimes: A Theoretical Consideration of Edgework and Gender." *Sociology of Sport Journal* 25(3): 293–309.

Lawrence et al. v. Texas 539 U.S. 558 (2003).

Lemert, Edwin M. 1967. *Human Deviance, Social Problems, & Social Control.* Englewood Cliffs, NJ: Prentice-Hall.

Lemke, J. 1995. *Textual Politics: Discourse and Social Dynamics.* London, UK: Taylor and Francis.

Levine, Nancy and Joan Silk. 1997. "Why Polyandry Fails: Sources of Instability in Polyandrous Marriages." *Current Anthropology* 38(3):375–398.

Ling, L. H. M. 1996. "Hegemony and the Internationalizing State: A Post-Colonial Analysis of China's Integration into Asian Corporatism." *Review of International Political Economy* 3(1):1–26.

Lithwick, Dahlia. 2004. "Slippery Slop." *Slate,* May 19, 2004. Retrieved June 2, 2009. (http://www.slate.com/id/2100824/).

Lofland, J. and L. Lofland. 1995. *Analyzing Social Settings: A Guide to Qualitative Observation and Analysis.* Boston, MA: Wadsworth.

Long, Judith and Pepper Schwartz. 1989. *Sexual Scripts: The Social Construction of Female Sexuality.* Hinsdale, IL: The Dryden Press.

Longmore, M. 1998. "Symbolic Interactionism and the Study of Sexuality." *The Journal of Sex Research* 35(1):44–57.

Lorber, Judith. 1995. *Paradoxes of Gender.* New Haven, CT: Yale University Press.

Lorentzen, Jorgen. 2007. "Masculinities and the Phenomenology of Men's Orgasms." *Men and Masculinities* 10(1):71–84.

Luker, Kristin. 2006. *When Sex Goes to School: Warring Views on Sex—and Sex Education—Since the Sixties.* New York: W. W. Norton & Company.

Malcolm, L. W. G. 1925. "Notes on the Seclusion of Girls Among the Efik at Old Calabar." *Man* 69(August):113–114.

Mao, Limin, John McCormick, and Paul Van de Ven. 2002. "Ethnic and Gay Identification: Gay Asian Men Dealing with the Divide." *Culture, Health & Sexuality* 4(4):419–430.

Martínez, Jorge Hernández and Mariana Ortega Breña. 2007. "U.S. Political Culture and Hegemony." *Latin American Perspectives* 34(1):46–52.

Matza, David. 1964. *Delinquency and Drift.* New York: John Wiley & Sons.

———. 1969. *Becoming Deviant.* Englewood Cliffs, NJ: Prentice-Hall.

McDermott, Elizabeth, K. Roen, and J. Scourfield. 2008. "Avoiding Shame: Young LGBT

People, Homophobia and Self-Destructive Behaviours." *Culture, Health & Sexuality: An International Journal for Research, Intervention and Care* 10(8):815–829.

McLelland, Mark. 2000. "Is There a Japanese 'Gay Identity'?" *Culture, Health & Sexuality* 2(4):459–472.

McLorg, Penelope A. and Diane E. Taub. 1987. "Anorexia Nervosa and Bulimia: The Development of Deviant Identities." *Deviant Behavior* 8:177–189.

McQueeney, Krista. 2009. "'We are God's Children, Y'All:' Race, Gender, and Sexuality in Lesbian and Gay-Affirming Congregations." *Social Problems* 56:151–173.

Mead, George Herbert. 1934. *Mind, Self, and Society: From the Standpoint of a Social Behaviorist. Volume 1,* edited by Charles W. Morris, with an introduction. Chicago, IL: University of Chicago Press.

———. 1964. "The Social Self." Pp. 142–149 in *Selected Writings,* edited by G. H. Mead. Chicago, IL: University of Chicago Press. First published 1913.

Medley-Rath, Stephanie R. 2007. "Am I Still a Virgin? What Counts as Sex in 20 Years of *Seventeen.*" *Sexuality and Culture* 11: 24–38.

Melton, J. G. 1999. *The Vampire Book: The Encyclopedia of the Undead.* Canton, MI: Visible Ink Press.

Ménard, A. and C. Cabrera. 2011. "'Whatever the Approach, Tab B Still Fits into Slot A': Twenty Years of Sex Scripts in Romance Novels." *Sexuality and Culture* 15(3): 240–255.

Ménard, A. and P. Kleinplatz. 2008. "Twenty-One Moves Guaranteed to Make His Thighs Go Up in Flames: Depictions of 'Great Sex' in Popular Magazines." *Sexuality and Culture* 12(1):1–20.

Merkin, Daphne. 1996. "Unlikely Obsession." *New Yorker,* February 26, 98.

Mestemacher, Rebecca A. and Jonathan W. Roberti. 2004. "Qualitative Analysis of Vocational Choice: A Collective Case Study of Strippers." *Deviant Behavior* 25:43–65.

Meston, Cindy M. and David M. Buss. 2007. "Why Humans Have Sex." *Archives of Sexual Behavior* 36:477–507.

Michael, Robert, John Gagnon, Edward Laumann, and Gina Kolata. 1994. *Sex in America: A Definitive Survey.* New York: Warner Books.

Mills, C. Wright. 1940. "Situated Actions and Vocabularies of Motive." *American Sociological Review* 5:904–913.

Morgan, D. 2011. "Framing Relationships and Families." Pp. 19–31 in *Researching Families and Relationships: Reflections on Process,* edited by L. Jamieson, R. Simpson, and R. Lewis. Hampshire, UK: Palgrave Macmillan.

Morrison, T. G., M. A. Morrison, M. A. Carrigan, and D. T. McDermott, eds. 2012. *Sexual Minority Research in the New Millennium.* New York: Nova Science.

Morrow, Lara Catherine. 2012. "Cyclical Role-Playing and Stigma: Exploring the Challenges of Stereotype Performance Among Exotic Dancers." *Deviant Behavior* 5:357–374.

Moser, Charles and Peggy Kleinplatz. 2005. "DSM-IV-TR and the Paraphilias: An Argument for Removal." *Journal of Psychology & Human Sexuality* 17(3/4): 91–109.

———. 2006. "Introduction: The State of Our Knowledge on SM." *Journal of Homosexuality* 50(2/3):1–15.

Mullaney, Jamie L. 2006. *Everyone Is NOT Doing It: Abstinence and Personal Identity.* Chicago, IL: The University of Chicago Press.

———. 2007. "'Unity Admirable But Not Necessarily Heeded': Going Rates and Gender Boundaries in the Straight Edge Hardcore Music Scene." *Gender & Society* 21:384–408.

———. 2012. "All in Time: Age and the Temporality of Authenticity in the Straight-Edge Music Scene." *Journal of Contemporary Ethnography* 41:611–635.

Murray, Samantha. 2004. "Locating Aesthetics: Sexing the Fat Woman." *Social Semiotics* 14(3):237–247.

———. 2005a. "(Un/Be) Coming Out? Rethinking Fat Politics." *Social Semiotics* 15(2):153–163.

———. 2005b. "Doing Politics or Selling Out? Living the Fat Body." *Women's Studies: An Interdisciplinary Journal* 34(3/4): 265–277.

Mutchler, M. 2000. "Young Gay Men's Stories in the States: Scripts, Sex, and Safety in the Time of AIDS." *Sexualities* 3(1):31–54.

Myers, Garth Andrew. 1998. "Intellectual of Empire: Eric Dutton and Hegemony in British Africa." *Annals of the Association of American Geographers* 88(1):1–27.

Nash, Catherine Jean and Alison Bain. 2007. "'Reclaiming Raunch'? Spatializing Queer Identities at Toronto Women's Bathhouse Events." *Social & Cultural Geography* 8(1):47–62.

Nelson, M. 2010. *Parenting Out of Control: Anxious Parents in Uncertain Times.* New York: New York University Press.

Nestle, Joan. 1997. "Restriction and Reclamation: Lesbian Bars and Beaches of the 1950s." Pp. 61–68 in *Queers in Space: Communities, Public Places, Sites of Resistance,* edited by Yolanda Retter, Anne-Marie Bouthillette, and Gordon Brent Ingram. Seattle, WA: Bay Press.

Newmahr, Staci. 2008. "Becoming a Sadomasochist: Integrating Self and Other in Ethnographic Analysis." *Journal of Contemporary Ethnography,* 37:619–641.

———. 2010a. "Power Struggles: Pain and Authenticity in SM Play." *Symbolic Interaction* 33(3):389–411.

———. 2010b. "Rethinking Kink: Sadomasochism as Serious Leisure." *Qualitative Sociology* 33(3):313–331.

———. 2011. *Playing on the Edge: Sadomasochism, Risk, and Intimacy.* Bloomington: Indiana University Press.

———. 2013. "Sadomasochistic Selves: Dramaturgical Dimensions of SM Play." Chapter 16 in *The Drama of Social Life: A Dramaturgical Handbook,* edited by Charles Edgley. Surrey, UK: Ashgate Publishing Co.

Norton, Aaron and Gregory Herek. 2013. "Heterosexuals' Attitudes Toward Transgender People: Findings From a National Probability Sample of U.S. Adults." *Sex Roles* 68(11/12):738–753.

Nin, A. 2004. *Delta of Venus.* Orlando, FL: Harcourt.

O'Brien, Jodi. 2004. "Wrestling the Angel of Contradiction: Queer Christian Identities." *Culture and Religion* 5:179–202.

O'Doherty, Tamara. 2011. "Criminalization and Off-Street Sex Work in Canada." *Canadian Journal of Criminology and Criminal Justice* 53(2):217–245.

Okazaki, Sumie. 2002. "Influences of Culture on Asian Americans' Sexuality." *The Journal of Sex Research.* 39(1):34–41.

Oldenburg, Ray. 1999. *The Great Good Place: Cafes, Coffee Shops, Bookstores, Bars, Hair Salons, and Other Hangouts at the Heart of a Community.* 3rd ed. Cambridge, MA: Da Capo Press.

O'Reilly, Bill and Martin Dugard. (2012). *Killing Kennedy, the End of Camelot.* New York: Henry Holt and Company.

Orne, Jason. 2011. "'You Will Always Have to "Out" Yourself'": Reconsidering Coming Out Through Strategic Outness." *Sexualities* 14:681–703.

Page, Amy Dellinger and James R. Peacock. 2013. "Negotiating Identities in a Heteronormative Context." *Journal of Homosexuality* 60(4):639–654.

Pan'sShadow, July 2013. Re: "Asexual With a Sexual Spouse, and I hope to Include You in My Journey" [Online forum comment]. Retrieved from http://www.asexuality.org/en/topic/89348-asexual-with-a-sexual-spouse-and-i-hope-to-include-you-in-my-journey/

Pascoe, C. J. 2007. *Dude, You're a Fag: Masculinity and Sexuality in High School.* Berkeley, CA: University of California Press.

Pasko, Lisa. 2002. "Naked Power: The Practice of Stripping as a Confidence Game." *Sexualities* 5:49–66.

Picart, C. J. and C. Greek. 2003. "The Compulsion of Real/Reel Serial Killers and Vampires: Toward a Gothic Criminology." *Journal of Criminal Justice and Popular Culture* 10:39–68.

Plante, Rebecca F. 2006. "Sexual Spanking, the Self, and the Construction of Deviance." *Journal of Homosexuality* 50(2/3):59–79.

———. 2007. "In Search of Sexual Subjectivities: Exploring the Sociological Construction of Sexual Selves." Pp. 31–48 in *The Sexual Self: The Construction of Sexual Scripts,* edited by Michael Kimmel. Nasvhille, TN: Vanderbilt University Press.

Plummer, Ken. 1995. *Telling Sexual Stories: Power, Change and Social Worlds*. London, UK: Routledge.

———. 2002. "Symbolic Interactionism and Sexual Conduct: An Emergent Perspective." Pp. 20–32 in *Gender and Sexuality,* edited by Christine L. Williams and Arlene Stein. Malden, MA: Blackwell.

———. 2003. "Queers, Bodies and Postmodern Sexualities: A Note on Revisiting the 'Sexual' in Symbolic Interactionism." *Qualitative Sociology* 26(4):515–530.

———. 2007. "Queers, Bodies and Postmodern Sexualities: A Note on Revisiting the 'Sexual' in Symbolic Interactionism." Pp. 16–30 in *The Sexual Self,* edited by Michael Kimmel. Nashville, TN: Vanderbilt University Press.

Popovic, M. (2006). "Psychosexual Diversity as the Best Representation of Human Normality Across Cultures." *Sexual and Relationship Therapy* 21: 171–186.

Przybylo, E. 2011. "Crisis and Safety: The Asexual in Sexusociety." *Sexualities,* 14(4):444–461.

Pyke, Karen D. and Denise L. Johnson. 2003. "Asian American Women and Racialized Femininities: 'Doing' gender Across Cultural Worlds." *Gender and Society* 17(1):33–53.

Query, Julia and Vicki Funari. 2002. "Live Nude Girls Unite." Videocassette, 70 min. Produced by Julia Query and John Montoya. (www.livenudegirlsunite.com). West Glen Communications, Inc., 1430 Broadway, New York, NY 10018.

Quinlan, Todd B. 1998. "Big Whigs in the Mobilization of Irish Peasants: An Historical Sociology of Hegemony in Prefamine Ireland (1750s-1840s)." *Sociological Forum* 13(2):247–264.

Richters, Juliet, Richard de Visser, Chris Rissel, Andrew Grulich, and Anthony Smith. 2008. "Demographic and Psychosocial Features of Participants in Bondage and Discipline, 'Sadomasochism' or Dominance and Submission (BDSM): Data from a National Survey." *Journal of Sexual Medicine* 5:1660–1668.

Ritchie, Ani and Meg Barker. 2006. "'There Aren't Words for What We Do or How We Feel So We Have to Make Them Up': Constructing Polyamorous Languages in a Culture of Compulsory Monogamy." *Sexualities* 9(5):584–601.

Ronai, Carol Rambo. 1998. "Sketching With Derrida: An Ethnography of a Researcher/ Erotic Dancer." *Qualitative Inquiry* 4(3):405–520.

Ronai, Carol Rambo and Carolyn Ellis. 1989. "Turn-Ons for Money: Interactional Strategies of the Table Dancer." *Journal of Contemporary Ethnography* 18:271–298.

Rosario, M., E. Schrimshaw, J. Hunter, and L. Braun. 2006. "Sexual Identity Development Among Lesbian, Gay, and Bisexual Youths: Consistency and Change Over Time." *Journal of Sex Research* 43(1):46–58.

Rothblum, E. and K. Brehony, eds. 1993. *Boston Marriages: Romantic but Asexual Relationships Among Contemporary Lesbians*. Amherst: University of Massachusetts.

Rowe, A. C. 2012. "Erotic Pedagogies." *Journal of Homosexuality,* 59(7):1031–1056.

Rubin, G. S., (1993). "Thinking Sex: Notes for a Radical Theory of the Politics of Sexuality." Pp. 3–44 in *The Lesbian and Gay Studies Reader,* edited by H. Abelove, M. A., Barale, and D. M. Halperin. New York: Routledge.

Rubin, Gayle. "The Valley of the Kings: Leathermen in San Francisco, 1960–1990."

PhD dissertation, University of Michigan, 1994.

Rubington, Earl and Martin S. Weinberg. 2008. *Deviance: The Interactionist Perspective.* 10th ed. New York: Allyn and Bacon.

Rutherford, Markella B. 2011. *Adult Supervision Required: Private Freedoms and Public Constraints for Parents and Children.* New Brunswick, NJ: Rutgers University Press.

Ryan, C. and C. Jethá. 2010. *Sex at Dawn: The Prehistoric Origins of Modern Sexuality.* New York: Harper.

Rye, B. J. and Glenn J. Meaney. 2007. "The Pursuit of Sexual Pleasure." *Sexuality & Culture* 11(1):28–51.

Sabina, Chiara, Janis Wolak, and David Finkelhor. 2008. "The Nature and Dynamics of Internet Pornography Exposure for Youth." *Cyberpsychology & Behavior* 11(6):1–3.

Salter, Brian and Charlotte Salter. 2007. "Bioethics and the Global Moral Economy: The Cultural Politics of Human Embryonic Stem Cell Science." *Science, Technology, & Human Values* 32(5):554–581.

Sandstrom, Kent, Daniel D. Martin, and Gary Alan Fine. 2010. *Symbols, Selves, and Social Reality: A Symbolic Interactionist Approach to Social Psychology and Sociology.* 3rd ed. New York: Oxford University Press.

Santtila, P., N. K. Sandnabba, L. Alison, and N. Nordling. 2002. "Investigating the Underlying Structure in Sadomasochistically Oriented Behavior." *Archives of Sexual Behavior* 31(2):185–196.

Savin-Williams, Ritch. 2005. *The New Gay Teenager.* Cambridge, MA: Harvard University Press.

Schalet, Amy. 2009. "Subjectivity, Intimacy, and the Empowerment Paradigm of Adolescent Sexuality: The Unexplored Room." *Feminist Studies* 35(1):133–160.

Scherrer, K. 2008. "Coming to an Asexual Identity: Negotiating Identity, Negotiating Desire." *Sexualities* 11(5):621–641.

———. 2010a. "Asexual Relationships: What Does Asexuality Have to Do With Polyamory?" Pp. 154–159 in *Understanding Non-Monogamies,* edited by M. Barker and D. Langdridge. London, UK: Routledge.

———. 2010b. "What Asexuality Contributes to the Same-Sex Marriage Discussion." *Journal of Gay & Lesbian Social Services* 22:1/2, 56–73.

Schrock, Douglas, Daphne Holden, and Lori Reid. 2004. "Creating Emotional Resonance: Interpersonal Emotion Work and Motivational Framing in a Transgender Community." *Social Problems* 51:61–81.

Schwalbe, Michael and Douglas Mason-Schrock. 1996. "Identity Work as a Group Process." *Advances in Group Processes* 13:113–147.

Schweingruber, David and Nancy Berns. 2011. "Organizing Door-to-Door Sales: A Symbolic Interactionist Analysis." Pp. 305–325 in *Illuminating Social Life: Classical and Contemporary Theory Revisited.* 5th ed., edited by P. Kivisto. Los Angeles, CA: Sage.

Scott, Gini Graham. 1993. *Erotic Power: An Exploration of Dominance and Submission.* New York: Citadel Press.

Scott, Marvin and Stanford Lyman. 1989. *A Sociology of the Absurd.* 2nd ed. Dix Hills, NY: General Hall Publishing Co.

Scott, S. 2007. *Shyness and Society: The Illusion of Competence.* Basingstoke, UK: Palgrave.

Scott-Dixon, Krista. 2008. "Big Girls Don't Cry: Fitness, Fatness, and the Production of Feminist Knowledge." *Sociology of Sport Journal* 25:22–47.

Seidman, S. 2010. *The Social Construction of Sexuality.* New York: W.W. Norton.

Semiel. June 15, 2011. *Intimacy Cartography.* "What a Poly, Aromantic Relationship Looks Like" [Web log post]. Retrieved from http://intimacycartography.wordpress.com/

Sheff, Elisabeth. 2005. "Polyamorous Women, Sexual Subjectivity and Power." *Journal of Contemporary Ethnography* 3(34): 251–283.

———. 2007. "The Reluctant Polyamorist: Auto-Ethnographic Research in a Sexualized Setting" Pp. 111–118 in *Sex Matters: The*

Sexuality and Society Reader, edited by M. Stombler, D. Baunach, E. Burgess, D. Donnelly, and W. Simonds. 2nd ed. New York: Pearson, Allyn, and Bacon.

———. 2013. *The Polyamorists Next Door: Inside Multiple Partner Families and Relationships.* Lanham, MD: Rowman and Littlefield.

Sheff, Elisabeth and Corie Hammers. 2011. "The Privilege of Perversities: Race, Class, and Education among Polyamorists and Kinksters." *Sexuality & Psychology* 2(3):198–223.

Shilling, C. and P. A. Mellor. 2010. "Sociology and the Problem of Eroticism." *Sociology* 44(3):435–452.

Shokeid, Moshe. 2001. "You Don't Eat Indian and Chinese Food at the Same Meal: The Bisexual Quandry." *Anthropological Quarterly* 75(1):63–90.

Shostak, Marjorie. 1981. *Nisa, the Life and Words of a !Kung Woman.* New York: Vintage Books.

Simmel, Georg. 1950. *The Sociology of Georg Simmel,* ed. and translated by K. Wolff. New York: Free Press.

Simon, W. 1996. *Postmodern Sexualities.* London, UK: Routledge.

Simon, William and John H. Gagnon. 1984a. "Sexual Scripts." *Society* (November/December): 54–60. New Brunswick, NJ: Rutgers University Press.

———. 1984b. "Sexual Scripts: Permanence and Change," *Archives of Sexual Behavior* 15(2):97–120.

———. 1987. "A Sexual Scripts Approach." Pp. 363–383 in *Theories of Human Sexuality,* edited by J. Geer and W. O'Donohue. New York: Plenum.

———. 2003. "Sexual Scripts: Origins, Influences and Changes," *Qualitative Sociology* 26(4):491–497.

Singh, Devendra, Peter Renn, and Adrian Singh. (2007). "Did the Perils of Abdominal Obesity Affect Depiction of Feminine Beauty in the Sixteenth to Eighteenth Century British Literature? Exploring the Health and Beauty Link." *Proceedings of the Royal Society B: Biological Sciences* 274(1611):891–894.

Smith, Christian, Michael Emerson, Sally Gallagher, Paul Kennedy, and David Sikkink. 1998. *American Evangelicalism: Embattled and Thriving.* Chicago, IL: University of Chicago Press.

Smith, Elizabeth A. 1989. "Butches, Femmes, and Feminists: The Politics of Lesbian Sexuality." *NWSA Journal* 1(3):398–421.

Solebello, Nicholas and Sinikka Elliott. 2011. "'We Want Them to Be as Heterosexual as Possible': Fathers Talk About Their Teen Children's Sexuality." *Gender & Society* 25(3):293–315.

Southgate, Dora Hilda. 1938. *Root in the Rock, an Indian Saga, 1876–1936.* New York: A. A. Knopf.

Springer, Claudia. 1996. *Electronic Eros: Bodies and Desire in the Postindustrial Age.* Austin, TX: University of Texas Press.

Stein, Arlene. (1997). *Sex and Sensibility: Stories of a Lesbian Generation.* Berkeley, CA: University of California Press.

Stewart, G. L. 1972. "On First Being a John." *Journal of Contemporary Ethnography,* 1(3):255–274.

Stokes, C. 2007. "'Representin' in Cyberspace: Sexual Scripts, Self Definition and Hip Hop Culture in Black Adolescent Girls' Homepages." *Culture, Health and Sexuality* 9(2):169–184.

Stone, G. 1962. "Appearance and the Self." Pp. 86–118 in *Human Behavior and Social Processes,* edited by A. Rose. Boston, MA: Houghton-Mifflin.

Storr, Merl. 2002. "Classy Lingerie." *Feminist Review* 71:18–36.

———. 2003. *Latex and Lingerie: Shopping for Pleasure at Ann Summers Parties.* Oxford, UK: Berg Publishers.

Stryker, S. 1980. *Symbolic Interactionism: A Social Structural Version.* Menlo Park, CA: Benjamin-Cummings Publishing Company.

Sumerau, J. Edward. 2012. "'That's What Men are Supposed to Do': Compensatory

Manhood Acts in an LGBT Christian Church." *Gender & Society* 26:461–487.

Sumerau, J. Edward and Douglas P. Schrock. 2011. "'It's Important to Show Your Colors': Counter-Heteronormative Embodiment in a Metropolitan Community Church." Pp. 99–110 in *Embodied Resistance: Challenging the Norms, Breaking the Rules,* edited by Christina Bobel and Samantha Kwan. Nashville, TN: Vanderbilt University Press.

Tang, D. T-S. 2011. *Conditional Spaces: Hong Kong Lesbian Desires and Everyday Life.* Hong Kong: Hong Kong University Press.

Tapestry. September 2010. Re: "Fellow Sexuals" [Online AVEN forum comment]. Retrieved from http://www.asexuality.org/en/topic/51754-fellow-sexuals/

Taylor, Gary W. and Jane M. Ussher. 2001. "Making Sense of S&M: A Discourse Analytic Account." *Sexualities* 4(3):293–314.

Texas Penal Code. 2012. Prostitution 43.02.

Thio, Alex 2010. *Deviant Behavior.* 10th ed. Boston, MA: Allyn and Bacon.

Thomas, W. I. 1931. *The Unadjusted Girl.* Boston, MA: Little, Brown. First published 1923.

Thomas, W. I. and D. S. Thomas. 1928. *The Child in America: Behavior Problems and Programs.* New York: Knopf. First published 1923.

Thompson, Wendy M. 2001. "Going Undercover." Pp. 201–205 in *Yell-Oh Girls!,* edited by Vickie Nam. New York: Quill, HarperCollins.

Torkelson, Jason. 2010. "Life After (Straightedge) Subculture." *Qualitative Sociology* 33:257–274.

Trautner, Mary Nell and Jessica L. Collett. 2010. "Students Who Strip: The Benefits of Alternate Identities for Managing Stigma." *Symbolic Interaction* 33(2):257–279.

Vaccarro, Christian, Douglas P. Schrock, and Janice McCabe. 2011. "Managing Emotional Manhood: Fighting and Fostering Fear in Mixed Martial Arts." *Social Psychology Quarterly* 74:414–437.

Valentine, David. (2003). "'I Went to Bed with My Own Kind Once': The Erasure of Desire in the Name of Identity." *Language & Communication* 23:123–138.

Valkenburg, Patti and Jochen Peter. 2010. "Online Communication Among Adolescents: An Integrated Model of Its Attraction, Opportunities, and Risks." *Journal of Adolescent Health* 48(2):121–127.

Valocchi, Stephen. 2005. "Not Yet Queer Enough: The Lessons of Queer Theory for the Sociology of Gender and Sexuality." *Gender & Society* 19(6):750–770.

Vance, C. 1998. "Social Construction Theory: Problems in the History of Sexuality." Pp. 160–172 in *Social Perspectives in Lesbian and Gay Studies,* edited by P. Nardi and B. Schneider. London, UK: Routledge. First published 1989.

———. 2013. "Prostitution Push and Pull: Male and Female Perspectives." *Journal of Sex Research* 50(1):11–16.

Walker, Shelley, Lena Sanci, and Meredith Temple-Smith. 2011. "Sexting and Young People." *Youth Studies Australia* 30(4):8–16.

Warner, Michael. 1999. *The Trouble With Normal: Sex, Politics and the Ethics of Queer Life.* New York: Free Press.

Waskul, Dennis. 2002. "The Naked Self: Being a Body in Televideo Cybersex." *Symbolic Interaction* 25(2):199–227.

———, (ed). 2004a. *Net.seXXX: Readings on Sex, Pornography, and the Internet.* New York: Peter Lang.

———. 2004 b. "Sex and the Internet: Old Thrills in a New World; New Thrills in an Old World." Pp. 1–8 in *Readings on Sex, Pornography, and the Internet,* edited by D. Waskul. *Net.SeXXX.* New York: Peter Lang.

———. 2006. "Internet Sex: The Seductive 'Freedom to.'" Pp. 262–270 in *Handbook of the New Sexuality Studies,* edited by Nancy Fisher, Steven Seidman, and Chet Meeks. New York: Routledge.

Waskul, Dennis, Mark Douglass, and Charles Edgley. 2000. "Cybersex: Outercourse and the Enselfment of the Body." *Symbolic Interaction.* 23(4):375–397.

Waskul, Dennis and Justin Martin. 2010. "Now the Orgy Is Over." *Symbolic Interaction.* 33(2):297–318.

Waskul, Dennis and Cheryl Radeloff. 2009. "'How do I Rate?' Nude 'Rate Me' Websites and Gendered Looking Glasses." Pp. 202–216 in *Porn.Com: Making Sense of Online Pornography,* edited by Feona Attwood. New York: Peter Lang.

Waskul, Dennis and Phillip Vannini. 2008. "Ludic and (Ludic)rous Relationships: Sex, Play, and the Internet." Pp. 241–261 in *Remote Relationships in a Small World: Empirical Research Online,* edited by Sam Holland. New York: Peter Lang.

Waskul, Dennis, Phillip Vannini, and Desiree Wiesen. 2007. "Women and Their Clitoris: Personal Discovery, Signification, and Use." *Symbolic Interaction* 30(2):151–174.

Weber, Sandra and Shanly Dixon, eds. 2010. *Growing Up Online: Young People and Digital Technologies.* New York: Palgrave Macmillan.

Weeks, J., B. Heaphy, and C. Donovan. 2001. *Same Sex Intimacies: Families of Choice and Other Life Experiments.* London, UK: Routledge.

Weinberg, Martin, Colin J. Williams, and Charles Moser. 1984. "The Social Constituents of Sadomasochism." *Social Problems* 31(4): 379–389.

Weinberg, Thomas S. 1983. *Gay Men, Gay Selves: The Social Construction of Homosexual Identities.* New York: Irvington Publishers, Inc.

—. 1994a. *Gay Men, Drinking, and Alcoholism.* Carbondale: University of Southern Illinois Press.

—. 1994b. "Sociological Theories of Sexuality," Pp. 564–567 in *Human Sexuality: An Encyclopedia,* edited by Vern L. Bullough and Bonnie Bullough. New York: Garland.

—. 2006. "Sadomasochism and the Social Sciences: A Review of the Sociological and Social Psychological Literature." *Journal of Homosexuality* 50(2/3):17–40.

Weiss, Margot. 2006. "Working at Play: BDSM Sexuality in the San Francisco Bay Area." *Anthropologics* 48(2):229–245.

Wellings, K., K. Nanchahal, W. Macdowall, S. McManus, B. Erens, C. H. Mercer, A. M. Johnson, A. J. Copas, C. Korovessis, K. A. Fenton, and J. Field. 2001. "Sexual Behaviour in Britain: Early Heterosexual Experience." *Lancet* 358; 1843–1850.

Weston, Kath. 1991. *Families We Choose: Lesbians, Gays, Kinship.* New York: Columbia University Press.

Whitman, Walt. 1986. *Walt Whitman: The Complete Poems,* edited by Francis Murphy. New York: Penguin Books.

Whittier, D. and W. Simon. 2001. "The Fuzzy Matrix of 'My Type' in Intrapsychic Sexual Scripting." *Sexualities* 4(2):139–165.

Wilcox, Melissa M. 2009. *Queer Women and Religious Individualism.* Bloomington: Indiana University Press.

Williams, D J 2008. "Contemporary Vampires and (Blood-Red) Leisure: Should We Be Afraid of the Dark?" *Leisure/Loisir* 32(2):513–539.

Williams, J. Patrick. 2006. "Authentic Identities: Straightedge Subculture, Music, and the Internet." *Journal of Contemporary Ethnography* 35:173–200.

Williams, J. Patrick and Heith Copes. 2005. "'How Edge Are You?': Constructing Authentic Identities and Subcultural Boundaries in a Straightedge Internet Forum." *Symbolic Interaction* 28:67–89.

Williams, R. 2000. *Making Identity Matter.* Durham, NC: Sociology Press.

Williamson, Celia and Lynda M. Baker. 2009. "Women in Street-based Prostitution: A Typology of Their Work Styles." *Qualitative Social Work* 8:27–44.

Wolkomir, Michelle. 2006. *Be Not Deceived: The Sacred and Sexual Struggles of Gay and Ex-gay Christian Men.* New Brunswick, NJ: Rutgers University Press.

Wood, Robert T. 2006. *Straightedge Youth: Complexity and Contradictions of a Subculture.* New York: Syracuse University Press.

World Health Organization (WHO). 2006. *Defining Sexual Health: Report of a Technical Consultation on Sexual Health, January 28–31 2002, Geneva.* Geneva, Switzerland: Author.

Wosick-Correa, Kassia. 2007. "Identity and Community: The Social Construction of Bisexuality in Women." Pp. 42–52 in *Sex Matters: The Sexuality and Society Reader,* edited by Mindy Stombler, Dawn M. Baunauch, and Elisabeth O. Burgess. New York: Pearson.

Ybarra, Michele and Kimberly Mitchell. 2005. "Exposure to Internet Pornography Among Children and Adolescents: A National Survey." *Cyberpsychology* 8(5):473–486).

Yost, Megan R. 2007. "Sexual Fantasies of S/M Practitioners: The Impact of Gender and S/M Role on Fantasy Content." Pp. 135–154 in *Safe, Sane, and Consensual: Contemporary Perspectives on Sadomasochism,* edited by D. Langdridge and M. Barker. New York: Palgrave MacMillan.

Zhao S., S. Grasmuck, and J. Martin. 2008. "Identity Construction on Facebook: Digital Empowerment in Anchored Relationships." *Computers in Human Behavior* 24(5):1816–1836.

Zimman, Lal. (2009). "'The Other Kind of Coming Out': Transgender People and the Coming Out Narrative Genre." *Gender & Language* 3(1):53–80.

INDEX

About the Contributors

Alison Better is an Assistant Professor of Sociology at CUNY Kingsborough Community College. Her research focuses on women's sexual agency, sex stores, and reimagining sexual categories. She is a member of Brooklyn Public Scholars and co-organizes the Women's and Gender Studies Faculty Interest Group at Kingsborough. Publications include "Redefining Queer: Women's Relationships and Identity in an Age of Sexual Fluidity" in *Sexuality & Culture* and "Pleasure for Sale: Feminist Sex Stores" in *Introducing the New Sexualities Studies, 2nd Edition.*

Tanya Bezreh wrote a spanking musical called *The Naughty Garden* for HBO Real Sex in 2003. Her video diary piece "Coming out Spanko" won best documentary short at CineKink 2008, was selected for the 2011 Kinsey Juried Art Show, and has toured internationally. Her research into the disclosure support needs of kinky people, "BDSM Disclosure and Stigma Management: Identifying Opportunities for Sex Education," was published in the *American Journal of Sexuality Education.*

Chris Brickell is Associate Professor in Gender Studies at Otago University, New Zealand. He has published extensively in the sociology and history of sexuality. Recently he has been exploring histories of adolescence, masculinities, and affect.

Matt Dawson (matt.dawson@glasgow.ac.uk) is a Lecturer in Sociology at the University of Glasgow, with research interests in asexuality, social theory, individualization, socialism and political sociology. He is the author of "Late Modernity, Individualization and Socialism: An Associational Critique of Neoliberalism" (2013, Palgrave Macmillan) and is currently preparing a book on normative theory and the social alternatives offered by sociology throughout the discipline's history. He has also published articles on Zygmunt Bauman, Émile Durkheim, individualization, and contemporary politics in a variety of journals. Matt is involved in a research project (funded by the Leverhulme Trust) with Susie Scott and Liz McDonnell (both at the University of Sussex) looking at asexual lives.

Charles Edgley is Adjunct Professor of Sociology and Anthropology at the University of Arkansas at Little Rock where he was lured out of retirement after a long career at Oklahoma State University. Dr. Edgley has written, edited, or revised nine books, as well as publishing numerous articles in *Symbolic Interaction*. He has written extensively on the health and fitness movement, on the sociology of sexuality, and does regular editorial work for the journal *Symbolic Interaction*. He currently serves as co-editor (with Jeff Nash) of *The Journal of Contemporary Ethnography*. He is also the author of *Life as Theater: A Dramaturgical Sourcebook* (with the late Dennis Brissett), a book that has become a standard reference in dramaturgical social psychology. The second edition of *Life as Theater* was released in a new printing by Aldine/Transaction Books with a new introduction by Robert A. Stebbins. His most recent publication is an edited handbook entitled *The Drama of Social Life: A Dramaturgical Handbook*. That book is a part of Ashgate Publishing Company's *Interactionist Currents* series edited by Dennis Waskul and Phillip Vannini.

Sinikka Elliott is an assistant professor of sociology at North Carolina State University where she teaches and researches topics related to gender, sexuality, inequality, and family. She is the author of the book *Not My Kid: What Parents Believe about the Sex Lives of Their Teenagers,* published in 2012 by New York University Press. Her research has also been published in top journals, including *Gender & Society, Journal of Marriage and Family,* and *Sexuality Research and Social Policy.*

Clare Forstie is a PhD student in the Sociology department at Northwestern University and a member of the interdisciplinary Gender and Sexuality Studies Cluster at Northwestern. Her research interests include the sociology of emotions, culture, identities, gender, sexualities, technology, and space and place. Her primarily qualitative research focuses on the social practice and memory of emotion in public spaces and private relationships and the related impact on self, identities, and communities. Her dissertation articulates the relationship between close, adult friendships and identity formation, in particular, gender and sexuality. She received an M.A. in American and New England Studies from the University of Southern Maine and an A.B. in Sociology and Women's Studies from Bowdoin College.

Petula Sik Ying Ho is Associate Professor in the Department of Social Work and Social Administration at the University of Hong Kong. Her current projects include using documentary films to explore the integration of arts and scholarship. They include: *22 Springs: The Invincible; Whatever Will Be Will Be; Hong Kong Calling Tokyo*; and *The 'Kong-lo' Chronicles*. She is co-author with Ka Tat Tsang of *Love and Desire in Hong Kong,* published in English and Chinese by Hong Kong University Press and China Social Science Press in 2012. She is currently working with Stevi Jackson on a book provisionally entitled *Women Doing Intimacy: Gender, Family and Modernity in Hong Kong and Britain* for Palgrave Macmillan.

Stevi Jackson is Professor of Women's Studies and Director of the Centre for Women's Studies at the University of York, UK. Her books include *Heterosexuality in Question* (Sage 1999), *Theorizing Sexuality* (with Sue Scott; Open University Press, 2010), and *Gender and Sexuality Sociological Approaches* (with Momin Rahman; Polity 2010). She is co-editor, with Liu Jieyu and Woo Juhyun, of *East Asian Sexualities* (Zed 2008). She is currently working, with Sik Ying Ho, on a book provisionally entitled *Women Doing Intimacy: Gender, Family and Modernity in Hong Kong and Britain,* to be published by Palgrave Macmillan.

Don Kulick is professor of anthropology in the department of Comparative Human Development at the University of Chicago. His books include *Travesti: Sex, Gender and Culture among Brazilian Transgendered Prostitutes* (University of Chicago Press, 1998), *Fat: The Anthropology of an Obsession* (edited with Anne Meneley, Tarcher/Penguin 2005), and *Fucked: Sex, Disability and the Ethics of Engagement* (with Jens Rydström, Duke University Press, 2014).

Misty Luminais, PhD., is currently a Research Associate and Project Coordinator for the Voicing and Action Project at Case Western Reserve University. As a cultural anthropologist, her areas of expertise include urban studies, gender, sexuality, public health, and ethnography. Her contribution is drawn from her dissertation, which focuses on how sexuality is used to both resist and reinforce hegemonic ideals of embodiment. Her other work focuses on the material culture, ritual, and morality of queer practices.

Josephine Ngo McKelvy is a graduate student at North Carolina State University in Raleigh, North Carolina. Her research interests include gender, family, the life course, and identity. She is currently a research assistant with Voices into Action (a USDA grant to conduct research on families, food, and health) with co-author Dr. Sinikka Elliott.

Stella Meningkat graduated from Buffalo State College with a Bachelors of Science Degree in Women, Gender and Diversity Studies. She currently works as an organizer for an affiliate of the American Civil Liberties Union. Stella is also the founding member of the Young Feminists of Buffalo and works diligently on local and national campaigns to achieve equality for all. Stella thanks her family, friends and colleagues for all of the support and guidance. She would also like to say a special and heartfelt thank you to her two beautiful children and loving partner for giving her the strength and love to make this world a brighter place.

Jamie L. Mullaney is associate professor and chair in the Department of Sociology and Anthropology at Goucher College. In addition to numerous journal articles, she is the author of two books: *Everyone is NOT Doing It: Abstinence and Personal Identity* (University of Chicago Press, 2006) and *Paid to Party: Working Time and Emotion in Direct Home Sales* (with Janet Shope, Rutgers University Press, 2012). Her research interests and projects largely focus around issues of time, emotion, and identity.

John P. is a recent graduate of the State University of New York, College at Buffalo, where he studied journalism and sociology. His academic interests include group-dynamics, micro-aggressions, and sociolinguistics. His research was presented at a recent conference sponsored by the New York State Sociological Association. Currently he resides in Buffalo, NY, where he is a columnist for numerous local publications. In his spare time John is active in the LGBT community and presently doing independent research on the high rates of HIV infection among African-American gay men.

Giselle Ridgeway received her BA in Psychology from Buffalo State College and is currently working towards a PhD in Transnational Studies at the University at Buffalo. Giselle is a two time recipient of the SUNY Chancellor's Award. She is a former McNair scholar and a current Arthur Schomburg Fellow. Her current research interests include transgender rights and transgender feminism in multinational contexts.

Susie Scott is a Reader in Sociology at the University of Sussex, UK, with research interests in self-identity and interaction, Goffman's dramaturgical theory, and symbolic interactionism. She is the author of *Shyness and Society* (Palgrave 2007), *Making Sense of Everyday Life* (Polity 2009) and *Total Institutions and Reinvented Identities* (Palgrave 2011). She has also published empirical research articles on topics including shyness and social interaction, identities in mental health, total institutions, and swimming pool behaviour.

Elisabeth Sheff has a BA in modern dance, women's studies, and communications (California State University Sonoma 1994) and a PhD in Sociology (University of Colorado Boulder 2005), as well as certifications as a Guardian Ad Litem (Fulton County Georgia) and a Certified Sex Educator (American Association of Sexuality Educators, Counselors, and Therapists). She is a noted sociological researcher in the areas of intersecting identities and relational diversity. CEO and Senior Legal Consultant for Sheff Consulting Group, Sheff is an expert witness, continuing educator, and educational/legal advocate for sexual minorities. She is the author of *The Polyamorists Next Door: Inside Multiple-Partner Relationships and Families,* a summary of her 15-year longitudinal study of polyamorous families published by Rowman and Littelfield.

Brandy L. Simula is a Visiting Assistant Professor of Sociology at Emory University. Her research focuses on the intersections of gender, sexuality, and power in interaction. Her publications include "Does Bisexuality 'Undo' Gender?: Gender, Sexuality, and Bisexual Behavior Among BDSM Participants" *Journal of Bisexuality* (2012) and "Queer Utopias in Painful Spaces: BDSM Participants Resisting Heteronormativity and Gender Regulation" in *Somewhere Over the Rainbow: A Critical Inquiry into Queer Utopias* (2013).

J. Edward Sumerau is a Visiting Assistant Professor of Sociology at the University of Tampa. Zir teaching and research focuses on the intersection of sexualities, gender, religion, and health in the lives of religious and sexual minorities and in relation to shifting historical and cultural patterns of social organization.

Beverly Yuen Thompson is an Assistant Professor of Sociology at Siena College. She earned her MA and PhD from the New School for Social Research in New York City. She also earned a Master's Degree in Women's Studies from San Diego State University, where she studied the intersections of gender, race and sexuality. She is also a documentary filmmaker.

Dennis D. Waskul is Professor of Sociology at Minnesota State University Mankato. He has conducted numerous empirical studies on various forms of cybersex, authored the book *Self-Games and Body-Play* (Peter Lang 2003) and edited *net.SeXXX* (Peter Lang 2004). He has also published extensively in the sociology of the body, including his co-authored books *Body/Embodiment* (Ashgate 2006) and *The Senses in Self, Culture, and Society* (Routledge 2011).

D J Williams, PhD, is the Director of Research for the Center for Positive Sexuality in Los Angeles and the Director of Social Work at Idaho State University. His research focuses on specific topics related to deviant leisure, alternative sexualities, and leisure and crime relationships, and his work has been published in numerous academic journals and books.